Critical Essays on
Willa Cather

Critical Essays on
Willa Cather

John J. Murphy

G. K. Hall & Co. • **Boston, Massachusetts**

Library of Congress Cataloging in Publication Data
Main entry under title:

Critical essays on Willa Cather.

 (Critical essays on American literature)
 Includes index.
 1. Cather, Willa, 1873–1947—Criticism and interpretation—Collected works. I. Murphy, John J. (John Joseph),
1933–   . II. Series.
PS3505.A87Z593   1984   813'.52   83–12612
ISBN 0–8161–8676–6

CRITICAL ESSAYS ON AMERICAN LITERATURE

This series seeks to anthologize the most important criticism on a wide variety of topics and writers in American literature. Our readers will find in various volumes not only a generous selection of reprinted articles and reviews but original essays, bibliographies, manuscript sections, and other materials brought to public attention for the first time. John J. Murphy's volume on Willa Cather is a welcome addition to our list in that it is the most substantial collection of scholarship yet assembled on this important writer. Among the thirty-five essays are reprinted articles and reviews by Katherine Anne Porter, Eudora Welty, H. L. Mencken, Bernice Slote, Blanche H. Gelfant, and Leon Edel. In addition, there is a lengthy introduction by John J. Murphy and Kevin A. Synnott that provides a history of scholarship on Cather, as well as original essays by David Stouck, James Woodress, Paul Comeau, and John J. Murphy. We are confident that this collection will make a permanent and significant contribution to American literary study.

James Nagel, GENERAL EDITOR

Northeastern University

For a wife and children
who support my Cather efforts,
And in memory of my father,
who brought me my first Cather novel,
And Virginia Faulkner,
who brought professionalism to Cather studies

CONTENTS

INTRODUCTION

The Recognition of
Willa Cather's Art

Two facts of Willa Cather's life, one somewhat legendary and the other somewhat prosaic, defined her as an artist. The legendary one, her uprooting in 1883 at the age of nine from the green Virginia hills to the rugged Nebraska prairie, sparked her creativity. The more prosaic fact, her journalistic and editorial apprenticeship in Lincoln, Pittsburgh, and New York, disciplined that creativity. One forgets in entertaining our favorite image of a girl making the rounds on her horse from one old Czech housewife to another old Swedish one that Cather spent several years as managing editor of *McClure's*, dealing with established authors as well as literary neophytes before going into fiction full time at age thirty-nine. The experimental nature of her fiction is as little recognized as her extended apprenticeship by the general reader, but one need merely consider the variety of fictional shapes of books as diverse as *Death Comes for the Archbishop, The Professor's House,* and *My Ántonia* (to name her best), and the half century of practice transforming the slickness of "Paul's Case" into the comfortable flow of "The Best Years," or compare the self-conscious style of the early magazine fiction to the effortless storytelling of *A Lost Lady.*

Cather has survived her season of neglect; her fiction during the past dozen years has generated significant criticism and analysis (a generous sampling of which is contained in this volume). While the total effect of this renewed activity is yet to be felt, perhaps the coming generation will witness the classroom fulfillment of Henry James biographer Leon Edel's prophecy: "I'm going to put myself out on a limb, but I think the time will come when she'll be ranked above Hemingway. . . . But I've got her below Faulkner."[1] One is reminded at this point of Wallace Stevens' estimate of Cather to a friend: "We have nothing better than she is. She takes so much pains to conceal her sophistication

1

that it is easy to miss her quality."[2] Much recent criticism has been devoted to revealing that sophistication and quality. Veteran Cather scholar Bernice Slote, whose tireless efforts have been so directed, cautions us that Cather is a writer of apparent simplicity, actual complexity, that we "have handicapped ourselves by fashionable judgments; by critical assumptions made, held, and never reexamined; by our own ignorance of the nineteenth-century milieu in which Cather developed (who now reads Alphonse Daudet, Alexandre Dumas, Pierre Loti, or George Sand?); and by the neglect of clues and allusions within the work that in T. S. Eliot's *The Waste Land* (to give only one example) would have drawn forth tomes of analysis."[3]

THE CRITICAL RECEPTION

Cather began and ended her career in fiction with short story collections, the first of which, *The Troll Garden* (1905), contained such staples as "Paul's Case," "The Sculptor's Funeral," and "A Wagner Matinee." The *Dial* singled out the second story as "vivid" and detected the theme that would occupy this author for the next forty years, the contrasting of "noble artistic ideals and the crassest commercialism."[4] *Bookman* saw the same story and "Paul's Case" as exceptions among unwholesome freak stories with mere dummies for characters, and the *Independent* reviewer, while detecting a note of Maupassant, also judged the collection depressing, preferring instead the hopefulness of William Allen White. The *New York Times* and the *Critic* found more promise than fulfillment in the pieces, both preferring "Flavia and Her Artists," a Jamesian piece, to the others. The *Atlantic Monthly* reviewer Mary Moss compared the style to Wharton's but claimed more sympathy and depth for the younger writer.

Cather's two "first novels" (as she later designated them), *Alexander's Bridge* (1912) and *O Pioneers!* (1913), her first Nebraska novel, received moderate national attention. The earlier work was praised for its elegant style, the *Living Age* reviewer comparing it to a fine engraving and H. L. Mencken labeling it "promising" in *Smart Set* and detecting similarities to Wharton. His reservation that Cather avoided resolving her hero's problem by killing him off in the collapse of his bridge echoed earlier comments in *Outlook* about the novel's futility and grimness. Mencken also observed greater success with female than male characters, anticipating the women dominating *O Pioneers!* The contrasting of heroines in that Nebraska novel impressed the *Herald Tribune* writer, and their originality as representatives of a big new country was commended by other reviewers. The large-scale landscape more than the characters impressed most, however, and the *Nation* was typical in praising the rendering of "big primitive fecund America." The *Boston Evening Transcript* noted the book's multiple "missions" (continuing to occupy scholars): "it is a disclosure of the splendid resources in our immigrant population; it is the revelation of a changed and changing country; it is, indirectly perhaps, an embodiment of the feminist theory. . . ."[5] Frederick Taber Cooper discussed this scattered effect structurally as a "series of separate scenes . . . a rude touch might almost be expected to shatter. . . ."[6] He also noticed "a touch of Maupassant" in the killing of the lovers but had difficulty relating their story to the main one of land conquest.

The increased attention given *The Song of the Lark* (1915) attested to Cather's growing stature as a novelist. Mencken responded positively and negatively in *Smart Set*, enthusiastically comparing the novel to the Cinderella fable and heroine Thea's worshipping males to Galahads but restricting his endorsement to the first half. The *Herald Tribune* admired the hardening of the woman and artist into the professional yet complained about the length, and H. W. Boynton applauded the attempt to trace the "genesis of genius" rather than merely depict a pretty woman idolized by two continents. He also felt Cather had set an example of sound realism in not sensationalizing Thea's vacation and flight with Fred and in rooting her heroine's strength in the soil—her town, mother, and friends of childhood.[7] Indeed, the *Boston Evening Transcript* saw the theme as what Thea took from her mother and four men, and the *Catholic World* reviewer felt unsympathetic toward the self-centered heroine and preferred the supporting characters. The most thorough statement on the collapse of the book appeared in the *New Republic*: "the last two parts seem an act of laborious creation, carried through after the author is bored with her story."[8] This would bear out what Cather herself later admitted as the book's "chief fault . . . a descending curve."[9] Finally, and perhaps more disturbingly, Edward E. Hale complained in the *Dial* about the skipping structural method and habit of explaining rather than depicting.

Having produced three noteworthy novels, Cather now became the subject of a fuller consideration by H. W. Boynton in the *New York Evening Post*.[10] Pursuing the provincial theme of his review of *Song*, he saw her work as embodying the best in fiction because rooted in the soil, although not in the local color sense. He clarified Sarah Orne Jewett's role in directing her from the studied brilliance of *Bridge* to the simple and sincere depiction of familiar materials in subsequent work. He compared Alexandra and Thea as types of feminine greatness, praised Cather's perspective on sexual episodes, and, more significantly (in terms of later criticism), credited her imagination with embracing both the real and ideal.

Boynton followed up this praise in his *Bookman* review of *My Ántonia* (1918), noting the "higher realism" which eschews both the "machinery of dramatic action" and the trappings of the obvious success story. In the *Globe and Commercial Advertiser* (New York), N. P.

Dawson stressed the role of memory in softening the realism and also the structural principle of stories within stories, "all as neatly unfolding as a set of Chinese boxes." Randolph Bourne, anticipating Cather's own pronouncements on writing, appreciated her "scraping" away of irrelevancies to achieve a spontaneous effect and also her gift of sympathy, the understanding that goes to the heart of the lives of her characters.[11] For this sympathy, he felt, rather than for illustrations of eternal truths or a crowded gallery of society, we read Cather. Also, he recognized narrator Jim's vision as romantic, a "discovery" repeatedly made by subsequent critics.

Bourne's feeling that with *Ántonia* this author left the ranks of the provincials and joined the class of modern world authors was shared by two influential critics, Mencken and Carl Van Doren, who now felt the need to evaluate her career. In *The Borzoi, 1920* Mencken credited her with detecting beneath the tawdry surface of Middle Western barbarism human beings in conflict with the gods.[12] This depth plus a confident style and instinct for form made her the glory of Midwestern literature, which might well become the national literature. Mencken apologized for affixing to her the Wharton label in his review of *Bridge*. Van Doren was more insightful if less extravagant in his 1921 article in the *Nation* (revised a year later for *Contemporary American Novelists, 1900–1920*).[13] He distinguished her work from Jewett's in depicting instead of echoing heroic activities but recognized that Cather's Whitmanesque feeling for life had been disciplined by the taste and intelligence she shared with Jewett. He also noted what later became a reason for her neglect, that she was difficult to place. Her preference for artists and pioneers unencumbered by bourgeois conditions put her squarely outside the somewhat uncritical revolt from the village school.

A second collection of stories, *Youth and the Bright Medusa*, Knopf's first Cather publication, appeared in 1920, gathering four selections from *The Troll Garden* and four newer stories, including "Coming, Aphrodite!" and "The Diamond Mine." In *Smart Set* Mencken acknowledged an unusual talent for representing artists on their own terms and also the increasingly firm grasp on character the newer stories displayed, a development also noticed by *Bookman's* Blanche C. Williams, who felt, however, that Cather had compromised her short story talent, that the later pieces were condensed novels rather than short stories. In the *New Republic* Francis Hackett discussed the depth of her understanding of the artist, of the great-hearted as well as the opportunistic, of the character employed inside the medium of self-expression.[14] Hackett also noted the "remarkable magazine-craft," her ability to manage the reader, yet lamented that her inspiration could be kept coolly in hand, that her genius was not the most exciting kind. The *Dial* reviewer echoed this sentiment, characterizing these stories of ambition in women as scrupulous analyses too coolly cerebral to satisfy the reading public.

Such fine self-discipline represented the "triumph of mind over Nebraska," said the *Nation* reviewer, who joined the *Freeman* reviewer in regarding the collection as an American debate between body and soul on the questionable compatibility of American ideals and the development of the artist.[15]

When *One of Ours* appeared in 1922 Cather experienced her first dose of adverse criticism, a fact which might have contributed to her later statement that the world broke in two that year.[16] In *Smart Set* even the supportive Mencken could not recommend the war section and felt it suffered by comparison to Dos Passos' *Three Soldiers*. Heywood Broun was less gentle, calling it deadly dull and ridiculous in theme—as if the purpose of the war was to get farm boys out of Nebraska.[17] Cather simply "does not know enough of the situations concerning which she writes in the latter part of the book." The *Springfield Republican* reviewer and Ludwig Lewisohn in the *Nation* objected to the use of the war as *deus ex machina* and felt the problems of the hero unsolved. R. D. Townsend seconded this in *Outlook* and added that the book broke in two. H. W. Boynton in the *Independent*, usually sympathetic, thought it extended beyond meaning, that it should have ended with the departure for France; significant in terms of recent criticism, he saw the war section as a tour de force of "revolting" naturalism. Sinclair Lewis in the *New York Evening Post* admitted disappointment in the opportunities for character development wasted in moving the action to France, while Edmund Wilson bordered on cruelty in *Vanity Fair*, wondering whether Mencken had been mistaken about Cather's significance and rejecting her novel as a flat failure, a waste of provocative material that could have become a document of national significance.[18] Also, Wilson repeated Hale's earlier reservation about *Song*, that the author failed to depict characters, that we do not partake of their experiences. Finally, there was one curious variation among these negative reviews: Louie M. Field in *Literary Digest International* felt the war section the best part of a tedious, pessimistic production.

More positive reactions appeared in the *San Francisco Chronicle*, which detected masculine qualities in Cather and distinguished between her own and hero Claude's views on the war, and in the *Des Moines Register*, which noted temperamental differences between Claude and the hero of *Three Soldiers* and said that most readers had misunderstood the novel. Claude's difference occupied Gamaliel Bradford, who saw the resolution as the "sanctification of glory over duty done" and was reminded of the final stanza of "Evening Song" in Cather's early poems, *April Twilights* (1903).[19] Reviewers in the *Greensboro Daily News* and *Survey* agreed with Burton Rascoe on the national meaning of the theme, that Claude's Nebraska origins were merely incidental. Dorothy Canfield Fisher's *New York Times* review was the most balanced; she felt the novel level-headed about Middle Western life and indicated the irony of Claude's starvation in a land of plenty as well as the significance of his New England ancestry.

Several months after this flurry and after *One of Ours* won the Pulitzer Prize, Herbert S. Gorman surveyed Cather's career in the *New York Times Book Review*, singling out her ability to combine place and character ("the impingement of spirit and environment") in the tradition of Hardy.[20] Gorman also compared Claude and Ántonia as molded in opposite ways by the soil and concluded that while no psychologue Cather was gifted in revealing character through "expositional narrative form" and deserved her award.

A Lost Lady (1923) restored reviewers' faith, and they suggested a variety of approaches to this novel—several still unpursued. John Farrar in *Bookman* saw Marian Forrester as a terrifying pivotal figure around which swung several types of men and classified the work as an allegory of love in its various phases. *World* reviewer Heywood Broun termed "shrewd" the device of telling the story from Niel's perspective and thereby insulating Marian from the harsh judgments of readers. He praised the novel as an exquisite blend of romance and realism, a combination also acknowledged in the *New York Times* by Henry James Forman, who labeled the realism "Russian." Edmund Wilson said in his *Dial* review that the book atoned for *One of Ours* but its secondhand method of telling reflected Cather's inability (one she shared with James) to depict emotions firsthand; however, he credited her with a unique ability to overlay Midwestern life with "artistic patina." The most helpful reviews were by H. W. Boynton and Joseph Wood Krutch. Boynton saw Marian and Ántonia as complementary types presented through male consciousnesses—"the woman who exists and delights, and the one who warms and sustains."[21] He also recognized Marian as supported by the Victorian code, that her power of Venus depended as much on poise as abandon, and that Niel had survived his bitterness to express thankfulness that she had a hand in breaking him into life. Krutch qualified Marian's guilt as aesthetic rather than moral, as a violation of the lady as artistic creation.[22] He admired Cather's ability to suggest moral without sermon and character without psychological treatise, and to integrate character and scene. Memory, he concluded, is the "mother of her muse."

Two general articles of significance appeared in 1924. Lloyd Morris argued in the *North American Review* that Cather had turned from pioneers to artists in depicting the universal struggle to dominate space because she failed to discover a national faith or destiny in contemporary America.[23] Between her pioneer and artistic characters were the victims of this failure, those like Claude at a loss to direct their energies and idealism. Percy Boynton in the *English Journal* offered advice that would contradict estimates by influential critics in the next decade: Cather "was at her best when she was not distracted by the consciousness of current events or current problems. There are plenty of writers of less distinction to dabble in these."[24] The struggle toward self-realization on the prairies was her proper theme, and the confusions of recent years have led her astray in both *One of Ours* and *A Lost Lady.* Boynton particularly singled out the accomplishment in *Ántonia* of emphasizing triumph rather than defeat or sacrifice in the "vital experience of mothering a family."

The Professor's House (1925) generated an unusual number of negative reviews. The *New York Times* found the "Tom Outland's Story" section "an amateurish essay in archeological adventure" and accused Cather of being "out of her philosophic depth" in the concluding section.[25] "No philosopher who pretends to the name," continued the reviewer on Godfrey St. Peter's brush with death, "takes the hemlock by mere accident." In a second *Times* review Lloyd Morris added that the novel was inadequate in design, uncertain in effect, and ignored the problems it raised. The *Springfield Republican* remained unconvinced that St. Peter was either a genius or thwarted by his wife and dismissed the Outland adventure as irrelevant and "anemic." James Linn, cruelest of all, ridiculed Tom Outland as "a spinster school teacher's dream of a Zane Grey cowboy."[26] Edwin Muir in the *Nation and Athenaeum* complained about the distance and coldness of the characters, and the *Nation* reviewer Joseph Wood Krutch insisted that Cather's intuitive method failed her on this occasion and found Outland a flat abstraction inferior to Louie Marsellus as a character.

A positive verdict came from Laura Benet in *Commonweal,* although she lamented the gallery of well-drawn characters allowed to "scatter" before the memory of Outland, Cather's symbol for the pioneer America that civilization had strangled. Henry Canby labeled the novel a real pioneering book and Cather the first since Hawthorne to detect profundity in American life.[27] He saw the story as the "slow discovery by Professor St. Peter—of himself." An equally complex view was Dorothea Mann's in the *Boston Evening Transcript*: caught in a domestic groove never intended for him, St. Peter tried to justify his sacrifice by sustaining the illusion of family dependence. Schuyler Ashley noted in the *Kansas City Star* the connection to Anatole France's *Le Mannequin d'Osier* and felt St. Peter's character a significant achievement. Herschel Brickell in *Bookman* and James Ford in *Literary Digest International* judged this the best Cather yet, while *Survey* reviewer Walter Millis attempted to define the work as modern because pointless and escapist.

Reviews of *My Mortal Enemy* (1926) were as mixed. The *Chicago Tribune's* Fanny Butcher, always faithful and enthusiastic, detected beneath the spare style and wreckage of two lives the fundamental hatred and irresistible attraction between the sexes. The *Time* reviewer saw pride turned upon itself as central and praised Cather's ability to create a moving experience after the "Wordsworth formula" of recollected emotion. Economy of language and rigidly selected depictions of our mortal mystery were admired by Lee W. Dodd in the *Saturday Review of Literature*, and the *Herald Tribune*'s Isabel Patterson noted the outline of a great nature ruined by defeat, but felt the outline had not been filled in. Destructively brief was the verdict of Louis Kronenberger in the *New York Times*; to him, narrator Nellie lacked involvement enough to make Myra Henshawe convincing and Cather was as out of her depth here as in *House*. *Boston Evening Transcript*'s Sidney Homer indicated Nellie's inadequacies as narrator and the author's as explorer of shadowy realms of mind and soul. In the *New Republic* Robert Morss Lovett wondered why Cather constantly used characters like Nellie to distance herself from her subjects, but Joseph Wood Krutch in the *Nation* felt positive about Nellie, that her sadness was at the center of the book. *New York Evening Post*'s Walter Yust liked the intense glimpses of a courageous woman who could not endure her regret, while Keith Preston in the *Chicago Daily News* saw the studied prose as merely adding novelty to an old theme played out by storybook characters against a studio background.

Impatience with the overfastidious style colored Burton Rascoe's *Bookman* response to *Death Comes for the Archbishop* (1927). Cather's interest in cadenced, limpid prose rather than story or theme amounted, he said, to a sabbatical from serious fiction. Other skeptical reviewers like the *Spectator*'s Rachel Taylor, either perplexed about the genre of the book or Cather's intention, usually found good things to say about the execution. There was general relief that she had returned to storytelling after the structural experiment of *House*. In the *North American Review* Herschel Brickell viewed the book's clarity as a lesson to younger writers who think life can only be caught in "murky, obscure, amorphous prose," and a similar antimodern stand was taken by Edwin Edgett in the *Boston Evening Transcript*. Robert Morss Lovett in the *New Republic* praised the straightforward narrative, the achievement of remoteness in fairly recent events, the feel for the New Mexico landscape, and the interweaving of themes, narratives, and traditions. William Whitman III in the *Independent* saw the novel as the perfect vehicle for the author's unique gifts, those of a writer of short stories rather than conventionally structured novels. Frances Robbins classified her a hagiographer rather than novelist in *Outlook*, and in the *Nation* Joseph Wood Krutch classified her book a Celtic rather than Nordic epic because it softened and distanced events through memory. However, *Boston Evening Transcript*'s Dorothy Gilman liked the immediacy given to historical events. In an otherwise favorable review, Henry Longan Stuart was disquieted by the "superimposition of the novel upon history" and the "transposition of Latour for Lamy."[28]

Several reviewers took unusual approaches to the work. Robert O. Ballou in the *Chicago Daily News* noted the Western angle, that a real artist had invaded the territory of the brawny writers of the ride and shoot school, while Arnold Ronnebeck in the *Rocky Mountain News* compared Cather's approach to the bold New Mexico landscape to certain paintings of Frank Applegate. The Catholic press was understandably enthusiastic; *Commonweal's* Michael Williams, extolling the novel's profundity and simplicity as well as its use of the rich Catholic past of America, urged Catholics to support sales. A more tempered review in the *Catholic World* appreciated challenges successfully met in building a book around two missionaries and in restraining poet, philosopher, and preacher on the novelist's leash. This reviewer also acknowledged aspects of sociological change and the mingling of barbarism and civilization.

Novelist Rebecca West used the occasion of *Archbishop* for an essay on Cather in the *Herald Tribune*.[29] West confessed that Cather was not a writer like D. H. Lawrence and James Joyce to appeal to youth by extending the frontiers of humanity, but one like Marcel Proust to pave our journey with grace. Indeed, Cather remained curiously earthbound, the most sensuous of writers with uncanny ability to comprehend and clarify intricate aspects of consciousness yet failing to penetrate (although never denying) the darker mysteries.

In 1928 T. K. Whipple revised an earlier essay for *Spokesmen*, noting the deepening of Cather's art since her Jamesian period, that her intelligence enabled her to control sentimentality and adopt her method to her subject.[30] Whipple also commented on her ability to dramatize with austerity the experience of women, to explore character through implication and symbol (that is objectively rather than through analysis), and on the universal appeal of her theme—the tragedy of failing to live to the fullest, on primitive and sophisticated levels. In the same year Régis Michaud reviewed Cather's career in *The American Novel To-Day*, stressing the suppressed and limited lives of her characters, their need for romantic release and their tragedy of making virtue of necessity.[31] Regarding the use of the war in *One of Ours*, Michaud asked, "When are we going to have a Freudian interpretation of the war as a supreme and tragic derivative to inhibition?" Such tragic implications were expressed in Cather's books with a style and sympathy making her a relief in the Dreiserian desert and Andersonian jungle of imperfect art and unanimous, pitiless grieving. In 1929 an appreciative essay by Edward Wagenknecht in the *Sewanee Review* praised the fiction as "the surest touchstone of literary judgment in our contemporary American letters."[32] Wagenknecht saw her as fusing the worlds of Jewett and Whitman, as possessing an aesthetic sense to discipline her love for common things. She was of the frontier without being either blind to its faults or negative like Lewis and other revolters from the village.

Finally, in 1930, as if to cap the criticism of the previous decades, René Rapin completed the first book-length study of her works, *Willa*

Cather, for McBride's Modern American Writers series.[33] Hardly echoing previous verdicts, Rapin much preferred *One of Ours* to *Ántonia,* in which he felt the author had capitulated to sentimentality and realism after the first section by making her heroine conventional. The Frenchman found the French setting and war scenes in *One of Ours* powerful, compared the novel to *War and Peace* and grouped it with *Song, House* and *Archbishop* as one of Cather's big four. He felt *Lady* well-wrought but slight and *Enemy* a failure due to lack of character analysis, a weakness which, along with slackening tempo, marred Cather's fiction. Rapin's understanding of the effects of her Jamesian apprenticeship in delaying her literary discovery of Nebraska and restraining her tendency to romanticism is particularly shrewd, as is his appreciation of the range of her subjects and experimentations. Among the virtues that led Rapin to select *Archbishop* and *House* as the very best is her ability to combine in them the pioneer virtues of Alexandra and Ántonia with the restlessness of Carl Linstrum and Claude.

The 1930s proved less productive for Cather and less appreciative. Literary historians producing comprehensive surveys of American literature did not fail to acknowledge her contribution, although controversy arose in evaluating her use of the pioneer age and her "realism" in depicting it. V. L. Parrington summarized one view in saying that Cather "looks back lovingly to a pioneer West, as the cradle of heroic lives."[34] His annotations on Cather (addenda to the third volume of *Main Currents in American Thought*) suggest comparisons to Hamlin Garland and Upton Sinclair while judging her "unconcerned with problems" and neither naturalistic nor romantic. Annie Marble likened her to Hardy, noting locale as a factor in emotional crises, and Fred Pattee, placing Cather with Wharton, Glasgow, and other writers of "the feminine novel," delineated three periods in the work up to *Archbishop* and declared the Nebraska novels (those recounting "youth seen through the golden haze of later years, in far exile") as works of lasting value.[35] However, Pattee also felt her art incomplete and without "glow," even while acknowledging her fine craftsmanship, especially in characterizations ("sharp cut as cameos"). Percy Boynton continued to see nostalgia as the force in her work, describing the Nebraska novels as "chronicles of hard, dreary beginnings and ultimate success" but, due to their focus on artistic temperaments, lacking in "scrupulous realism, the conscientious exactitude of the expert court witness."[36]

Riding on the coattails of the favorable reception accorded *Archbishop, Shadows on the Rock* (1931) enjoyed the largest immediate sales of Cather's career, despite most reviewers ranking it below its predecessor. A few, *Commonweal*'s Michael Williams and the *Saturday Review of Literature*'s Wilbur Cross among them, detected its serious intent, that it was deeply rooted in the ultimate mystery of eternal shadows. Cross also addressed its art, distinguishing it from the traditional novel and comparing it to Sterne's *Sentimenal Journey*. However, Carl Van Doren in *Herald Tribune Books* felt it dramatically thin, a "domesticated" epic, the reverse of the Nebraska pioneer fiction; the author, he said, had played Miss Jewett to Quebec. Increasingly disparate, episodic, private, and without struggle was the *Nation* reviewer Dorothy Van Doren's verdict, to which John Chamberlain added "shrinking," lamenting that Cather had not employed the filter of poetic consciousness as Elizabeth Madox Roberts had in *The Great Meadow*, a Kentucky historical novel of the previous year. He speculated that Cather might be at the end of her rope, might have exhausted her limited experience.[37] Louis Kronenberger accused her in *Bookman* of creating private idylls rather than vital historical fiction like Sigrid Undset's, dealing with the collective experience of men. "At best," wrote Horace Gregory, *Shadows* is "an example of reaction against the tendency of the American novel to gain sociological importance" and at worst "a romantic if not completely sentimental dream of a lady novelist yearning for an ideal home in which all the elements of a pioneer tradition are refined beyond ultimate conviction."[38] To Newton Arvin in the *New Republic* the book was born dead, yet another indication of the author's failure to come to grips with the life of her time. He labeled the triumphs of her career evasions, her theme of self reliance a reaction rather than an expression of society, in effect, an abandonment of the middle class. Granville Hicks admitted in *Forum* that the novel was beautifully wrought and convincing but dismissed Cather as a minor artist, a local colorist too soft to be a modern novelist.

On the other side of the barricade, James Southall Wilson in the *Virginia Quarterly Review* saw the novel's spirit of humanity and compassion as springing from something hard and bitter, not from soft sentimentality but from the exaltation of courage, loyalty, and kindness, as in the tradition of *Beowulf*. The *Yale Review* responded similarly: *Shadows* was a humanistic plea in idyll form for what distinguishes human from brute life. Archer Wilson's review in *Bookman* was a rebuttal to the detractors.[39] Cather's ideas and themes, he argued, are neither precious nor affected by fads; they include divided loyalties, responsibility to self, women's strength of fortitude, the price life can exact, the establishment of a system of living, and the endurance of a civilization. Finally, Camille McCole defended the author in the *Catholic World* as a welcome exception to a Freudian, pseudo-sophisticated, inferior-language, tawdry literary age.

Several critics evaluated Cather's fictional techniques at this time. In a *New Yorker* essay Louise Bogan appreciated the fine crafting of the novels and gave the woman and her work the title "American Classic."[40] She described her narratives as "solid as a house, written in prose as surely counterpointed as music," and admired her depiction of "indestructible qualities in human nature." Constance Rourke formally aligned Cather with the American romance tradition, noting her reliance on basic literary forms—the romance, the cumulative tale, the saga, even the allegory—in capturing and evoking the pioneer experience.[41] William R. Blankenship praised Cather's restraint as an artist and recognized her essay "The Novel Démeublé" as key to appreciating her achievement.[42] Hers is a realism like Tolstoy's, he maintained, founded upon "the inner core of being and not upon surface manifestations." Avoiding the path of social documentary, she had depicted the clash of character and environment with "unhurried loveliness." Walter Myers acknowledged *Shadows* as approaching the ideal form, a fiction divested of obvious novelistic mechanical devices and stratagems, and engaging the reader creatively through suggestion.[43] Well-wrought speech and powers of description were factors determining Ludwig Lewisohn's choice of *Lady* and *Enemy* as the high points of Cather's career.[44]

Even the unsympathetic among reviewers were relieved when she returned to the American West in the three long stories making up *Obscure Destinies* (1932). Although Clifton Fadiman belittled her for idealizing in them a pioneer period that was really the "joint creation of masters and slaves" and built up by "blood and iron" rather than the "nicer Christian virtues," Helen MacAfee argued in her defense that death is the only escape from life and that involvement in religious affairs, science, and reading instead of business affairs, politics, and talking as survival activities until death is hardly escapist.[45] The most understanding estimate was Henry Seidel Canby's in the *Saturday Review of Literature*: Neighbour Rosicky and Mrs. Harris were, respectively, a smiling Bohunk and a prejudiced old woman but Cather was able to reveal their souls, could "make great souls where others deal in stereotype, caricature or studio photograph."[46] The *New Republic* reviewer expressed the general consensus in preferring "Old Mrs. Harris," which John Chamberlain in the *New York Times* recognized as a "subtle dissection of any American town in which infinitely repellant particles from all over the map have met and mingled and worked out a temporary adjustment."[47] "Two Friends," faulted for being too anecdotal and distanced from the characters, was generally felt below the standard of the other stories.

Clifton Fadiman followed up his somewhat condescending review of *Obscure Destinies* with a more reasoned estimate of Cather in the *Nation*, arguing that unlike her contemporaries she appeared to have "no report to make to us on the America of her time."[48] Her respect for conventional social order and her "puritan reticence" were transporting her, he felt, into a world of dreams, and her flight, a dangerous attempt to recapture childhood, would destroy the status achieved by *Ántonia* and *Song*, turning a major writer into a minor one. Granville Hicks echoed much of this a year later in his famous "Case Against Willa Cather" in the *English Journal*, charging that she had exploited the nostalgic and idealized frontier of her early Nebraska novels to create romantic escapes from her own problematic age.[49] Her failure to address the questions of her own time and her flight to the past led Hicks to conclude that she had traded realism for the "calm serenity of her dreams." However, it was the technical achievement of that serenity and those dreams that Pelham Edgar appreciated in his 1934 evaluation. *Archbishop* might be too brightly peopled to compare with "the delicate wash of Chavannes frescoes," he noted, but *Shadows on the Rock* was all its name implied.[50] Suggestion and picture are Cather's appeal; she understands and uses "the power of words to evoke and image."

Another crop of literary histories in the mid-1930s reaffirmed Cather's place in the American procession. Reuben Halleck mentioned her briefly in his study of romance in the American novel, reiterating the usual compliments for well-delineated characterizations, and Harlan Hatcher reemphasized the classical aspect of her work and termed her an escapist, albeit a successful one.[51] Harry Hartwick noted her symbol-making ability and persistence in representing superior individuals in conflict with an unworthy society, and Arthur Hobson Quinn in *American Fiction* (1936) advised against confining her to the West, since in his opinion she was "quite unprovincial."[52] Quinn was among the earliest to give close scrutiny to the fiction, providing insights into its recurrent themes. He offers particularly good commentary on *Bridge* and at several points draws interesting connections between the short stories and the novels. During the same year, however, Walter Taylor in *A History of American Letters* would persist in familiar and somewhat simplistic approaches to Cather as a traditionalist and novelist of the prairie.[53]

Response to *Lucy Gayheart* (1935) was neither as divided nor emotional as to *Shadows.* Cather had given her defenders less to defend and some of the more volatile voices had given up on her. Robert Cantwell recorded her collapse along with Ellen Glasgow's and E. M. Roberts' (*Vein of Iron* and *He Sent Forth a Raven* had appeared the same year) and called *Lucy* "maudlin" and "peopled with stock characters who move through stock situations and who die, unexpectedly and accidentally, to bring the story to a ramshackle conclusion."[54] John Slocum proved kinder in the *North American Review*, admitting she did well with an "absurdly mid-Victorian plot" but complaining that she left out too much, that we know too little about Lucy herself. Hollywood cinema stuff, another spoiled heroine too exquisite for her time and place, charged William Troy in the *Nation*. To Cyril Connolly the deaths seemed "introduced from laziness and a desire to round off the story rather than as the inevitable consequence of choosing such a subject."[55] Two reviewers admired the novel's structure, the *Chicago Tribune*'s Fanny Butcher noting its "daring" symphonic technique and Helen MacAfee in the *Yale Review* its rectilinear dimension, "twice stepped back, like a modern building," depicting the heroine's advance and then retreat and death. Both acknowledged the originality of the third section, as did Dorothea Brande, who felt it embodied the feeling of continuing life. Brande also recognized that the central character had not been killed off, that the "sense of life" was that character, but she admitted insufficient knowledge of Lucy and excessive ambiguity in her relationship with Sebastian.[56]

Several reviewers were reminded of other Cather novels. *Commonweal's* Charlotte Meagher thought *Lucy* reminiscent of but superior to *Song* and *Lady* in emotional depth and felt Harry Gordon the best character. The *San Francisco Chronicle* viewed the novel as a cross between *Ántonia* and *Lady*, adding that Lucy should have married Harry but had not been made for domestic happiness. Perfection of style and fine intuitive insight into the most opposite personalities was the verdict of Howard Mumford Jones in the *Saturday Review of Literature*, although he objected to Harry's sentimentality in the coda. The *Los Angeles Times* reviewer admired Cather's consistent ability to extract beauty from ordinary things, identifying the pains and problems in *Lucy* as other than of economic and class origins, and J. Donald Adams in the *New York Times* detected two common Cather themes: the passionate desire to win something satisfying from life and the grasping back at youth in middle age.

The latter half of the decade brought more specialized and probing assessments. Lionel Trilling suggested a modification of the standing perception of Cather as elegist of the pioneer, noting the complexity and realism of her characters and their destinies: "From *O Pioneers!* to *The Professor's House*, Miss Cather's novels portray [*Lady* most explicitly] the results of the pioneer's defeat, both in the thwarted pettiness to which he is condemned by his material failures and in the callous insensitivity produced by his material success."[57] Critical of the lack of dramatic relationships in the later works, Trilling suggested that her attempt to "make the most of things" in modern life had directed her philosophically to the "horizon of the spirit" and technically toward "the novel démeublé." The result, he concluded, was "life without its furniture . . . strangely bare." In a 1938 *American Literature* essay, Robert Footman analyzed her genius in terms of three basic qualities—the value of the individual, meaningful existence on every level, and evocative, suggestive style.[58] Only when the three converged did she produce a great novel, and in Footman's opinion this happened only twice, in *Ántonia* and in *Archbishop*. Howard Mumford Jones used the occasion of the Library Edition (1938) to refute the "escapist" label, crediting her with renewing a tradition of contemplative, sympathetic, and insightful characterizations.[59] He restated Bogan's use of the term "classic" to describe her work; no other writer seemed to him as truly deserving of the adjective.

The 1930s came to an end with an appreciative recognition by fellow travelers in the kingdom of art. Sinclair Lewis named Cather "the greatest American novelist," pointing out her quiet and solitary path: "The boys have roared and fought; they have left out the commas and added the hyphens; they have galloped to Paris or Moscow; they have dived into degeneracy or phony holiness; but quiet and alone, Willa Cather has greatly pictured the great life."[60] Steven and Rosemary Benet praised her work as thoroughly American and appreciated the high degree of civilization her novels depict.[61] The attitudes implied in both these comments are key to the expanding understanding of Cather in the 1940s. She was clearly seen as somehow different, perhaps out of step with the times, maintaining a relatively quiet existence in her own art, keeping faith with permanent and eternal truths in the face of increasing challenges. More and more, critics began to understand the work she had been about and assess it as a whole, seeing in it the development of an intense and dedicated artist.

Serenity and thoughtfulness characterized the reaction to her last novel, *Sapphira and the Slave Girl* (1940). Mary Ross recognized the "basic stuff of tragedy, the struggle of the individual to maintain personal integrity despite dissonance within and attack from without," as the theme, and Dorothy Canfield Fisher stressed the topical nature during the early days of World War II of a story of escape from human slavery.[62] Clifton Fadiman meanwhile in the *New Yorker* thought the book out of the mainstream of current fiction yet a serious consideration of the different ways individuals act when the system of slavery impinges on them. Harry Binsse echoed Fadiman in stressing the "psychological effect of slavery on both slave and master" and ranked it with Cather's best.[63] In his *Atlantic Monthly* column, Edward Weeks noted the tension between pulsating antagonisms and the calm surface. *Yale Review's* Robert Littel marveled at the author's ability to transform stereotypes and familiar incidents into a blend of reality and remoteness, austerity and life. Cather's trio of historical novels evoking the quality of life in particular regions is now complete, wrote an appreciative Henry Canby in the *Saturday Review of Literature*, grouping *Sapphira* with *Shadows* and *Archbishop*.

A less enthusiastic response came from J. Donald Adams in the *New York Times*, who felt uneasy about the resolution of the conflict between Sapphira and Henry Colbert, and from the *Time* reviewer, who appreciated the book's quality but called it dull. The *Christian Science Monitor* was baffled as well as disappointed: Sadness and slow decay were the book's residue, yet the portraits were skillful and difficult to forget. The *Catholic World* found the final, first-person section exasperating.

That same year Carl Van Doren explored Cather's early years in *The American Novel, 1789–1939*, taking note of her understanding of the immigrants in Red Cloud, her university days, and her admiration for Henry James.[64] He selected *Lady* ("short and flawless") her greatest success and affirmed the durability of the works in general: "Some of her books are powerful, some merely graceful. But they are always truthful. And hardly one of them has worn thin with time." In *America in Contemporary Fiction* Percy Boynton repeated some of his earlier opinions in offering a broader view of Cather's career.[65] He detected in her work an undue "zest for studio life" leading to overcrafting and a violation of verisimilitude. Even when she explored "through sympathetic observation" the arduous paths toward self-fulfillment of women "of heroic possibilities" in *Pioneers, Song* and *Ántonia*, the portraits lacked "scrupulous realism." In subsequent novels Boynton found the characters weak, faltering, and defeated. *Archibishop* and *Shadows* show a retreat to the past and deny "the fruitfulness of contemporary life." Halford Luccock was harsher. Within his limited view of literature as social reflector her work was dated and her career "one of the most conspicuous retreats from contemporary life of any first class artist in her time."[66] Philip Rahv reported much the same "slump" in American letters generally, noting that in the later works particularly Cather had turned from "vigorous, though subtle, realism" to "the serenity of pious meditation."[67]

However, George White honored her as "Emersonian" in his 1942 *Sewanee Review* essay because she had "described in permanent brilliance the importance of the affirmative, intelligent individual."[68] He applauded her stand against the topical literary vision of the day and her desire "to be experienced, not just talked about." Although her faith may lie in unmarketable things, it rests on the essential truth "that man has a spiritual responsibility to himself and to his world; that the responsibility is to create, regardless of art, the greatest 'good' he can." Alfred Kazin's *On Native Grounds* included perceptive distinctions between Cather's use of elegy as emotion and as theme.[69] Though she is a conscious traditionalist, Kazin maintained, she looks back to the pioneer age more philosophically and artistically than emotionally; rather than frontier institutions, she admires the human qualities of characters like Ántonia Shimerda, Thea Kronborg, and Godfrey St. Peter—qualities disintegrating in the modern age. The high point of her career came with *Lady* and *House*, novels counterposed between regret and resignation. To Kazin, Godfrey St. Peter's story is her "most elaborately symbolic version of the story of heroic failure" and can be taken as the story of "what Willa Cather herself has always hoped to be—a pioneer in mind, a Catholic by instinct, French by inclination, a spiritual aristocrat with democratic manners." In subsequent novels, however, she became a victim of her own traditionalism. In colonial New Mexico and Quebec her characters were safe from the doom awaiting their kind in an industrial culture.

Cather's death in 1947 occasioned considerable reconsideration and reappraisal of both the woman and her work. Henry S. Canby noted her fierce devotion to her art and her "sympathetic chronicles" of the clash

of character and environment in the American West.[70] Dayton Kohler
cited close-to-Nature ties and criticisms of the small Midwestern town
as consistent throughout her fiction.[71] He found the latter strain particularly striking in the stories of betrayal and corruption at the heart of
House, the protagonist of which, like the author herself in later works,
followed a path "into the region of imagination and history." Her eventual idealization and mourning of the world she earlier had attacked
so vigorously struck Morton Zabel as curious in his consideration of the
"pathos of distance" of time and place in her work.[72] Like most critics by
this time, Zabel admired the faith she had kept in the artist's struggle to
understand and create something of permanence, and he acknowledged
that, despite didacticism and nostalgia, she had written "a few books—
My Ántonia and A Lost Lady chief among them—that are American
classics and that still can tell us, in a time of sanctified journalism and
demoralized sophistication, how much of a lifetime it costs to make
that rare and expensive article." Her accomplishment he saw as comparable to that of Turgenev or Gogol.

Also in 1947, Maxwell Geismar's The Last of the Provincials offered
the first comprehensive assessment of Cather's fiction.[73] Geismar indicated a design in the body of work, consistency in a career that whatever
its limitations was beginning to be acknowledged as significant. He
appreciated the investment of a life in art, the attempt to find meaning
through art, the struggle to maintain values in hostile and threatening
times. As her life and work revealed, Cather's search stayed true to its
mark even if it directed her toward the past. She is, concluded Geismar,
"one of the most complex, if not difficult and contradictory, minds in
our letters."

Cather's last stories, The Old Beauty and Others (1948), appeared
posthumously and included besides the title story "The Best Years" and
"Before Breakfast." Some of the responses were eulogistic, especially
Fanny Butcher's in the Chicago Tribune, who lamented the passing of
an era of great writers while managing to detect the satirical nature of
"Before Breakfast." The San Francisco Chronicle reviewer, almost as
appreciative, saw the entire range of the novelist's themes and settings
summed up in the slim volume, which he felt would return readers to
earlier Cather. William Peden in the Saturday Review of Literature
singled out sympathy for characters as distinguishing her from our early
naturalists and her younger contemporaries.[74] The title story, he felt,
"captured the essence of an individual and a way of life"; he classified
"The Best Years" as a "tone poem, praising the 'home place' and family
ties," but felt "Before Breakfast" inferior, its central character a "puppet
rather than a human being." However, the Nation reviewer Margaret
Marshall felt this story the only original one in a book that otherwise gave
the "impression of being mementoes rather than new thrusts of Miss
Cather's talent."[75] Perhaps the most insightful review was Charles Poore's

in the *New York Times*. Poore saw these last stories as fulfilling Cather's principle of unnamed creation, depicting life in its tragic hardness, and expressing a preference for the past and humanity in "murmurs . . . incomparably clear."[76]

Critics now began to look with renewed interest on the products of the life in art Geismar had delineated so clearly. Two items in the *Explicator* proposed structural analyses of *My Ántonia* in attempts to relate the action of the various episodes and stories to a central theme.[77] In 1948, James Shively presented some of Cather's early writings from the *Hesperian*, the magazine she had edited at the University of Nebraska. Some of her early essays in the Lincoln press were cited in another article as evidence of originality of expression and clarity of style.[78] In less than three decades recognition of Cather had changed from a nodding glance in the pages of literary history to close examination of her uniquely American art.

TRENDS IN CATHER SCHOLARSHIP

Four biographical studies appeared within five years of Cather's death in 1947. Mildred Bennett's *World of Willa Cather* (1951) focused on the memories and incidents of the Red Cloud years as they related to the fiction.[79] Largely anecdotal, the book was difficult for scholars to use effectively until a later edition (1961) added notes and sources. *Willa Cather: A Critical Biography*, begun by E. K. Brown at the request of Edith Lewis, Cather's longtime companion and literary executor, and completed by Leon Edel, appeared in 1953.[80] The result of solid scholarship, it is valuable as a factual record as well as an examination of the autobiographical and psychological aspects of the fiction. Miss Lewis herself recorded "the memories and impressions that came to me spontaneously out of my long friendship with Willa Cather" in *Willa Cather Living* (1953), a companion volume to the critical biography.[81] Lewis' admiration and devotion are evident in the glimpses she gives us of her companion's daily life, which provide interesting connections between the people and places Cather knew and enjoyed and their part in her creative process. *Willa Cather, A Memoir* (1953) by Elizabeth S. Sergeant is the story of two literary lives crossing paths, although as the record of one writer's remembrances of another the true focus is often blurred.[82] Nevertheless, the discussion of Cather's interest in Sergeant's experiences in France during World War I is noteworthy.

James Woodress' *Willa Cather: Her Life and Art* (1970) updates the Brown/Edel biography, incorporating information from Cather letters unavailable to earlier biographers.[83] Woodress follows the Brown/Edel approach, examining the combination of life and art; he presents nothing startlingly new, but his work is solid and perceptive analysis. For those wishing to peruse Cather's letters on their own, Margaret Anne

O'Connor's invaluable 1974 "A Guide to the Letters of Willa Cather" identifies and comments on forty-three collections of Cather correspondence scattered throughout the country.[84] Published a year after the Woodress biography, *Willa Cather: The Woman and Her Works* by Marion M. Brown and Ruth Crone may prove of some interest to the layman, although it lacks both the scholarly and critical solidity of the other studies.[85] In a centennial essay publisher Alfred Knopf provides a revealing glimpse of Cather's professional attitude toward the printing and promotion of her books.[86]

Brown and Crone recently collaborated on a second biographical study, *Only One Point of the Compass: Willa Cather in the Northeast* (1980), which focuses primarily on Cather's summers on Grand Manan Island.[87] Again, lack of sound scholarship makes this volume like their earlier one unreliable. Another 1980 study, *Chrysalis: Willa Cather in Pittsburgh* by Kathleen D. Byrne and Richard C. Snyder, provides a factual record of an earlier phase of the career, concentrating on Cather's ten years in Pittsburgh as a journalist and high school teacher.[88] Long-standing biographical questions, especially concerning her relationship to the McClung family, are evaluated from as sound a basis of fact as possible.

The question of lesbianism has become a growing aspect of Cather biography and criticism, although her close guard on her private life limits conclusive evidence. In *Lesbian Images* (1975), Jane Rule sensibly warns against reading the fiction as autobiography and respects the author's desire to keep public and private lives separate.[89] Rather than restricting works to matters of sexual preference, Rule notes in the art "a capacity to transcend the conventions of what is masculine and what is feminine to see the more complex humanity of her characters." Quite another view is found in Deborah Lambert's 1982 article "The Defeat of a Hero: Autonomy and Sexuality in *My Ántonia*," which asserts that "Cather was a lesbian who could not, or did not, acknowledge her homosexuality and who, in her fiction, transformed her emotional life and experiences into acceptable, heterosexual forms and guises."[90] Simple assertion, however, neither answers the question nor establishes the fact. In "Cather and Her Friends" in the present volume James Woodress attempts to clarify the factual basis of this aspect of the life. Since lesbianism is likely to remain an important issue in Cather studies, one hopes that future critics will pursue it with an eye toward substantive understanding of the art rather than to make a case.

A fruitful outgrowth of these biographical studies has been recognition of the depth of Cather's interest in the dualism of the human psyche. The psychological complexity of Godfrey St. Peter in *House* has long captured Leon Edel's interest, serving for him as a standard example of the literary "case." The most recent elaboration of his views, appearing in *Stuff of Sleep and Dreams* (1982), is reprinted in this volume. Dorothy Van Ghent in her 1964 Minnesota pamphlet on Cather assessed the fiction in terms of two important psychological themes: the "theme of the lost self," that "self" of youth, "at once more generic and individual than the self allowed to live by the constrictions of American adulthood," and the theme of recovery—"to recover the ancestors, to redeem them from their forgotten places, to make them speak," thereby integrating "the self and the human past, in order that life may be affirmed and celebrated."[91]

Stanley Cooperman, Blanche Gelfant, and Kathleen L. Nichols (whose works appear in this volume) have examined psychological depths in several Cather males who are best understood in light of their frustrated and sublimated sexuality. Ellen Moers investigated similar depths in Cather women in her 1976 study *Literary Women*.[92] Discussing Cather with Colette, Woolf, and Stein, Moers sees her as the creator of modern heroines whose lives and passions can be viewed in terms of the Electra story. The demise of mother figures, Moers contends, causes great anguish for the narrative filters created by Cather in works such as *Lady* and *Enemy*. Sharon O'Brien subsequently examined dualism in the two narratives of Cather's first Nebraska novel in "The Unity of Willa Cather's 'Two-Part Pastoral': Passion in *O Pioneers!*," suggesting that the stories of Alexandra Bergson and of Marie and Emil are each a "parable about passion."[93] These stories represent "one of Willa Cather's most persistent fictional preoccupations: the insufficiency, even the danger, of sexual passion and the opposing grandeur of passion deflected from the personal to the impersonal object." Recently, in "Willa Cather's Women," Susan Rosowski explored the two-selves pattern within Cather heroines, limiting her thesis to how "a woman encounters contradictions between the human pattern of two selves and cultural myths that would limit her to only one of them."[94]

Critics have also provided significant insight into Cather's intense search for values, especially in traditions fast losing ground in modern, industrialized America. Howard Mumford Jones in *The Bright Medusa* (1952) reveals as a central theme in Cather's fiction the necessary accommodation the artist must make to survive in a world not committed to the pursuit of beauty.[95] In Francis X. Connolly's 1951 essay "Willa Cather: Memory as Muse," Cather is applauded for defending positive values and producing in her greatest work a record of "progress from one level of meaning and value to another; from the level of nature to the level of mind, and from the level of mind to the level of spirit."[96] In *The Twenties: American Writing in the Post-War Decade* (1954), Frederick Hoffman views *House* as a conflict between values past and present, noting the implications in Cather's handling of Godfrey St. Peter's attic study and the ironic disposition of Tom Outland's fortune.[97] It is an appreciation of Cather's strong sense of artistic integrity that George Greene offers in "Willa Cather at Mid-Century," particularly her "ideal of the artist as a bringer of truth."[98] In a 1960 Library of Congress lecture, Leon Edel considered such integrity as based on "unshakable faith in the old true things" despite life's constant changes.[99] Cather's own story, he suggests, is much like the patterned success and failure of her characters.

Cather's cognizance of values was examined two years earlier by Philip Gerber in terms of the rock as refuge in "Willa Cather and the Big Red Rock."[100] Gerber maintains that she is not so much out of step with her fellow writers as quite different, a representative of and believer in "the affirmative virtues of character, fidelity, idealism, civilization, culture, religion, ethics, and order. . . ." Her lifelong search for value is John Randall's subject in an exhaustive book-length study *The Landscape and the Looking-Glass* (1960), from which the summary comments on *Archbishop* have been included in the present volume. Randall attempts to look at the canon deeply and closely but ultimately raises as many questions as he answers, and readers will generally find his study confusing as well as provocative.

Studies focused toward values in particular works are probably more useful for clarifying or understanding Cather's artistic integrity. Sister Lucy Schneider's work with Cather's view of the land is adequately summarized in her 1972 article "Artistry and Instinct: Willa Cather's 'Land-Philosophy,'" which enumerates the seven basic tenets this critic elsewhere relates to specific texts, ranging from the land as a force working directly on man to land as source of man's transcendence.[101] In "Willa Cather and the Indian Heritage" (1976), David Stouck points out the feeling in Cather's fiction "which turns away from the American dream of selfhood toward the richness and complexity of the perceptual world, and which views art not as the product of self-expression but as a process of sympathy for people, places, and events."[102] Canadian cultural values attractive to Cather are noted in Benjamin George's "The French-Canadian Connection: Willa Cather as a Canadian Writer" (reprinted in this volume). He points specifically to tradition and societal involvement in *Shadows*, singling out the Canadian woodsmen who cherish their links to civilization.

A new dimension in Cather studies began in 1967 with the publication of *The Kingdom of Art* by the University of Nebraska Press. Edited by Bernice Slote, the volume gathered Cather's dramatic and literary criticism, 1893–96, and revealed both her intellectual complexity and the significant experience with the arts and world literature informing her fiction. This collection was followed in 1970 by Nebraska's two-volume *The World and the Parish*, edited by William Curtin, reprinting more journalistic writings, 1893–1902. *Willa Cather's Collected Short Fiction, 1893–1912* was revised in 1970 and supplemented three years later with *Uncle Valentine and Other Stories*, both Nebraska publications, restoring over fifty Cather stories to print. The surprising range of

Cather's sophistication and the exhaustive nature of her long apprenticeship were now completely at the service of critics, and Cather's works began to be considered in terms of sources, for echoes of other literatures, and in terms of literary forms. Some had anticipated this trend, among them Curtis Dahl, whose 1955 consideration of *Ántonia* assessed its Virgilian quality, and D. H. Stewart, who in 1966 viewed *Archbishop* as a truncated *Divine Comedy*.[103] In 1968 Nebraska published Richard Giannone's *Music in Willa Cather's Fiction*, which examines the novels not only from the perspective of musical references but from structural dimensions of musical techniques. Developed from a dissertation directed at Notre Dame by Joseph Brennan, who had published on the topic three years earlier, Giannone's thesis does not apply equally well to every novel, although Cather's deep knowledge of music and musicians becomes clear. (Giannone's analysis of *Song* is reprinted in the present volume.)

The activities surrounding Cather's centennial in 1973 contributed Donald Sutherland's fine exploration of influences from Greek and Latin literature, Bernice Slote's revelation of the web of literary associations (from Mickiewicz to Whitman) involved in Cather's creative process, and John Randall's argument that the novels are squarely within the pastoral tradition.[104] David Stouck's *Willa Cather's Imagination* (1975) considers the various modes through which the fiction moves (from pastoral to satiric), the literary forms she used to express her moral vision, and the art-life theme permeating her work.[105] Evelyn Helmick illustrated the courtly romance characteristics of *Lady* that same year, and Bernice Slote's introduction to the 1977 Bison edition of *Bridge* surveyed the mythological dimensions as well as image patterns of Cather's first novel. In the late 1970s *Western American Literature* published John Murphy's comparison of *Archbishop* and the *Aeneid* and also Ann Moseley's study of Dionysian and Apollonian polarities in *Song*.[106] (The Helmick, Slote, and Murphy essays are included in this volume.) Murphy's examination of *Lady*'s Niel Herbert and the hero of Euripides' *Hippolytus* appeared in *American Literature* in 1981, the same year Paul Olson made a valid case in *Prairie Schooner* for Cather's dependence on the *Aeneid*.[107] In the present volume, original essays by David Stouck and Paul Comeau exploring Cather's debt to French fiction fall within this critical category.

It is difficult to determine where such criticism by association leaves off and technical studies begin—it is merely a matter of emphasis, as in John Murphy's consideration in this volume of the role of biblical allusions and Whitman's poetry in integrating the "parts" of *Pioneers*, or Harry Eichorn's 1973 analysis (also included in this volume) of how Shakespearean references and Bellini's opera *Norma* supplement the narrator in *Enemy*. The first book-length study to focus on technique appeared in 1951, when David Daiches attempted an "appreciation" of the novels and short stories as prose fiction in *Willa Cather: A Critical Introduction*.[108] Although more at home with aesthetics, with narrative structures and the effects managed in landscapes and interiors, Daiches cautions against interpreting Cather too narrowly by not reading her carefully enough. A major study of narrative techniques as well as themes is Edward and Lillian Bloom's *Willa Cather's Gift of Sympathy* (1962); especially valuable is their chapter on literary theories and practices, and their analysis of Cather's use of W. J. Howlett's obscure biography of Denver's Bishop Machebeuf as a source for *Archbishop*. (The Blooms' concluding chapter is reprinted in this volume.) Three years later Clinton Keeler (in an essay also included here) assessed the contribution of painter Puvis de Chavannes' monumental style to Cather's treatment of westward movement and religion in *Archbishop*, and Isabel Charles explained how the tragic tale of the lovers contributes to the development of heroine Alexandra Bergson in *Pioneers*.[109] Terence Martin's 1969 *PMLA* article showed how narrator Jim's drama of memory gives structural coherence of *Ántonia*, such attention to formal matters continuing in Murphy's 1976 analysis of *Shadows* as a six-part composition of interwoven themes and Stouck's recent consideration of travel literature elements in *Archbishop*.[110] The 1982 *Great Plains Quarterly* Cather issue contains Susan Rosowski's examination of historical and symbolical narrative modes in *A Lost Lady* and Murphy's analysis of the handling of detail and character in *Ours*.[111] Use of landscape had been emphasized in Eudora Welty's centennial essay (included in this volume) on the physical quality of the world of the novels.

Cather's place in American literature and culture has been the subject of several studies, among them Bernard Baum's 1949 comparison of her and T. S. Eliot as waste-landers.[112] Philip Gerber's 1975 Twayne U.S. Authors Series *Willa Cather*, while disappointing in analyses of individual novels, is valuable for placing Cather in her literary milieu.[113] Gerber discusses the principles she shared with Howells as well as James, her anticapitalistic stance and ecological concerns. Several critics have considered relationships to the stages of the American frontier, among them James Miller, whose 1958 *Ántonia* essay examined cyclical patterns as the source of the book's emotional unity. [114] Marcus Cunliffe noted East-West tensions in Cather, and James Woodress her fusion of American experience and European culture in centennial essays.[115] John Murphy surveyed Cather's pioneer novels with Cooper's Leatherstocking and Littlepage novels as depictions of historian Frederick Jackson Turner's frontier thesis in a recent *Prairie Schooner* essay.[116]

In the 1972 Cather issue of *Western American Literature* Patricia Yongue described Niel Herbert's disillusionment at the end of the pioneer age in *Lady* as "suggestive" of Nick Carraway's loss of wonder in *The Great Gatsby*, and a comparison of Cather's and Hawthorne's handling of perennial American themes is John Murphy's subject in the 1975 *Renascence* Cather issue.[117] In 1968 Bruce Baker treated her changing attitude toward Nebraska and ability to translate provincial material into universal situations.[118] Bernice Slote followed up Baker's study in 1970 with a discussion of the regional material as timeless folk literature.[119] Wallace Stegner's essay on *Ántonia* in *The American Novel* (1965) considers Cather's discovery of what she was born to write in terms of Jim Burden's departure and return, "a demonstration of how such an American may reconcile the two halves of himself."[120]

Our survey of Cather criticism is representative rather than complete, and we refer readers to Bernice Slote's bibliographical essay on Cather in *Sixteen Modern American Authors* (1973) and to the "Fiction 1900–1930s" essays in the annual volumes of *American Literary Scholarship*.[121] A helpful companion volume to the present one is *Willa Cather and Her Critics* (1967), edited by James Schroeter, which offers general estimates by big-name critics from H. L. Mencken to Leon Edel.[122] Activity in the world of Cather studies has never been greater. A few among several instances of work recently completed or in process are novelist Doris Grumbach's biography of Cather, a book-length study (the first) of the short fiction by Marilyn Arnold (Ohio University Press), and University of Nebraska's *Willa Cather: A Bibliography* (of primary sources) by Joan Crane.

John J. Murphy
Kevin A. Synnott

ACKNOWLEDGMENTS

This volume could not have been prepared without the untiring efforts of my wife Sally, who types, retypes, and sustains my efforts, and Kevin Synnott, who shared the burdens of the Introduction and gave encouragement. I am especially indebted to David Stouck, James Woodress, and Paul Comeau, who wrote original essays for the collection, and to all who agreed to have their works reprinted. Elizabeth O'Brien of the McQuade Library, Merrimack College, was especially helpful in locating publishers and sources. My work was assisted by a fellowship from the National Endowment for the Humanities and a Merrimack College faculty development grant. Thanks are due as well to the many students who have studied Willa Cather with me over the years at Merrimack College.

John J. Murphy

Notes

1. "Definitions and Evaluations," in *The Art of Willa Cather*, ed. Bernice Slote and Virginia Faulkner (Lincoln: Univ. of Nebraska Press, 1974), p. 235.

2. *Letters of Wallace Stevens*, ed. Holly Stevens (New York: (Alfred A. Knopf, 1966), p. 381.

3. "An Exploration of Cather's Early Writing," *Great Plains Quarterly*, 2 (1982), 211.

4. Anon., 38 (June 1, 1905), 394. Notes are provided only for those reviews containing unique insights or quoted at some length. Most reviews cited are merely representative, indicating the general reception given individual works.

5. E. U. S., July 16, 1913, p. 18.

6. *Bookman*, 37 (Aug., 1913), 666–67.

7. *Nation*, 101 (Oct. 14, 1915), 461–62.

8. Anon., 5 (Dec. 11, 1915), 153–55.

9. See Cather's "Preface" to revised edition of *The Song of the Lark* (Boston: Houghton Mifflin, 1932), pp. v–vi.

10. "Chapters in 'Great American Novel,'" Nov. 13, 1915, Sec. 3, p. 7.

11. *Dial*, 65 (Dec. 14, 1918), 557.

12. (New York: Alfred A. Knopf, 1920), pp. 28–31.

13. (New York: Macmillan, 1922), pp. 113–22.

14. 25 (Jan. 19, 1921), 233–34.

15. Anon., *Nation*, 111 (Sept. 25, 1920), 352–53.

16. See "Prefatory Note," *Not Under Forty* (New York: Alfred A. Knopf, 1936), p. v.

17. *World* (New York), Sept. 13, 1922, p. 13.

18. Oct., 1922, pp. 26–27.

19. "Atlantic's Bookshelf," *Atlantic Monthly*, 130 (Nov., 1922), 16.

20. "Willa Cather, Novelist of the Middle Western Farm," June 24, 1923, p. 5.

21. *Independent*, 111 (Oct. 27, 1923), 198–99.

22. *Nation*, 117 (Nov. 28, 1923), 610.

23. "Willa Cather," in 219 (May, 1924), 641–52.

24. "Willa Cather," in 13 (1924), 373–80.

25. Sept. 6, 1925, p. 8.

26. *San Francisco Examiner*, Oct. 3, 1925, Editorial Page, n.p.

27. *Saturday Review of Literature*, 2 (Sept. 26, 1925), 151.

28. *New York Times Book Review*, Sept. 4, 1927, p. 2.

29. "Miss Cather's Business as an Artist," *New York Herald Tribune Books*, Sept. 11, 1927, pp. 1, 5–6; reprinted in *The Strange Necessity* (New York: Doubleday, Doran, 1928), pp. 233–48.

30. "Willa Cather," in *Spokesmen: Modern Writers and American Life* (New York: Appleton, 1928), pp. 139–60.

31. (Boston: Little, Brown & Co., 1928), pp. 238–48.

32. "Willa Cather," in 37 (1939), 221–39.

33. New York: Robert M. McBride, 1930.

34. *Main Currents in American Thought*, vol. 3 (New York: Harcourt, Brace & Co., 1930), pp. 382–83.

35. Marble, *A Study of the Modern Novel British and American since 1900* (New York: D. Appleton & Co., 1930), pp. 381–88; Pattee, *The New American Literature* (New York: Century Co., 1930), pp. 260–65.

36. *The Rediscovery of the Frontier* (Chicago: Univ. of Chicago Press, 1931), pp. 116–19.

37. *New York Times Book Review*, Aug. 2, 1931, p. 1.

38. *Symposium*, 2 (Oct., 1931), 551–54.

39. 74 (Mar., 1932), 634–40.

40. "American Classic," in 7 (Aug. 8, 1931), 19–22.

41. *American Humor* (New York: Harcourt, Brace & Co., 1931), pp. 220–21.

42. *American Literature As an Expression of the National Mind*, rev. ed. (New York: Holt, Rinehart and Winston, 1931, 1949), pp. 673–79.

43. "The Novel Dedicate," *Virginia Quarterly Review*, 8 (1932), 410–18.

44. *Expression in America* (New York: Harper and Brothers, 1932), pp. 538–43.

45. Fadiman, *Nation*, 135 (August 3, 1932), 107; Mac Afee, *Yale Review*, 22 (Autumn, 1932), vi.

46. 9 (Aug. 6, 1932), 29.

47. *New York Times Book Review*, July 31, 1932, p. 1.

48. "Willa Cather: The Past Recaptured," in 135 (Dec. 7, 1932), 563–65.

49. 22 (1933), 703–10.

50. *The Art of the Novel* (New York: Macmillan, 1933), pp. 255–67.

51. Halleck, *The Romance of American Literature* (New York: American Book Co., 1934), pp. 312–20; Hatcher, *Creating the Modern American Novel* (New York: Farrar, Strauss, 1935), pp. 58–71.

52. Hartwick, *The Foreground of American Fiction* (New York: American Book Co., 1934), pp. 389–404; Quinn, *American Fiction* (New York: D. Appleton & Co., 1936), pp. 683–97.

53. (Boston: American Book Co., 1936), expanded to *The Story of American Letters* (Chicago: Regnery, 1956), pp. 357–64.

54. *New Republic*, 85 (Dec. 11, 1935), 149–50.

55. *New Statesman and Nation*, 10 (Aug. 3, 1935), 166.

56. *American Review*, 5 (Oct., 1935), 625–29.

57. "Willa Cather," *New Republic*, 90 (Feb. 10, 1937), 10–13.

58. "The Genius of Willa Cather," in 10 (1938), 123–41.

59. "The Novels of Willa Cather," *Saturday Review of Literature*, 18 (Aug. 6, 1938), 3–4, 16.

60. "The Greatest American Novelist," *Newsweek*, 11 (Jan. 3, 1928), 29.

61. "Willa Cather: Civilized and Very American," *New York Herald Tribune Books*, Dec. 15, 1940, p. 6.

62. Ross, *New York Herald Tribune Books*, Dec. 8, 1940, p. 1; Fisher, *Book-of-the-Month Club News*, Dec., 1940, pp. 2–3.

63. *Commonweal*, 33 (Jan. 10, 1941), 306–07.

64. (New York: Macmillan Co., 1940), pp. 281–93.

65. (Chicago: Univ. of Chicago Press, 1940), pp. 150–63.

66. *American Mirror* (New York: Macmillan Co., 1940), p. 152.

67. "The Slump in American Writing," *American Mercury*, 49 (1940), 185–91.

68. "Willa Cather," in 40 (1942), 18–25.

69. (New York: Harcourt, Brace, 1942), pp. 247–57.

70. "Willa Cather (1876–1947)," *Saturday Review of Literature*, 302 (May 10, 1947), 22–24.

71. "Willa Cather, 1876–1947," *College English*, 9 (1947), 8–18.

72. "Willa Cather," *Nation*, 164 (June 14, 1947), 713–16; reprinted in *Craft and Character* (New York: Viking Press, 1957), pp. 264–75.

73. (Boston: Houghton Mifflin Co., 1947), pp. 153–220.

74. 31 (Sept. 18, 1948), 25.

75. 167 (Oct. 2, 1948), 376.

76. *New York Times Book Review*, Sept. 12, 1948, p. 3.

77. George Arms, item 35, and W. S. Scott, item 58, 5 (1947).

78. "Willa Cather's Juvenilia," *Prairie Schooner*, 22 (1948), 97–111; Flora Bullock, "Willa Cather: Essayist and Drama Critic, 1891–1895," *Prairie Schooner*, 23 (1949), 393–401.

79. Rev. ed. (Lincoln: Univ. of Nebraska Press, 1961).

80. New York: Alfred A. Knopf, 1953.

81. New York: Alfred A. Knopf, 1953.

82. Philadelphia: Lippincott, 1953; rpt. ed., Lincoln: University of Nebraska Press, 1963.

83. New York: Western Publishing Co., 1970; rpt. ed., Lincoln: University of Nebraska Press, 1975.

84. *Resources for American Literary Study*, 4 (1974), 145–72.

85. New York: Scribner's, 1970.

86. "Miss Cather," in *The Art of Willa Cather*, pp. 205–24.

87. Danbury, Conn.: Archer Editions, 1980.

88. Pittsburgh: Historical Society of Western Pennsylvania, 1980.

89. (Garden City, N.Y.: Doubleday, 1975), pp. 74–87.

90. *American Literature*, 53 (1982), 676–90.

91. *Willa Cather* (Minneapolis: Univ. of Minnesota Press, 1964).

92. (Garden City, N.Y.; Doubleday, 1976), pp. 230–42, 255–63.

93. *Studies in American Fiction*, 6 (1978), 157–70.

94. *Studies in American Fiction*, 9 (1981), 261–75.

95. Urbana: Univ. of Illinois Press, 1952.

96. In *Fifty Years of the American Novel*, ed. Harold C. Gardiner (New York: Scribner's, 1951), pp. 69–87.

97. Rev. ed. (New York: Free Press, 1962), pp. 181–90.

98. *Thought*, 32 (1957), 577–92.

99. *Willa Cather: The Paradox of Success* (Washington: Library of Congress, 1960).

100. *College English*, 19 (1958), 152–57.

101. *College Language Association Journal*, 16 (1973), 485–504.

102. *Twentieth Century Literature*, 22 (1976), 433–43.

103. "An American Georgic: Willa Cather's *My Antonia*," *Comparative Literature*, 7 (1955), 43–51; "Cather's Mortal Comedy," *Queen's Quarterly*, 73, (1966), 244–59.

104. Sutherland, "Willa Cather: The Classic Voice," in *The Art of Willa Cather*, pp. 156–79; Slote, "Willa Cather: The Secret Web," in *Five Essays on Willa Cather: The Merrimack Symposium*, ed. John J. Murphy (North Andover, Mass.: Merrimack College, 1974), pp. 1–19; Randall, "Willa Cather and the Pastoral Tradition," in *Five Essays*, pp. 75–96.

105. Lincoln: Univ. of Nebraska Press, 1975.

106. "The Dual Nature of Art in *The Song of the Lark*," in 14 (1979), 19–32.

107. "Euripides' *Hippolytus* and Cather's *A Lost Lady*," in 53 (1981), 72–86; "The Epic and Great Plains Literature: Rølvaag, Cather and Neihardt," in 55 (1981), 263–85.

108. (Ithaca: Cornell Univ. Press, 1951).

109. "Love and Death in Willa Cather's *O Pioneers!*," *College Language Association Journal*, 9 (1965), 140–50.

110. "The Drama of Memory in *My Ántonia*," in 84 (1969), 304–11; "The Art of *Shadows on the Rock*," *Prairie Schooner*, 50 (1976), 37–51; "Cather's *Archbishop* and Travel Writing," *Western American Literature*, 17 (1982), 3–12.

111. "Willa Cather's *A Lost Lady*: Art Versus the Closing Frontier," in 2 (1982), 239–48; "*One of Ours* as American Naturalism," pp. 232–38.

112. "Willa Cather's Wasteland," *South Atlantic Quarterly* 48 (1949), 589–601.

113. Boston: Twayne Publishers, 1975.

114. "*My Ántonia*, A Frontier Drama of Time," *American Quarterly*, 10 (1958), 476–84.

115. Cunliffe, "The Two or More Worlds of Willa Cather," in *The Art of Willa Cather*, pp. 21–42; Woodress, "Willa Cather: American Experiences and European Tradition," pp. 43–62.

116. "Cooper, Cather and the Downward Path to Progress," in 55 (1981), 168–84.

117. "*A Lost Lady*: The End of the First Cycle," in 7 (1972), 3–12; "Willa Cather and Hawthorne: Significant Resemblances," in 27 (1975), 161–75.

118. "Nebraska Regionalism in Selected Works of Willa Cather," *Western American Literature*, 3 (1968), 19–35.

119. "Willa Cather as a Regional Writer," *Kansas Quarterly*, 2 (1970), 7–15.

120. (New York: Basic Books, 1965), pp. 144–53.

121. "Willa Cather," in *Sixteen Modern American Authors*, ed. Jackson Bryer (New York: W. W. Norton, 1973), pp. 29–73; *American Literary Scholarship*, ed. J. Albert Robbins and James Woodress (Durham, N.C.: Duke Univ. Press, 1965–).

122. Ithaca, N.Y.: Cornell Univ. Press, 1967.

ESSAYS

General Essays

Critical Reflections on Willa Cather

Katherine Anne Porter*

I never knew her at all, nor anyone who did know her; do not to this day. When I was a young writer in New York I knew she was there, and sometimes wished that by some charming chance I might meet up with her; but I never did, and it did not occur to me to seek her out. I had never felt that my condition of beginning authorship gave me a natural claim to the attention of writers I admired, such as Henry James and W. B. Yeats. Some proper instinct told me that all of any importance they had to say to me was in their printed pages, mine to use as I could. Still it would have been nice to have seen them, just to remember how they looked. There are three or four great ones, gone now, that I feel, too late, I should not have missed. Willa Cather was one of them.

There exist large numbers of critical estimates of her work, appreciations; perhaps even a memoir or two, giving glimpses of her personal history—I have never read one. She was not, in the popular crutch-word to describe almost any kind of sensation, "exciting"; so far as I know, nobody, not even one of the Freudian school of critics, ever sat up nights with a textbook in one hand and her works in the other, reading between the lines to discover how much sexual autobiography could be mined out of her stories. I remember only one photograph—Steichen's—made in middle life, showing a plain smiling woman, her arms crossed easily over a girl scout sort of white blouse, with a ragged part in her hair. She seemed, as the French say, "well seated" and not very outgoing. Even the earnestly amiable, finely shaped eyes, the left one faintly askew, were in some mysterious way not expressive, lacking as they did altogether that look of strangeness which a strange vision is supposed to give to the eye of any real artist, and very often does. One doesn't have to be a genius absolutely to get this look, it is often quite enough merely to

*Afterword by Katherine Anne Porter from *The Troll Garden* by Willa Cather. Copyright (c) 1961 by Katherine Anne Porter. Reprinted by arrangement with the New American Library, Inc., New York, New York.

believe one is a genius; and to have had the wild vision only once is enough—the afterlight stays, even if, in such case, it is phosphorescence instead of living fire.

Well, Miss Cather looks awfully like somebody's big sister, or maiden aunt, both of which she was. No genius ever looked less like one, according to the romantic popular view, unless it was her idol, Flaubert, whose photographs could pass easily for those of any paunchy country squire indifferent to his appearance. Like him, none of her genius was in her looks, only in her works. Flaubert was a good son, adoring uncle of a niece, devoted to his friends, contemptuous of the mediocre, obstinate in his preferences, fiercely jealous of his privacy, unyielding to the death in his literary principles and not in the slightest concerned with what was fashionable. No wonder she loved him. She had been rebuffed a little at first, not by his astronomical standards in art—none could be too high for her—but by a certain coldness of heart in him. She soon got over that; it became for her only another facet of his nobility of mind.

Very early she had learned to reverence that indispensable faculty of aspiration of the human mind toward perfection called, in morals and the arts, nobility. She was born to the idea and brought up in it: first in a comfortable farmhouse in Virginia, and later, the eldest of seven children, in a little crowded ranch house in Nebraska. She had, as many American country people did have in those times and places, literate parents and grandparents, soundly educated and deeply read, educated, if not always at schools, always at their own firesides. Two such, her grandmothers, taught her from her infancy. Her sister, Mrs. Auld, in Palo Alto, California, told it like this:

"She mothered us all, took care of us, and there was a lot to do in such a big family. She learned Greek and Latin from her grandmothers before she ever got to go to school. She used to go, after we lived in Red Cloud, to read Latin and Greek with a little old man who kept a general store down the road. In the evenings for entertainment—there was nowhere to go, you know, almost nothing to see or hear—she entertained us, it was good as a theater for us! She told us long stories, some she made up herself, and some were her versions of legends and fairy tales she had read; she taught us Greek mythology this way, Homer, and tales from the Old Testament. We were all story tellers," said her sister, "all of us wanted to be the one to tell the stories, but she was the one who told them. And we loved to listen all of us to her, when maybe we would not have listened to each other."

She was not the first nor the last American writer to be formed in this system of home education; at one time it was the customary education for daughters, many of them never got to school at all or expected to; but they were capable of educating their grandchildren, as this little history shows. To her last day Willa Cather was the true child of her plain-living, provincial farming people, with their aristocratic ways of feeling and thinking; poor, but not poverty-stricken for a moment; rock-based in character, a character shaped in an old school of good manners, good morals, and the unchallenged assumption that classic culture was their birthright; the belief that knowledge of great art and great thought was a good in itself not to be missed for anything; she subscribed to it all with her whole heart, and in herself there was the vein of iron she had inherited from a long line of people who had helped to break wildernesses and to found a new nation in such faiths. When you think of the whole unbelievable history, how did anything like this survive? Yet it did, and this life is one of the proofs.

I have not much interest in anyone's personal history after the tenth year, not even my own. Whatever one was going to be was all prepared for before that. The rest is merely confirmation, extension, development. Childhood is the fiery furnace in which we are melted down to essentials and that essential shaped for good. While I have been reading again Willa Cather's essays and occasional papers, and thinking about her, I remembered a sentence from the diaries of Anne Frank, who died in the concentration camp in Bergen-Belsen just before she was sixteen years old. At less than fifteen, she wrote: "I have had a lot of sorrow, but who hasn't, at my age?"

In Miss Cather's superb little essay on Katherine Mansfield, she speaks of childhood and family life: "I doubt whether any contemporary writer has made one feel more keenly the many kinds of personal relations which exist in an everyday 'happy family' who are merely going on with their daily lives, with no crises or shocks or bewildering complications. . . . Yet every individual in that household (even the children) is clinging passionately to his individual soul, is in terror of losing it in the general family flavor . . . the mere struggle to have anything of one's own, to be oneself at all, creates an element of strain which keeps everybody almost at breaking point.

". . . Even in harmonious families there is this double life . . . the one we can observe in our neighbor's household, and, underneath, another—secret and passionate and intense—which is the real life that stamps the faces and gives character to the voices of our friends. Always in his mind each member is escaping, running away, trying to break the net which circumstances and his own affections have woven about him. One realizes that human relationships are the tragic necessity of human life; that they can never be wholly satisfactory, that every ego is half the time greedily seeking them, and half the time pulling away from them."

This is masterly and water-clear and autobiography enough for me: my mind goes with tenderness to the lonely slow-moving girl who happened to be an artist coming back from reading Latin and Greek with the old storekeeper, helping with the housework, then sitting by the fireplace to talk down an assertive brood of brothers and sisters, practicing her art on them, refusing to be lost among them—the longest-winged one who would fly free at last.

I am not much given to reading about authors, or not until I have read what they have to say for themselves. I found Willa Cather's books for myself, early, and felt no need for intermediaries between me and them. My reading went on for a good many years, one by one as they appeared: *O Pioneers!; The Song of the Lark; My Ántonia; Youth and the Bright Medusa; Death Comes for the Archbishop; Obscure Destinies;* just these, and no others, I do not know why, and never anything since, until I read her notebooks about two years ago. Those early readings began in Texas, just before World War I, before I left home; they ended in Paris, twenty years later, after the longest kind of journey.

With her first book I was reading also Henry James, W. B. Yeats, Joseph Conrad, my introduction to "modern" literature, for I was brought up on solid reading, too, well aged. About the same time I read Gertrude Stein's *Tender Buttons*, for sale at a little bookshop with a shoeshine stand outside; inside you could find magazines, books, newspapers in half-a-dozen languages, avant-garde and radical and experimental; this in a Texas coast town of less than ten thousand population but very polyglot and full of world travelers. I could make little headway with Miss Stein beyond the title. It was plain that she meant "tender buds" and I wondered why she did not say so. It was the beginning of my quarrel with a certain school of "modern" writing in which poverty of feeling and idea were disguised, but not well enough, in tricky techniques and disordered syntax. A year or two after *Tender Buttons* I was reading Joyce's *Dubliners*, and maybe only a young beginning writer of that time, with some preparation of mind by the great literature of the past, could know what a revelation that small collection of matchless stories could be. It was not a shock, but a revelation, a further unfolding of the deep world of the imagination. I had never heard of Joyce. By the pure chance of my roving curiosity, I picked up a copy of the book at that little shoeshine bookstore. It was a great day.

By the time I reached Paris, I had done my long apprenticeship, published a small book of my own, and had gone like a house afire through everything "new"—that word meant something peculiar to the times—absolutely everything "new" that was being published; also in music; also painting. I considered almost any painting with the varnish still wet, the artist standing by, so to speak, as more interesting than anything done even the year before. But some of the painters were Klee, Juan Gris, Modigliani. . . . I couldn't listen to music happily if it wasn't hot from the composer's brain, preferably conducted or played by himself. Still, some of the music was Stravinsky's and Béla Bartók's and Poulenc's. I was converted to the harpsichord by the first New York recital of Wanda

Landowska. In the theater I preferred dress rehearsals, or even just rehearsals, to the finished performance; I was mad about the ballet and took lessons off and on with a Russian for two years; I even wrote a ballet libretto way back in 1920 for a young Mexican painter and scene designer who gave the whole thing to Pavlova, who danced it in many countries but not in New York, because the scenery was done on paper, was inflammable and she was not allowed to use it in New York. I saw photographs, however, and I must say they did not look in the least like anything I had provided for in the libretto. It was most unsatisfactory.

What has this to do with Willa Cather? A great deal. I had had time to grow up, to consider, to look again, to begin finding my way a little through the inordinate clutter and noise of my immediate day, in which very literally everything in the world was being pulled apart, torn up, turned wrong side out and upside down; almost no frontiers left unattacked, governments and currencies falling; even the very sexes seemed to be changing back and forth and multiplying weird, unclassifiable genders. And every day, in the arts, as in schemes of government and organized crime, there was, there had to be, something New.

Alas, or thank God, depending on the way you feel about it, there comes that day when today's New begins to look a little like yesterday's New, and then more and more so; you begin to suffer slightly from a sense of sameness or repetition: that painting, that statue, that music, that kind of writing, that way of thinking and feeling, that revolution. that political doctrine—is it really New? The answer is simply no, and if you are really in a perverse belligerent mood, you may add a half-truth—no, and it never was. Looking around at the debris, you ask has newness merely for its own sake any virtue? And you find that all along you had held and wound in your hand through the maze an unbreakable cord on which one by one, hardly knowing it, you had strung your life's treasures; it was as if they had come of themselves, while you were seeking and choosing and picking up and tossing away again, down all sorts of by-paths and up strange stairs and into queer corners; and there they were, things old and new, the things you loved first and those you loved last, all together and yours, and no longer old or new, but outside of time and beyond the reach of change, even your own; for that part of your life they belong to was in some sense made by them; if they went, all that part of your life would be mutilated, unrecognizable. While you hold and wind that cord with its slowly accumulating, weightless, unaccountable riches, the maze seems a straight road; you look back through all the fury you have come through, when it seemed so much, and so dismayingly, destruction, and so much just the pervasively trivial, stupid, or malignant-dwarfish tricks: fur-lined cups as sculpture, symphonies written for kitchen batteries, experiments on language very similar to the later Nazi surgical experiments of cutting and uniting human nerve ends never meant to touch each other: so many perversities crowding in so close you could hardly see beyond them. Yet look, you shared it, you were part of it, you even added to the confusion, so busy being new yourself. The fury and waste and clamor was, after all, just what you had thought it was in the first place, even if you had lost sight of it later— life, in a word, and great glory came of it, and splendid things that will go on living cleared of all the rubbish thrown up around their creation. Things you would have once thought incompatible to eternity take their right places in peace, in proper scale and order, in your mind—in your blood. They become that marrow in your bones where the blood is renewed.

I had liked best of all Willa Cather's two collections of short stories. They live still with morning freshness in my memory, their clearness, warmth of feeling, calmness of intelligence, an ample human view of things; in short the sense of an artist at work in whom one could have complete confidence: not even the prose attracted my attention from what the writer was saying—really saying, and not just in the words. Also I remember well my deeper impression of reserve—a reserve that was personal because it was a matter of temperament, the grain of the mind; yet conscious too, and practiced deliberately: almost a method, a technique, but not assumed. It was instead a manifesting, proceeding from the moral nature of the artist, morality extended to aesthetics—not aesthetics as morality but simply a development of both faculties along with all the others until the whole being was indivisibly one, the imagination and its expression fused and fixed.

A magnificent state, no doubt, at which to arrive; but it should be the final one, and Miss Cather seemed to be there almost from the first. What was it? For I began to have an image of her as a kind of lighthouse, or even a promontory, some changeless phenomenon of art or nature or both. I have a peculiar antipathy to thinking of anyone I know in symbols or mythical characters and this finally quietly alienated me from her, from her very fine books, from any feeling that she was a living, working artist in our time. It is hard to explain, for it was a question of tone, of implication, and what else? Finally, after a great while, I decided that Miss Cather's reserve amounted to a deliberate withholding of some vital part of herself as artist; not as if she had hidden herself at the center of her mystery but was still there to be disclosed at last; no, she had absented herself willfully.

I was quite wrong of course. She is exactly at the center of her own mystery, where she belongs. My immoderate reading of our two or three invaluably afflicted giants of contemporary literature, and their abject army of camp followers and imitators, had blurred temporarily my perception of that thin line separating self-revealment from self-exhibition. Miss Cather had never any intention of using fiction or any other form of writing as a device for showing herself off. She was not Paul in travesty, nor the opera singer in "The Diamond Mine," nor that girl with the clear eyes who became an actress: above all, not the Lost Lady. Of course she was all of them. How not? She made all of them out of herself, where else could they have taken on life?

Her natural lack of picturesqueness was also a good protective coloring: it saved her from the invasive prying of hangers-on: and no "school" formed in her name. The young writers did not swarm over her with flattery, manuscripts in hand, meaning to use her for all she was worth; publishers did not waylay her with seductions the instant her first little book appeared; all S. S. McClure could think of to do for her, after he published *The Troll Garden*, was to offer her a job as one of his editors on *McClure's Magazine*, where she worked hard for six mortal years before it seems to have occurred to her that she was not being a writer, after all, which was what she had started out for. So she quit her job, and the next year, more or less, published *Alexander's Bridge*, of which she afterward repented, for reasons that were to last her a lifetime. The scene, London, was strange and delightful to her; she was trying to make a novel out of some interesting people in what seemed to her exotic situations, instead of out of something she really knew about with more than the top of her mind. "London is supposed to be more engaging than, let us say, Gopher Prairie," she remarks, "even if the writer knows Gopher Prairie very well and London very casually."

She realized at once that *Alexander's Bridge* was a mistake, her wrong turning, which could not be retraced too instantly and entirely. It was a very pretty success, and could have been her finish, except that she happened to be Willa Cather. For years she still found people who liked that book, but they couldn't fool her. She knew what she had done. So she left New York and went to Arizona for six months, not for repentance but for refreshment, and found there a source that was to refresh her for years to come. Let her tell of her private apocalypse in her own words: "I did no writing down there, but I recovered from the conventional editorial point of view."

She then began to write a book for herself—*O Pioneers!*—and it was "a different process altogether. Here there was no arranging or 'inventing'; everything was spontaneous and took its own place, right or wrong. This was like taking a ride through a familiar country on a horse that knew the way, on a fine morning when you felt like riding. The other was like riding in a park, with someone not altogether congenial, to whom you had to be talking all the time."

What are we to think? For certainly here is a genius who simply will not cater to our tastes for drama, who refuses to play the role in any way we have been accustomed to seeing it played. She wrote with immense sympathy about Stephen Crane: "There is every evidence that he was a reticent and unhelpful man, with no warmhearted love of giving out opinions." If she had said "personal confidences" she could as well have been writing about herself. But she was really writing about Stephen Crane and stuck to her subject. Herself, she gave out quite a lot of opinions, not all of them warmhearted, in the course of two short little books, the second a partial reprint of the first. You hardly realize how many and how firm and how cogent while reading her fine pure direct prose, hearing through it a level, well-tempered voice saying very good, sensible right things with complete authority—things not in fashion but close to here and now and always, not like a teacher or a mother—like an artist—until, after you have closed the book, her point of view begins to accumulate and take shape in your mind.

Freud had happened: but Miss Cather continued to cite the old Hebrew prophets, the Greek dramatists, Goethe, Shakespeare, Dante, Tolstoy, Flaubert, and such for the deeper truths of human nature, both good and evil. She loved Shelley, Wordsworth, Walter Pater, without any reference to their public standing at the time. In her essay, "The Novel Démeublé," she had the inspired notion to bring together for purposes of comparison Balzac and Prosper Merimée; she preferred Merimée on the ground quite simply that he was the better artist: you have to sort out Balzac's meanings from a great dusty warehouse of misplaced vain matter—furniture, in a word. Once got at, they are as vital as ever. But Merimée is as vital, and you cannot cut one sentence without loss from his stories. The perfect answer to the gross power of the one, the too-finished delicacy of the other was, of course, Flaubert.

Stravinsky had happened; but she went on being dead in love with Wagner, Beethoven, Schubert, Gluck, especially *Orpheus*, and almost any opera. She was music-mad, and even Ravel's *La Valse* enchanted her; perhaps also even certain later music, but she has not mentioned it in these papers.

The Nude had Descended the Staircase with an epoch-shaking tread but she remained faithful to Puvis de Chavannes, whose wall paintings in the Panthéon of the legend of St. Geneviève inspired the form and tone of *Death Comes for the Archbishop*. She longed to tell old stories as simply as that, as deeply centered in the core of experience without extraneous detail as in the lives of the saints in *The Golden Legend*. She loved Courbet, Rembrandt, Millet and the sixteenth-century Dutch and Flemish painters, with their "warmly furnished interiors" but always with a square window open to the wide gray sea, where the masts of the great Dutch fleets were setting out to "ply quietly on all the waters of the globe. . . ."

Joyce had happened: or perhaps we should say, *Ulysses*, for the work has now fairly absorbed the man we knew. I believe that this is true of all artists of the first order. They are not magnified in their work, they disappear in it, consumed by it. That subterranean upheaval of language caused not even the barest tremor in Miss Cather's firm, lucid sentences.

There is good internal evidence that she read a great deal of contemporary literature, contemporary over a stretch of fifty years, and think what contemporaries they were—from Tolstoy and Hardy and James and Chekhov to Gide and Proust and Joyce and Lawrence and Virginia Woolf, to Sherwood Anderson and Theodore Dreiser: the first names that come to mind. There was a regiment of them; it was as rich and fruitfully disturbing a period as literature has to show for several centuries. And it did make an enormous change. Miss Cather held firmly to what she had found for herself, did her own work in her own way as all the others were doing each in his unique way, and did help greatly to save and reassert and illustrate the validity of certain great and dangerously threatened principles of art. Without too much fuss, too—and is quietly disappearing into her work altogether, as we might expect.

Mr. Maxwell Geismar wrote a book about her and some others, called *The Last of the Provincials*. Not having read it I do not know his argument; but he has a case: she is a provincial; and I hope not the last. She was a good artist, and all true art is provincial in the most realistic sense: of the very time and place of its making, out of human beings who are so particularly limited by their situation, whose faces and names are real and whose lives begin each one at an individual unique center. Indeed, Willa Cather was as provincial as Hawthorne or Flaubert or Turgenev, as little concerned with aesthetics and as much with morals as Tolstoy, as obstinately reserved as Melville. In fact she always reminds me of very good literary company, of the particularly admirable masters who formed her youthful tastes, her thinking and feeling.

She is a curiously immovable shape, monumental, virtue itself in her art and a symbol of virtue—like certain churches, in fact, or exemplary women, revered and neglected. Yet like these again, she has her faithful friends and true believers, even so to speak her lovers, and they last a lifetime, and after: the only kind of bond she would recognize or require or respect.

Willa Cather and the Tradition
Edward A. and Lillian D. Bloom*

There is a steadiness about Willa Cather's fiction that defies the crosscurrents of the literary age in which she lived and wrote. Like many conscientious American writers, she was profoundly aware of the grow-

*From *Willa Cather's Gift of Sympathy* by Edward A. and Lillian D. Bloom, pp. 237–50. Copyright © 1962 by Southern Illinois University Press. Reprinted by permission of Southern Illinois University Press and the authors.

ing cleavage in her society between moral values and expedient action. Dislocations following the military and economic disasters she witnessed in her lifetime caused her to share a widespread fear that the future was bleakly uncertain, that a spiritual chaos threatened the central purpose of existence. More than most thoughtful Americans, perhaps, she was personally sensitive to devalued conduct and customs. Because she had consciously built her life upon a structure of traditions, and because she had preferred the solid virtues of an inspiriting past to the mercurial shifts of practical reality, she suspiciously resisted change. From time to time she protested against the violation of durable truths, although rarely in the clamorous voice used by many contemporary writers. Looking backward to the fixed values of a satisfying past, she reaffirmed the moral standards she cherished, thus ultimately denying they could be destroyed by temporary upheavals. In so doing, she committed herself to a pattern of continuity and became part of an exclusive but nevertheless great tradition of American writing.

Given fullest expression in the nineteenth century, the tradition is synthesized in the fiction of Cooper, Hawthorne, Melville, and James. Although they differed in their reactions to the convulsions afflicting an America in flux, they are unified by certain connections of personal responsibility. In the opinion of Marius Bewley (*The Complex Fate*, New York, 1954, pp. 3–4), these authors "form a line in American writing based on a finely critical consciousness of the national society." Although all of them drew upon America as the source of their creative purpose, they resembled each other in their awareness of national exigencies rather than in any superficial resort to a common region or even set of circumstances.

Admiring the potential greatness of their country, they at the same time recognized certain shortcomings and imperfections which menaced that greatness. Their art, which makes their union in a tradition relevant, was derived from a conflict between apprehension and conviction. Their tradition was compounded of earnest, mutual concern for the realization of an American destiny. Because they identified their fears with their hopes, they felt obliged to acknowledge that the positive advances of which their nation was capable were too frequently accompanied by attrition. In order to nullify, or at least retard, negative developments, they often spoke out against them in sharply critical fashion. Constructive criticism became one of their means of asserting optimistic conclusions.

In every essential detail, Willa Cather aspired toward the ethical and creative goals of the great tradition, consequently becoming the twentieth-century successor of these four nineteenth-century novelists. Miss Cather's novels are still relatively recent, and historical perspective may not yet permit an ultimate evaluation of her literary position. We do have standards of continuity by which we may measure her achievement, however, and if these standards have any critical validity then Miss Cather is surely in the line of succession. More notably even than Cooper, and with a moral intensity comparable to that of Hawthorne, Melville, and James, Miss Cather has represented the tensions of American existence in the late nineteenth and early twentieth century. Like her predecessors—especially the last three—she is a commentator on the prevailing American condition. Sometimes urgent in her fears but always ardent in her faith, she constantly held before herself the vision of realizable ideals. Out of inspired singleness of conviction grew a distinguished art. To a greater degree than any of the four traditionalists except James, Willa Cather was absorbed in the total identification of an esthetic with moral purpose. Great achievement in the fusion of two inalienable ideals sets her apart from her own contemporaries and fixes her in a continuity of distinguished American writing whose practitioners are few.

With the United States as a common subject, and with its frustrations and destiny as a common theme, the tradition makes comparisons inevitable. But even within the limits of an idealized cause, the writers assert their separateness, demonstrating in their respective works of fiction that individual talents must search through varieties of conscience, and of literary modes and incidents for answers to the riddles of being. The changing mask of America furthermore exacts from each writer attention to problems which, at least in an exterior fashion, are significantly focal in his age and in no other. The frontier which Cooper writes about in the first half of the nineteenth century is obviously different from that with which Willa Cather concerns herself in the twentieth. The Calvinistic or Puritanical assumptions of sin which beset Hawthorne and Melville have a theological basis which is not directly germane to the esthetically controlled questions of Miss Cather. Yet she is no less engaged by the meaning of the frontier than Cooper, nor any more casual about human salvation or destiny than are Hawthorne and Melville. The denominators are common but the point of view is individual. The inner-directed concentration which each serious artist brings to an understanding of certain universal conditions is in a large measure the unifying force of the tradition. Each was driven by a need to deal earnestly and artistically with large, pervasive issues.

At first glance, Miss Cather would appear by virtue of her frequently used frontier subjects to be closest to Cooper. In fact, however, the frontier provides only a superficial resemblance, and Cooper was the writer most distant from her in temperament even as he was in time. That they were alike at all in aim is the result of the fact that they were deeply engrossed in the solution of American crises, each in his own way. Yvor Winters (*Maule's Curse*, Norfolk, Conn., 1938, p. 29) has said of Cooper that his "concern was primarily for public morality; it was the concern of the statesman, or of the historian, first, and of the artist but secondarily." This statement of Cooper's literary interests, acutely defensible, it appears to us, shows the polarity between him and Willa Cather. National morality was, to be sure, intensely part of her fiction of the frontier. But in Cooper's intention we find a reversed image of Miss Cather's. She was the artist, and—more significantly—the moral artist, first. It was only after she had appeased her esthetic-moral sense that she spoke as the historian, and then but to give fuller definition to her primary intention. Dealing with ethics rather than with manners, dedicated to a personal, nondoctrinal concept of salvation, she drew her characters as moral agents, somewhat as abstractions, if more balanced in physical properties than Hawthorne's.

Sharing with Hawthorne and Melville a moral propensity that is unusual in the twentieth century, Miss Cather built her novels along allegorical lines which we have described in our opening chapter. ["Regarded in their totality, Miss Cather's novels of the frontier comprise an allegory of quest—the individual's seeking and finding a direction of life."] Without engaging in tedious, inconclusive comparisons or judgments of ultimate worth, however, we suggest that the parallels, as in the case of Cooper, must be limited because of differences in concepts of the novel.

Essentially an allegorist, and hence essentially a moralist, Hawthorne deliberately restricted his artistic materials for maximum concentration upon his moralistic intention. He used the exterior circumstances of physical reality, but he made them shadowy symbols of profoundly inner necessity. His selection of details was rigorous in order that each physical moment be allowed to direct most searching attention to its moral equivalent. The seriousness with which he viewed the relationship between facts and the ultimate truths of being is apparent in the short story "Wakefield," where he described his concept of fiction. His starting point would be a private symbol in which he had discovered eternal, salutary meaning. From the symbol he would proceed to the construction of a narrative through whose constituent parts he translated the moral in terms related to the experiences of his readers. In this sense, which is consistent with his usual practice, Hawthorne's allegorized stories became processes of correlation between inner truth and outer matter. As Miss Cather observed about *The Scarlet Letter*, in "The Novel Démeublé": "The material investiture of the story is presented as if unconsciously; by the reserved, fastidious hand of an artist, not by the gaudy fingers of a showman or the mechanical industry of a department-store window-dresser."

Our examination of Miss Cather's novels reveals a concern which differs mainly in degree and intention. In her tendency to allegorize her moral searchings, she like Hawthorne never lost sight of her function as a creative artist. Indeed, she devoted herself to the notion that only through the highest expression of art could she give worthy representation to her inner desire. More specifically than Hawthorne, she cherished people as people and incidents as incidents. She softened the lines of her figures and actions, but she never clothed them in such abstractions that they lost verisimilitude. She respected the varieties of human emotions and meant them to be credible aspects of daily, familiar experience.

She was furthermore acutely conscious of artistic techniques, giving her search for esthetic perfection equality with her yearning for inner meaning. With regard to artistic credibility, she was closer to Melville than to Hawthorne, for like the former she sought a more immediate equation between physical reality and spiritual significance. As is true of Melville, she portrayed phenomenal reality and human beings in readily identifiable proportions. She made them agents of an ultimate truth but always invested them with properties which could be accounted for immediately at the conscious level of perception as well as at the somewhat mystic level of moral insight. If she was less visionary than Hawthorne and Melville, and less profound in her moral intensity, she was the more accomplished technician and consequently the more readable novelist.

But among the major writers in the tradition, Henry James undoubtedly bears the closest creative resemblance to Miss Cather. Both as an artist and as a moral realist he was the literary personality who figured most prominently among the influences shaping her artistic development. Greatly respectful of his esthetic achievements, she was attracted to his singularity of purpose, to the manner in which he made an art form cohesive with serious thematic details. James was so evidently the novelist she herself cared to be that she imitated him unsuccessfully in *Alexander's Bridge*. Her blunder, as she realized, was the attempt to capture a style in which meaning was not appropriately related to personal experience. But if James ceased to function as her model for the execution of idea and form, he left a permanent impression upon her because of the purity of aim which she always venerated as the essence of her own practice. Although they dealt with comparable themes somewhat divergently, each drawing upon his particular genius, the subtle likenesses between them make their exterior differences relatively unimportant.

What is important, in the present connection, is the attitude which they took toward their art. It is an attitude of moral sobriety, a deeply serious concern with quintessential American problems. Basic to this commitment is an esthetic sensibility which transfigures ethical responsibility into organic narrative situations. Both Henry James and Willa Cather believed that without appropriately conceived shape the novel fails to represent in true essence the inner experience which is the only justifiable substance of fiction. For each, therefore, a moral sense is powerfully one with an esthetic sense. Concept and form admit of no separation, the two growing simultaneously in the created work, inevitably and rightly. With respect to technical virtuosity, James and

Miss Cather progressed beyond the earlier writers. In their fusion of moral idea and physical reality, they acknowledged to a remarkable degree the demands of their art, and then went on to fulfill the obligations to which they had committed themselves.

James and Miss Cather, furthermore, are related in the subjects they chose, although they attacked them from different angles. Yvor Winters (p. 170) has pointed out that James wrote about "the spiritual antagonism which had existed for centuries between the rising provincial civilization and the richer civilization from which it has broken away, an antagonism in which the provincial civilization met the obviously superior cultivation of the parent with a more or less typically provincial assertion of superiority." Whereas for James the antagonism lay between an ancient European culture and an upstart American culture, for Miss Cather the rift existed at times as an exclusively American phenomenon. That is, she focused her frontier novels on the divisions existing among native cultural forms. She may be said to have narrowed her view intensively, looking to the frontier first as a reaffirmation of traditional American values, and then to its development as a corruption of those values. As a further point of comparison, however, it must not be forgotten that even in the frontier novels, such as *O Pioneers!* and *My Ántonia*, she often considered with affection the traditions the first-generation pioneers had brought with them from Europe. But whether James and Willa Cather treated American themes as outgrowths of cultural divisions between nations or within the nation, they always did so with a moral responsiveness. Each brought to his novels a personal commitment which wedded feeling with insight, although Miss Cather's sympathies for America were the more immediate and direct.

As a traditionalist in an age which had no reverence for tradition, Miss Cather was a lonely figure. The moral integrity of the individual implied an exaltation of personality, even of egoism, which collided with the mass standardization and rapidly shifting values of mechanistic progress. To resist in a practical sense was, of course, vain. But the convictions of writers such as Miss Cather and James, as well as of Hawthorne and Melville, transcended practicality. Thus, Miss Cather, who formed very few intimate alliances in her lifetime, clung to a somewhat solitary position from which she idealized universal truth and frequently denounced temporization. Like Thoreau she challenged her own society, and like him she demanded a return to good purpose. "Turn to the old; return to them," he wrote in *Walden*. "Things do not change: we change."

Her attitude has implicitly the same insistence upon values which Irving Babbit and Paul Elmer More enunciated in their doctrine of neo-humanism. They preached moderation, abhorring the excesses of both naturalism and asceticism. While they sought a mean between amoral action promoted by animal instinct and the profound introspection often attendant upon organized religion, they optimistically looked for a balance point in existence. The fulcrum, they decided, must be within the individual; it must be based upon awareness of the human condition, it must incorporate the better properties of instinct and faith, and it must be controlled judiciously and wisely by means of an inner check. Man, mature and responsible, is thus the measure of this demanding philosophy. As Stuart Sherman summed it up (*On Contemporary Literature*, New York, 1917, p. 17), the neo-humanistic position urged "the desirability of continuing to work out in the world that ideal pattern which lies in the instructed and disciplined heart."

Miss Cather did not subscribe formally to the tenets of this philosophy, which had arisen out of protests against the irritations of a prevailing naturalistic temper. But her fiction is ample evidence of her privately and esthetically derived humanism. She was consistently moderate, but she never doubted that within the cares of real human problems individuals could and should work toward positive values. To this end she identified her art with a moral realism, even as James had, which helps to clarify her distinctive contribution to literature. The kind of realism she practiced is usefully defined by Sherman (p. 101) in his sharp attack on "The Barbaric Naturalism of Theodore Dreiser." Finding Dreiser devoid of moral value and esthetic worth, Sherman proposed a separation between the naturalistic and realistic novel. "Both are representative of the life of man in contemporary or nearly contemporary society, and both are presumably composed of materials within the experience and observation of the author. But the realistic novel is a representation based upon a theory of human conduct. . . . A naturalistic novel is a representation based upon a theory of animal behavior. Since a theory of animal behavior can never be an adequate basis for a representation of the life of a man in contemporary society, such a representation is an artistic blunder."

This is not an occasion for judging the naturalistic novel or the realistic novel, but Sherman's description of the latter genre is very much to the point, in that Miss Cather also drew upon her experiences and observations to formulate in fiction a theory of human conduct. Furthermore, she repudiated contemporary naturalism, artistically expressing her distaste for a theory of animal behavior applied to human beings. She was repelled not only by the premise of action determined wholly by raw instinct, but also by the relentless inclusiveness of details which was the hallmark of naturalism. Of the early naturalists, only Stephen Crane seemed to her to be free of this creative flaw. Indeed, she admired him as "one of the first post-impressionists," as one "who never tried to make a faithful report of everything else within his field of vision, as if he were a conscientious salesman making out his expense-account." But for the naturalistic movement in general, with its divorce from humane and esthetic principles, she harbored contempt.

Although she considered certain American writers of the 1930's—

notably, Hemingway, Wilder, Fitzgerald, and Lewis—to be genuine artists, she thought the fiction of that period was largely without purpose. Yet, if she was hostile to the overt tone of pessimism and cynicism which pervaded much of contemporary fiction, she was closer in spirit to this literature of harsh reality than she herself would have cared to admit. For all the external disapprobation and negativeness of such writers as Dos Passos, the early Faulkner and Steinbeck, Caldwell, Farrell, and many others, they are innately idealists. They are idealists because they imply the possibility of something better and do not lean back upon the comfortable false optimism of settled peace and contentment that could be illusory at best. The positive goal is there, but it is implicit as a reaction against those very qualites and subjects of which each author writes.

Even in the primitive, naturalistic concept the stringent sense of determinism—handed down from Crane, Norris, London, and Dreiser—does not totally conceal hope. Steinbeck, for instance, is thematically close to Miss Cather because he has a high regard for the life of simple necessity and because he shows us that depite economic disaster it is still possible for men to retain at least vestiges of their traditions, to seek a social and even spiritual well-being, and to have respect for the inherent dignity of man. And Faulkner, likewise—especially in the later phases of his career—appears to conclude that man is worthy; that he is capable of dignified and even noble action; that, in short, he will endure and prevail. Wolfe bears another kind of resemblance to Miss Cather because of his profound respect for the artistic temperament.

All the serious writers who were contemporary with her share an awareness of the brotherhood of man. The principles of Darwin, Marx, Freud, Einstein, and the new atomism have, to be sure, tended to supplant the old orthodoxies. The urgencies imposed by the mechanics of the new science, the law of survival of the fittest, biological determinism—all these have taken away much of the awe and wonder of existence and have replaced them with a fear and contempt of the finite and material. But the strong sense of mechanical determinism after all underscores rather than denies the need for values that transcend the temporal.

Because of her morally sentimental attachment to the traditional past, however, Willa Cather was less adaptable to the present than most of her contemporaries. Because the note of protest is less frequent in her writings than in those of other novelists, when it occurs its contrast with her customary tranquillity makes it all the more pronounced. One of her protests is directed against science and scientific materialism, and its major occurrence is in *The Professor's House* and *One of Ours.* Unlike most of the naturalistic writers who deal with this debilitating phenomenon through satire or the inevitable tragedy of determinism, Miss Cather speaks out with an unusual bluntness which is the testimony of her personal grievance. In this respect she is more akin to several distinguished poets, who were more inclined to voice a spiritual distress, than to the sociologically minded naturalists. E. A. Robinson, Robert Frost, and T. S. Eliot have, each in his own way, developed a thesis of the negative effect of science on modern morality, a thesis which complements Miss Cather's own displeasure (see Hyatt H. Waggoner's *The Heel of Elohim*, Norman, Okla., 1950). Here, too, is a tradition of idealistic protest which may be traced to the nineteenth century, especially to the writings of Thoreau.

But science was only one aspect of what seemed to Willa Cather to be a universally hollow condition. As far as she was willing to see, existence in her times had become spiritually devitalized and values meaningless in a wasteland of conformity and aimless enterprise. The implications were immediate enough for her, even though the notion of futility is given expression in numberless idealistic contexts. Surrender to this kind of inner exhaustion had been described by Shelley as moral death and by Arnold as philistinism. Depleted and insecure, the victims of this waste—to borrow from Thoreau—"lead lives of quiet desperation. What is called resignation is confirmed desperation."

The particular phenomenon of modern times which aroused Miss Cather to explicit statement was the rise of small towns in the wake of westward expansion. As a result—most pronounced in *My Ántonia* and in several bitter short stories—she challenged the spiritual aridity of a narrowly conformist society. Thus she takes a place alongside Sinclair Lewis and Sherwood Anderson, among others, in her attack upon smug provincialism. She was irritated by the complacent inertness of those people who accepted the material comforts handed down to them by their hard-working parents, as in the frontier novels, or by men of vision and accomplishment like Tom Outland in *The Professor's House*. Both contemptuous and grieved because of wooden acceptance, she gradually visualized it as an infection spreading even to the large, established communities of America and Europe. Her attack upon conformity at all levels of society is consistent with a widely shared theme of contemporary literature. It is reminiscent, for instance, of Marquand's more specifically contrived ridicule of New England sameness. The fact that Miss Cather's buoyant spirit generally causes an optimistic note to prevail in her fiction by no means lessens the seriousness of her inner fears.

Throughout her novels, then, Miss Cather is in the curiously ambivalent position of standing apart from her contemporaries, and yet at the same time of sharing many of the immediate moral problems which they had made their responsibility. Although she directed her vision to a traditional past, as they did not, she was nonetheless able to assess the dilemma of modern times through a conjunction of tradition with present reality. The important thing for her, of course, was that values may never be divorced from art. But it must also be acknowledged that for most serious writers of modern times moral or social responsibility must coincide with esthetic awareness. Willa Cather addresses herself most memorably to a tradition of conscience and hope; in this respect she is in the main stream of great American literary achievement. But she also addresses herself trenchantly, if in a minor key, to affairs of material reality. Eloquently joining past and present, affirmation and censure, she has memorialized herself as an American classic.

Willa Cather and the Impressionist Novel

David Stouck*

Willa Cather's essay "The Novel Démeublé," published in the *New Republic*, 12 April 1922, represents her mature reflections on the nature of fiction. It provides at once a statement of her literary ideals and a guide to her techniques as a novelist. The essay is also one of the last summary statements of impressionist and symbolist theory as related to the novel, coming near the close of a tradition of critical thought that spanned more than five decades. The essay points to Cather's roots in the nineteenth century, particularly in the French novel. Not surprisingly the concepts Cather set down in this formal essay were ones that she had been applying twenty-five years earlier, when she wrote over two hundred critical pieces as a collegiate journalist in Lincoln and was first entranced by the masters of French fiction. In this essay I will look closely at some of the French writers with whom Cather had such close affinities, and then consider the critical theory of impressionism and symbolism that helped shape those works Cather admired and chose as models for her own work. The differences between impressionism and symbolism serve, I think, to clarify some of the strengths and weaknesses in Cather's writing.

I

Willa Cather seems to have admired almost all the French writers of the nineteenth century, from the romantics Hugo and Dumas to Zola, the father of literary naturalism. But only a small group can be said to have influenced her technically. The author whose theory and practice are held up as exemplary in "The Novel Démeublé" is Prosper Mérimée (1803–70). To provide a fundamental critical principle she quotes Mérimée's statement from his essay on Gogol that the art of choosing from all the details that life affords is much more difficult than careful observation and faithful reportage. And when she gives an example of a perfectly wrought piece of fiction from which not a word could be cut, it is Mérimée's *Carmen*. E. K. Brown tells us that Cather

*This essay was written for this volume and is published by permission of the author.

became acquainted with Mérimée's work while she was still at the university and that she felt a close affinity to his mind.[1] It was an abiding sympathy, for in a letter as late as November 1929 she singles out Mérimée as the author she most admires.[2] Reading through his fiction and critical writings one feels that here indeed was a writer whose work would have had a powerful and lasting influence on Willa Cather. His aesthetic ideals of organic unity, restraint, and apparent simplicity are those which inform Cather's writing at its best.

Mérimée believed that the selection of significant detail ("le trait qu'il faut") was the crucial act in all artistic creation, hence the importance of the phrase quoted by Cather, "l'art de choisir." Mérimée disliked excessive detail, however, and in the Gogol essay he reproaches Rabelais for failing to choose from among many brilliant details, and complaining that the reader of his work becomes sated, fatigued, and that the narrative goes flat. Many details that offer themselves, he argues, must be excluded or subordinated, set in relief, so that an organic whole is achieved that is greater than the sum of its parts.[3] Certainly this was a concern of Cather's from the outset. In a newspaper book review in 1896 she complained that the author under scrutiny, Mrs. Humphrey Ward, had formidable powers of description but not the power to make a whole picture stand out by a few masterly strokes.[4] After she had herself written *O Pioneers!* she said in an interview that instead of adding detail, the artistic process involves eliminating and continually simplifying. Referring to Millet's painting *The Sower*, she says "the composition is so simple that it seems inevitable. It was probably the hundred sketches that went before that made the picture what it finally became—a process of simplifying all the time—of sacrificing many things that were in themselves interesting and pleasing, and all the time getting closer to the one thing—It."[5]

Apparent simplicity and inevitability were artistic goals Cather shared with Mérimée, and both achieved those goals through restraint. References to Mérimée in Cather's essay on the unfurnished novel are very much to the point. Few writers have exercised such economy in storytelling as Mérimée, whose novellas are as brief and austere as Cather's *My Mortal Enemy*. Both writers were by disposition romantics attracted to material with strong emotional content, and they both achieved their special effects by using classical forms and a reserved, often laconic style. Mérimée's subjects approach the melodramatic: *Tamango* tells of the tragic fate of a cargo of Negro slaves adrift on the ocean; *Colomba* is an unrelenting tale of feuding families, while *Mateo Falcone* is the story of a man who willfully slaughters his only son. But the strong feelings in these stories are held in check by the austere, apparently indifferent narrative voice and a corrective irony that pervades even the smallest details. In *Mateo Falcone*, for example, there is a documentary account of the area (thick underbrush on the island of Corsica) which stands in juxtaposition to the killing of the boy. And much explosive feeling is packed into a few deceptively casual lines at the story's close when Falcone sends for his son-in-law to be his new heir. Mérimée even tried to undercut the powerful emotion of *Carmen*. As narrator in his fictions he liked to pose as a scholar or historian, and in the 1847 revised version he does not end the tragic love story with the account of Carmen's murder but with a pedantic disquisition on the language of the Gypsies.

Cather's effects are more muted but technically similar. As a frame around *My Ántonia*, the author has a lawyer friend bringing her a memoir he has written about his childhood in Nebraska. This creates a distance between the author and her nostalgic narrative, the content of which is largely autobiographical. In a letter Cather refers to her "introduction" as a device employed by French authors when they wanted their narrative to be colored by a certain mood throughout.[6] Like most of Mérimée's works, *Death Comes for the Archbishop* and *Shadows on the Rock* are carefully researched books in which the personal and emotional contents are muted by historical transposition and potentially melodramatic scenes undercut by the long summary view of history. For example, after telling in *Death Comes for the Archbishop* the lurid story of the degenerate murderer Buck Scales and his captive wife Magdalena, Cather concludes the chapter with a brief, documentary account of their fates—Scales after a short trial is hung and his wife becomes a housekeeper for a group of nuns.

Mérimée thought of the writer as a dissembler, similar to a woman doing her makeup or an actor preparing his costume, but warned that the ideals of simplicity and inevitability were spoiled if the reader became aware of the artifice and calculation involved. He felt that the writer in every respect must remain behind the scenes. Like Cather, Mérimée took every precaution to keep the prying gaze of the public away from his emotions and private life.

Gustave Flaubert (1821–80), a writer whose influence on Cather has been more fully documented,[7] was the French novelist who made the impersonality of the writer a central part of his artistic credo and an imperative for his followers. He believed passionately that writers should represent the world objectively and that great art stands above personal affections and susceptibilities. He wrote that "the artist should so arrange things as to make posterity believe that he has never lived. The less I can form an idea of him, the greater he seems to me."[8] And elsewhere he made his famous statement that "the artist in his work should be like God in creation, invisible and all powerful; his presence should be felt everywhere, but he should not be seen."[9] This conviction was reinforced by his idea that a work of art should exhibit the precision of the physical sciences; every word should be the exact word, "le mot juste."

Cather admired Flaubert from her university days onward, which

explains her great excitement late in life at meeting his niece.[10] Critics
have seen similarites between Cather's work and Flaubert's, comparing
A Lost Lady to *Madame Bovary*, and *Obscure Destinies* to *Trois Contes*.
Certainly Cather like Flaubert took great pains to hide herself from the
reader, and using the male point of view in *My Ántonia* and *A Lost Lady*
was one such strategy. But similarities between the authors go further
than similarity of content and authorial reticence. Flaubert's appeal to
Cather was in his use of carefully chosen details that focus the emotion
and the action of the story in an unforgettable image. *L'Éducation senti-
mentale* seems to have been very suggestive for Cather when she was
writing *A Lost Lady*. Frederic Moreau and Niel Herbert, both semi-
orphaned and halfhearted law students, are subject to the treacheries of
sex and beauty in women they romantically idealize. Both of the idealized
women are married to men of declining means, and appearances are hard
to maintain. One of the earliest images that the young men associate
with their romantic ideals is an ivory-handled parasol, and for both young
men a bouquet of roses thrown in the mud expresses disenchantment. The
latter might easily represent a direct borrowing by Willa Cather from
Flaubert. A detail from *Madame Bovary* which must have appealed
strongly to Cather and carried over to *A Lost Lady* is that of the adolescent boy, Justin, who is infatuated with Emma Bovary and lovingly
cleans her shoes caked in mud from one of her rendezvous. Cather created
a similar point of view in the German boy Adolph Blum.

Flaubert had learned much about writing from Mérimée, but the
latter criticized Flaubert for including too much detail in his novels, for
indulging in what he called "tableaux." The use of local color had become a popular convention in the nineteenth century, and vivid presentation of "scenes" was a significant aspect of Flaubert's art. Although
Mérimée, with his concern for classical form, held local color in contempt,
Cather was frequently concerned to convey the spirit of place in her books
and admired Flaubert's detailed rendering of locale. Indeed *Salammbô*,
which she cited as her favorite novel by Flaubert,[11] could be described
as one magnificent, extended tableau. However, it was imperative for
Flaubert, and subsequently for Cather, that every detail help create and
sustain the mood or "illusion" being created by the work of art.

Spareness and precision were aesthetic ideals Cather admired in
these French writers and applied to her own work. Flaubert's disciple,
Guy de Maupassant (1850–93), whom Cather included with the great
French writers, wrote an essay on the novel which summarizes many aspects of Mérimée's and Flaubert's aesthetics and anticipates Cather's
"Novel Démeublé."[12] Indeed, Cather's essay in places seems to echo de
Maupassant directly. Apparent simplicity is the highest goal an author
can reach according to de Maupassant, who continues that the artist "must
construct his work with such skill, such hidden art and such seeming
simplicity, that it is impossible to detect and sketch the plan, or discern

the writer's purpose." Selectivity is the essential act in the artistic process: "from among the numberless trivial incidents of daily life the artist must know how to eliminate all which do not serve his end." Applying this precept specifically to those writers who call themselves realists he states: "The realist, if he is an artist, will endeavor not to show us a commonplace photograph of life, but to give us a presentiment of it which shall be more complete, more striking, more cogent than reality itself. To tell everything is out of the question; it would require at least a volume for each day to enumerate the endless, insignificant incidents which crowd our existence. A choice must be made." Once the choice of subject is made, the artist must "select only such characteristic details as are of use to it, from this life overladen with chances and trifles, and must reject everything else, everything irrelevant." Again selection is specified as the highest aesthetic imperative.

II

Cather probably learned much about formal structure from Mérimée and about image and scene from Flaubert, but her special technique of suggestion would have had its roots in those large movements in the arts in the late nineteenth century—impressionism and symbolism. Certainly Flaubert and his followers had much to do with the emergence of the new aesthetic (when de Maupassant says that writers should give a "presentiment" rather than a photograph of life, he directly anticipates Cather's statement that authors "should present their scene by suggestion rather than by enumeration"), but these ideas about the art of suggestion were refined in the late nineteenth century and joined to the importance of point of view, so that when Cather discusses the place of literal detail in her essay on the novel she situates its significance in perception, in "the emotional penumbra of the characters."

Impressionism was a term first applied to a style of painting concerned to capture the evanescent effects of light and movement in a landscape. What was being conveyed was a perceived reality, the subjective truth of appearances. Walter Pater was one of the first critics to formulate the implications of this style; he wrote that "the first step towards seeing one's object as it really is, is to know one's own impression as it really is."[13] Since reality is determined by perception, the artist conveys not simply an object, but the emotional and intellectual excitement that accompanies the perception of that object. Accordingly, it is the artist's particular impression of the appearance of things, not his ability to transcribe their substance in detail, which counts in a work of art. Henry James expressed his adaptation of this assumption in his famous statement that "a novel is in its broadest definition a personal, a direct impression of life; that, to begin with, constitutes its value, which is greater or lesser according to the intensity of the impression."[14]

Impressionism was most completely translated from painting to prose in the writings of Joseph Conrad (1857–1924) and Ford Madox Ford (1873–1939). These novelists, who were brought together by a mutual admiration for Flaubert and de Maupassant, tried to formulate an aesthetic which would describe the important role of subjective "truth" in art. They grounded their theory in Flaubert's concept of *le mot juste*, interpreting that phrase as referring not to the precision of accurate scientific description but to the exact rendering of impressions experienced by the writer. Conrad and Ford jointly held that "the general effect of a novel must be the general effect that life makes on mankind."[15] Life, they argued, does not narrate, but makes impressions on the brain and the novel should duplicate this process. The impressionist painters, they felt, had approached the physical process of seeing in their art by breaking color down into its constituent hues and vividly rendering the variety and irregularity that strikes the eye. They sought an analagous manner of representation in fiction. They were aware of the fragmentary nature of conscious experience and of the fact that the mind orders events according to its own individual laws. For the painter's bewildered eye they substituted the novelist's memory and to render the confusing, fragmented nature of experience they rearranged linear time, more nearly approaching the psychological process of remembering. They insisted of course on fidelity to the viewpoint of the central consciousness narrating the tale and on careful selection of detail to render exact impressions of perceived experience. Juxtaposition of images, scenes, and events was also an important technique for rendering impressions vividly without explanation or judgment. They sought a "progression d'effet"—a gradual revelation of character, of the conflict to be narrated, of its symbolic meaning. Good prose succeeds, wrote Ford, by "a succession of tiny, unobservable surprises."[16]

As *progression d'effet* structures, both Cather's *My Ántonia* and *A Lost Lady*, each telling the story of a woman who has made a powerful and lasting impression on a young boy growing up in the pioneer Midwest, are clear examples of the impressionist novel. In *My Ántonia* the story is told in the first person as Jim Burden's memoir; in *A Lost Lady* it is told in the third person but centered in Niel Herbert's consciousness. The controlling structural principle is the act of remembering and, although the material in both books is presented roughly in chronological order, it is shaped (perhaps even distorted) by the fragmented and imperfect process of memory. Jim Burden appears to be aware of this in the "Introduction" when he gives the author his manuscript about Ántonia and says it probably hasn't any form: "I didn't take time to arrange it; I simply wrote down pretty much all that her name recalls to me." Accordingly, we learn the details about Ántonia's life in the same manner that we make an acquaintance—through gradual revelation, through association and "flashbacks." For example, the novel has progressed through several chapters before we learn anything about the Shimerdas' life in Bohemia and the circumstances that brought them to America. In *A Lost Lady* it is not until the penultimate chapter that we learn about Marian Forrester's early life, about the scandal surrounding her first engagement to be married, and about her rescue in the mountains by Captain Forrester. More important than chronology and the literal action in both novels are images and scenes which fuse together the significant symbolic elements in the story and leave a vivid, indelible impression on the reader's mind: the plough against the sun witnessed by Jim Burden; Niel Herbert's throwing a bouquet of roses into the mud or cutting the telephone wire to save his "lost lady."

Conrad gives much weight to impressionist theory in his preface to *The Nigger of the "Narcissus,"* where he argues that art appeals primarily to the senses, that the artist in words must make sensory appeal if he is to touch the deepest spring of human emotions.[17] To achieve something akin to the color of painting or the suggestiveness of music the literary artist creates impressions conveyed through the senses and attends to the shape and ring of sentences so that "the light of magic suggestiveness may be brought to play for an evanescent instant over the commonplace surface of words." An artist, says Conrad, appeals not to our intelligence so much as to our emotional capacities. The "truth" of art, he posits, is the "attempt to find in [the visible universe], in its forms, in its colours, in its light, in its shadows, in the aspects of matter and in the facts of life, what of each is fundamental, what is enduring and essential." The impressionist writer seeks "truth" not through intellectual discovery but through responsive emotions, through temperament. Ford said, "the accuracies I deal in are the accuracies of my impressions, I really don't deal in facts . . . I try to give you what I see to be the spirit of an age, of a town, of a movement."[18] He evocatively states that the impressionist is concerned to capture moments of time and convey exactly the sense of fleeting light and shadow which gives "certain moods and certain aspects of the earth a rare and tender pathos."[19] Both Conrad and Ford, in response to the naturalist writers, urged that the artist's goal was not to seek out the laws of nature and society, like the scientist, but to appreciate life itself.

These are the assumptions of Willa Cather's art—the contempt for verisimilitude, the concern for "the verbal mood, the emotional aura of the fact or the thing or the deed."[20] In a fragment of critical writing published posthumously as "Light on Adobe Walls," Cather defines art as impressions, resorting to painting to illustrate her point. There she says that an artist can never give an exact scientific representation of the sun or even of sunlight, "he can only paint the tricks that shadows play with it, or what it does to forms." She qualifies the artist's capacity even further and points out that the product on the canvas is purely subjective: "He cannot even paint those relations of light and shade—he

can only paint some emotion they give him, some man-made arrangement of them that happens to give him personal delight. . . . At bottom
all he can give you is the thrill of his own poor little nerve—the projection in paint of a fleeting pleasure in a certain combination of form and
colour, as temporary and almost as physical as a taste on the tongue."[21]

Not surprisingly, Cather admired Conrad and acknowledges his importance in her essay on Sarah Orne Jewett in *Not Under Forty*,[22] but
the writer who I believe had a more direct influence on Cather in the
area of sensory appeal is the Provençal author Alphonse Daudet (1840–
97). It is not the custom in literary history to designate Daudet an impressionist, but simply a late romantic; the term, however, as discussed
above applies fittingly to much of his work, particularly the prose
sketches of his native region. Although Cather hesitated to place him
in the front rank of French novelists,[23] she clearly had a special affinity
for both the author and his works (in her journal articles she refers to him
more frequently than to any other French writer).[24] Her piece on the
occasion of Daudet's death singles out the novel *Sapho* as the one work
in which the author achieved greatness and by which he would live on.[25]
One can easily appreciate that judgment in the light of Cather's own
novels, for Daudet's masterpiece tells the story of a young student, a
less donnish version of Jim Burden, who is in love with two women. One
of these is the eponymous heroine, the student's mistress in Paris, the
other is a strong, maternal peasant woman who is married to his uncle.
There are scenes of disillusionment when the young student, like Cather's
Jim Burden or Niel Herbert, discovers his aging mistress to be shallow
and unfaithful; there is also a fine dawn scene when the student is home
in Provence and his uncle's wife approaches him with a reaping hook
in hand—a configuration of images that anticipates *My Ántonia*.

But the volume by Daudet which Cather would have loved best is
Lettres de mon moulin, which in fact is Daudet's most widely read book
today. She quotes from the book and alludes to its content several times
in her 1902 travel letter from Provence, published in the *Nebraska State
Journal* as "In the Country of Daudet."[26] *Lettres de mon moulin* could
easily be compared to Sarah Orne Jewett's *The Country of the Pointed
Firs*, a book which Cather admired greatly. Both volumes celebrate the
region of the author's birth in an intimate and quietly lyrical fashion.
Both books are framed by the author's retreat from the bustle of the
world to a remote dwelling in which to write (for Jewett the schoolhouse,
for Daudet the mill), and both convey the life of the region through
character studies, accounts of travel, and anecdotal tales. The narrators
remain only peripherally involved in the local scene and at the close
reveal that the world they have described belongs largely to the past,
is essentially the world of their childhood. Cather, who read Daudet at
university, would have read *Letters de mon moulin* before *The Country
of the Pointed Firs*, which was not published until 1896. Since this kind

of writing exerted a significant influence on Cather, Daudet's book is worth consideration here.[27]

His deep and lasting affection for Provence would have recommended Daudet's work to Cather, who continually returned in her own fiction to the part of the country where she grew up. Pleasure in the physical properties of the landscape and its people is the real essence of Daudet's *Lettres*, love of the hot southern sun, the vineyards and olive trees, the dusty roads, the cicadas, the mistral, the shepherds and farmers. What would have influenced Cather is the structure of Daudet's book, for it became a formal model that she used herself when she wrote *Death Comes for the Archbishop* and *Shadows on the Rock*. Instead of telling the story of a place in an extended tale of heroic action, Daudet combines local legends and anecdotes with character sketches and personal observations to create a mosaic of the country which is larger than its individual pieces. One feels a whole world has been created, a landscape and a way of life captured, yet the individual parts, whether a reflection on a deserted inn, a visit to an elderly couple, or the comic legend of Father Gaucher's Elixir are anecdotal, almost inconsequential. In *Death Comes for the Archbishop* Cather constructed her portrait of the Southwest in the same manner; establishing Father Latour, the French missionary priest, as a point of view for her narrative, she compiles legends, character sketches, and descriptions of landscape that would have constituted the Southwest as the priest experienced it.

The narrator's emotional response is a component in the descriptions and anecdotes—technically that is what makes this kind of writing impressionistic. In Daudet's writing, as later in Willa Cather's, there is what Stephen Tennant calls "the burden of unspent feeling," something held back which keeps the emotion fresh, "almost denied one."[28] This gives the style, the very sentences, their special structure and rhythm. One of Daudet's *lettres* is a fantasy on oranges, beginning:

> In Paris oranges have the sad look of windfalls picked up beneath the tree. At the season at which we receive them, midwinter, with its rain and cold, their bright skin and their scent which, in those northern countries of mild flavours, seems a little overdone, give them a strange, rather bohemian, look. On misty evenings they lie sadly along the pavement's edge, piled up on their little coster barrows, under the dim light of a red paper lantern. A harsh, monotonous cry accompanies them, a cry that is lost amid the noise of carriage-wheels and the clatter of omnibuses:
> "Sweet Valencia oranges, a penny each!"[29]

The author's feeling, which is never specified, is homesickness for the South and nostalgia for the romance of youthful travels in the Mediterranean. In Paris things from the South are misfit, strange-looking, their value unappreciated in the harsh, abrasive world of a cold northern city.

The pathos evoked in the author by oranges in Paris is focused in the fruit vendor's cry smothered by the noise of the traffic. But in a subsequent paragraph the author thinks about oranges in their Mediterranean setting and his exquisite pleasure emerges in the rich description:

> the Mediterranean . . . that's where they are beautiful! Amid the dark, lustrous, varnished foliage the fruit had the sparkle of stained glass, and made the surrounding air golden with that halo of splendour that surrounds all vivid flowers. Here and there gaps between the branches give a glimpse of the ramparts of the little town, the minaret of a mosque, the dome of a shrine. . . .

The narrator's eye finally comes to rest on the snow-covered peaks of the Atlas Mountains. The sketch is slight, yet rich in elusive feeling. Daudet, however, is reticent to specify the emotions that made him compose a "fantasy" on oranges; he conveys instead its sensuous lineaments.

Cather modulates the descriptive passages in her fiction in much the same way, so as to convey their emotional content, like color in painting or tone in music. In *Shadows on the Rock* there is a description of an autumn sunset which strives for something like painterly accuracy. It is witnessed by the two children of the novel.

> They sat down in the blue twilight to eat their bread and await the turbid afterglow which is peculiar to Quebec in autumn; the slow, rich, prolonged flowing-back of crimson across the sky, after the sun has sunk behind the dark ridges of the west. Because of the haze in the air the colour seems thick, like a heavy liquid, welling up wave after wave, a substance that throbs, rather than a light.[30]

There is color, texture, even movement, in this description, but there are also the unstated emotional connotations of death and dispersal. It makes the girl Cécile think of the martyrs in the forests to the west, but its deepest meaning for her is not the death of the priests in Huronia but in her own threatened removal from Quebec, the only home she has known. The throbbing of the light focuses objectively for the reader the inner turmoil of the child. She says the sunset and thoughts of the martyrs make her feel happy, but the complexity of that feeling is only fully revealed when she says she will come back some day to see the city and forest covered in the gold of another sunset.

Cather's short story "Two Friends" is a vivid "impression" from childhood of a friendship between two small-town businessmen, a relation that was rare and seemingly inviolable but which was ultimately broken. This memory, at once pleasurable and sad, is evoked through images compounded of all the senses:

> Those April nights, when the darkness itself tasted dusty (or, by the special mercy of God, cool and damp), when the smell of burning grass was in the air, and a sudden breeze brought the scent of wild

plum blossoms,—those evenings were only a restless preparation for the summer nights,—nights of full liberty and perfect idleness. . . . All day long there had been the excitement that intense heat produces in some people,—a mild drunkenness made of sharp contrasts; thirst and cold water, the blazing stretch of Main Street and the cool of the brick stores when one dived into them. By nightfall one was ready to be quiet. My two friends were always in their best form on those moonlit summer nights, and their talk covered a wide range.[31]

The darkness, the heat, the smell of burning grass and wild plum blossoms, the dusty taste of the air and the sound of the two men's voices all merge in synaesthesia to give that fleeting moment in time "a rare and tender pathos." The truth in this story has little to do with the political differences that terminated the friendship, but with the imaginative wonder of a child on a hot summer night in tension with the disillusionment and nostalgia of the adult narrator. This double perspective converges in the moonlight, at once a source of enchantment and nostalgia. Interestingly, according to E. K. Brown, Cather told Alfred Knopf that "Two Friends" was a painter's subject, that she had the paintings of Courbet in mind when she wrote the story.[32]

III

The aesthetic of impressionism, with its appeal to the senses, does not wholly account for Cather's theory of art. When she refers to "[w]hatever is felt upon the page without being specifically named there," she is using the language of symbolism, another late romantic movement in the arts with its chief exponents in France. Symbolism, as compared to impressionism, was a psychology rather than a style: the symbolist, to use French terminology, sought *connaissance* beyond *volupté*. For the symbolist feelings were not enough; a work of art should move ultimately toward the expression of an idea, one that cannot be stated directly in words. Impressionism and symbolism are not easily distinguished for they are both concerned with the aesthetics of suggestion and evocation, but when Cather refers to the presence in art of "the thing not named" she reveals an affinity with the symbolists, a concern that art approach something that partakes of the mysterious and infinite.

The broad base of Cather's symbolism lies in her youthful reading of Thomas Carlyle (1795–1881) who in *Sartor Resartus* wrote, "the universe is but a vast symbol of God; nay, if thou wilt have it, what is man himself but a symbol of God."[33] Carlyle identified art and religion as being the same and argued that symbols in art allow eternity to become visible: "For is not a symbol ever, to him who has eyes for it, some dimmer or clearer revelation of the God-like? . . . Of this latter sort are all those works of art; in them (if thou know a work of art from a daub of artifice) wilt thou discern eternity looking through time; the God-like rendered visible."[34]

The joining of religion and art, God and Beauty, appears often in Cather's journalist writing; her essay on Ruskin endorses this view at great length. Cather continued to entertain this equation: in *The Professor's House* Godfrey St. Peter tells his students that art and religion "are the same thing, in the end,"[35] and in her 1936 letter to *Commonweal* titled "Escapism" Cather writes that "religion and art spring from the same root and are close kin."[36] For the symbolist, the work of art is a bridge between time and eternity, and the artist or priest reveals life's highest values and mystery through "correspondences."

Music offered the symbolists the perfect analogue for feeling which shapes itself toward an inarticulate and infathomable Idea. Again Carlyle, in *Heroes and Hero-Worship*, wrote that music "leads us to the edge of the Infinite, and lets us for a moment gaze into that." He stated, "All deep things are Song. It seems somehow the very central essence of us, Song."[37] The idea goes back to Plato and the Pythagoreans who held that the universe was constructed around music and that the human soul was similarly formed. Later the Neoplatonists argued that although man is physically not capable of hearing the music of the spheres, he responds to music because of the memory of celestial music. Internal song is thus a higher form than audible music; or as Keats phrased it in "Ode to a Grecian Urn":

> Heard melodies are sweet, but those unheard
> Are sweeter; Therefore, ye soft pipes play on;
> Not to the sensual ear, but, more endear'd,
> Pipe to the spirit ditties of no tone.

In "The Novel Démeublé" Willa Cather refers to something similar with the phrase, "the overtone divined by the ear but not heard by it."

The symbolist poets were preoccupied with achieving the effects of music (Pater had said that "all art aspires to music"). They argued that intimations of a higher reality were too vague and fleeting to be conveyed by direct statement or description, but that a succession of words or images might suggest it to the reader. Stéphane Mallarmé, the French poet whose essays and letters constitute the central body of symbolist thought, argued that the One (or the Absolute) and the correspondences between the One and the many, could only be approached through an art of suggestion. In a lecture titled "Music and Literature" he stated: "It is not *description* which can unveil the efficacy and beauty of monuments, seas, or the human face in all their maturity and native state, but rather *evocation, allusion, suggestion*."[38] For Mallarmé, to name or specify the object would be to destroy its imaginative power. In an essay that reads in places like Cather's "The Novel Démeublé," Mallarmé wrote:

"To evoke...the unmentioned object, by allusive, never direct, words, that all amount equally to expressions of silence, is to attempt something which comes close to an act of creation."[39] Cather's phrasing of this idea, which she called the thing not named, goes: "Whatever is felt upon the page without being specifically named there—that, one might say, is created."[40] Cather does not mention Mallarmé in any of her published or unpublished writings. She knew and admired the work of other symbolist poets such as Verlaine, but would probably have found Mallarmé too abstract for her tastes. They nonetheless shared a similar belief in the aesthetic power of suggestion.

Many of the central statements in Cather's mature critical writings are extensions of symbolist thought. When she defends the arts as a form of escape without practical value, she does so by reminding the reader that "they sprang from an unaccountable predilection of the one unaccountable thing in man."[41] The mystery and allusiveness of the aesthetic impulse, according to Cather, must also characterize its finest productions. A great story, she says, "must leave in the mind of the sensitive reader an intangible residuum of pleasure," something as elusive as a remembered melody or a garden's summer perfume.[42] This aesthetic pleasure in something evoked but never objectified remains a sure critical touchstone for Cather. She does not consider Defoe's *Roxanna* a work of imaginative literature because nothing emerges beyond the level of the text; in *Pilgrim's Progress* by contrast, "little is said but much is felt and communicated."[43] In the essay "On the Art of Fiction" she formalizes this preference as an art of simplification, of "finding what conventions of form and what detail one can do without and yet preserve the spirit of the whole—so that all one has suppressed and cut away is there to the reader's consciousness as much as if it were in type on the page."[44] Her fondness for Katherine Mansfield rests in this achievement, that "she communicates vastly more than she actually writes." The reader, says Cather, might look through the text for something that has been said and will not find it. It is there, nonetheless, she says, "though no typesetter will ever set it."[45]

This art of ellipsis is most strikingly apparent in Cather's *My Mortal Enemy*, the brief novel whose very title remains ambiguous and elusive. It is the story of a woman whose potential greatness is never realized, but whose frustrated ambitions are felt on every page. Myra Henshawe is a worldly, headstrong heiress who married against her uncle's wishes (Henshawe was the son of her uncle's enemy) and thereby condemned herself to a life of threadbare gentility. Myra has an insatiable desire for wealth and social prominence as well as romance, and when she is eclipsed socially by an acquaintance passing through the park in a carriage she laments bitterly to the narrator of the story, "it's very nasty, being poor!"[46] Beneath the civilized exterior of her charming manners,

Myra is a frustrated, tyrannical woman. While the narrator does not understand her, she nevertheless senses "something in her nature that one rarely saw, but nearly always felt" (48). Cather never explains her heroine but through allusions to power and greatness in history, art, and religion makes us feel that "compelling, passionate, overmastering something" for which the narrator has no name. We are told, for example, that Myra's head "would have graced one of the wickedest of the Roman emperors" (63), but the allusions to Marie Stuart, Katharine of Aragon, Richard II, and King John (all figures of worldly power and ambition) bespeak the irony of an ambitious woman who will have no place in history.

The intensity of Myra's personality is probably registered most powerfully in the scene where, on New Year's Eve, Madame Modjeska's friend from the opera sings the aria "Casta Diva" from Bellini's *Norma*. One feels that Myra, like the Druid priestess, would perjure herself for love and die in order to be revenged. Through association this scene conveys much more than is ever stated; it has the power of a great aria itself and extends its mood over the whole narrative. Its effect cannot be explained. Here is a splendidly realized instance of the symbolists' desire for literature to approximate music. Also, Myra's Christian reckoning at the end of the book is similarly conveyed indirectly through allusions to Heine, King Lear, and the saints of the early church.

There were dangers, however, for Willa Cather in symbolism. When she sought to convey indirectly a strong emotion through association and suggestion her writing is natural and very moving, but when she tried to shape that emotion toward the expression of an idea, some elusive truth, then her writing becomes contrived and opaque. Examples of Cather's flawed art can be found in *The Professor's House* and the short story "The Old Beauty," two pieces of fiction in which conflict is resolved by an idea.

When Cather started *The Professor's House* she wrote to her friend Dorothy Canfield that she had taken to bed in order to work out an idea for her new novel.[47] This is the first time that she referred to fiction in terms of ideas rather than emotions or memories. Although she cautioned Robert Frost that *The Professor's House* was not a philosophical book,[48] she was concerned nonetheless to bring the protagonist to a certain degree of wisdom. The elusive idea that hovers over the text is perhaps best described as the paradox of Christian faith—that one must lose one's life to gain it. This idea informs the lives of both Godfrey St. Peter and his student Tom Outland whose stories are yoked together in what Cather referred to as the French device of inserting a *nouvelle* into a *roman*.[49] It emerges in Tom Outland's story after the Indian artifacts have been taken away from the mesa and the disillusioned youth comes to accept the loss:

Something had happened in me that made it possible for me to co-
ordinate and simplify, and that process, going on in my mind, brought
with it great happiness. It was possession. The excitement of my first
discovery was a very pale feeling compared to this one. For me the
mesa was no longer an adventure, but a religious emotion.[50]

Although the idea of gain through loss is suggested more specifically in
the subsequent paragraph where Outland reflects, "I wakened with the
feeling that I had found everything, instead of having lost everything,"
the transition is not explained. A mystery has been unveiled for the
idealistic youth, but like the symbolist poets the author can only suggest
its impact in such unyielding phrases as "something had happened . . . a
great happiness . . . a religious emotion."

The attempt to convey through symbolism a parallel experience in
the professor's life involves Cather in not only stylistic opacity but contrivance of plot. The despondent professor almost literally loses his life
before he can take possession of himself and go forward again. He had
"let something go" we are told, but the import of that relinquishment
is explained no further. The novel's plot is flawed artistically. The reader
is warned at the beginning of the story that the gas stove in the professor's study leaks, that a gust of wind could put out the flame, and a
deeply absorbed man could be asphyxiated. This is precisely what happens when the professor is in the depths of despair over his family and
career, but he is miraculously rescued by the stoical and devout dressmaker, Augusta. Cather's best writing is never dependent on twists of
plot but on the natural and inevitable character of people and places
remembered, undramatic episodes, little anecdotes. There is a *deus ex
machina* quality to the professor's delivery which is not wholly required
on either the literal or symbolic level of the story. *The Professor's House*
is one of Cather's most important books but it is not without flaws.

Much less successful is "The Old Beauty," whose plot is conceived
entirely in terms of symbolic action. In this 1936 story, written the same
year as she published her manifesto against the present in *Not Under
Forty*,[51] Cather was clearly grappling with her own sometimes irritable
conservatism and nostalgia for the past. The heroine, Gabrielle Longstreet, is repelled by the dress and manners of the Jazz Age and clings
fiercely to everything the Victorian and Edwardian periods represented.
Henry Seabury, the old beauty's admirer and central consciousness for
the story, says that he is grateful to have survived the holocaust of war
and to be sitting in a comfortable French hotel; but Gabrielle replies,
"Are you grateful? I am not. I think one should go out with one's time."[52]

Her death follows a series of symbolic incidents. Seabury takes the
old beauty and her companion on a drive in the mountains to the
Grande-Chartreuse. Seabury feels the drive on a perfect fall day to be
"strangely impersonal" as if they were leaving everything behind. The

autumnal journey which suggests a ritual preparation for death brings the three friends to a monastery which, like the heroine, is in ruins but is also somehow a significant "destination," although its significance is not made clear and grows even more elusive as the heroine probes the depths of the monastery well with sunlight reflected from a mirror. Seabury notices from a distance that there is "a faintly contemptuous smile on her lips" (64). Does the deep well in the earth suggest to Gabrielle the grave and is the smile her contempt for man's mortal condition? Or is she probing the recesses of her soul and her chequered past?

On the return to the hotel the automobile in which the friends are traveling narrowly misses a collision with a car driven by two swaggering, cross-dressed American women. Gabrielle is badly shaken by this incident (not by the bruises, she says, but by the dirty white breeches), and before dawn the next morning she dies in her hotel room. We are left to ask whether the encounter on the road amounted to a moment of brutal self-confrontation (her thoughtless youth, her repressed sexuality) or a confirmation of her desire to die rather than live on in a discordant and vulgar present. The suggestions are interesting but the action is contrived, the meaning of the story personal in an idiosyncratic fashion. The story is ultimately one of Cather's least satisfying fictional contributions.

I have titled this paper "Willa Cather and the Impressionist Novel" because I feel Cather's achievement is best described by the impressionists' goal to convey a sensuous appreciation of life, to seek "truth" not through intellectual discovery but responsive emotions, through temperament. This is Thea Kronborg's understanding of art in *The Song of the Lark* when she spends time alone in Panther Cañon:

> Here she could lie for half a day undistracted, holding pleasant and incomplete conceptions in her mind—almost in her hands. They were scarcely clear enough to be called ideas. They had something to do with fragrance and colour and sound, but almost nothing to do with words. She was singing very little now, but a song would go through her head all morning, . . . and it was like a pleasant sensation indefinitely prolonged. It was much more like a sensation than like an idea, or an act of remembering.[53]

The symbolists' desire to create something as suggestive and unalloyed as music was a significant part of Cather's aesthetic, but reaching out to an inarticulate and ultimately unfathomable "Idea" betrayed Cather's special talent and led her to contrived and sometimes unintelligible writing. It is grudging perhaps to conclude this essay with an examination of the author's weaknesses but, as Willa Cather herself wrote, "to note an artist's limitations is but to define his genius."[54]

Notes

1. E. K. Brown, *Willa Cather: A Critical Biography* (New York: Alfred A. Knopf, 1953), p. 47. Brown notes in passing that Cather had a close and lasting affinity with Mérimée's mind and art, but critics have not explored that relationship any further. James Woodress simply includes Mérimée in a list of authors that Cather read while she was a university student; see his *Willa Cather: Her Life and Art* (New York: Pegasus, 1970), p. 90. Bernice Slote, who has written extensively on Cather's reading and European influences in *The Kingdom of Art: Willa Cather's First Principles and Critical Statements* (Lincoln: Univ. of Nebraska Press, 1966), surprisingly does not mention Mérimée at all.

2. Letter to Albert Feuillerat, dated 6 Nov. 1929, in Sterling Memorial Library, Yale University.

3. A story that Mérimée recommends highly in this essay and one that would have pleased Cather is Gogol's "Old-World Landowners." The story is a small masterpiece in Mérimée's view because all the details contribute to the general effect, nothing is superfluous. Cather would also have admired it for the content—a description of an elderly couple (their archetypes are Baucis and Philemon) who live for each other, have no worldly ambitions although they are landowners, and who take great pleasure in eating, teasing each other, and playing with their pets. When the wife dies the husband is unconsolable until his own death—a testament to the perfection of their marriage. One is reminded particularly of the Cuzaks in *My Ántonia* and the Rosickys in *Obscure Destinies*. See Prosper Mérimée, *Études de littérature russes*, II (Paris: Librairie Ancienne Honoré Champion, 1932), pp. 3–12.

4. See Slote, ed., *The Kingdom of Art*, p. 375.

5. Ibid., p. 447.

6. Letter to Will Owen Jones, 20 May 1919, in University of Virginia Library.

7. See, for example, Brown, *Willa Cather*, pp. 47, 224.

8. *Oeuvres complètes de Gustave Flaubert* (Paris: Libraire de France, 1909–53); *Corréspondance* II, 380; my translation.

9. *Oeuvres complètes de Gustave Flaubert, Corréspondance*, IV, 164.

10. See "A Chance Meeting," in *Not Under Forty* (New York: Alfred A. Knopf, 1936), pp. 3–42.

11. Ibid., p. 22.

12. This essay was published as a preface to his novel *Pierre et Jean* and can be found in *The Portable Maupassant*, ed., with intro., by Lewis Galantière (New York: Viking Press, 1947), pp. 668–70.

13. Quoted by Geoffrey Tillotson in *Criticism and the Nineteenth Century* (London: Althone, 1951), p. 104.

14. Henry James, "The Art of Fiction," in *The Art of Fiction and Other Essays*, ed. Morris Roberts (New York: Oxford Univ. Press, 1948), p. 8.

15. Ford Madox Ford, *Joseph Conrad: A Personal Remembrance* (New York: Octagon Books, 1965), p. 192.

16. Ibid., p. 211.

17. The following quoted matter is from Joseph Conrad's preface to *The Nigger of the "Narcissus"* (New York: Harper and Brothers, 1951), pp. xxxvii–xlii.

18. Ford Madox Ford, *Memories and Impressions A Study in Atmospheres* (New York: Harper & Brothers, 1911), p. xviii.

19. Ford Madox Ford, *The Pre-Raphaelite Brotherhood* (London: Duckworth, 1907), p. 165.

20. Willa Cather, "The Novel Démeublé," in *Willa Cather on Writing* (New York: Alfred A. Knopf, 1949), pp. 41–42.

21. Cather, "Light on Adobe Walls," in ibid., p. 124.

22. Cather, "Miss Jewett," in *Not Under Forty*, p. 90.

23. See *The World and the Parish: Willa Cather's Articles and Reviews, 1893–1902*, ed., with commentary, by William M. Curtin (Lincoln: Univ. of Nebraska Press, 1970), p. 574; hereafter cited as *W&P*.

24. James Woodress writes that Daudet was "the writer of all French writers she loved the most." See Woodress, *Willa Cather: Her Life and Art*, p. 103.

25. *W&P*, p. 575.

26. Ibid., pp. 946–51.

27. Literary impressionism is a good description for *The Country of the Pointed Firs* as well as *Lettres de mon moulin*. Henry James points to exactly those characteristics of Jewett's work when in his review of her historical novel, *The Tory Lover*, he advises her to return to "the palpable present *intimate*" of *The Country of the Pointed Firs*. See Leon Edel's *Selected Letters of Henry James* (New York: Farrar, Straus and Cudahy, 1955), p. 203.

28. Stephen Tennant, "The Room Beyond," a foreword to *Willa Cather on Writing*, p. xiv.

29. Alphonse Daudet, *Letters from My Mill*, trans. John P. MacGregor (New York: Taplinger Publ. Co., 1966), pp. 136–37.

30. Willa Cather, *Shadows on the Rock* (New York: Alfred A. Knopf, 1931), p. 233.

31. Willa Cather, "Two Friends," in *Obscure Destinies* (New York: Alfred A. Knopf, 1932), pp. 209–10.

32. Brown, *Willa Cather*, p. 292.

33. Thomas Carlyle, *Sartor Resartus* (London: Walter Scott, 1888), p. 198.

34. Ibid., p. 201.

35. Willa Cather, *The Professor's House* (New York: Alfred A. Knopf, 1925), p. 69.

36. Cather, "Escapism," in *Willa Cather on Writing*, p. 27.

37. Thomas Carlyle, *Heroes and Hero-Worship*, ed., with intro., by Carl Niemeyer (Lincoln: Univ. of Nebraska Press, 1966), p. 83.

38. Stéphane Mallarmé, "Music and Literature," first appeared in *La Revue blanche*, Oct. 1894. Collected in *Mallarmé: Selected Prose Poems, Essays and Letters*, trans. with intro., by Bradford Cook (Baltimore: Johns Hopkins Press, 1956), pp. 43–55.

39. Stéphane Mallarmé, "Magie," collected in *Stephané Mallarmé: Oeuvres complètes*, ed. Henri Mondor and G. Jean-Aubry (Paris: Editions Gallimard, 1945), p. 400; my translation. Mallarmé's essay in the original reads: "Évoquer . . . l'objet tu, par des mots allusifs, jamais directs, se réduisant à du silence égal, comporte tentative proche de créer."

40. Cather, "The Novel Démeublé" in *Willa Cather on Writing*, p. 41.

41. Cather, "Escapism," in ibid., p. 19.

42. Cather, "The Best Stories of Sarah Orne Jewett," in ibid., p. 50.

43. Cather, "Defoe's *The Fortunate Mistress*," in ibid., p. 79.

44. Cather, "On the Art of Fiction," in ibid., p. 102.

45. Cather, "Katherine Mansfield," in ibid., p. 110.

46. Willa Cather, *My Mortal Enemy* (New York: Random House, 1961), p. 41; references are to this text.

47. Letter to Dorothy Canfield Fisher, 29 Nov. 1923, in the Guy Bailey Memorial Library, University of Vermont.

48. See Elizabeth S. Sergeant, *Willa Cather: A Memoir* (Philadelphia: J. B. Lippincott, 1953), p. 215.

49. Cather, "On *The Professor's House*," in *Willa Cather on Writing*, p. 30.

50. Cather, *The Professor's House*, pp. 250–51.

51. Cather, Prefatory note to *Not Under Forty*, p. v.

52. Willa Cather, *The Old Beauty and Other Stories* (New York: Alfred A. Knopf, 1948), p. 46; references are to this text.

53. Willa Cather, *The Song of the Lark*, Sentry Edition (Boston: Houghton Mifflin, 1963), p. 373.

54. Cather, "The Best Stories of Sarah Orne Jewett," in *Willa Cather on Writing*, p. 54.

The House of Willa Cather   Eudora Welty*

Your invitation to come to the International Seminar of writers, scholars, and critics in commemoration of the centennial of Willa Cather's birth, to speak as a writer of fiction on the fiction of Willa Cather, brings me the very highest honor. I am grateful and filled with humility and pride together in coming before you. The great prize couched in the invitation has come from the incentive it gave me to read all her work again, read it from the beginning. How she refreshes the spirit! The quality that struck me with the strongest force as I read is what I should like to speak about as we meet to celebrate her—the remarkable, and rewarding, physical quality of her work.

"More than anything else I felt motion in the landscape; in the fresh, easy-blowing morning wind, and in the earth itself, as if the shaggy grass were a sort of loose hide, and underneath it herds of wild buffalo were galloping, galloping...."[1] All Willa Cather's prose, like this passage in *My Ántonia*, speaks of the world in a way to show it's alive. There is a quality of animation that seems naturally come by, that seems a born part of every novel. Her own living world is around us as we read, present to us through our eyes and ears and touch.

*Originally published in *The Art of Willa Cather* (Lincoln: University of Nebraska Press, 1974), pp. 3–20. Reprinted by permission of Russell & Volkening, Inc. as agents for the author. Copyright © 1974 by Eudora Welty.

Of course it doesn't escape us that this physical landscape is brought home to us in a way that is subjective. "Overhead the stars shone gloriously. It was impossible not to notice them." Thus she rivets our eyes. "The summer moon hung full in the sky. For the time being it was the great fact in the world."[2] Willa Cather would like our minds to receive what she is showing us not as its description—however beautiful—but as the thing described, the living thing itself. To this end she may eliminate its picture, the better to make us see something really there. It was her observation that "whatever is felt upon the page without being specifically named there—that, one might say, is created."[3] "There were none of the signs of spring for which I used to watch in Virginia," says the narrator. "There was only—spring itself; the throb of it.... If I had been tossed down blindfold on that red prairie, I should have known that it was spring."[4]

And so the texture, that informs us of so much in her prose, owes more than a little to its function. "It was over flat lands like this...that the larks sang."[5] Now we see the land. And hear the lark.

What she has given us is of course not the landscape as you and I would see it, but her vision of it; we are looking at a work of art.

There is something very special, too, about its composition. Look at the Nebraska of her novels as a landscape she might have addressed herself to as an artist with a pencil or a brush. There is the foreground, with the living present, its human figures in action; and there is the horizon of infinite distance, where the departed, now invisible ancients have left only their faint track, cliff dwellings all but disappeared into thin air, pure light. But there is no intervening ground. There is no generation preceding the people now here alive, to fill up the gap between, to populate the stretch of emptiness. Nobody we can see, except the very youngest child, has been born here. Fathers and mothers traveled here, a few hardy grandparents who kept up will survive the life a little while too, and the rest of the antecedents have been left in their graveyards the width of the continent behind.

In this landscape we are made as aware of what isn't as of what is. There is no recent past. There is no middle distance; the perspectives of time and space run unbroken, unmarked, unmeasured to the vanishing point. With nothing in between, the living foreground and that almost mythological, almost phantasmagorical background are all but made one, as in a Chinese painting—and exactly as in one of the mirages that Willa Cather's people often meet, quite casually, in the desert:

> ...a shallow silver lake that spread for many miles, a little misty in the sunlight. Here and there one saw reflected the image of a heifer, turned loose to live upon the sparse sand grass. They were magnified to a preposterous height and looked like mammoths, prehistoric beasts standing solitary in the waters that for many thousands of years actu-

ally washed over that desert: the mirage itself may be the ghost of that long-vanished sea.[6]

Or that ancient life may be discovered through profound personal experience, through one of her "opening windows." Willa Cather brought past and present into juxtaposition to the most powerful effect. And that landscape itself must have shown her this juxtaposition. It existed in the world where she lived, she had the eyes to see it, and she made it a truth of her art. When the sword of Coronado and the plow against the sun are fused into one in *My Ántonia*, we are seeing another vision of it.

The past can be seen—she lets us see it—in physical form. It can be touched—Thea can flake off with her thumb the carbon from the rock roof that came from the cooking stove of the Ancient People. Thea comes to have intuitions about their lives so close to heart that she could walk the trail like the women whose feet had worn it, "trying to walk as they must have walked, with a feeling in her feet and knees and loins which she had never known before. . . . She could feel the weight of an Indian baby hanging to her back as she climbed."[7] And so Niel, of a later day, in *A Lost Lady*, feels in saying goodbye to it: "He had seen the end of an era, the sunset of the pioneer. He had come upon it when already its glory was nearly spent. So in the buffalo times a traveller used to come upon the embers of a hunter's fire on the prairie, after the hunter was up and gone; the coals would be trampled out, but the ground was warm, and the flattened grass where he had slept and where his pony had grazed, told the story."[8]

She saw the landscape had mystery as well as reality. She was undaunted by both. And when she writes of the vast spaces of the world lying out in the extending night, mystery comes to her page, and has a presence; it seems to me a presence not too different from that called up by Turgenev in his magical "Behzin Meadow."

Willa Cather saw her broad land in a sweep, but she saw selectively too—the detail that made all the difference. She never lost sight of the particular in the panorama. Her eye was on the human being. In her continuous, acutely conscious and responsible act of bringing human value into focus, it was her accomplishment to bring her gaze from that wide horizon, across the stretches of both space and time, to the intimacy and immediacy of the lives of a handful of human beings.

People she saw slowly, with care, in their differences: her chosen characters. They stood up out of their soil and against their sky, making, each of them and one by one, a figure to reckon with.

"For the first time, perhaps, since that land emerged from waters of geologic ages," she says of Alexandra in that memorable passage in *O Pioneers!*, "a human face was set toward it with love and yearning. It seemed beautiful to her, rich and strong and glorious. Her eyes drank in the breadth of it, until her tears blinded her. Then the Genius of the

Divide, the great, free spirit which breathes across it, must have bent lower than it ever bent to a human will before. The history of every country begins in the heart of a man or a woman."[9]

And the farther and wider she could see when she started out, the closer it brought her, we feel, full circle—to the thing she wanted, the living, uncopyable *identity* of it that all her working life she wrote in order to meet, to face, to give us as well as she knew it in stories and novels.

The lack of middle distance may have something to do with the way the characters in the foreground cast such long, backreaching shadows. In that lonely stretch of empty and waiting space, they take on heroic stature. And so, Jim Burden tells us—and this has been earned; we have almost reached the end of her novel: "Ántonia had always been one to leave images in the mind that did not fade—that grew stronger with time.... She lent herself to immemorial human attitudes which we recognize by instinct as universal and true. She was a battered woman now, not a lovely girl; but she still had that something which fires the imagination, could still stop one's breath for a moment by a look or gesture that somehow revealed the meaning in common things. She had only to stand in the orchard, to put her hand on a little crab tree and look up at the apples, to make you feel the goodness of planting and tending and harvesting at last. All the strong things of her heart came out in her body.... She was a rich mine of life, like the founders of early races."[10]

A writer uses what he's been given. The work of William Faulkner—another writer of Southern origin, who was destined himself to live in the thick of his background and who had his own abiding sense of place and time and history—is packed most densely of all at the middle distance. The generations clustered just behind where the present-day characters are in action are in fact the tallest—and the most heavily burdened with that past. Faulkner's ancient peoples, his Indians, whose land was taken away by unjust treaty, who were expelled from their own, their race dispersed and brought to nothing, have made the land inimical to the white man. The slave has cursed him again. History for Faulkner is directly inherited; it has come down to the present with the taint of blood and the shame of wrongdoing a part of it. Along with the qualities of nobility and courage and endurance, there were for him corresponding qualities of guilt; there is torment in history and in Faulkner's wrestling with it, in his interpretation of it. Willa Cather's history was not thus bonded to the present; it did not imprison the present, but instructed it, passed on a meaning. It was pure, remained pure, and in its purity could come and go in crystal air. It had the character and something of the import of a vision. The spirit, and not the blood, received it.

In the world of her novels, history lies in persistence in the memory, in lost hidden places that wait to be found and to be known for what they are. Such history is barely accessible, the shell of it is only frailly held together, it will be loseable again. But the continuity is *there*.

Where does the continuity lie, then? It is made possible, it is carried out, is lived through, by the pioneer. And it is perceived by the artist. And even more profoundly, it exists, for Willa Cather, as a potential in the artist himself; it is his life's best meaning, his own personal, and responsible, connection with the world.

"That stream"—Thea is meditating in Panther Canyon—"was the only living thing left of the drama that had been played out in the cañon centuries ago. In the rapid, restless heart of it, flowing swifter than the rest, there was a continuity of life that reached back into the old time. . . . The stream and the broken pottery: what was any art but an effort to make a sheath, a mould in which to imprison for a moment the shining, elusive element which is life itself—life hurrying past us and running away, too strong to stop, too sweet to lose? The Indian women had held it in their jars. . . . In singing, one made a vessel of one's throat and nostrils and held it on one's breath, caught the stream in a scale of natural intervals."[11]

When Thea holds the ancients' pottery in her hands, her feeling for art is born. When Willa Cather makes her novel one about art, she chooses art not of the word, but of the voice. And not the song, but the voice. She has been able to say everything—it is a dazzling translation— in terms of the human being in a physical world.

The whole work of Willa Cather is an embodiment. The great thing it embodies is, of course, passion. That is its vital principle.

She did not come out of Virginia for nothing, any more than she grew up in Nebraska for nothing. History awed and stirred Willa Cather; and the absence of a history as far as she could see around her, in her growing up, only made her look farther, gave her the clues to discover a deeper past. The scarcity of people, a sense of absence and emptiness, set to work in her mind ideas not of despair but of aspiration, the urgency to make out of whatever was there *something*—a thing of her own. She opened her mind to the past as she would to a wise teacher. When she saw the connections, the natural channels opening, she let the past come flooding into the present.

"To people off alone, as we were, there is something stirring about finding evidences of human labour and care in the soil of an empty country. It comes to you as a sort of message, makes you feel differently about the ground you walk over every day,"[12] says Tom Outland, in *The Professor's House.*

Willa Cather's story conceptions have their physical bases, and their physical counterparts. The shift that took place in her own life when her family moved from its settled home in Virginia to the unbroken prairie of the Divide came about when she was nine years old, so likely to be the most sensitive, most vulnerable year of childhood. Its wrench to the spirit was translated over and over again into the situations in her novels and stories. The shift from one home to another, the shift of feeling, must have become in itself the source of a distinctive fictional pattern which was to fall into place for her; it is the kaleidoscopic wrench to the heart that exposes the deeper feeling there. Not impossibly, the origin of her technique of juxtaposition lay in the Virginia–Nebraska move, too. She worked out some of her most significant effects by bringing widely separated lives, times, experiences together—placing them side by side or one within the other, opening out of it almost like a vision—like Tom Outland's story from *The Professor's House*—or existing along with it, waiting in its path, like the mirage.

Personal history may turn into a fictional pattern without closely reproducing it, without needing to reproduce it at all. Essences are what make patterns. Fictional patterns may well bite deeper than the events of a life will ever of themselves, or by themselves, testify to. The pattern is one of interpretation. There, the connections are as significant as what they join together, or perhaps more so. The meaning comes through the joined and completed structure, out of the worthiness of its accomplishment.

In the novel, relationships, development of acts and their effects, and any number of oblique, *felt* connections, which are as important and as indispensable as the factual ones, in composing the plot, form a structure of revelation. The pattern is the plot opened out, disclosing—this was its purpose—some human truth.

Of course it is a pattern uniquely marked by its author's character; the nature of personal feeling has given it its grain. Willa Cather's revered Flaubert said in a letter, "The secret of masterpieces lies in the concordance between the subject and the temperament of the author." The events of a story may have much or little to do with the writer's own life; but the story *pattern* is the nearest thing to a mirror image of his mind and heart.

The artist needs and seeks distance—his own best distance—in order to learn about his subject. To open up the new, to look back on the old, may bring forth like discoveries in the practice of art. Whether the comprehension keeps to the short perimeter around the present, or runs far back into the past, is secondary to the force, impellment, of human feeling involved: *this* determines its reach.

We need to know only what the work of Willa Cather in its course has to tell us—for it's a great deal—about her independence and courage of mind to guess that Miss Jewett's well-known advice—"You must find a quiet place. . . . You must find your own quiet centre of life and write from that"—would not have been the sign to her it was, unless she had arrived at that fact for herself, deep in her own nature. How could she not have? It was central to her life, basic to her conception of character, of situation, in fiction: the writing of one novel had been able to teach that. When she read that truth of Miss Jewett's, isn't it likely that she simply *recognized* it? As she recognized, in the Dutch masters when she saw them in Paris, her own intention in a book to come:

"Just before I began the book [*The Professor's House*]," runs a well-known letter she wrote, "I had seen, in Paris, an exhibition of old and modern Dutch paintings. In many of them the scene presented was a living-room warmly furnished, or a kitchen full of food and coppers. But in most of the interiors, whether drawing-room or kitchen, there was a square window, open, through which one saw the masts of ships, or a stretch of grey sea. The feeling of the sea that one got through those square windows was remarkable, and gave me a sense of fleets of Dutch ships that ply quietly on all the waters of the globe."[13]

It is not surprising that the act of recognition is one of the touch-stones of her fiction. We see her writing in *The Song of the Lark*: "The faculty of observation was never highly developed in Thea Kronborg. A great deal escaped her eye as she passed through the world. But the things which were for her, she saw; she experienced them physically and remembered them as if they had once been part of herself. The roses she used to see in the florists' shops in Chicago were merely roses. But when she thought of the moonflowers that grew over Mrs. Tella-mantez's door, it was as if she had been that vine and had opened up in white flowers every night." And, "Here, in Panther Cañon, there were again things which seemed destined for her."[14] And before that, "When the English horns gave out the theme of the Largo [this is Thea hearing Dvořák's *New World Symphony* for the first time], she knew that what she wanted was exactly that. Here were the sand hills, the grasshoppers and locusts, all the things that wakened and chirped in the early morning; the reaching and reaching of high plains, the immeasurable yearning of all flat lands. There was home in it, too; first memories, first mornings long ago; the amazement of a new soul in a new world; a soul new and yet old, that had dreamed something despairing, something glorious, in the dark before it was born; a soul obsessed by what it did not know, under the cloud of a past it could not recall."[15]

Recognition, we feel, was for Willa Cather a learning process that didn't stop; and Willa Cather was a born learner. The beautiful early story "The Enchanted Bluff" about the boys whose whole wish was to escape from home and who fail in their lives when they never make the break, turned into a chapter of *My Ántonia* that is more beautiful. Here, as in "The Enchanted Bluff," we have children listening and dreaming as a story is being told to them; Jim tells the children about the coming of Coronado and his search for the Seven Golden Cities in the early days, coming right here to Nebraska, where a sword with the name of its Spanish maker was turned up by a farmer breaking sod. And

Presently we saw a curious thing: There were no clouds, the sun was going down in a limpid, gold-washed sky. Just as the lower edge of the red disk rested on the high fields against the horizon, a great black figure suddenly appeared on the face of the sun. We sprang to our feet, straining our eyes toward it. In a moment we realized what it was. On some upland farm, a plough had been left standing in the field. The sun was sinking just behind it. Magnified across the distance by the horizontal light, it stood out against the sun, was exactly contained within the circle of the disk; the handles, the tongue, the share—black against the molten red. There it was, heroic in size, a picture writing on the sun.

Even while we whispered about it, our vision disappeared; the ball dropped and dropped until the red tip went beneath the earth. The fields below us were dark, the sky was growing pale, and that forgotten plough had sunk back to its own littleness somewhere on the prairie.[16]

The author has come to her quiet center. Nebraska, when she left it, was "Siberia"; now, for her writer's eyes, it is a radiant force of life itself.

The birth of Willa Cather came, as it happens, in the year Mark Twain began writing *Huckleberry Finn*. The authors' worlds were different, their frontiers were different—the events in *Huck* went back, of course, to the 1830s and '40s—but they worked, in a way that came naturally to them both, to something of the same scale. They stand together in *bigness*—their sense of it, their authority over it. The difference I want to mention is not in scale or in authority over it, but in the fictional uses to which the world is put.

Through each of their lands there flows a river. Mark Twain's Mississippi is the wider and muddier. It is the route and channel of adventure to Huck; around every bend as he takes it, the river is both what he's looking for and what he dreads, and it's got for him what he'd not dreamed of till he finds it. It's *experience* he's on raft-level with; it can wash him overboard, he can plunge for it too, and endanger himself and refresh himself and cleanse himself or hide himself, or defy it, or live off it, dream on it, or show off on it. It is his to live through, and he lives through it—comes out at the other end alive, and ready to take off for a new frontier if they try too hard again to civilize him.

Willa Cather's river is filled with grandeur and power too; it too is both danger and rescue, the demander of courage and daring, of sacrifice and reverence and awe; it stirs the heart to a sense of destiny. But the river that waters the plains for Willa Cather is the pure stream of art.

The works of these two are totally unlike except in their very greatest respects, except in being about something big, in the apprehension of the new, and in movement, tireless movement in its direction. And both great writers say: Who can move best but the inspired child of his times? Whose story should better be told than that of the youth who has contrived to cut lose from ties and go flinging himself might and main, in every bit of his daring, in joy of life not to be denied, to vaunt himself in the love of vaunting, in the marvelous curiosity to find out everything, over the preposterous length and breadth of an opening new world, and in so doing to be one with it? The Mississippi River and the unbroken Prairie; comedy and tragedy; and indeed all destinies and destinations, all come subordinate to the charge of life itself. The two novelists remain a world apart, and yet both, at their best, celebrate through the living presence of that world, an undeniable force—the pursuit of truth. They recognize and confront a common evil—the defiling of the proud human spirit.

It is in looking back on Willa Cather's work that we learn how the vast exterior world she shows us novel by novel, a world ever-present and full of weight and substance and stir, visible to us along differing perspectives and in various mutations of time, has been the deliberately fitted form for each novel's own special needs. This world is here to serve her purpose by taking a fictional role, allying itself more or less openly with human destiny. It appears, according to role, a world with the power to crush and suffocate, and the power to give back life; a world to promise everything, and to deny everything; a world to open a way for living, or to close in life's face. It is all her great, expanding on-moving world; she has made it hers to take at its own beginnings and follow to its slow eclipse; and, in the full circle of it, to bring home the significance of the solitary human spirit which has elected to bring itself there, in its will and its struggle to survive.

She sought for the wholeness of the form—the roundness of the world, the full circle of life. The vital principle, this passion, has of its own a life—a seed, a birth, a growth, a maturing, a decline and sinking into death, back into the earth; it carries within it the pattern of life on earth, and is a part of the same continuity. It is "the old story writing itself over. . . . It is we who write it, with the best we have,"[17] says Alexandra, at the conclusion of *O Pioneers!*

The emotions of Willa Cather's characters, too, have deep roots in the physical world—in that actual physical land to which they were born. In such a land, how clear it is from the start that identity—self-identity—is hard to seize, hard to claim, and hard to hold onto.

Another of the touchstones of her work, I think, is her feeling for the young. "There is no work of art so big or so beautiful," she writes, "that it was not once all contained in some youthful body, like this one [it is Thea's] which lay on the floor in the moonlight, pulsing with ardour and anticipation."[18] The burning drive of the young, the desire to live, to do, to make, to achieve, no matter what the sacrifice, is the feeling most surpassingly alive to the author, most moving to us. Life has made her terribly certain that being young in the world is not easy. "If youth did not matter so much to itself, it would never have the heart to go on,"[19] she says, as Thea starts from home. And Doctor Archie, old friend and traveling companion, "knew that the splendid things of life are few, after all, and so very easy to miss."[20] In *O Pioneers!* we read that "there is often a good deal of the child left in people who have had to grow up too soon."[21] Miss Cather has a number of ways to tell us that life is most passionate in the promise, not in the fulfillment.

A strenuous physical life is lived throughout every novel, whether it is the struggle for survival or the keen experience of joy in simple physical well-being; it may reach in some characters the point of total identification with the living world around. It is a form of the passion that is all through Willa Cather's work; her work is written out of it. We see it in many modulations: desire—often exalted as ambition; devotion; loyalty; fidelity; physical nearness and kindness and comfort when it lies at rest. Love? It is affection that warms the life in her stories and hate that chills it. There is reconcilement, and there is pity. There is obsession here too, and so is the hunger for something impossible: all of these are forms of love. And there is marriage, though the marriages that occur along the way of the novels are milestones, hardly destinations; as required in the careful building of her plots, they are inclined to be unavailing. Sexual love is not often present in the here and now; we more often learn of it after it is over, or see it in its results. My own feeling is that along with her other superior gifts Willa Cather had a rare sureness as to *her* subject, the knowledge of just what to touch and what not to touch in the best interests of her story.

What her characters are mostly meant for, it seems to me, is to rebel. For her heroines in particular, rebelling is much easier than not rebelling, and we may include love, too, in not rebelling. It is the strong, clear impulse in Willa Cather's stories. It is the real springwater. It is rebelling, we should always add, not for its own sake as much as for the sake of something a great deal bigger—for the sake of integrity, of truth, of art. It is the other face of aspiration. Willa Cather used her own terms; and she left nothing out. What other honorable way is there for an artist to have her say?

The novels have the qualities and the components of love in proportions all their own, then; and I believe this may point again to the thought that they are concerned not with *two* but with *one*, in the number of human beings—not, finally, with relationships but with the desire in one heart and soul to claim what is its own, to achieve its measure of greatness, to overcome any terrible hardship, any terrible odds; and this desire is served by love, rewarded by love (but its absence or failure never compensated for by love); and most of the time, and at its highest moments, the desire is its own drive, its own gratification. One of its forms is indeed pride; and pride is not punished in Willa Cather's novels, it can be deserved.

"Her voice . . . had to do with that confidence, that sense of wholeness and inner well-being that she had felt at moments ever since she could remember. . . . It was as if she had an appointment to meet the rest of herself sometime, somewhere. It was moving to meet her and she was moving to meet it. That meeting awaited her, just as surely as, for the poor girl in the [train] seat behind her, there awaited a hole in the earth, already dug."[22] And then in the city, at the concert, hearing the music that is to change her life, Thea says, "As long as she lived that ecstasy was going to be hers. She would live for it, work for it, die for it; but she was going to have it, time after time, height after height. . . . She would have it, what the trumpets were singing! She would have it, have it—it!"[23]

How does Willa Cather make this an emotion for which we have such entire sympathy? Its intensity, I think, is the answer—Thea's intensity partaking of Willa Cather's. Thea's music teacher says of her, " 'Her secret? It is every artist's secret—passion. That is all. It is an open secret, and perfectly safe. Like heroism, it is inimitable in cheap materials.' "[24]

This high desire, when merged into other than itself, merges into the whole world. An individuality can be made willing to lose itself only in something as big as the world. It *was* the world, in *O Pioneers!* and *My Ántonia*. It was not the world itself, except in magnitude and undeniability, in *The Song of the Lark* and, consummately, in *The Professor's House*: it was art.

For this novelist, art, as she saw it and perfected it, always kept the proportions of the great world and the undeniability of the world, and it lived for her as certainly as this world lived. And the strongest *felt* relationship, a reader may come to believe, might not be any of those between the characters but the one their creator feels for them, for their developing, passionate lives.

In a landscape this wide and pulsing, it seems not at all out of keeping that the greatest passions made real to us are those *for* greatness, and for something larger than life. Men and women do of course fall in love in Willa Cather's novels and their relationship is brought into clear enough focus for us to put good reliance on; but the desire to make a work of art is a stronger one, and more lasting. In the long run, love of art—which is love accomplished without help or need of help from another—is what is deepest and realest in her work.

There is not a trace of disparagement in her treatment of the least of her characters. The irony of her stories is grave, never belittling; it is a showing of sympathy. She *contended* for the life of the individual. Her attack was positive and vigorous and unflinching and proud of winning. This contending was the essence of her stories, formed her plots, gave her room for action. And she did it without preaching. She lacked self-righteousness, and she just as wholly lacked bitterness. It is impossible to think of diminishment in anything she thought or wrote. She conceived of character along heroic lines. For her, the heroic life is the artist's as it is the pioneer's. She equated the two.

Set within the land is the dwelling—made by human hands to hold human life. As we know, the intensity of desire for building the house to live in—or worship in—fills all the Cather novels. It fills the past for her, it gives the present meaning; it provides for a future: the house is the physical form, the *evidence* that we have lived, are alive now; it will be evidence some day that we were alive once, evidence against the arguments of time and the tricks of history.

In her landscape, we learn from both seeing what is there and realizing what is not there; there is always felt the *absence* of habitation. We come to know what degrees there are of the burrow and the roof. "The houses on the Divide were small and were usually tucked away in low places; you did not see them until you came directly upon them," we read of the Scandinavian settlement in *O Pioneers!* "Most of them were built of the sod itself, and were only the unescapable ground in another form."[25] Mrs. Archie, in *The Song of the Lark*, of whom we are told "such little, mean natures are among the darkest and most baffling of created things," liked to "have her house clean, empty, dark, locked, and to be out of it—anywhere."[26] The Professor's house, shabby and outgrown as it is, is a dated house; but the cliff house, almost older than time, is timeless.

"I wish I could tell you what I saw there, just *as* I saw it, on that first morning, through a veil of lightly falling snow," Tom Outland says, in his story within the story. "Far up above me, a thousand feet or so, set in a great cavern in the face of the cliff, I saw a little city of stone, asleep.... It all hung together, seemed to have a kind of composition.... The tower was the fine thing that held all the jumble of houses together and made them mean something.... I felt that only a strong and aspiring people would have built it, and a people with a feeling for design." "The town hung like a bird's nest in the cliff, ... facing an ocean of clear air. A people who had the hardihood to build there, and who lived day after day looking down upon such grandeur, who came and went by those hazardous trails, must have been ... a fine people." "'I see them here, isolated, cut off from other tribes, working out their destiny,'" said Father Duchene, the scholar, "'making their mesa more and more worthy to be a home for man.... Like you,'" he tells Tom Outland, "'I feel a reverence for this place. Wherever humanity has made that hardest of all starts and lifted itself out of mere brutality, is a sacred spot.... They built themselves into this mesa and humanized it.'"[27]

The Professor's House is a novel with a unique form, and to read it is to see it built before our eyes: the making of two unlike parts into a whole under a sheltering third part which defines it and is as final as that verse that comes to recite itself to the Professor's mind. The construction is simple, forthright, and daring. By bringing the Professor's old house and the cliff dwellers' house in combination to the mind, Willa Cather gives them simultaneous existence, and with the measure of time taken away we may see, in the way of a mirage, or a vision, humanity's dwelling places all brought into one. And it was there all the time:

> For thee a house was built
> Ere thou wast born;
> For thee a mould was made
> Ere thou of woman camest.[28]

Tom Outland's story, set into *The Professor's House* like the view from the casement of that Dutch interior, is the objectively told, factual-seeming counterpart of Thea's experience in the Ancient People's cliff houses in *The Song of the Lark*, which was published ten years earlier. Tom Outland's story has a further difference: the tragic view.

It is the objective chronicler for whom the story comes to a tragic end. For Thea, who has seen in her discovery of the Ancient People something totally and exclusively her own, and her own secret, it remained undamaged as a dream. She apprehended it in her own mind, and her own body, as a message for her. Tom Outland's Cliff City was there in the world, and he wanted the world to discover it as he had, to study it, venerate it, share it; and it was taken away from him, broken and desecrated; it brought about not the self-discovery of Thea, but a crisis and a lasting sorrow in human relationship. In the end, it is more of an interior story than Thea's ever was.

"Tom Outland's Story" is written with a compression and strength that the author had already showed us in *A Lost Lady*, and achieves a simplicity that, as it seems to me, nothing else she wrote ever surpassed. Such simplicity is not what a writer starts with; it is what the writer is able to end with, or hopes to be able.

The Professor's House in whole might show us that the novel, in its excellence as a work of art, stands, itself, as a house finished. In so much as it has perfection, perfection has not sealed it, but opened it to us.

A work of art is a *work*: something made, which in the making follows an idea that comes out of human life and leads back into human life. A work of art is the house that is *not* the grave. An achievement of order, passionately conceived and passionately carried out, it is not a thing of darkness. When it is finished, if it is good and sound, somehow all opacity has left it. It stands as clear as candor itself. The fine physical thing has become a transparency through which the idea it was made to embody is thus made totally visible. It could not have been this visible before it was embodied. We see human thought and feeling best and clearest by seeing it through something solid that our hands have made.

"Artistic growth is, more than it is anything else, a refining of the sense of truthfulness." This is said at the end of *The Song of the Lark.* "The stupid believe that to be truthful is easy; only the artist, the great artist, knows how difficult it is."[29] And, Thea's teacher has told her, " 'Every artist makes himself born. It is very much harder than the other time, and longer.' "[30]

In the Cather novels, there is a setting apart of the artist in value, a setting apart of his life from that of other people. Artists, in her considered and lifelong view, are perhaps greater and more deserving to be made way for than other human beings. This could never have been a popular view, but in trying to understand it I think she extolled the artist not for what would seem vanity, or for anything less than a function he could perform—the great thing that only an artist would be able, in her eyes, to do. The artist has a role. Thea, meditating on this role, thought, of the people who cared about her singing, "Perhaps each of them concealed another person in himself, just as she did. . . . What if one's second self could somehow speak to all those second selves?"[31] At base, I think this is an aspect of the Cather sense of obligation to give of oneself. "If he achieves anything noble, anything enduring, it must be by giving himself absolutely to his material. And this gift of sympathy is his great gift," Willa Cather said; "it is the fine thing in him that alone can make his work fine."[32] The artist is set apart the more entirely, all but symbolically, to give himself away, to fulfill the ultimate role of dedication.

Today, neither the artist nor the world holds this idea, and it has faded, along with some of her other strong beliefs (the hero and the heroine, the sanctity of the family), from our own view. Our ideas of history and art are different from hers, as tomorrow's will be different from today's. We have arrived at new places to stand to obtain our own viewpoint of history. Art, since it grows out of its times, is of itself, and by rights, a changing body. But truth?

Truth is the rock. Willa Cather saw it as unassailable. Today the question is asked if this is indeed so. Many of us align ourselves with Willa Cather—I do—in thinking the truth will hold out; but there are many who feel another way, and indeed, I believe, many who would not feel life was over if there were no truth there.

One of the strangest things about art, nevertheless, is that the rock it is built on is not its real test. Our greatest poem made a mistake about the construction of the universe, but this will never bring the poem down.

Yet plain enough is the structure Willa Cather built on these rocks she herself believed were eternal. Her work we, today, see entirely on its own, without need of that support. It holds itself independently, as that future church appears to be doing above the dreaming head of Saint Francis of Assisi in Giotto's fresco. Her work has its own firm reason for existence. And here it stands, a monument more unshakable than she might have dreamed, to the independent human spirit she most adored.

She made this work out of her life, her perishable life, which is so much safer a material to build with than convictions, however immutable they seem to the one who so passionately holds them. It is out of our own lives that we, in turn, reach out to it. Because the house of Willa Cather contained, embodied, a spirit, it will always seem to us inhabited. There is life in that house, the spirit she made for it, made it out of; it is all one substance: it is her might and her heart and soul, all together, and it abides.

Notes

1. *My Ántonia* (Boston: Houghton Mifflin Company, Sentry Edition, 1961), p. 16.

2. *The Song of the Lark* (Boston: Houghton Mifflin Company, Sentry Edition, 1963), pp. 6, 51.

3. "The Novel Démeublé," in *Willa Cather on Writing: Critical Studies on Writing as an Art* (New York: Alfred A. Knopf, 1949), p. 41.

4. *My Ántonia*, pp. 119–20.

5. *The Song of the Lark*, p. 276.

6. Ibid., pp. 59–60.

7. Ibid., p. 376.

8. *A Lost Lady* (New York: Alfred A. Knopf Vintage Book edition, 1972), p. 168.

9. *O Pioneers!* (Boston: Houghton Mifflin Company, Sentry Edition, 1962), p. 65.

10. *My Ántonia*, pp. 352–53.

11. *The Song of the Lark*, p. 378.

12. *The Professor's House* (New York: Alfred A. Knopf Vintage Book edition, 1973), p. 194.

13. "On *The Professor's House*," in *Willa Cather on Writing*, p. 31.

14. *The Song of the Lark*, p. 374.

15. Ibid., p. 251.

16. *My Ántonia*, p. 245.

17. *O Pioneers!*, p. 307.

18. *The Song of the Lark*, p. 177.

19. Ibid., pp. 198–99.

20. Ibid., p. 199.

21. *O Pioneers!*, p. 17.

22. *The Song of the Lark*, p. 272.

23. Ibid., pp. 254–55.

24. Ibid., pp. 570–71.

25. *O Pioneers!*, p. 19.

26. *The Song of the Lark*, p. 42.

27. *The Professor's House*, pp. 201 (3), 203–204, 213, 220, 221.

28. Ibid., p. 272.

29. *The Song of the Lark*, p. 571.

30. Ibid., p. 221.

31. Ibid., p. 273.

32. "The Best Stories of Sarah Orne Jewett," in *Willa Cather on Writing*, p. 51.

Cather and Her Friends   James Woodress*

The frank treatment of sexual relations (hetero- and homo-) that our culture currently tolerates in public discussion has inevitably broadened to include academic discourse. Sessions on homosexual and lesbian literary subjects are now a staple of the many-ringed circus that goes on annually at the conventions of the Modern Language Association. Sexuality, of course, is a subject of immediate and universal interest, and one should not be surprised that readers want to know about the sexual preferences of their favorite authors. The life and works of Willa Cather have generated their own considerable amount of sex-oriented scrutiny. It came as no surprise to the members of the faculty at the 1981 Cather seminar held in Hastings, Nebraska, to be asked about Cather's sex life. It is my purpose in this essay to say what can be said on this topic by way of introducing a survey of Cather's relationships with her three closest women friends. That these relationships were important to her personally and had an impact on her work is beyond question.

At the end of the Cather seminar all students were invited to submit questions to be answered by the faculty at an open meeting. The majority of the queries had to do with sex. The students wanted to know if Cather ever considered herself a lesbian, and if so, how did this affect her work, or how did her sexual preference influence the creating of character in her fiction? In short, was she a lesbian? The questions led to an hour-long discussion but to no answers, nor can one ever expect definitive answers to these queries. Documentary evidence does not exist to dispose of the question in one way or another. The panelists agreed that they did not believe Cather ever thought of herself as lesbian, but whether she was or not will have to remain moot.

The absence of evidence, however, does not keep people from drawing conclusions. In a seminar paper I received recently there was this sentence: "That Willa Cather was a lesbian is more than hinted by biographical fact." The paper went on to quote from my biography of

---

*This essay was written for this volume and is published by permission of the author.

Cather two comments regarding the relationship between Cather and Isabelle McClung: that their friendship "grew to be a great love that lasted a lifetime" and that the relationship "quite literally changed her [Cather's] life."[1] I think that these statements are accurate, but my student's inductive leap to her conclusion was really only a guess. In Jane Rule's *Lesbian Images* (1975) one finds a chapter on Cather that assumes her lesbianism. This book also charges with male bias disparaging comments by Lionel Trilling and John H. Randall III on Cather's treatment of heterosexual relations: "No lesbian can write about heterosexual experience without 'dangerous idiosyncrasy' [Randall's term] which must therefore be found in Willa Cather's work whether it is there or not."[2] In a recent article Deborah Lambert finds "many strange flaws and omissions" in *My Ántonia* because "Cather was a lesbian who could not, or did not, acknowledge her homosexuality and who, in her fiction, transformed her emotional life and experiences into acceptable, heterosexual forms and guises."[3] Lillian Faderman in her recent history of lesbianism argues that Cather perhaps felt the need to be reticent about love between women in her fiction because "she bore a burden of guilt for what came to be labeled perversion," and she adds that "Cather characters that are suspiciously autobiographical, such as the narrator in *My Ántonia*, appear as male whenever they show love interest in females."[4]

Jane Rule also speculates that Cather's burning of her letters to McClung and her refusal to let her letters be published "were minor gestures in a whole pattern of protecting her personal life so that she and those she loved could live without the invasion and distortions of fame."[5] That she guarded her privacy zealously is not to be disputed, but the ban on posthumous publication of letters sprang from another motive. Cather wanted to be known only by the work of her artistic maturity, the work that she had prepared for publication and sometimes revised substantially. She never wanted to reprint most of her early stories, and she refused all offers (except one that she regarded as a mistake) to turn her fiction into dramatic scripts or movie scenarios. Her letters were ephemeral, not written for posterity, and therefore not to be published.

Deducing biographical data from fiction is a nonproductive business, and biographers and critics should be wary of attempting it. If we had every letter that Cather ever wrote, I am sure that we would be no closer than we are now to knowing anything about Cather's sex life or sex preference. I have read most of her extant letters, and I cannot conceive of Cather's ever committing to paper anything so personal. Thus we are left with conjecture, and the lesbian image of Jane Rule, Deborah Lambert, and Lillian Faderman is in the eye of the beholder. However, if one defines lesbianism as Faderman does, the problem becomes simple: " 'Lesbian' describes a relationship in which two women's strongest emotions and affections are directed toward each other. Sexual contact may be part of the relationship to a greater or lesser degree, or it may be entirely absent."[6] By this definition Cather's friendship with McClung certainly was a lesbian relationship, and her long association with Edith Lewis also may have been.

This statement, however, does not get us very far in understanding the passion and dedication that went into Cather's fiction. It is my belief that Cather's sexual impulses were channeled into her work. On numerous occasions throughout her career she stated that art was a merciless taskmaster, that an artist could not be successful without pouring all of his/her energy and emotion into art. During her freshman year in college she wrote an essay on Shakespeare and *Hamlet* in which she argued: "If an artist does any good he must do it alone. No number of encouraging or admiring friends can assist him. . . . He must go off alone with his own soul and they too must labor and suffer together."[7] Twenty-four years later she had Thea Kronborg, her Wagnerian soprano, say in *The Song of the Lark*: "Your work becomes your personal life. You are not much good until it does. It's like being woven into a big web. You can't pull away, because all your little tendrils are woven into the picture. It takes you up, and uses you, and spins you out; and that is your life."[8]

This is not to say that Cather did not have time in her life for love. There were a good many people that she loved, male and female; but she never entered into an emotional attachment that kept her from her work. There is no evidence that she ever seriously considered getting married, though she did have chances. During her Pittsburgh years when she was in her mid-twenties, she did a lot of socializing and received at least two proposals of marriage in rapid succession. But the men she was closest to in her life were those she did not have to consider living with— her father, her older brothers Roscoe and Douglass, and S. S. McClure, her employer with whom she had a close avuncular relationship. She also was devoted to her publisher Alfred Knopf (nineteen years her junior) and her younger brothers, for whom she was more aunt than sister. I find it impossible to say whether Cather's sexual preference for women resulted from inherent tendencies or from the fact that emotional ties with women avoided domestic entanglements with male egos or children.

Cather was convinced that art and marriage did not mix. When actress Mary Anderson retired from the stage to get married, Cather reflected on the demands of career and matrimony. Mary Anderson was not a great artist, and for her perhaps the happiness of married life was the better choice. Yet for the greatest of women artists, women like "Sappho and the two great Georges [Sand and Eliot]," only art could satisfy.[9] On another occasion, when Helena von Doenhoff retired from the operatic stage to marry, Cather wrote a sort of obituary. The artist, she declared, must love his art above all things and must say to it, as Ruth said amidst the alien corn: "Where thou goest, I will go, and where thou lodgest I will lodge . . . thy people shall be my people, and thy God my God." To this she added "married nightingales seldom sing."[10] When actress Marie Burroughs' divorce was announced in the papers, Cather wrote in her column that Marie wanted to be free for her work and free from the obligation of matrimony. The fact that her husband had been her teacher and coach made her ungrateful, but then all actresses are ungrateful. "If they are actresses worthy of the name, they always have a *premier amour* to whom they return, their work."[11] Another sentence she was fond of quoting: "He travels the swiftest who rides alone."[12] Cather, however, was perfectly happy to congratulate her artist friends when they embarked on matrimony, and when Zoë Akins got married at forty-six Cather wrote her rather wistfully about this development. Zoë, she said, was never afraid to take a chance and if anyone could make matrimony go, she could. Cather was sorry she was not planning to visit California that year to see Zoë in her new home and to hear all about her marriage.

In my view there is no evidence from the fiction that Cather's sexual preference influenced her writing. In her novels and stories she is completely androgynous. She creates memorable women characters such as Alexandra Bergson, who is relatively sexless, and Ántonia Shimerda, who is a richly fulfilled mother and wife. She depicts Myra Henshawe, an unhappy, deluded woman whose marriage is a failure, and Marian Forrester, whose life is full of extramarital heterosexual activity. She also draws convincing portraits of Professor St. Peter, who grows weary of his materialistic wife and children, the young idealist Claude Wheeler, who dies in World War I, and the devoted archbishop and his vicar, whose nonsexual male friendship unfolds glowingly in *Death Comes for the Archbishop.* She also could enter into the consciousness of a male narrator with complete success, as she does with Jim Burden in *My Ántonia,* or tell her story through the eyes of a young woman, as with Nellie Birdseye in *My Mortal Enemy.* The gallery of characters is large and full of variety.

Faderman in her book believes that "there is absolutely no suggestion of same-sex love in Cather's fiction."[13] She is talking about female relationships here, but she is clearly wrong. There are at least two friendships that come to mind immediately: the relationships between Marie Shabata and Alexandra Bergson in *O Pioneers!,* and Cherry Beamish and Gabrielle Longstreet in "The Old Beauty." And what is more, Cather treats these two friendships as admirable. At the same time, there are two overt examples of homosexuality that she treats very negatively in her fiction: the glimpse of the two American women who cause the accident in "The Old Beauty" and the relationship between Clement Sebastian and James Mockford in *Lucy Gayheart.*

Although Cather was totally committed to her art and did not let friends keep her from working, she valued certain friendships highly and drew on them for support. The three most significant friendships, all with women, sustained her from the beginning of her career to the end of her life. None of them covered the entire span of years, but all of them were of long duration. The friends were Isabelle McClung, whom she met in Pittsburgh in 1898 or 1899; Edith Lewis, with whom she lived for thirty-nine years until her death in 1947; and Elizabeth Sergeant, journalist and writer, who met Cather when she submitted an article to *McClure's Magazine* in 1910.[14]

When Cather was writing drama criticism for the *Pittsburgh Leader*, one of her friends was Lizzie Collier, the leading lady of the Pittsburgh Stock Company and a very popular actress. Cather wrote in her paper on one occasion: "I never come out of the theater with her after a matinee that there is not a string of carriages lined up in front of the stage entrance full of worshipful girls, who wave and smile at her and gaze at me with green-eyed jealousy and deep-seated loathing."[15] Among those worshipful girls was Isabelle McClung, who managed one night to get into Lizzie Collier's dressing room backstage after a performance. Cather also was there, and from this chance meeting sprang the most important relationship of Cather's life.

Somewhat younger than Cather, McClung was the tall, handsome daughter of a socially prominent judge. The two women were immediately drawn to each other, and the friendship that began on that night grew into a great love that lasted nearly four decades. This relationship is the one great romance in Cather's life. The two women became inseparable companions during the balance of Cather's years in Pittsburgh, and two years after this meeting Cather began living in the McClung house. Even after she left Pennsylvania for New York in 1906, she returned often to Pittsburgh to stay with her friend.

Samuel McClung was a dour Presbyterian of Scottish background and a judge of impeccable probity. As a conservative, upper-class Pittsburgher, he lived expansively in a large house on Murray Hill Avenue and expected his children to conduct themselves as well-bred young socialites. Isabelle, however, had her father's strong will and character but not his tastes. She was interested in art and music and cultivated theater people, writers, and musicians. She had no artistic abilities herself but found in Cather someone she could love and whose artistic career she could help promote.

By the time Cather moved into the McClung house she had left journalism and begun teaching high school. One of her reasons for leaving the paper was to give herself more time for writing, which she would do chiefly in the summers. The McClung household was a perfect place to do this. The house was in the fashionable east end of Pittsburgh and commanded a magnificent view from its hilltop site. It had solidity, elegance, comfort. Operated by a staff of servants, it provided luxuries that Cather never before had experienced. The contrast with her boardinghouses, where cooking odors permeated the bedrooms and one stood in line to use the bathroom, was very sharp.

A family battle apparently preceded Cather's change in living arrangements. At least this is the report of Edith Lewis, who succeeded McClung as Cather's inseparable companion, and one suspects there may be some jealousy tincturing the memory: "Isabelle McClung's parents at first wondered at the propriety of having Willa Cather come to reside in their household, though they welcomed her as their daughter's friend. The daughter promptly threatened to leave home if she could not have her way; her parents yielded."[16] At least they agreed that Cather could stay temporarily; but she actually lived there more than five years.

A good picture of Cather and McClung at this time is supplied by Elizabeth Moorhead, a Pittsburgh writer who knew them both: "The two young women would forsake the family group soon after dinner, and evening after evening would go upstairs to the bedroom they shared to read together in quiet. This room was at the back of the house and its wide low windows gave on a downward slope across gardens and shaded streets toward the Monongahela River and green hills rising beyond. There were no close neighbors to destroy their sense of privacy. Here the friends spent many happy and fruitful hours."[17] To facilitate Cather's writing, McClung fixed up a study in the attic, a former sewing room, to which Cather could retire on week ends and summers to work.

From this beginning an intimate relationship continued during the following years. In 1902 Cather and McClung went to Europe together for three months, visiting England and France and returning in September for Cather's teaching job at Central High School. They went back to Europe in 1908 after Cather had joined the staff of *McClure's* and then traveled to Italy. About this time Cather began sharing an apartment with Edith Lewis, but McClung visited New York frequently, and Cather went back to Pittsburgh when she could get away. When Cather finally felt able in 1911 to cut loose from journalism and free lance, she and McClung went off together to Cherry Valley, New York, in the Finger Lakes region. There Cather worked for three months and discovered for the first time her real subject—Nebraska. Those three months in the autumn of 1911 were pivotal in Cather's career, and the presence of McClung as devoted companion and guardian of privacy facilitated the creative process. Isabelle's mother had grown up in that region, and Isabelle, who loved the area, had found them a quiet, secluded house. During this period Cather wrote "The Bohemian Girl" and a story, "Alexandra," which grew into her first Nebraska novel, *O Pioneers!* The following year the McClung home in Pittsburgh was Cather's headquarters for six months while she worked on the novel.

After publishing *O Pioneers!* in 1913, Cather discovered the subject for her next novel in the career of Olive Fremstad, the reigning Wagnerian soprano at the Metropolitan Opera. Freed from the drudgery of editing *McClure's*, she could settle down to sustained periods of writing. In the fall of 1914 she went back to her attic study in Pittsburgh and in four weeks produced the first twenty-eight thousand words of her new novel. McClung was there, of course, giving her support and company. Then she went back to New York in the winter but returned to Pittsburgh in May and finished the novel there. This period marks the culmination of Cather's relationship with McClung, and *The Song of the Lark* is dedicated to her:

> On uplands
> At Morning,
> The world was young, the winds were free;
> A garden fair,
> In that blue desert air,
> Its guest invited me to be.

The relationship, however, was soon to undergo a radical change. Judge McClung died in November 1915, and since Isabelle's mother had predeceased him, Isabelle finally was freed of parental domination and possessed of independent means. After a sad Christmas in the old house on Murray Hill Avenue with Isabelle, Cather wrote her Aunt Franc in Nebraska that the kind and hospitable house which had been a home to her for fifteen years would probably be sold and that this was the last Christmas she ever would have there. The shock of losing this old refuge, however, was nothing compared to the crisis that followed sometime later that winter when McClung informed Cather that she was going to be married. The announcement shattered Cather physically and mentally. The paralyzing effect may be judged by a letter Cather wrote some weeks later in mid-March to her old friend Dorothy Canfield Fisher. She reported laconically that she was unable to start a new book because of the death of Judge McClung and Isabelle's marriage. Elizabeth Sergeant, who heard of McClung's defection as she walked with Cather on an icy day in Central Park, reported that as Cather broke the news her face was bleak and her eyes vacant: "All her natural exhuberance had drained away."[18]

Cather picked herself up after the shock, however, and that summer she went to New Mexico with Edith Lewis. She also visited her brother Roscoe in Wyoming, whence she wrote in August that Isabelle's marriage was still a hard blow to take and always would be, but the rest of the world was beginning to look as it used to. That she snapped out of her depression at the loss of McClung is apparent from the fact that she was well into the writing of *My Ántonia* by the end of the year. The reconciliation with McClung and the acceptance of Jan Hambourg, her husband, followed slowly in the years after 1916. By the summer of 1917

Cather was able to visit the Hambourgs in Jaffrey, New Hampshire, where they were vacationing. She saw them again in Toronto, where they lived, in 1922, and again the next year in Europe after they had bought a villa outside of Paris. McClung hoped that Cather would visit them in France several months a year, and she fixed up a study for her. But it was not like the old attic study in Pittsburgh, and Cather was unable to work there. It does not seem to have been the presence of Jan Hambourg that distracted her, because she was not able to work in Paris either. She had to get back to the Bank Street apartment in Greenwich Village that she shared with Lewis in order to work. By this time she had accepted Jan and an altered relationship with Isabelle, but the friendship remained strong and affectionate, though it was mostly carried on by correspondence for the next decade and a half.

It is unfortunate for the biographer that most details of the Cather–McClung relationship come from secondhand sources. The hundreds of letters that passed between these two friends were destroyed deliberately. After McClung died in 1938 Cather retrieved her letters and burned them; she also destroyed all McClung's letters to her. At least she thought she had, but recently three of McClung's letters have turned up. Apparently they were left behind among abandoned papers when World War II made it impossible for Cather and Lewis to return to their summer cottage on Grand Manan Island in New Brunswick, and when the war ended, Cather was too infirm to go back to the cottage. These letters show convincingly that the relationship had continued as an intimate friendship, even though McClung had long been married and lived abroad.[19]

There would be no question about the durability of this relationship, however, because in 1935 Cather devoted much of the year to attending her friend. McClung and her husband came to the United States to consult American doctors about her deteriorating health. Cather spent most of April and part of May visiting McClung in a New York hospital. Then when she insisted on going to Chicago where her husband was to teach a summer course, Cather accompanied her. In August the Hambourgs returned to Europe and Cather followed and visited them in France. When she returned to the United States, she knew that she probably would not see her friend again. In April before going to Europe Cather had written Zoë Akins in California that McClung was the sweetest and most appreciative invalid and one of the noblest creatures in the world. To look out for her was one of the deepest satisfactions of her life. When McClung died in Sorrento three years later, Cather thought she could not go on living; but she pulled herself together once more. In her final reflections on the long relationship Cather came to believe that McClung had been the one person for whom all of her books had been written.

Cather's relationship with Edith Lewis was a far different affair from her friendship with McClung. It began as an ordinary acquaintance when Cather met Lewis in Lincoln in the summer of 1903. Lewis had come home after graduating from an Eastern college, and Cather was visiting friends in the Nebraska capital during her summer holidays from teaching in Pittsburgh. At the end of the summer Lewis returned to the East and got a job with the Century Publishing Company. Cather visited her the following summer of 1904 in New York, and after McClure invited Cather to join his staff in 1906 she and Lewis were thrown together a great deal. Lewis soon took a proofreading job at *McClure's* at Cather's suggestion and Cather moved into a studio apartment at 60 Washington Square South in the building where Lewis lived. When McClure sent Cather to Boston during her early months on the magazine to work on a life of Mary Baker Eddy that he planned to publish, Lewis was sent up from New York with proof, which the two women read together, a practice they continued after Cather began writing novels.

The relationship grew steadily the longer they were colleagues and neighbors. It took a more serious turn in 1908 when Cather and Lewis decided to share an apartment at 82 Washington Place, and from this beginning grew a life-time companionship. Cather and Lewis lived together until Cather died in 1947, and she made her friend one of her literary executors. They moved from Washington Place in 1913 to 5 Bank Street where they lived for the next fourteen years. When the construction of a subway forced them to find lodging elsewhere, they transferred to the Grosvenor Hotel on Fifth Avenue. They lived there for five years until they found an apartment on Park Avenue, which was their final home.

Even though Cather and Lewis lived together after 1908, McClung remained Cather's most intimate friend; Lewis never replaced her in Cather's affections. The shared apartment was an arrangment of convenience. Cather was thirty-five when she and Lewis moved in together, and the relationship was more like a comfortable middle-aged marriage than anything else, though Lewis was about ten years younger. It was perhaps something like the Gertrude Stein–Alice B. Toklas relationship. Lewis was content to handle many of the dull domestic details involved in running an apartment and to allow Cather the freedom of mind and spirit that she needed. Elizabeth Sergeant, who knew them both well, described the relationship in nautical terms: "A captain . . . must have a first officer, who does a lot the captain never knows about to steer the boat through rocks and reefs."[20] Lewis was the subordinate who always deferred to her more illustrious companion, and being Cather's junior, there also was an element of hero-worship in the relationship. She was in addition very protective of Cather's reputation and privacy. This is clearly seen in the memoir that she wrote after Cather's death for E. K. Brown to use in writing Cather's biography. It is an admiring, informative account of Cather's life and work, but the picture is retouched, and it still remains for some future biographer to restore completely the real Cather.

There must have been some rivalry between Lewis and McClung for Cather's affections during those years between 1908 and 1916. One senses it in the passage from the Brown biography I have already quoted regarding Cather's going to live with the McClungs. There also must have been some tension in the summer of 1915, when Cather was invited by S. S. McClure, who then edited the *New York Evening Mail*, to go to Germany to do some reporting. Although World War I had been going on for a year, Cather agreed to go and asked McClung to accompany her. Just what Cather was supposed to write, the surviving records do not say, and why an ardent Francophile would go to Germany then, one cannot imagine. Fortunately for Cather, Judge McClung, who ran his family with an iron hand, said no, and the trip was canceled. Cather then went to the Southwest for the summer with Lewis, and it was only a few months later that the Judge died, Isabelle came into her inheritance, and Cather was deserted for Jan Hambourg. Was the summer in the Southwest a crucial moment for the triangular relationship of McClung, Lewis, and Cather? One wonders.

As time went on, Lewis became more and more the dependable, in fact, indispensable, first officer. In the early days on Bank Street when Lewis had a nine-to-five job, Cather did the marketing before she settled down at her desk to write. Later Lewis took over all the routine. She was always able to get away in the summers when they traveled to Europe or the Southwest, and after she and Cather built a cottage on Grand Manan in 1925, they summered there together. In the later years Lewis made the travel plans, looked up schedules, bought the tickets, did the shopping, dealt with the cleaning woman, and at Grand Manan walked down the road to get the mail. She fended off visitors and curiosity seekers, and, of course, was always on hand to read proof. The two grew old together in a comfortable, intimate relationship.

Cather's friendship with Elizabeth Sergeant is well documented. Sergeant also wrote a memoir of Cather, and because she outlived her friend Cather's letters to her have survived. Whereas neither McClung nor Lewis was a writer, Sergeant made her living as a journalist and author. She alone among this trio was able to discuss literary technique and artistic problems with Cather. During the early years of Cather's career Sergeant was privy to Cather's plans and saw at least one of her novels in manuscript before publication. The relationship did not remain as close as it had been when the two women grew older, for Sergeant became an ardent New Dealer and champion of avant garde movements in the thirties, while Cather remained a rock-ribbed Midwest Republican and retreated into the past. They visited each other only occasionally during Cather's last decade and a half, but for about twenty years the friendship was strong and important.

Sergeant was born in Massachusetts into an old family and grew up in the New England that Cather discovered through her friendship with Annie Fields and Sarah Orne Jewett. This was the world of literary Boston that looked back to the golden age of Hawthorne, Lowell, Emerson, and Holmes. Cather, who had a Midwesterner's reverence for the writers of New England's flowering, rather envied Sergeant's background. Sergeant also had a common interest with Cather in France. She had gone to France after graduating from Bryn Mawr and her first book, *French Perspectives* (1916), reflected her life in France as a young woman. After returning from Europe, she settled in New York and began writing muck-raking articles that revealed a well-developed social conscience. This was definitely not Cather's interest, even though she was managing editor of the leading muck-raking magazine. It was, however, the activity that brought the two together.

In January 1910, Sergeant took an article she had written on sweated tenement workers, along with a letter of introduction to Cather, to the offices of *McClure's*. Cather read the piece, commented favorably on the style and objectivity, but was not much pleased by the subject. "'Tell me,' Miss Cather suddenly exploded, 'why you joined the reforming pamphleteers? This all has its place—it's good—but aren't short stories more in your line? I don't mean tenement stories—you look like a Jamesian—am I right?' "[21] As Sergeant remembered the situation, Cather did not like having to think about the plight of New York's unassimilated European immigrants who were being exploited in the then-unorganized garment industry. But she took Sergeant in to meet the boss, S. S. McClure, and they accepted her article, which appeared as the lead piece in the magazine in July.

What Cather really was interested in was building up the belletristic content of the magazine. McClure, who also was interested in publishing good fiction as well as muck-raking articles, had sent Cather to Europe twice on buying trips. Cather told Sergeant that McClure had lost more money publishing Joseph Conrad than any other editor alive. From that point on the two women discovered that they shared many literary interests: Flaubert, Tolstoy, James, and (especially important) Jewett. When Cather learned that Sergeant had given a copy of *The Country of the Pointed Firs* to a French critic, who had compared it to Turgenev's *A Sportsman's Sketches*, Cather was delighted. Thus begun, a strong intellectual relationship developed, particularly during the following decade. Cather was soon to leave *McClure's* and needed a sympathetic fellow writer to listen to her.

During Cather's first trip to the Southwest in the spring of 1912 she wrote her new friend frequently. Her letters are filled with the excitement of discovering a new world, something totally different from Nebraska or the Eastern cities. She visited Indian missions and cliff-dwellings for the first time and was captivated by Mexican culture.

Her letters for the next three months are filled with accounts of this experience, especially of a marvelous Mexican named Julio, who sang and played for her, told her stories, took her to a Mexican dance, and looked like something out of an Aztec sculpture. She urged Sergeant to come to the Southwest, which Sergeant did after World War I when she bought a house in Santa Fe.

Cather did not make literary use of her Southwestern experience until she wrote *The Song of the Lark* (1915), but she plunged into writing *O Pioneers!* with unusual vigor after her vacation. Having completed the story "Alexandra" in Cherry Valley, she got the idea for another tale, "The White Mulberry Tree," and wrote Sergeant that the idea had come to her on the edge of a wheat field during her visit to Nebraska that summer. The two stories combined became the novel, and when it was finished she sent the manuscript to Sergeant for criticism, saying that Sergeant was one of three people whose judgment she valued. "She begged me to hand her the unvarnished truth," Sergeant wrote.[22] Cather needed reassurance that the novel was all right, and Sergeant gave it to her.

Sergeant did not see *The Song of the Lark* until after it was published, but she was in on the creation of *My Ántonia* at the beginning. During a visit to Sergeant's apartment one day Cather took an old Sicilian apothecary jar filled with flowers and set it in the midst of a bare, round, antique table: "I want my new heroine to be like this— like a rare object in the middle of a table, which one may examine from all sides . . . I want her to stand out—like this—because she is the story."[23] Cather did not talk about her books while she was writing them, and Sergeant, who was in Europe as a correspondent for the *New Republic* while *My Ántonia* was taking shape, had no further contact with the novel until it appeared. When Sergeant returned to America after the war, Cather was already deep into her war novel, *One of Ours*, and wanted information about "shell shock." She also was eager to hear about new French writers.

During the twenties, however, these two friends began to draw apart. Cather was ill at ease in the postwar world. Her mind began to dwell more and more on the past, while Sergeant, some ten years younger and caught up in the new movements in art and literature, lived in the present. They argued about Freud, to whom Cather had taken an instinctive dislike, and when Sergeant said she had to read him because he belonged to today's world, the two friends had to agree to disagree. "Willa," wrote Sergeant, "like the Pueblo Indians who—I am told in New Mexico—had no word for 'future,' looked backward with regret. Our present lay about us in ruins but we had, she wistfully remarked, a beautiful past."[24] Although they could and did talk about books, they disagreed again over Sinclair Lewis' *Main Street* and John Dos Passos' *Three Soldiers*. Later when Sergeant developed a passion for O'Neill's plays, Cather said she would not go around the corner to see one of his productions at the nearby Sheridan Square Theater. But they did meet at a fiftieth birthday dinner for Robert Frost, a writer whom they both admired.

At the end of the twenties Sergeant went back to Europe for two years, and when she returned the depression was in full swing. Cather soon moved into her Park Avenue apartment, a pretentious place Sergeant disliked, with all its uniformed attendants who probably would not have allowed Neighbour Rosicky or Grandma Harris beyond the lobby. Still the old friends occasionally met for tea, and later when Sergeant took an apartment in the East Seventies Cather and Lewis came to dinner. The friendship never ended, but during World War II the two women seldom met. Telephone conversations kept the relationship alive until Cather's death in 1947, after which Sergeant prepared an affectionate, generous tribute to her friend in the memoir she published in 1953.

McClung, Lewis, and Sergeant do not exhaust the list of Cather's close women friends. There are at least five more important relationships that extended over many years: Carrie Miner Sherwood and Irene Miner Weisz, friends from Cather's childhood in Red Cloud; novelist Dorothy Canfield Fisher, whose friendship began during Cather's college days; playwright Zoë Akins, who, like Sergeant, met Cather during her *McClure's* period; and to these names one should add the most famous friend of all, Annie Sadilek Pavelka, whose luminous portrait is preserved for posterity in *My Ántonia*. This last friendship, which did not produce many letters, was renewed in person whenever Cather visited Nebraska. The relationships with the Miner sisters did elicit a long correspondence that fortunately has survived, as both women outlived Cather and had the good sense to keep their letters.

The Fisher and Akins friendships are important ones of the same nature as the Sergeant relationship. Cather and Dorothy Canfield met at the University of Nebraska, collaborated on a story published in the college yearbook, and during their early years saw a good bit of each other. Dorothy's father became chancellor of Ohio State University when Cather was working in Pittsburgh, and the two friends visited back and forth. Later they met in Europe during Cather's summer trip with McClung in 1902, and as Dorothy was working on a doctorate in Romance languages and knew France and French very well, she and Cather shared a strong interest in French civilization. Later Dorothy became a novelist and the two friends often discussed their work. But by 1907 she was married and settled in Vermont, and the relationship was carried on mostly by correspondence. Zoë Akins came into Cather's life in 1909 when she submitted some verse to *McClure's*. Cather rejected it but found Akins a delightful person, twenty-three years old, a St. Louisan who had come to New York to be a writer. Cather always felt, as she wrote many years later, that there was a golden glow about Akins. When Cather turned down the verse, she told Akins she really ought to become a playwright, which she actually did, and during the twenties and thirties she wrote one successful play after another, finally winning a Pulitzer Prize in 1935. Cather and Akins carried on a lifelong correspondence, and because Akins outlived Cather her letters also survive. During the twenties Akins lived in New York and the two friends saw each other often, but in the thirties Akins moved to California and thereafter there were fewer meetings. When Cather's mother was dying in a Pasadena sanitorium, however, the two friends got together, and when Akins visited New York for the opening of her plays, there were annual meetings at least. This friendship, like those with Sergeant and Fisher, was an intellectual and literary relationship as well as one of compatible personalities. Cather's letters to Akins, like those to Sergeant and Fisher, dealt frequently with writing plans and problems.

The calendar of Cather letters extant in libraries from Vermont to California clearly establishes that Cather's important friendships with her contemporaries were with women.[25] (I exclude from this generalization correspondence with her brothers and her Pittsburgh friend George Seibel, whose letters from Cather were always addressed to his wife as well.) That Cather needed and sought emotional attachments is abundantly supported by the biographical record. The inescapable conclusion to be drawn from this survey of her personal relationships is that Cather derived her greatest comfort, pleasure, moral support, and satisfaction from friendships with members of her own sex.

Notes

1. James Woodress, *Willa Cather; Her Life and Art* (New York: Pegasus, 1970), p. 91.

2. Jane Rule, *Lesbian Images* (Garden City, N.Y.: Doubleday & Co., 1975), p. 76.

3. Deborah G. Lambert, "The Defeat of a Hero: Autonomy and Sexuality in *My Ántonia*," *American Literature*, 53 (1982), 676.

4. Lillian Faderman, *Surpassing the Love of Men: Romantic Friendship and Love between Women from the Renaissance to the Present* (New York: William Morrow & Co., 1981), p. 201.

5. Rule, *Lesbian Images*, p. 78.

6. Faderman, *Surpassing the Love of Men*, pp. 17–18.

7. This essay was published in the *Nebraska State Journal*, 1, 8 Nov. 1891 pp. 16, 11; reprinted in Bernice Slote, ed., *The Kingdom of Art: Willa Cather's First Principles and Critical Statements, 1893–1896* (Lincoln: Univ. of Nebraska Press, 1966), pp. 434–35.

8. *The Song of the Lark* (Boston: Houghton Mifflin, 1963), p. 546.

9. Originally published in the *Journal*, 3 May 1896, p. 13, reprinted in *The*

Kingdom of Art, ed. Slote, p. 158. It is interesting to note that Cather here lumps together one lesbian, one heterosexual (Eliot), and one bisexual (Sand). Incidentally, for many years Cather kept an engraving of Sand on her mantel. The important thing for Cather was that nothing deterred these three from their artistic enterprises.

10. Originally published in the *Journal*, 25 Jan. 1895, p. 13; reprinted in William M. Curtin, ed., *The World and the Parish: Willa Cather's Articles and Reviews, 1893–1902* (Lincoln: Univ. of Nebraska Press, 1970), I, 176.

11. Originally published in the *Journal*, 10 March 1895, p. 13; reprinted in *The World and the Parish*, ed. Curtin, I, 193.

12. Ibid., p. 194.

13. Faderman, *Surpassing the Love of Men*, p. 201.

14. A brief fourth relationship with fellow University of Nebraska student Louise Pound, later a distinguished folklorist, is of interest for the study of Cather's sexual orientation. That it was a very strong romantic attachment is clear from Cather's letters to Pound now available to scholars in the Duke University Library. It was shattered when, for some mysterious reason, Cather wrote a nasty profile of Louise's brother Roscoe in a university publication. See Phyllis Robinson's *Willa: The Life of Willa Cather* (Garden City, N.Y.: Doubleday, 1983), pp. 58–62.

15. Originally published in the *Journal*, 30 May 1897, p. 13; reprinted in *The World and the Parish*, ed. Curtin, I, 443.

16. E. K. Brown, *Willa Cather: A Critical Biography* (New York: Knopf, 1953). p. 97. In her memoir, *Willa Cather Living* (New York: Knopf, 1953), Lewis merely says: "She apparently had no difficulty in persuading her father and mother to invite Willa Cather to become a member of the McClung household." But Brown got his information from Lewis, and this statement must have come from her in conversation.

17. Elizabeth Moorhead, *These Too Were Here: Louise Homer and Willa Cather* (Pittsburgh: Univ. of Pittsburgh Press, 1950), pp. 49–50.

18. Elizabeth Shepley Sergeant, *Willa Cather: A Memoir* (Philadelphia: J. B. Lippincott & Co., 1953), p. 140.

19. These letters are published in Marion Marsh Brown and Ruth Crone, *Only One Point of the Compass: Willa Cather in the Northeast* (Danbury, Conn.: Archer Editions, 1980).

20. Sergeant, *Willa Cather*, p. 202.

21. Ibid., p. 35.

22. Ibid., p. 92.

23. Ibid., p. 139.

24. Ibid., p. 164.

25. See Margaret O'Conner, "A Guide to the Letters of Willa Cather," *Resources for American Literary Study*, 4 (1974), 145–72.

Alexander's Bridge

[Review of *Alexander's Bridge*]   H. L. Mencken*

Alexander's Bridge, by Willa S. Cather, has the influence of Edith
Wharton written all over it, and there is no need for the canned review on the cover to call attention to the fact—the which remark, let
me hasten to add, is not to be taken as a sneer but as hearty praise,
for the novelizing novice who chooses Mrs. Wharton as her model is
at least one who knows a hawk from a handsaw, an artist from an
artisan. The majority of beginners in this fair land choose E. Phillips
Oppenheim or Marie Corelli; if we have two schools, then one is the
School of Plot and the other is the School of Piffle. But Miss Cather,
as I have said, is intelligent enough to aim higher, and the thing she
offers must be set down a very promising piece of writing. Its chief
defect is a certain triteness in structure. When Bartley Alexander, the
great engineer, discovers that he is torn hopelessly between a genuine
affection for his wife, Winifred, and a wild passion for his old flame,
Hilda Burgoyne, it seems a banal device to send him out on his greatest bridge a moment before it falls, and so drown him in the St. Lawrence. This is not a working out of the problem; it is a mere evasion of
the problem. In real life how would such a man solve it for himself?
Winifred, remember, is in Boston and Hilda is in London, and business takes Bartley across the ocean four or five times a year. No doubt
the authentic male would let the situation drift. In the end he would
sink into the lean and slippered pantaloon by two firesides, a highly
respectable and reasonably contented bigamist (unofficially, of course),
a more or less successful and satisfied wrestler with fate. Such things
happen. I could tell you tales. But I tell them not. All I do is to throw
out the suggestion that the shivering of the triangle is far from inevitable.
Sometimes, for all the hazards of life, it holds together for years. But
the fictioneers are seldom content until they have destroyed it by catastrophe. That way is the thrilling way, and more important still, it is
the easy way.

*Originally published in *Smart Set*, 38 (December 1912), 156–57.

Aside from all this, Miss Cather gives a very good account of herself indeed. She writes carefully, skillfully, artistically. Her dialogue has life in it and gets her story ahead. Her occasional paragraphs of description are full of feeling and color. She gives us a well drawn picture of the cold Winifred, a better one of the emotional and alluring Hilda and a fairly credible one of Bartley himself—this last a difficult business, for the genius grows flabby in a book. It is seldom, indeed, that fiction can rise above second rate men. The motives and impulses and processes of mind of the superman are too recondite for plausible analysis. It is easy enough to explain how John Smith courted and won his wife, and how William Jones fought and died for his country, but it would be impossible to explain (or, at any rate, to convince by explaining) how Beethoven wrote the Fifth Symphony, or how Pasteur reasoned out the hydrophobia vaccine, or how Stonewall Jackson arrived at his miracles of strategy. The thing has been tried often, but it has always ended in failure. Those supermen of fiction who are not mere shadows and dummies are supermen reduced to saving ordinariness. Shakespeare made Hamlet a comprehensible and convincing man by diluting that half of him which was Shakespeare by a half which was a college sophomore. In the same way he saved Lear by making him, in large part, a silly and obscene old man—the blood brother of any average ancient of any average English taproom. Tackling Caesar, he was rescued from disaster by Brutus's knife. George Bernard Shaw, facing the same difficulty, resolved it by drawing a composite portrait of two or three London actor-managers and half a dozen English politicians.

Introduction to *Alexander's Bridge*   Bernice Slote*

Alexander's Bridge, the story of a bridge builder divided in himself between his youth and his maturity, veering restlessly between his mistress in London and his wife in Boston, and finally destroyed in the fall of his greatest bridge, was published by Houghton Mifflin Company in April 1912. (In England it was brought out by Heinemann as *Alexander's Bridges*.) This book was Willa Cather's first published novel, though she later preferred to consider *O Pioneers!* (1913) as more spiritually "first." *Alexander's Bridge* was not, however, the first novel she had written. After more than a dozen years of writing short fiction for magazines and the publication of two books—the poems of *April Twilights* in 1903 and the stories of *The Troll Garden* in 1905—she had in the summer of

*Reprinted from *Alexander's Bridge*, by Willa Cather, by permission of the University of Nebraska Press. Introduction copyright © 1977 by the University of Nebraska Press.

1905 completed a novel set in Pittsburgh.[1] She had promised it for publication to S. S. McClure, but, for whatever reason, the book did not
appear. Only stories seemed to surface—and few of them—during the
six years she worked in New York on the editorial staff of *McClure's Magazine*, but by 1911 there was indeed the manuscript of another novel.

In her Preface to the 1922 edition of *Alexander's Bridge* Willa Cather
says that she wrote the book in 1911. By that fall she had submitted it
to Houghton Mifflin, whose files include mentions of the book as early as
November; reports from Ferris Greenslet, a Houghton Mifflin editor who
had known Willa Cather from the periods she had spent in Boston on
editorial business for *McClure's*, noted the excellence of the novel, its
"spiritual sense of life."[2] But at about the same time she had also submitted the book to *McClure's Magazine*, where, under the title of "Alexander's Masquerade," it was published as a three-part serial in February,
March, and April of 1912. The *McClure's* submission was indirect. Early
in January the *Nebraska State Journal*, after announcing the forthcoming magazine appearance of the story, added a note on Catherian devious-
ness: "To test the real quality of her work, Miss Cather mailed it from
St. Louis under the nom de plume of Miss Fanny Cadwallader. Only
after it had been strongly endorsed by the censor and Mr. McClure
himself did she let them know the truth." It is not certain that she herself had been in St. Louis, but it would not have been necessary; she
did have connections there through Lincoln friends and a new friend,
Zoë Akins, whose home was in St. Louis. After twenty years of volumin-
ous writing a nom de plume had become a familiar comfort as well as a
business necessity for Willa Cather. This time "Miss Fanny Cadwallader"
had grown as large as life.

Reviews of *Alexander's Bridge* were generally favorable, commenting, as in the *Outlook*, on "the fine skill which stamps this first long story
as a piece of exceptionally well conceived and well written fiction. Miss
Cather has gone far, and will go farther" (April 20, 1912). The story is
"told with some force" (*Athenaeum*, August 31, 1912), and "with a good
deal of charm and skill" (*New York Times Book Review*, May 12, 1913).
Slightly more specific comments are made in one of the longer reviews,
in *Current Literature* (September 1912), which quotes from other notices
of the book: It is a "condensed novel" (*Boston Transcript*); it "suggests
a portrait group . . . whose personages are presented with such intensity,
with such feeling for character, as to make the canvas lose a moment its
static quality, the figures seem but caught a moment in the scene of a
drama" (*Louisville Courier–Journal*); and she was already being praised
for the "exquisite fitness" and clarity of her style: "There are wordy
writers sometimes called great . . . to whom should be taught the lessons
which *Alexander's Bridge* may teach of the power and blessedness of
simplicity" (*New York World*).

In some of the articles it is evident that Willa Cather was being placed in the school of Henry James and Edith Wharton. Just how this was managed is suggested in the *Current Literature* review, which identified three kinds of writers: "American writers of fiction seem to group themselves into the crude and purposeful, the frankly and engagingly commercial, and—the 'lesser Henry Jameses.' To the last-named group, some of the reviewers think, belongs Willa Sibert Cather, the remarkable young poet and story writer whose first long work in prose 'Alexander's Bridge' (Houghton Mifflin Company) is now given to the public in book form." A note on the dust jacket had referred to the influence of Edith Wharton—and this other general link was praised by H. L. Mencken in the *Smart Set* (December 1912). But Mencken and others who spoke of James and Wharton in connection with Willa Cather were speaking only of the general alliances of good literature, placing her with writers of the time who were recognized for their literary excellence. Later critics have repeated the "Jamesian" definition of Willa Cather's early work without sufficiently weighing its origin.[3]

Mencken was not satisfied with the structure of the book, suggesting that the "shivering of the triangle" of Bartley Alexander, Winifred Alexander, and Hilda Burgoyne was "far from inevitable." Men do hold on to two lives very comfortably, he says—and for a lifetime. But his praise for Cather's skill is seriously put: She "gives a very good account of herself indeed. She writes carefully, skillfully, artistically. Her dialogue has life in it and gets her story ahead. Her occasional paragraphs of description are full of feeling and color. She gives us a well drawn picture of the cold Winifred, a better one of the emotional and alluring Hilda and a fairly credible one of Bartley himself—this last a difficult business, for the genius grows flabby in a book." Mencken's interest in *Alexander's Bridge* led to his continued critical approval of Willa Cather's fiction through 1920, and some of the warmest praise she was to receive for *My Ántonia.*

One of the most interesting notices is that which appeared in the "Books" section of *McClure's* in July 1912, as an interpretation of the nuances and emphases of the book. "'Alexander's Bridge' (Houghton, Mifflin), by Willa Sibert Cather, is the story of a great engineer who has reached the crisis in his life when success and responsibility have begun to fret and weary a restless, energetic nature inherently impatient of restraint. Alexander tries to shake himself free, to go back to the time when life was at its highest, most adventurous pitch. He rebels against life and life defeats him. The story is a love story, for it is in his relations with two women, Winifred, his wife, and Hilda, a young Irish actress, that Alexander learns to know himself. His pursuit of Hilda, begun in a spirit of adventure, grows into a destroying obsession. It yields him intoxicating moments of delight, in which he recaptures the sense of youthful freedom and power; but it torments him more and more with the consciousness of an ever-growing breach in his own inner integrity. The situation is developed with a dramatic skill that holds one's absorbed attention throughout. It is a story of brilliant and unusual power." Although Willa Cather was not officially working for *McClure's* in the spring of 1912 when this issue was being prepared, she might well have had a hand in it, just as she sometimes later helped with the blurbs on the jackets of her books.

We do have three statements by Willa Cather on *Alexander's Bridge*: a 1912 interview, the Preface to the new edition of the book published by Houghton Mifflin in 1922, and a shorter piece in the *Colophon* in 1931 ("My First Novels [There Were Two]").⁴ The first account appeared in the *New York Evening Sun* in 1912, probably shortly after the publication of the book. I am using the undated clipping which Willa Cather marked with heavy black lines and sent home to her family. The piece is titled "Explaining the Novel." In it Willa Cather is quoted as saying, "This is not the story of a bridge and how it was built, but of a man who built bridges. The bridge builder with whom this story is concerned began life a pagan, a crude force, with little respect for anything but youth and work and power. He married a woman of much more discriminating taste and much more clearly defined standards. He admires and believes in the social order of which she is really a part, though he has been only a participant. Just so long as his ever kindling energy exhibits itself only in his work everything goes well; but he runs the risk of encountering new emotional as well as new intellectual stimuli." There are other comments on the industrial novel ("That is one kind of a story, this is another"), and on the characters as composites.

By 1922 Willa Cather had published three more novels—*O Pioneers!* (1913), *The Song of the Lark* (1915), and *My Ántonia* (1918)—all in the vein of early personal experience and chiefly in the settings she knew while she was a child. (Another Nebraska novel, *One of Ours*, came out in the fall of 1922). The Western world of memory, she thought, was her true road, and her first use of Boston and London material in *Alexander's Bridge* had begun to bother her. It "does not deal with the kind of subject-matter in which I now find myself at home," she wrote in the 1922 Preface. The people and places of the story, she said, interested her intensely at the time, because they were new and engaging and fresh for discovery. However, they lay outside her deepest experience, or the things the writer knows best, the things that feed him.

Her last statement in 1931 in the *Colophon* is similar: "My first novel, *Alexander's Bridge*, was very like what painters call a studio picture. It was the result of meeting some interesting people in London. Like most young writers, I thought a book should be made out of 'interesting material,' and at that time I found the new more exciting than the familiar." In both of these statements Willa Cather is talking about her "material," not what she did with it; and even granting her preference for the later novels, there are still other turns of the glass through which one might view *Alexander's Bridge*.

Willa Cather's longtime friend Edith Lewis was one of the first to find in *Alexander's Bridge* a deeper quality, a more personal engagement, than the author had admitted. Reading it over again, Edith Lewis felt that Willa Cather had never done the book justice. There are faults, she admits, but concludes that "when it at last moves into its true theme, the mortal division in a man's nature, it gathers an intensity and power which comes from some deeper level of feeling. . . . It is as if her true voice, submerged before in conventional speech, had broken through, and were speaking in irrepressible accents of passion and authority."[5] I believe Edith Lewis refers not to the sections of dialogue, which often seem staged, like scenes in a play, and give a theatrical aura to the book, but to the two narrative sections which probe Alexander's psychological dilemma (his early days in London and his winter voyage across the Atlantic) and particularly the final scenes of the collapse of the bridge, when the waters closed over his life. It may be significant that though Willa Cather made stylistic changes from the printing of "Alexander's Masquerade" in *McClure's* to the final version in the book, there are almost no corrections in the last two chapters. The conclusion was the reason for the book, and she had it right from the first.

Two subjects, then, can be useful in a consideration of *Alexander's Bridge*: What events, what interesting people and places did Willa Cather use as her material? And in what way did she give this material her own accent? For I think she did make the real body of *Alexander's Bridge* her own; its deepest forms follow the configuration of the passions and concerns meshed in herself. The real subject matter was truly her own. And the proof can be found in the many repetitions of themes and motifs related to *Alexander's Bridge* throughout her work.

First, we may look at some of the new sources Willa Cather found interesting. In 1907–1908 she was on assignment for *McClure's* in Boston. For part of the time she had an apartment on Chestnut Street, where *Alexander's Bridge* begins, a "slanting street, with its worn paving, its irregular, gravely colored houses" just above Charles Street, Brimmer Street, and the Charles River. In Boston she came to know many literary and other distinguished people, including Mr. and Mrs. Louis (later Justice) Brandeis, through whom she met new friends who soon became dear to her—Mrs. James T. Fields, widow of the late publisher (of Ticknor and Fields), and the writer Sarah Orne Jewett. Mrs. Fields, in her house at 148 Charles Street, with its long drawing-room overlooking a garden and the river,[6] along with Miss Jewett, represented a rich, assured, and permanent link with a past of distinction and beauty, a way of life that on the surface had little to do with the restless, driving force Willa Cather had known in her Nebraska youth during the 1880s and

1890s, and even later during her journalistic and teaching years in crudely strong, industrial Pittsburgh—though there in Pittsburgh she had found her closest friend, Isabelle McClung, a tall, beautiful, poised young woman who in her way could persuade one to elegance and riches. Bostonian order is the world of the tall, beautiful, and serene Winifred Alexander on Brimmer Street, who, one feels, must be something of a portrait of Isabelle. Winifred Alexander is one side of Bartley's dilemma. At forty-three, he surveys the world of his maturity, a grace he owes to his wife and the generations she represents: "the harmony of beautiful things that have lived together without obtrusion of ugliness or change . . . those warm consonances of color had been blending and mellowing before he was born" (9–10). The feeling is Willa Cather's for the houses she came to know well—not only that of Mrs. Fields in Boston but the Jewett home in South Berwick, Maine. This was civilization, in its best sense.

The pagan energy and force of Alexander's youth which he tries to recapture in London is represented by the Irish actress Hilda Burgoyne, once his love a dozen years ago when they were young in Paris, but since forgotten. In London Willa Cather had in actuality found the "interesting people" who also suggested characters, scenes, and places for *Alexander's Bridge*. During May and June 1909 she was in London acquiring material for *McClure's*, returning to New York in the middle of July. Edith Lewis says that she returned to London for a second business trip in the next year or two (76). In London she went about a good deal with the English critic (and *McClure's* author) William Archer, and met literary people like Sydney Colvin, Edmund Gosse, Ford Madox Ford (then Hueffer), William Butler Yeats, Lady Gregory, Katherine Tynan, and H. G. Wells. Particularly, she went to the theatre, and once, says Edith Lewis, she "sat in Yeats' box with Lady Gregory at one of the early performances of the Irish players. There was a gifted young actress in the cast whose beauty and engaging personality vividly impressed her; it was from her that she drew the figure of *Hilda Burgoyne*" (68).

The Irish actress Miss Lewis referred to was undoubtedly the beautiful and talented Maire O'Neill; in June 1909 Willa Cather had many opportunities to see her (and the equally talented Sara Allgood) as the Irish National Theatre Society from the Abbey Theatre, Dublin, presented two series of plays, between June 7 and June 26 at the Royal Court Theatre. The first program on June 7 was a combination of Lady Gregory's short play *Dervorgilla* and Synge's *The Playboy of the Western World*,[7] in which Maire O'Neill played Pegeen Mike. There were six performances of *Playboy* (June 7, 9, 10, 12, 17, and 21). Maire O'Neill also played in Synge's *In the Shadow of the Glen* on June 9 and 12. Among other plays given in the June season were Yeats's *Kathleen ni Houlihan*, Synge's *The Well of the Saints* and *Riders to the Sea*, Lady Gregory's *Hyacinth Halvey*, *Spreading the News*, and *The Rising of the*

Moon, and, in the last series beginning on June 23, Yeats's *Deirdre*, with Mrs. Patrick Campbell.

In *Alexander's Bridge* it is a new comedy by Hugh MacConnell, *Bog Lights*, in which Hilda Burgoyne stars poetically as a donkey girl who sings "The Rising of the Moon." The play is at the Duke of York's Theatre. What is described suggests much of the quality of the Irish plays Willa Cather had certainly seen.

But there were other conjectures about the actress Hilda Burgoyne. What about the English actress Hilda Trevelyan, Willa Cather was asked in her 1912 *Sun* interview: " 'Is the actress in the story meant to be much like Hilda Trevelyan? Certainly not. Miss Trevelyan is a different sort of person. I tried, however, to give the actress in this story certain qualities which I have found oftener in English actresses than in our own.' " As a matter of fact, Hilda Trevelyan was playing in London when Willa Cather was there—in a long run of Barrie's *What Every Woman Knows,* and at the Duke of York's Theatre. (In a later season she played Wendy in *Peter Pan.*) One can fairly say that the theatrical references in *Alexander's Bridge* are a composite. Hugh MacConnell is playwright *something like* Barrie and Synge and Yeats—the play and the actors the same. Willa Cather found the originals interesting, but she filtered them through her imagination.

There may have been long-range harmonies. Reviewers noted qualities in the Irish plays that blend in spirit with Willa Cather's artistic preferences. Even when she is excited, Pegeen Mike's voice is "softer, rounder, and richer than the English voice in ordinary conversation." (Hilda Burgoyne "has the Irish voice" [24]). And the Irish actors "are sparing of movement and gesture; everything is quieter, more static." The performance was "artfully simple," "pleasantly strange."[8]

Other places in London stirred her imagination, and they appear as settings—Westminster, the Embankment and the Thames, the Temple, Bedford Square, the British Museum (with its mummy room). These combine with the great houses of Boston and its silvery river to catalogue the places Willa Cather had in recent years found both beautiful and stirring. One must add, too, the ship and the ocean voyage which formed a bridge across the Atlantic. These are vividly recreated. And the crucial event of the book, the collapse of Alexander's last great Canadian bridge at Moorlock, "the longest cantilever in existence" (37), was modeled in many ways on a real event, the collapse of the Quebec Bridge.

The long cantilever bridge under construction over the St. Lawrence near Quebec collapsed late on the afternoon of August 29, 1907. Half of it, according to the *New York Times* of August 30, "crumpled up and dropped into the water." Men were still at work on the span when "there came a grinding sound from the bridge at midstream." Though they rushed shoreward, the distance was too great, and "the fallen section of the bridge dragged others after it, the snapping girders and cables booming like a crash of artillery." More than eighty died, including the chief engineer at the site, who had gone out on the bridge just before it fell. Wounded men were pinned in the wreckage near the shore. Later accounts gave other details: that the warning of danger had reached the engineer too late, that construction had been hampered by insufficient funds, and that wrong estimates had been used.[9] This situation is repeated in *Alexander's Bridge*, with one difference. Alexander's failure to receive the message of danger in time was his own fault, a result of his turning again to Hilda when she comes to him in New York.

The second kind of interest in *Alexander's Bridge* is in the way Willa Cather gave it her personal voice. We can begin with some obvious long ranges of her experience. Stories of the theatrical world, for example, are common with her. The stage and its artists were for years the source of some of her most passionate engagements with art while she was a drama critic in Lincoln, Nebraska, and in Pittsburgh. And she had always been a voracious and free-wheeling reader. No doubt works like Ibsen's *The Master Builder* are valid parallels to *Alexander's Bridge*, and one is tempted to guess that *The Education of Henry Adams*, privately printed in 1907 and passed around in literary circles, had somehow reached her. The portrayal of Alexander as a "natural force" (15), a "powerfully equipped nature" (17), one with machinery pounding in him always (13), reminds one of Henry Adams's emphasis on energy, force, the dynamo.[10] There may even be a slanting influence from Henry James. In an 1896 review of James's *The Other House* she writes of one of his characters, Anthony Bream, as "a new subject in fiction, this big, blonde, easy-going comely fellow, without a touch of romance in him for whom women go mad and commit murder."[11] The Greeks used him, though, and she cites Theseus, Jason, Adonis. Alexander is not "easy-going," but he can be associated with one of those strong, independent Greek heroes— tall and glowing, with "rugged, blond good looks." His head seems "as hard and powerful as a catapult" (9), his shoulders strong enough to support bridges.

One personal source of material for Willa Cather is always myth. Alexander's name, of course, touches immediately on Greek history and mythology. He is not only the great conqueror (a tamer of rivers) but mythically his story repeats in several ways the story of Paris (also called Alexander), the nymph Oenone (his wife), and Helen of Troy, for whom he deserts his wife. Paris is repeatedly referred to as Alexander in the Greek text of the *Iliad*. In the triangle of *Alexander's Bridge* some qualities are exchanged (the wife Winifred is more queenly, the mistress Hilda more nymph-like), but many elements of the Paris-Alexander story are followed. In both, for example, are scenes in which the bereft wife mourns by the body of her husband.

The moon-myth had a special power for Willa Cather, its light shining variously through almost all of her work. In *Alexander's Bridge* the invocations are insistent, beginning with the reflection of the story of Endymion and Diana. As Endymion yearned for the moon, so Bartley Alexander desired the magic of youth and its representative in Hilda Burgoyne, who thus becomes Diana (or Cynthia). Allusions are frequent in details of the fairy play, *Bog Lights*, and in Alexander's relation to the Irish Hilda, even to the golden aura in which she often appears. The Diana-Cynthia role of Hilda is made especially clear as Bartley Alexander also speaks in the role of Actaean: "And what have you to do, Hilda, with this ugly story? Nothing at all. The little boy drank of the prettiest brook in the forest and he became a stag" (102). The texture of myth is allusive in *Alexander's Bridge*, but its power seems deliberately invoked in Willa Cather's true language.[12]

There are other characteristic techniques. The action of *Alexander's Bridge* takes place within the cycle of one year, from April to April. This turn of seasons in a rounding flow gives structure to many of her other works, *O Pioneers!* and *My Ántonia* especially. Contrast also gives form (angles within the circle), including the opposition, on an axis of ocean, of the old world and the new, the two women, the two cities, and even the two rivers near them. From her early days as a drama critic Willa Cather had admired "that telling element of contrast."[13]

Color reinforces emotion with symbolic meaning. Gold, associated in Cather with love and sexuality, highlights Hilda's appearance as moon goddess. When Alexander first meets her in London she wears a "primrose satin gown" and yellow slippers. In their first time alone in her apartment she wears, and he notices, the same yellow gown and "canary slippers." There are yellow irises, and, for dinner, a "dry yellow Rhone wine," which Bartley holds against the yellow lights of the candles (49–58). Gold had lifted the London air as Alexander first began to think of Hilda again. The towers "were washed by a rain of golden light. . . . The yellow light poured through the trees. . . . the laburnums were dripping gold" (35). Later, after a happy day in the country, Bartley and Hilda return to a "gold-washed city" where vapors became "fluttering golden clouds" and all the city was held in "aureate light," floating "in a golden haze" (92). Willa Cather had used such a yellow motif before and would again. The story "On the Gulls' Road" (1908) is filled with details describing Alexandra Ebbling—"red-gold hair," "yellow-hazel eyes"— and the world about her—the golden light on Vesuvius, yellow headlands, yellow and umber rocks, a yellow afternoon. And especially there is a memory: "'We have a yellow vine at home that is very like your hair. . . . We call it love vine.'" In "The Joy of Nelly Deane" (1911) Nelly has the eyes which reappear in other heroines (like Marie Shabata in *O Pioneers!*)—"yellow-brown eyes, which . . . sparkled with a kind of golden effervescence."[14] And there is in *O Pioneers!* Alexandra's dream of being lifted and carried away by a man who was "yellow like the sunlight" (206).

In contrast with the more centrally placed gold motifs of *Alexander's Bridge* are the gray and watery elements of its opening and its close. When Professor Lucius Wilson walks down Chestnut Street to visit the Alexanders, he sees the river at the foot of the hill, the "silvery light" fades into "watery twilight"; he descends "into cooler and cooler depths of grayish shadow." Wood smoke is in the air, and "the odor of moist spring earth" (2). In one of the last episodes Hilda comes to Bartley's New York apartment soaked and dripping with rain. The final scene of the drowning is harsh with grinding and breaking of ironwork as the bridge falls, and with it Alexander dark in the waters that closed over him. Death by drowning may go to the heart of one of Willa Cather's most persistent personal images. Its principal appearance is in one of her last books, *Lucy Gayheart* (1935), but there are many other linked references, like the dangerous river the slave Nancy has to cross to freedom in *Sapphira and the Slave Girl* (1940). Alexander himself crosses the Atlantic in sometimes stormy waters. An early clue to the importance of drowning water is a phrase Willa Cather used for personal catastrophe—"to go under." When she saw the new land of Nebraska in 1883 and heard the larks, she recalled, she was filled with homesickness: "I thought I should go under."[15] In its final form in *Alexander's Bridge* one sentence reads, "A million details drink you dry" (12). It was in a more horrific form in its first version—"A million details swallow you."

Of all the elements in *Alexander's Bridge*, the subject matter that is most deeply Willa Cather's own is the central concept of the book—the divided self. Professor Wilson first speaks of it in terms of an old fear for Alexander, that in his dazzling front there would appear " 'a big crack zigzagging from top to bottom. . . . then a crash and clouds of dust' " (12). The eventual repetition of the image in the collapse of Alexander's Moorlock Bridge and his own destruction is a surface parallel: the split inside Alexander is more subtle, but also more intensely the theme of the book. He is torn not primarily because of Hilda, but because oncoming middle age and the absorption of his life in the machinery of work and success have obliterated his real sense of himself, his "continuous identity" (39). To hear of Hilda again in London merely triggers a turn to what he once was, to his youth. He had not thought of Hilda for years; he had actually forgotten her (28, 29). In his long walks through London, before he approached her again, "he walked shoulder to shoulder with a shadowy companion—not little Hilda Burgoyne, by any means, but some one vastly dearer to him than she had ever been" (40). And, for him, "this youth was the most dangerous of companions" (41). Yet it gave him the feeling of intense life, of limitless possibilities.

The theme of double selves is pervasive in Cather's works. In *The Song of the Lark* (1915), for example, Thea often feels something different, warm, and personal within her—"that warm sureness, that sturdy little companion with whom she shared a secret" (199). And, thinks

Thea, all her friends must have something else concealed within them: "What if one's second self could somehow speak to all these second selves? . . . How deep they lay, these second persons, and how little one knew about them, except to guard them fiercely" (273). Claude Wheeler in *One of Ours* (1922) senses a more spiritual duality, that "inside of living people, too, captives languished. Yes, inside of people who walked and worked in the broad sun, there were captives dwelling in darkness,— never seen from birth to death." Those with imprisoned spirits were children of the moon, "with their unappeased longings and futile dreams" (207–208). And of Claude and his mother: "For a moment they clung together in the pale, clear square of the west window, as the two natures in one person sometimes meet and cling in a fated hour" (87). In *Lucy Gayheart* Pauline was "always walking behind herself. The plump, talkative little woman one met on the way to choir practice, or at afternoon teas, was a mannikin which Pauline pushed along before her; no one had ever seen the pusher behind that familiar figure, and no one knew what that second person was like" (168). Doubleness is also achieved by creating contrasting characters, like Ántonia Shimerda and Jim Burden in *My Ántonia* (1918) or Father Latour and Father Vaillant in *Death Comes for the Archbishop* (1927). But these are general patterns of the theme introduced in *Alexander's Bridge*: a more exact counterpart is in the 1925 novel, *The Professor's House*, and a story which preceded it, "Her Boss" (1919).[16]

In both the novel and the story there is the almost archetypal renewal of a middle-aged man through memories of his youth and a sense of an earlier reality through some figure who represents that youth. Like Bartley Alexander, Godfrey St. Peter in *The Professor's House* feels the impotence of his own spirit as the clutter of age bears heavily upon him; he is renewed through his alter ego, the young Tom Outland, whose life of creative discovery seems to extend the Professor's feeling for the life of his youth. Eventually there does return that youth of his original state, his "twin" whom he had left behind in Kansas while his changing self went on to maturity (like Alexander who forgot Hilda and had to be reminded of his young self). So St. Peter "remembered that other boy very rarely" (264). St. Peter and that boy "had meant . . . to live some sort of life together. . . . They had not shared much together, for the reason that they were unevenly matched" (263–64). But the "primitive" self does return to St. Peter's consciousness one summer. He was wise; he "seemed to be at the root of the matter" (265). Man does have a new self—a social, sexual creature—grafted on to his original being, thinks the Professor. In Alexander, the violent youth who takes over his personality is "some resolute offshoot of himself" (114). When the original self returned, St. Peter "did not regret his life, but he was indifferent to it. It seemed to him like the life of another person" (267). His "career, his wife, his family, were not his life at all, but a chain of events which had happened to him" (264). The concept of the second self in *The Professor's House* is much more complex than in *Alexander's Bridge* and, in some ways, different. Yet the two are so close as to suggest that the second book is something like a re-trial of the first. The outer circumstances of place and situation are different, but the heart of the "subject matter"—the division of selves—is at the center of Willa Cather's imagination.

The connection between *Alexander's Bridge* and *The Professor's House* can be observed in yet another way. There are the balances between a wife and a figure representing the protagonist's youth, the ending of a life work, and, in a subtle reminder of water imagery, the Professor surviving his crisis with the relief one might have after a difficult sea voyage—"he felt the ground under his feet" (283). And in two instances ballad-like repetitions direct the theme.

In both books an episode of youth in Paris is remembered, though with mirror-images. In *Alexander's Bridge* Bartley and Hilda recall one spring when they bought lilacs and then, walking by the river, met a woman crying bitterly. Hilda gave her a spray of lilac, Bartley a franc, and the woman blessed them with " 'God give you a happy love!' " It was a voice of the woman's sorrow, "vibrating with pity for their youth and despair at the terribleness of human life" (55). *The Professor's House* has a related scene in Paris (both occurring near the Rue St. Jacques). But what was spring and the beginning of love for Hilda and Bartley is now fall, as St. Peter recalls it: All Souls' Day. It is raining and there are mourning colors—black, gray, and wood-ash—on the "bleak, silvery, deserted streets" instead of the lilac-colored sky of the first episode. St. Peter buys a bouquet of pink dahlias and "fresh green chestnut-leaves" from a young family (parents and child); he tries to give it to a pretty, young girl in a group from a charity school, but "just as he put out his hand with the bouquet one of the sisters flapped up like a black crow and shut the girl's pretty face from him" (104). Where the old woman in *Alexander's Bridge* gave a blessing out of sorrow, youth and beauty in the later book are cut down with an ominous gesture, almost like a curse. The correspondences are so insistent that it is almost as if the second scene had been written with the first in mind.

Both books, too, have Christmas jewel-giving scenes, indirectly linking Winifred Alexander with St. Peter's wife, Lillian, and his daughter, Rosamond. At Christmas Bartley gives his wife earrings "of curiously worked gold, set with pearls." They go " 'only with faces like yours,' " he says, " '—very, very proud, and just a little hard' " (67). In *The Professor's House* the gift is from Marsellus to his wife, Rosamond, who is said to be her mother's "second self" (66), and, after her youth with Tom Outland, also a little hard. Rosamond's gift is an old green-gold necklace, to be set with emeralds. When she wears it for Christmas there is also the recollection of a softer jewel from the past, the turquoise bracelet Tom Outland gave her when they were young, "a turquoise set in silver. . . . Yes, a turquoise set in dull silver" (107). It is, like the lilac-colored sky, a gentle brightness remembered in a harder season.[17]

In 1905, as an epigraph to her book of short stories, *The Troll Garden*, Willa Cather had used a passage from Charles Kingsley's *The Roman and the Teuton*,[18] a book in which he shows allegorically the Romans as "Trolls" in their civilized, busy world, and the strong but raw Teutons as "Forest-Children," or Barbarians, who try to and sometimes do enter the garden and palace of the Trolls. Some of Cather's early writing, even in the design of *The Troll Garden*, uses thematically this division of types and extends it to an East (Troll)–West (Forest-Child) dichotomy. There is more than a little of this conflict in the personal dilemma of Bartley Alexander (who was originally from the West), as Willa Cather suggests in her 1912 *Sun* comment on the book. The young Bartley, she says, "began life a pagan, a crude force." The revealing terms "pagan" and "crude force" ally that youth to the Forest-Children, or the Barbarian Teutons. His wife, Cather says, is of "more discriminating taste" and "more clearly defined standards." She is really part of a "social order" in which he only participates. Eventually in Bartley it is the pull between old but violent freedoms and new, restrained order. There is no question but that Willa Cather presents the young Bartley who takes over his personality as a harmful, destructive force. (Here the youth is different from the primitive young self who returned to Godfrey St. Peter, the difference between wild force and earth-wisdom.) "Something had broken loose" in Alexander, something "of which he knew nothing except that it was sullen and powerful, and that it wrung and tortured him. . . . Always, now, it brought with him a sense of quickened life, of stimulating danger" (68). At first Bartley's other self (the "second man" that had been grafted into him) seemed only "a pleasure-loving simpleton," but then he became "strong and sullen": "'he is fighting for his life at the cost of mine. . . . Eventually, I suppose, he will absorb me altogether'" (102). And because Alexander is with Hilda and not where a telegram can find him, he does not reach his bridge in time to save it. It was "some resolute offshoot of himself" (114) that did in fact spoil his life for him.

Alexander's Bridge is, as some have called it, a psychological novel, but not only in the psychology of its protagonist. The book also reflects in one form Willa Cather's own division of spirit, and in her voice the language moves with passion. But it also reflects large human concerns—the quality of Greek tragedy with its flawed hero, the pagan in civilization, the difficult marriage of freedom and order. And perhaps *Alexander's Bridge* does take the bittersweet side of order. If so, its crisply balanced form is the body chosen carefully to support its theme.

Notes

1. Notes in the *Nebraska State Journal* during July and August 1905 said that it was "the first long story she has written."

2. E. K. Brown, *Willa Cather: A Critical Biography*, completed by Leon Edel (New York: Alfred A. Knopf, 1953), pp. 153, 159.

3. I would not, as some critics have, call *Alexander's Bridge* "Jamesian" because the scene is international (though superficially so), or because there are psychological explorations in it. My own opinion is that *O Pioneers!* and *My Ántonia* go more to the heart of the Jamesian "organic" critical theory of the novel, and in this sense might even with validity be called "Jamesian."

4. *Colophon*, part 6, no. 4, 1931, p. 21. Reprinted in *Willa Cather on Writing: Critical Studies on Writing as an Art* (New York: Alfred A. Knopf, 1949).

5. Edith Lewis, *Willa Cather Living: A Personal Record* (New York: Alfred A. Knopf, 1953), p. 78. Hereafter pagination is given in the text.

6. See Willa, Cather's "148 Charles Street," in *Not Under Forty* (New York: Alfred A. Knopf, 1936).

7. Brown, *Willa Cather*, p. 147, says that *The Rising of the Moon* was the curtain-raiser for *Playboy*, but the programs as listed in the *London Times* do not show that combination at any time. *The Rising of the Moon* was first given on June 25 with *Deirdre* and *Hyacinth Halvey*.

8. "Royal Court Theatre," *London Times*, June 8, 1909, p. 12.

9. Useful summaries are in John P. Hinz, "The Real Alexander's Bridge," *American Literature* 21 (January 1950): [473]–76, and Brown, *Willa Cather*, pp. 157–59.

10. See also "The Joy of Nelly Deane" (1911): "We heard it throbbing like great engines, and calling to us, that faraway world"; and in "Behind the Singer Tower" (1912), the concept of generating human power, "the output of energy." Both stories reprinted in *Willa Cather's Collected Short Fiction, 1892–1912*, ed. Virginia Faulkner (Lincoln: University of Nebraska Press, 1965). A more certain link than Adams, however, is Kipling, whose *The Day's Work* was reviewed by Willa Cather in the *Courier*, March 4, 1899 (reprinted in *The World and the Parish: Willa Cather's Articles and Reviews, 1893–1902*, ed. William M. Curtin [Lincoln: University of Nebraska Press, 1970], p. 555), noting Kipling's devotion to energy, the "worship of force:" One story in Kipling's book is "The Bridge Builders."

11. *Nebraska State Journal*, December 20, 1896. Reprinted in *The World and the Parish*, p. 552.

12. For a fuller discussion of the moon-myth and the Paris-Alexander connections see *The Kingdom of Art: Willa Cather's First Principles and Critical Statements, 1893–1896*, ed. Bernice Slote (Lincoln: University of Nebraska Press, 1966), pp. 97–103.

13. *The Kingdom of Art*, p. 179.

14. "On the Gulls' Road" and "The Joy of Nelly Deane" are reprinted in *Collected Short Fiction*. The "yellow vine" reference occurs on p. 87.

15. Interview, "Willa Cather Talks of Work," *Philadelphia Record*, datelined August 9, 1913, reprinted in *The Kingdom of Art*, p. 448.

16. "Her Boss" is collected in *Uncle Valentine and Other Stories: Willa Cather's Uncollected Short Fiction, 1915–1929*, ed. Bernice Slote (Lincoln: University of Nebraska Press, 1973). For a more complete discussion of the connections between the story and *The Professor's House* see Introduction to this collection.

17. For the correspondences of the mirror-images and for some of the mythological elements discussed here I have drawn on an unpublished article by Professor Virginia Faulkner.

18. "A fairy palace, with a fairy garden; . . . Inside the Trolls dwell, . . . working at their magic forges, making and making always things rare and strange." For a fuller discussion of the Kingsley connection see *The Kingdom of Art*, pp. 93–97.

O Pioneers!

[Review of *O Pioneers!*]   Frederick Taber Cooper*

O Pioneers!, by Willa Sibert Cather, is quite as local in theme and in characters as any volume that Mr. [John] Fox [Jr., author of *The Heart of the Hills*, etc.] ever wrote. It is a study of the struggles and privations of the foreign emigrant in the herculean task of subduing the untamed prairie land of the Far West and making it yield something more than a starvation income. Miss Cather has an unquestioned gift of observation, a keen eye for minute details and an instinctive perception of their relative significance. Every character and every incident in this slow-moving and frankly depressing tale give the impression of having been acquired directly through personal contact, and reproduced almost with the fidelity of a kodak picture or a graphonola record. And yet the net result strikes one, on second thought, as rather futile. The story opens practically at the deathbed of a middle-aged Swede, prematurely worn out with his vain struggle against inclement weather, the failure of crops and the burden of mortgages. He leaves behind him some incompetent sons and one splendid, dauntless amazon of a daughter, Alexandra, who dedicated her youth and strength and beauty to the hopeless drudgery of carrying on the task that had slain her father. We get brief glimpses of her early blunders and discouragements; the grudging help and secret antagonism of her brothers, and the departure of her young neighbour, who, although a lad several years her junior, was the only person who gave her sympathy. Now, the story of how Alexandra fought her battle and won it might have been well worth the telling; but this is precisely the part of her history which Miss Cather has neglected to chronicle. Instead, she has passed over it in leaps and bounds, and when we once more meet Alexandra, it is in the midst of prosperity, with all her brothers save the youngest happily married, her land increased by hundreds of acres, all yielding fabulous harvests, and Alexandra herself on the threshold of her fortieth year, and, with

*Originally published in *Bookman*, 37 (August 1913), 666–67.

all her success, keenly conscious of the emptiness of her life, the craving for the love of husband and of children. Of course, it requires no keen guess-work to foresee that the young neighbour of her youth will ultimately return and the discrepancy of their ages will be forgotten. But somehow the reader cannot bring himself to care keenly whether the young neighbour returns or not, whether Alexandra is eventually happy or not,—whether, indeed, the farm itself prospers or not. The conscious effort required to read to a finish is something like the voluntary pinch that you give yourself in church during an especially somnolent sermon. The book does have its one big moment; but it is due to an incident that lies outside of the main thread of the story. Alexandra's youngest brother falls in love with Marie Shabata, the wife of a big, hot-tempered Bohemian; and one night the two forget discretion and are found in the orchard by the infuriated husband, who wreaks prompt vengeance. The swift, sharp picture which follows has a touch of Maupassant in it.

> He did not see anything while he was firing. He thought he heard a cry simultaneously with the second report, but he was not sure. He peered again through the hedge, at the two dark figures under the tree. They had fallen a little apart from each other, and were perfectly still—no, not quite; in a white patch of light, where the moon shone through the branches, a man's hand was plucking spasmodically at the grass.

But this incident, perfect as it is by itself, lies outside the main story, outside the history of the conquest of prairie land. And for that matter, the whole volume is loosely constructed, a series of separate scenes with so slight cohesion that a rude touch might almost be expected to shatter it.

A Comprehensive View of
Cather's *O Pioneers!*

John J. Murphy*

The dual nature of Willa Cather's *O Pioneers!* (1913) has occupied its critics from the beginning, from *Bookman* reviewer Frederick Taber Cooper's backhanded admiration for Emil and Marie's passionate affair as a vivid touch of Maupassant unfortunately outside the plodding main story to more thoughtful considerations by subsequent generations.[1] Cather herself described her work as a "two-part pastoral" developed from two stories—the earlier one titled "Alexandra" and the later "The White Mulberry Tree" and agreed with Elizabeth Sergeant that lack of a sharp skeleton was a weakness.[2] The contrasting moods

*This essay was written for this volume and is published by permission of the author.

of the two seminal stories she announced in "Prairie Spring," a poem included after the title and dedicatory pages of *O Pioneers!* The first nine lines of the poem tell of the harsh land and toil of Alexandra Bergson's story, and the remaining ten of the fierce necessity of youthful passion—the romance of Marie Shabata and Emil Bergson. David Stouck notes that "[t]he two stories woven together in *O Pioneers!* stretch back to Genesis. Alexandra's is the story of creation, the story of a human civilization being shaped out of a land as flat and formless as the sea. Emil and Marie's is the story of lovers cast from the earth's garden through sin."[3] However, there are more than two "parts" to *O Pioneers!*; the novel attests to Cather's surprising eclecticism as a writer, her ability to combine literary traditions and styles successfully. Between Alexandra's epic taming of the wild land and her final recognition of its eternity, Cather interweaves domestic drama and social satire, stories of friendship love and illicit passion, manslaughter and spiritual struggle. Developing from individual to universal concerns, the novel espouses the themes of Whitman's poetry, especially that of life everlasting in *Leaves of Grass*.[4] The encompassing character of Alexandra becomes the integrating factor; through it Cather achieves unity despite her novel's dualistic beginnings and consequent lack of a "sharp skeleton."

THE GENESIS DIMENSION

O Pioneers! opens on a January day in 1883 with a description of the embryonic settlement of Hanover, Nebraska, trying not to be blown away in the wind. The sea of prairie and sky are gray and dwarf the place, and snowflakes curl and eddy about haphazardly scattered dwellings "straying off by themselves, headed straight for the open plain."[5] The suggestion of chaos as described in Genesis is obvious: "the earth was without form and void, with darkness over the face of the abyss, and a mighty wind that swept over the surface of the waters."[6] This atmosphere established, Cather introduces her principals. Five-year-old Emil cries for his kitten and is given sweets by seven-year-old Marie, who has "tiger-eye" streaks in her eyes. Fifteen-year-old Carl Linstrum comes to the aid of Alexandra, four years his senior, already matronly and capable of Amazonian fierceness. While Marie flirts with Emil and her uncle's cronies, Alexandra and Carl share their loneliness and sustain each other. The relationships Cather will develop she thus defines within the context of the creation theme. The first chapter concludes with Alexandra, burdened with the sad knowledge that her father will soon die, rattling through the swirling darkness in a wagon with a lamp at her feet, making "a moving point of light along the highway, going deeper and deeper into the dark country" (18). She will be the creative force, bringing order to chaos: "God said, 'Let their be light,' and there was light; and God saw that the light was good, and he separated light from darkness" (Genesis 1:3–4).

In a low log homestead on a wintry waste without human landmarks patriarch John Bergson lies on his deathbed contemplating the futility of his efforts to make a country out of the wild land. So far, "[t]he record of the plow was insignificant, like the feeble scratches on stone left by prehistoric races, so indeterminate that they may, after all, be only the markings of glaciers.... [The land] was still a wild thing that had its ugly moods.... Its genius was unfriendly to man" (19–20). Yet Bergson believes in the land's potential and recognizes Alexandra as the "one among his children to whom he could entrust the future of his family and the possibilities of his hard-won land" (24). He sees her outlined in the light of a lamp behind her and has her pledge to keep her brothers on the land—a pledge that will determine and limit her life. Unlike Isaac, who was tricked by his wife, Bergson deliberately entrusts the heritage to the unexpected one, his daughter rather than his eldest son, Oscar. In light too dim for him to see their faces, he tells Oscar and his younger brother Lou to be guided by their sister. They will bear a grudge against her like Esau bore against Jacob "because of the blessing which his father had given him...." (Genesis 27:41).

Six months after Bergson's death, Alexandra, her brothers, and Carl make their way to Crazy Ivar's to buy a hammock and get advice on hog raising. As they enter rough and less populated country, "all broken up with hillocks and clay ridges" (35), they discuss Ivar's fits and communings with the Lord, and his gifts for doctoring animals. A powerful dwarflike man with a face shining with happiness as he contemplates Psalm 104 (a creation hymn), Ivar resembles Noah. Gentle and protective toward all God's creatures, he is especially solicitous about the shooting of birds and warns the boys that "these wild things are God's birds. He watches over them and counts them..." (41). As Alexandra approaches Ivar's cave, its single window and door visible at the end of a broad, flooded pond suggest the ark; indeed, in describing a visit from a sea gull, Ivar explains, "Maybe she thought my house was a boat, she was such a wild thing" (40). God gave Noah charge over "all wild animals on earth" and "all birds of heaven" after the flood, and in establishing the covenant with Noah and "living things of every kind" discouraged the eating of meat (Genesis 9:1–17).[7] Ivar "never ate meat, fresh or salt" (43). As an otherworldly man in communion with universal rhythms, Ivar will be used to contrast with the family bickering of the ensuing domestic drama and recall the cosmic atmosphere of the novel's opening.

Three years go by; harder times come to the Divide, and people are selling out, including the Linstrums. When Carl brings Alexandra the news that he will no longer be around to comfort her, she is standing in a dry garden patch, "[h]er thick, reddish braids, twisted about her head, fairly [burning] in the sunlight" (49). Still the creative force, she is distinguished from her neighbors and her brothers by her tenacity in staying: "Like most of their neighbors, [the Bergson boys] were meant to follow in paths already marked out for them, not to break trails in a new country.... A pioneer should have imagination, should be able to enjoy the idea of things more than the things themselves" (47–48). Alexandra possesses this pioneer imagination, and after convincing her brothers not to leave with the others, she experiences what Edward and Lillian Bloom term "mystic insight into divine causes,"[8] enabling her to persuade her brothers to invest in more land and fulfill their father's dreams. Her face is radiant and turned toward that land "with love and yearning"—perhaps the first human face to so respond "since that land emerged from the waters of geologic ages.... It seemed beautiful to her, rich and strong and glorious. Her eyes drank in the breadth of it, until her tears blinded her" (65). The Genius of the Divide, previously "unfriendly to man" (20), now "bent lower than it ever bent to a human will before." The creative order Alexandra represents is now obvious in the comfort she takes in the stars, in "their vastness and distance, and . . . ordered march" (70).

In part 2, "Neighboring Fields," set thirteen years later, order has indeed come to the wild land—creation is complete and the earth fruitful. The drab land and sky have been replaced by a colorful checkerboard of wheat and corn that "seems to rise a little to meet the sun" (76). The chaos evident in the opening section has developed into the geometrical precision of Midwestern roadways, complete with corresponding telephone wires. The wind has been harnessed to serve the new order: "light steel windmills tremble throughout their frames and tug at their moorings, as they vibrate in the wind that often blows from one week's end to another...." The earth itself responds to the plow "with a soft, deep sigh of happiness" (75–76). "Then God said, 'Let the earth produce fresh growth, let there be on the earth plants bearing seed, fruit-trees bearing fruit each with seed according to its kind.' So it was; the earth yielded fresh growth, plants bearing seed according to their kind and trees bearing fruit each with seed according to its kind; and God saw that it was good" (Genesis 1:11–12).

Carl returns in this section to focus on Alexandra's character and accomplishments, and it is through him that Cather manages the transition from the story of creation to that of the fall. Rising one morning before dawn, he climbs the hill where he and Alexandra used to milk together and recalls his favorite image of her—one he renews each time he sees the sunrise: with "her skirts pinned up, her head bare, a bright pail in either hand, and the milky light of the early morning all about her . . . she looked as if she had walked straight out of the morning itself" (126). Like the generating light God made to govern the day, the sympathy evident in Alexandra's radiant face has made the wild land prolific, and the field Carl sits in is teeming with life: "Birds and insects without number begin to chirp, to twitter, to snap and whistle, to make all manner of shrill noises. The pasture was flooded with light . . ." (126–27). Carl then walks toward a pasture pond and sees Marie and Emil, who is breaking Crazy Ivar's law by shooting ducks. The bloody birds, "too happy to kill" (128), prefigure the violent deaths of the lovers. In this way Cather directs us toward the love story which will dominate part 4, "The White Mulberry Tree." The Genesis implications of this story are simple and obvious—the lovers sin beneath a tree in an orchard and are then killed by Marie's jealous husband. Earlier, when Emil came to cut grass in the orchard, Marie joined him there and then left his side to pick cherries, saying "I'll call you if I see a snake" (151). The destruction of Alexandra's Eden is announced by Ivar after he discovers the bodies: "Mistress, mistress, . . . it has fallen! Sin and death for the young ones! God have mercy upon us!" (271).

DOMESTIC DRAMA AND SOCIAL SATIRE

Cather's account of creation and fall, of pioneering and its aftermath, is largely a domestic drama of Bergson family fortunes. As appointed head of the family Alexandra must cajole her reluctant brothers into cooperating with her schemes. Comments about Alexandra's mind being "slow, truthful, steadfast," without "the least spark of cleverness" (61) and possessing little imagination (203) can be misleading, for they do not apply to her efforts to fulfill her pledge to her father. She is able to dissuade her brothers from selling out by using their mother against them and by appealing to Lou's fear of being cheated, explaining how a local land dealer is capitalizing on the discouragement of their neighbors. Having accomplished this much, she maneuvers them into selling cattle and taking loans to buy the Linstrum, Crow, and Struble farms. She has it all figured out—the duration of two loans, the amount of land to be purchased from each neighbor, the value of the land by the time the mortgages are due, etc. When Lou, who is envious of the wealthy and anxious to get ahead, balks, Alexandra applies family pride, that the Bergsons are better quality than their neighbors: "We *ought* to do more than they do, and see further ahead" (68–69). With Oscar, who is dull-witted and plodding, she applies sympathy, explaining that her plans will make life easier for him: "I don't want you to have to grub for every dollar" (70). Thirteen years later we are not surprised that Alexandra's is the most prosperous farm in the area, and that she experiments with new farming methods and has the first silo on the Divide. Seated at the head of a long table having dinner with her men, she is a boss lady, a successful business woman settling into the ample physical proportions of middle age.

The Bergson clan now includes the three families Cather assembles for a dinner party in Alexandra's dining room, which the Hanover furniture dealer "had conscientiously done his best to make...like his display window" (97). This setting of "highly varnished wood and colored glass and useless pieces of china...conspicuous enough to satisfy the standards of the new prosperity" is appropriate to Cather's criticism of the petty jealousies, suspicions, and material concerns characterizing the successful Bergsons. Their talk is in English because they have grown ashamed of their Swedish origins. Oscar, affluent but still dull, is jealous because Alexandra is buying a piano for Lou's daughter. Lou, affluent but still suspicious, fears gossip about Alexandra's keeping Ivar, now old and dependent, on her farm. Lou's wife Annie, an overdressed social climber, boasts of their new bathtub and daughter Milly's piano talents, pries into Alexandra's domestic economies to her own advantage, and tries to keep secret Alexandra's gifts to her children. Within view in an adjoining room the portrait of pioneer John Bergson, with "sad eyes that looked forward into the distance, as if they already beheld the New World" (104), gazes down on the bickering. Ivar had anticipated their complaints and expressed his fears about being sent to an asylum, telling Alexandra that conformity is now the ideal: "The way here is for all to do alike" (92). There is no longer a place "if a man is different in his feet or in his head," or for those "who had been touched by God, or who had seen things in the graveyard at night and were different afterward."

Cather reintroduces Carl Linstrum at this point to develop his relationship with Alexandra and provide an outside perspective on the changes that have come with prosperity. A failure according to the standards of this new country, he is on his way to Alaska to make his fortune. Lou and Oscar immediately sense a threat to Alexandra's share of the property and are decidedly unfriendly, while Annie takes pains to primp herself, boast about Milly's talents in piano and wood-burning ("You wouldn't believe what she can do with her poker" [110]), Lou's success, and that they will be moving into town "as soon as her girls are old enough to go out into company" (113). When Annie steps inside to prepare to depart, Lou begins to swagger about William Jennings Bryan and how the West "is going to make itself heard" (112). In the midst of this tirade, Annie reappears "in a hat that looked like the model of a battleship" (113). The scene, anticipating Sinclair Lewis, is a masterpiece of satire on the Midwestern inferiority complex, a combination of resentment toward outsiders and misguided attempts to impress them. The nastiness of the condition is exposed when Lou draws Alexandra aside and asks, "What do you suppose he's come for?" (113). Oscar, rousing himself from his dullness, adds "solemnly, as from the depths of a cavern[,] 'He never was much account.' "

Alexandra's difference is, of course, a major theme of this aspect of

O Pioneers! She has little interest in the showy side of prosperity, which explains her victimization by the local furniture dealer and the unfinished state of her house. Her favorite rooms are the kitchen and the sitting room containing the family furniture from the old log house and a few treasures from Sweden. Unlike Annie, she has little concern for clothes or hiding from Oscar what she chooses to buy for Lou's children. She is unaware of the social distinction of having a bathtub, and her reasons for wanting a piano for Milly are winsome for their honesty and innocence. Milly deserves a piano, she explains, because of "[a]ll the girls around here... taking lessons for years,... Milly is the only one ...who can ever play anything when you ask her. I'll tell you when I first thought I would like to give you a piano, Milly, and that was when you learned that book of old Swedish songs that your grandfather used to sing" (103). Her attitude toward gossip is evident when she tries to quiet Ivar's fears about the asylum: "Let people go on talking as they like, and we will go on living as we think best" (94).

Cather does not create a perfect heroine, however. Like Lou and Oscar, Alexandra has shortcomings; unlike them, she is aware of her own and theirs. She confides to Carl that she has little to do with her brothers and that her independent ways alienate them. She fails to protest when Carl says he liked the old Lou and Oscar better, and she admits to the limiting effects of life on the land: "We grow hard and heavy here," she says, "and our minds get stiff" (124). Confessing a preference for Carl's freedom from the land, she equates purpose and survival with a sense of the larger world: "If the world were no wider than my cornfields, if there were not something beside this, I wouldn't feel that it was much worth while to work." She is conscious of the adverse effects of her sacrifices in fulfilling her pledge to her father, and tells Lou and Oscar in her eventual falling out with them over Carl, "I certainly didn't choose to be the kind of girl I was. If you take even a vine and cut it back again and again, it grows hard, like a tree" (171).

Alexandra depends too much on her brother Emil and neighbor Marie to compensate for her deprivations. Providing for Emil gives her purpose, and his education and opportunities satisfy her need for the larger world. In fact, she denigrates her pioneer efforts by applying them exclusively to his future: "He shall do whatever he wants to," she tells Carl. "He is going to have a chance, a whole chance; that's what I've worked for" (117). Their unique brother and sister relationship is poignantly dramatized when Emil prepares to leave for Omaha and Michigan to study law. Unknown to Alexandra, he is actually fleeing Marie and not very confident about his future. She, however, is full of confidence. "She felt no anxiety about Emil. She had always believed in him, as she had believed in the land." (239). When he expresses discouragement, that Lou and Oscar would be better off poor, that "it gets worse as it goes on" (239), she cites Milly's generation and her father to bolster his hope and pride. She must believe in this brother's future; it is a matter of her own purpose and survival.

Alexandra's need for Marie is, first of all, for the confidante Carl had been before he moved and Emil before he left for college. Marie is also her intimate companion (as the maid Signa becomes after Marie's death). Marie and Alexandra enjoy each other's company and demonstrate their affection physically. This is not to suggest, as a recent critic has, that theirs is a lesbian affair in which Alexandra's passion for the younger woman is satisfied vicariously through Emil.[9] What is satisfied vicariously is Alexandra's need for what Marie embodies and what Alexandra temporarily lacks or has sacrificed to pioneering on the land. She has Marie in mind when she tells Carl, "The young people, they live so hard. And yet I sometimes envy them" (119). She then lists examples of "hard" living: Marie's running away at eighteen to marry Frank, her refusal to be dampened by her husband's moods, her ability to work all day and dance all night, etc. "She's too young and pretty for this sort of life," Alexandra comments. "We're all ever so much older and slower" (121). The complementary nature of the women's relationship is suggested when Carl observes them seated together in Marie's orchard like an impressionist painter's study:

> Alexandra took off her shade-hat and threw it on the ground. Marie picked it up and played with the white ribbons, twisting them about her brown fingers as she talked. They made a pretty picture in the strong sunlight, the leafy pattern surrounding them like a net; the Swedish woman so white and gold, kindly and amused, but armored in calm, and the alert brown one, her full lips parted, points of yellow light dancing in her eyes as she laughed and chattered. (135)

Marie shares with Carl the ability to appreciate Alexandra in ways her brothers cannot. When Lou and Oscar begin to suspect she might marry Carl, they try to argue her out of property rights (because she "always took it pretty easy" [170]) and ridicule her wanting to marry such "a tramp" (167) at her age: "[E]verybody's laughing to see you get took in. . . . Why, Alexandra, you are forty years old!" (172). She breaks with them at this point and suggests they see a lawyer. Adding to her disappointment, Emil also fails to understand her need for Carl; involved in his own difficulties with Marie, "[h]e felt that there was something indecorous in [Alexandra's] proposal, and she did seem to him somewhat ridiculous. There was trouble enough in the world, he reflected, . . . without people who were forty years old imagining they wanted to get married" (179). Marie, however, disagrees with Emil's view that his sister "wouldn't know how to go about" falling in love: "Oh, you don't know Alexandra as well as you think you do!" (154). She realizes that Carl appreciates Alexandra more than her family does, a fact established soon after his arrival, when he tells Alexandra, "You've seen yourself for so long in the dull minds of the people about you, that if I were to tell you how you seem to me, it would startle you" (132). After Lou and Oscar convince him to leave, he explains Alexandra's dilemma and includes himself among the deficient for letting them unnerve him: "What a hopeless position you are in. . . . It is your fate to be always surrounded by little men. And I am no better than the rest" (181). As during the early years of creation, Alexandra towers above the others during the period of prosperity when the Bergson family collapses about her. What remains for her to achieve is the love she deserves and a vision of life suitable to her heroic stature.

THE LOVE STORIES

The love theme of *O Pioneers!* contrasts friendship (Alexandra and Carl's) and passion (Marie and Emil's) and contributes to Alexandra's vision of life. While both love affairs are announced in the first chapter, when Alexandra seeks Carl's help and shares with him the bad news about her father's health, and the child Marie offers sweets to little Emil, the theme's connection to Alexandra's vision begins after she returns from Ivar's with advice on hog raising. She sits on the doorstep "dreamily" watching the boys swimming in the moonlit pasture pool and then directs her eyes to the sorghum patch where she will build her new pig corral (46). Her efforts must be directed away from herself—or, at least, substitute for more usual forms of self-realization—in order for her to fulfill her pledge to her father. Her accomplishment will depend on the channeling of sexual passion to the detriment of the conscious sexual self. This explains her surprising unawareness of Emil's affair with Marie and the nature of her own relationship to Carl.

By omitting the years between "The Wild Land" and "Neighboring Fields" sections when such self-discipline would be most difficult, Cather avoids presenting Alexandra's conflict, merely suggesting it in her recurring erotic fantasy of being carried across the fields by a gigantic man. Alexandra recovers from such lapses of independence and integrity by "pouring buckets of cold well-water over her gleaming white body . . ." (206). Her sense that this male figure is "yellow like the sunlight, and [has] the smell of ripe cornfields about him" suggests the extension of her sexual self to the land. During her happiest days she feels "close to the flat, fallow world about her, and [feels], as it were, in her own body the joyous germination in the soil" (204)—a sensation obviously related to the description at the opening of "Neighboring Fields": "The brown earth, with such a strong, clean smell, and such a power of growth and fertility in it, yields itself eagerly to the plow; rolls away from the shear, not even dimming the brightness of the metal, with a soft, deep sigh of happiness" (76).

This channeling of passion through the extension of self to land defines the Alexandra Carl meets when he returns. When he stops her from carrying his suitcase for him, she explains, "You see, I give myself away. I have only women come to visit me, and I don't know how to behave" (107). Her response to his hope that having Marie at the end of the old Linstrum path is not quite the same as having him there is a surprised look and confusion: "Why, no, of course not. Not the same. She could not very well take your place, if that's what you mean" (130). Carl becomes concerned about this unawareness of womanhood and draws her out accordingly:

> "But you must see that you astonish me. You must feel when people admire you."
>
> Alexandra blushed and laughed with some confusion. "I felt that you were pleased with me, if you mean that."
>
> "And you've felt when other people were pleased with you?" he insisted.
>
> "Well, sometimes. The men in town, at the banks and the country offices, seem glad to see me. I think, myself, it is more pleasant to do business with people who are clean and healthy-looking," she admitted blandly. (132)

Even when Alexandra contemplates marrying Carl her love for him is still essentially Platonic. In the "Winter Memories" section, long after he has departed to prove himself and have something to offer her, we are told that she "had never been in love, she had never indulged in sentimental reveries. Even as a girl she had looked upon men as work-fellows" (205). Alexandra is disappointed when Carl admits he is not big enough to live off her fortune and must wait a year to prepare for marriage, but she fails to realize that she too is deficient and must become aware of sexual love.

In sharp contrast to the quiet companionship shared by Alexandra and Carl, Marie and Emil's love blazes like the flaming wild roses among the bunchgrass in the Shabata orchard. Through this illicit affair, as Isabel Charles notes, "the passionate love of men and women . . . manifest[s] itself to Alexandra Bergson."[10] It also functions as the most dramatic element in a four-part pattern devoted to aspects of heterosexual relationships. In "Neighboring Fields" Cather carefully alternates between the two major love affairs and introduces those of Angelique and Amedee Chevalier and Signa and Nelse Jensen to reflect on various situations of love and marriage. When Marie reveals impatience with Signa for marrying the domineering Nelse instead of the Smirka boy she seems fond of, Alexandra explains that Swedish girls marry for practical reasons: "I guess we think a cross man makes a good manager" (229). Having eloped at her first infatuation and now deeply involved in another, Marie is irritated at this and stalks home. Discouraged when the happy newlywed Amedee pressures him about getting married, Emil compares his friend's hopeful situation and his own hopeless one to two grains of corn, one shooting toward the light and the other rotting in the earth. Amedee and Angelique are indeed enviable, balance passion and spiritual sharing, and find expression in a boy child. But Amedee dies of a ruptured appendix weeks after his son is born. The relationship is perhaps too perfect to survive in this world; the names even suggest otherworldliness, as does Cather's restriction of the couple to Sainte Agnes Church activities.

The hazards of relationships based on passion are evident in Marie's love for Emil and her marriage to Frank. Both are doomed to follow the route of infatuation, resentment, and violence. Marie's enthusiasm for life and refusal to be dampened by Frank's moods is a major cause of their trouble, and Emil, like Frank, a violent type susceptible to moods (Alexandra, for example, is frightened by his violent feelings [117]), resents Marie's light spirits at the Sainte Agnes fair while he suffers the agony of their love. When he accuses Marie of being shallow-hearted and flirting with other young men, she is as flippant with him as she is with Frank: "Perhaps I am," she says. "What do you want me to do? Sit around and cry all day?" (230). Since passion is ungovernable all partners are insecure. Marie, for example, is as unreasonably possessive about Emil as Frank is about her and gets angry when Emil teases Angelique and stops with the French boys instead of rushing to her at the church supper. She admits being spoiled, of getting everything she ever wanted, from the Turkish lady toy to Frank Shabata, and becomes petulant when Emil allows one of his turquoise shirt studs to be auctioned off instead of giving it to her.

Waste and illusion define both Marie's marriage and her illicit affair. She surprises Emil by admitting that she was "[v]ery much in love" with Frank and that her way of perceiving him is really all that has changed: "Frank is just the same now as he was then, only then I would see him as I wanted him to be. I would have my own way" (231). Frank is guilty of similar self-deception; in the heat of his passion and frustration at Marie's banishment to a convent, he made her his destiny: "whereas he had been only half in love with her before, he now persuaded himself that he would not stop at anything" (145). Having experienced infatuation with Frank, Marie recognizes the ephemeral nature of her relationship with Emil. As a Catholic caught in a marriage based on long dead passion, she feels her life is over, considers Emil an exciting diversion, and finds it "pleasant to let the mind wander forth and follow a young adventurer who has life before him" (200). Although deeply infatuated with Emil, she tries to make him understand that their feeling for each other "won't last. It will go away, and things will be as they used to" (157). He, of course, rejects her estimate of the nature of their love.

Cather embellishes this romance with a variety of literary devices to indicate its escapist nature. Marie and Emil's scenes together are either among flaming roses, beneath the white mulberry tree, in costume (he as a Mexican and she a Gypsy fortune teller) at the Sainte Agnes Church supper, or in the wheatfields with fireflies twinkling and darting in the background. The consummation of their love is approached through a series of erotic gestures: early in the relationship Emil spills a handful of the "sweet, insipid fruit,—the long ivory-colored mulberries, tipped with faint pink"—(153), into her lap; later he performs the same gesture with "a handful of uncut turquoises, as big as marbles" (224). After Marie declares her love, she reflects, "They couldn't meet any more. They had spent the last penny of their small change; there was nothing left but gold" (249). When they do meet again beneath the white mulberry tree, the scene is reminiscent of Keats's "The Eve of St. Agnes," a poem Cather might have had in mind when she named the French Church for this saint. As Marie lies in the orchard apparently asleep, her breast rising and falling faintly, Emil approaches: "The blood came back into her cheeks, her amber eyes opened slowly, and in them Emil saw his own face and the orchard and the sun. 'I was dreaming this,' she whispered, hiding her face against him, 'don't take my dream away!'" (259). In the poem, Porphyro blends with Madeline's dream of him, although the distinction between dream and reality is established, and the lovers flee into the reality of the storm. In Cather's novel, no such distinction is made, and the lovers never leave the orchard. Their discovery and killing by Frank recalls the tale told by Francesca da Remini in canto 5 of Dante's *Hell*, how she and her young brother-in-law Paolo were killed by her husband Gianciotto when he discovered them in the act of love.

Throughout the romance of Marie and Emil, Alexandra functions as a mundane figure of reality having a chilling effect on their love. During the church supper, Marie stiffens at her touch: "There was about Alexandra something of the impervious calm of the fatalist, always disconcerting to very young people, who cannot feel that the heart lives at all unless it is still at the mercy of storms; unless its strings can scream to the touch of pain" (226). She anticipates seamstress Augusta in Cather's later novel *The Professor's House*, who is "like the taste of bitter herbs. . . . Seasoned and sound and on the solid earth she surely was, and, for all her matter-of-factness and hard-handedness, kind and loyal."[11] Surrounded by the ruin left in the wake of Marie's, Frank's, and Emil's passion, Alexandra and Carl survive to develop an older relationship based on friendship.

THE WHITMAN DIMENSION

The fireflies, wheatfields, mulberries, wild roses, and lush grass surrounding Marie and Emil's lovemaking also suggest inevitablity and naturalism. The dark stains on the orchard grass and the attitudes of the bodies in death tell "only half the story. Above Marie and Emil, two white butterflies from Frank's alfalfa field were fluttering in and out among the interlacing shadows; diving and soaring, now close together, now far apart; and in the long grass by the fence the last wild roses of the year opened their pink hearts to die" (270). This other half of the story is one of instinct and necessity. Marie's prayers and religion are powerless before the attraction she and Emil feel for each other. Although Ivar cries sin as he brings Alexandra the news that shatters her world, the lovers are finally absolved by Carl, who compares their relationship to "something one felt in the air, as you feel the spring coming, or a storm in summer" (305). Attempting to soften Alexandra's bitterness toward Marie, he explains that she and Emil tried hard to control their feelings but that some women "spread ruin around them through no fault of theirs, just by being too beautiful, too full of life and love. They can't help it. People come to them as people go to a warm fire in winter" (304). Cather's passionate romance thus dramatizes the natural law, while the story of Alexandra framing it celebrates the law of restraint. The same kind of sympathetic dualism is evident throughout *The Scarlet Letter*. When his lovers decide to flee and the sun floods the forest, Hawthorne comments on the two laws: "Such was the sympathy of Nature—that wild, heathen Nature of the forest, never subjugated by human law, nor illumined by higher truth—with the bliss of these two spirits!"[12]

The cosmic vision advanced by the tragic circumstances in *O Pioneers!* and ultimately by Carl is unquestionably informed by the poetry of Walt Whitman. Not only did Cather take her title from Whitman's "Pioneers! O Pioneers!," but her prose approximates his free verse in lyric passages devoted to what he describes in paragraph 3 in "Song of Myself" as "The procreant urge of the world. / Out of the dimness opposite equals advance, always substance and increase, always sex. . . ."[13] At the beginning of "Neighboring Fields," for example, air and earth "are curiously mated and intermingled, as if the one were the breath of the other" (77); also, the responsive earth "yields itself eagerly to the plow; rolls away from the shear, not even dimming the brightness of the metal, with a soft, deep sigh of happiness" (76). This creative urge explains Alexandra's sensation of germinating soil, her fantasy of being carried across the fields by a gigantic earth figure, and her spiritual communion with the Genius of the Divide. The "love and yearning" she feels for the "free spirit which breathes across" the land (65) resembles the intercourse between poet and soul in Whitman's paragraph 5, which concludes with the insight that creation is one, "that the spirit of God is the brother of my own," and relates the universal spirit to the common grass "sprouting alike in broad zones and narrow zones . . ." (91–109).

Alexandra's consciousness of social ostracism and death as well as illicit passion is managed through other people, as in Whitman's poem, where the persona first observes and then becomes those involved in a full range of life experiences. During her visit to the graveyard a few months after Emil's death Alexandra feels carried back into the dark before birth: "Maybe it's like that with the dead," she tells Ivar. "If they feel anything at all, it's the old things, before they were born . . ." (281).

Her realization that death is not painful or frightening results from Whitmanlike introjection, as in "The Sleepers," where the persona identifies with the dead state: "A shroud I see and I am the shroud, I wrap a body and lie in the coffin, / It is dark here under ground, it is not evil or pain here, it is blank here, for reasons" (66–67). Alexandra's conjoining of birth and death is a major insight in paragraph 49 in "Song of Myself," although reversed:

> To his work without flinching the accoucheur comes,
> I see the elder-hand pressing receiving supporting,
> I recline by the sills of the exquisite flexible doors,
> And mark the outlet, and mark the relief and escape. (1289–93)

The earth lover of Alexandra's fantasy is revealed after the graveyard episode. As he stands in the doorway of her room with his head covered she recognizes him as Death, "the mightiest of all lovers" (283). Such conjoining of love and death is a favorite Whitman theme, basic to "Song of Myself" and the particular subject of "Out of the Cradle Endlessly Rocking," where the poet fuses the love song of the grieving bird with the "strong and delicious word" death whispered by the sea (174–83).

Having identified Death, Alexandra decides to visit Frank Shabata in the State Penitentiary in Lincoln, where she experiences his revulsion at his deed, his confusion between the wife he loved and the woman who wronged him, and the guilt he feels for neglecting Marie. Alexandra is able to identify with this changed, not altogether human prisoner, and share his lack of future and feeling of imprisonment: "A disgust of life weighed upon her heart..." (298). In spite of her despair, however, she will petition for the release of this man who killed her brother. As when she protects Ivar from those who would have committed him, she uplifts and speaks for the downtrodden, the ostracized, as the poet in paragraph 24 of "Song of Myself": "Through me many long dumb voices, / ... of prisoners and slaves, / ... of thieves and dwarfs..." (508–10).

Carl returns to Nebraska to rescue Alexandra from her dark night of the soul and help her toward the cosmic vision for which her experiences have prepared her. After changing from mourning clothes to a white dress, she walks the sunny fields with him and discusses the inevitability of passion and the future. She reveals that on the train from Lincoln she felt again the spirit of the land, its comfort and freedom. She realizes now that the land has a wider future than the Bergson family, that her efforts were not confined to Emil: "We come and go, but the land is always here. And those who love it and understand it are the people who own it—for a little while" (308). Cather's final words, that the land will receive hearts like Alexandra's to give them out again in various forms of life, echo the conclusion of Whitman's great poem: "I bequeath myself to the dirt to grow from the grass I love, / If you want me again look for me under your boot-soles" (1339–40).

Alexandra Bergson, then, unifies *O Pioneers!* Hers is the creative force bringing wild land to productive order. Aside from pampering Emil, she remains uncorrupted by the materialism of success evident in Lou and Oscar. Her blindness toward her own accomplishments and toward relationships beyond friendship between men and women is challenged by the tragic affair which deprives her of Emil and exposes Marie's destructive passion. Finally, passing through a dark night of the soul and sharing Frank's horror, she is led by Carl to a new, universal vision of the land and its people.

Notes

1. Cooper's review appeared in *Bookman*, 37 (Aug. 1913), 666–67. Among recent critics, David Daiches in *Willa Cather: A Critical Introduction* (Ithaca, N.Y.: Cornell Univ. Press, 1951) sees the first part of the novel as arising "from a different impulse and . . . built on different underlying rhythms than later sections which deal with the love of Emil and Marie . . ." (p. 22); John Randall in *The Landscape and the Looking Glass: Willa Cather's Search for Value* (Boston: Houghton Mifflin, 1960) detects the logical sequence of the two parts, that Cather turned to spontaneity in human relationships "after exploring spontaneous emotion in relation to nature and the land . . ." (p. 76).

2. Elizabeth Shepley Sergeant in *Willa Cather: A Memoir* (Lincoln: Univ. of Nebraska Press, Bison Books, 1963) describes Cather's recognition of the dualistic nature of the novel (pp. 86, 91).

3. David Stouck, *Willa Cather's Imagination* (Lincoln: Univ. of Nebraska Press, 1975), p. 31.

4. James Woodress notes the Whitman connection in *Willa Cather: Her Life and Art* (New York: Western Publishing Company, 1970), pp. 158–59, as does Bernice Slote in "Willa Cather: The Secret Web," in *Five Essays on Willa Cather: The Merrimack Symposium*, ed. John J. Murphy (North Andover, Mass.: Merrimack College, 1974), pp. 11–12.

5. Willa Cather, *O Pioneers!*, Sentry Edition (Boston: Houghton Mifflin, 1962), p. 3; hereafter cited in the text.

6. Genesis 1:1–2; subsequent references are to *The New English Bible with the Apocrypha: Oxford Study Edition*, ed. Samuel Sandmel, M. Jack Suggs, and Arnold J. Tkacik (New York: Oxford Univ. Press, 1976).

7. Ibid., notes to Genesis 9:1–17, pp. 8–9.

8. Edward A. and Lillian D. Bloom, *Willa Cather's Gift of Sympathy* (Carbondale: Southern Illinois Univ. Press, Arcturus Books, 1964), p. 18.

9. Deborah G. Lambert, "The Defeat of a Hero: Autonomy and Sexuality in *My Ántonia*," *American Literature*, 53 (Jan. 1982), 682.

10. Isabel Charles (Sister Peter Damian), "Love and Death in Willa Cather's *O Pioneers!*," *CLA Journal*, 9 (Dec. 1965), 144–45.

11. Willa Cather, *The Professor's House* (New York: Random House, Vintage Books, 1973), pp. 280–81.

12. Nathaniel Hawthorne, *The Scarlet Letter: A Norton Critical Edition*, 2nd ed., ed. Sculley Bradley et al. (New York: W. W. Norton, 1978), pp. 145–56.

13. Walt Whitman, "Song of Myself" (ll. 45–46), in *Leaves of Grass: A Norton Critical Edition*, ed. Sculley Bradley and Harold W. Blodgett (New York: W. W. Norton, 1973); hereafter cited in the text.

The Song of the Lark

[Review of *The Song of the Lark*]   Anonymous*

It seems a far journey back to the rare imaginative quality of *O Pioneers!*, the story by Miss Cather of young life in the Nebraska prairie with its beautiful and tragic denouement. *O Pioneers!* had a warm unity of tone, a youthful wistfulness, that made it appealing. One could scarcely believe it was not the work of a writer who was going to do great things in that imaginative realism which our current American fiction still so stupidly lacks. The appearance of dramatic imagination in any form in this country is something to make us all drop our work and run to see. It is the thing to keep straining our eyes for. One hoped that the adulation which greeted Mr. Ernest Poole's timid *The Harbor*, where the imagination was swabbed on from the outside rather than run as a vital current through the veins, would encourage more of the younger novelists to let themselves go, and stir us by a representation of life that is fearlessly bathed in a glow of youth and generous ideals. This is why it is so disappointing to find Miss Cather, with her rare promise, running now prudently to cover.

It is difficult, from *The Song of the Lark*, to reconstruct that lyric preface to the former book, the "Prairie Spring," which sang the very theme of the book, and made at least one Dakotan youth quite weak with homesickness. This very title suggests a play to sentimental chords on the style of the unspeakable "Rosary." One could forgive it perhaps if the song of the lark were actually the *leitmotif* of the story. But it is not. Thea Kronborg sees the picture in the Chicago Art Museum, feels that it is her picture. "The flat country, the early morning light, the wet fields, the look in the girl's heavy face," were "all hers." But never again does either Miss Cather or Thea think of the picture, and the imagination simply refuses to relate the tense and golden Thea, ambitious, quiet, and a little fierce, to the placid and thickly knit girl of Breton's popular canvas.

*Originally published in the *New Republic*, 5 (11 December 1915), 153–54.

The suspicious rift of artistic defect which this title discloses continues to widen through the story. Miss Cather's imagination seems acceleratedly to miss fire, until the last two parts seem an act of laborious creation, carried through after the author is really bored with her story. The early chapters—the little Swede girl's childhood in the Colorado town, her quaint pastoral family, the old musician, her early musical studies in Chicago—are delightfully done. So are scenes like the Mexican dance, where Thea's artistic soul rises against the disapproving conventionality of the little town. There is air and sun in the Arizona cliff summer. All this is real because it is part of the Thea that Miss Cather is writing about, and part of Miss Cather's own assimilated experience. It is warm with the hard little golden fire that was at Thea's heart, and which drove her on and on in her quest.

In this fair and self-centred girl with her passion for music, with that clutch at her soul which held her aloof from every environment, that urge which impelled her to realize her very self though it meant shutting out the whole world, Miss Cather had a great story. Such a story could have been a crescendo of interpretation, with the contrast between the inner clutch and the conventional appeals of life made ever more inescapable. But Thea's actual success limps very badly. The inner fire becomes smothered in wearisome objective detail of the operatic life and the uninteresting friends that she does not really need. The story could have worked up to the climax of Thea's cool flight to Mexico with the young Ottenburg, Thea inexorably true to her art, taking passion as an interesting but indispensable incident of life. There the story could have broken off with a leap. Our imagination would have easily supplied the finished career. Miss Cather does not mean to spell deterioration for Thea, and yet so unskilful is the handling of these later chapters that it is almost impossible to find in the bourgeoise Madame Kronborg the same Thea, with her "loyalty of young hearts to an exalted ideal, and the passion with which they strive." In the inscrutable epilogue Miss Cather seems simply to throw to the winds what she is trying to do. Her story was the progress of a peculiarly arresting youthful talent. The epilogue acts as if she were writing a sociological treatise of the town of Moonstone, Colorado, in which every last citizen of the girl's early environment is to be accounted for to the anxious reader.

Yet few novels give so tell-tale a pattern of the difficulties that beset the imaginative writer, and the narrow way that must be walked. Miss Cather would perhaps be shocked to know how sharp were the contrasts between those parts of her book which are built out of her own experience and those which are imagined. Her defects are almost wholly those of unassimilated experience. The musical life of this opera singer who has so fascinated her she has admired, but she has not made it imaginatively her own. She has contented herself with the fascination and has not grasped the difficulty of reading herself into this other life and making it so much hers that the actual and the imagined are no longer separable. This is almost the whole cunning of the novelist's art. *O Pioneers!* was artistic because it was woven all of a piece of imaginatively interpreted experience. Its charm made one want to put Miss Cather's next book among that very small group of epics of youthful talent that grows great with quest and desire. But in that little library one cannot give even temporary place to *The Song of the Lark*. Resentment of this unpleasant fact is perhaps the greatest compliment one could pay to its author's genuine talent.

The Lyric Artist   Richard Giannone[*]

I

Of the three American singers about whom Willa Cather wrote appreciatively while they reigned during the Metropolitan Opera's golden age, one commands her total favor. Louise Homer, a contralto born in Pittsburgh, famous for her Orpheus, had power and persuasion, "but she had set for herself no goal that it would break her heart to lose."[1] Geraldine Farrar, a soprano from Massachusetts, was known for the lyric sensuousness of her interpretation and had that personal quality of voice which her great teacher, Lilli Lehmann, taught the world to prize. Farrar gave fresh feeling to her roles, but even in her full vocal measure the emotion she gained was at the expense of "the intellectual side" of music. Neither the " 'frozen heights' " of talent (as Madame Farrar called the region where one risks being stupid in order to be sublime) nor the idea behind the music intimidated Olive Fremstad, the Swedish-born Wagnerian soprano who was reared in Minnesota. She overreached for the one and dug for the other, and her voice could accommodate both intentions. She was Willa Cather's artist *par excellence*—powerful, passionate, daring, intellectual.

Madame Fremstad's expansive vocal range, intelligent singing, and sheer melodic beauty were reasons enough for esteem, but as always it was the force behind the instrument that fascinated Willa Cather. The history of artists whom she greatly admired offered her a possible way into the mystery of artistic creativity; also, she learned from analyzing her own experience. She did not hesitate to put her own ideas in the mouths of others, and frequently the pronouncement that issues from a personality she is interviewing echoes what she herself has written

[*]From *Music in Willa Cather's Fiction*, by Richard Giannone, pp. 83–99. Reprinted by permission of the University of Nebraska Press and the author. Copyright © 1968 by the University of Nebraska Press.

earlier.[2] In "Three American Singers," the profile of Olive Fremstad has elements of projection, but it also has something more. The homage derives from a meeting of two minds which think and feel alike. The diva had large, strong ideas and she was enjoying the highest success. For once, there is not the slightest hint of superiority in Cather's attitude, not a trace of disapproval. Several of Fremstad's quoted observations would fit neatly in such early stories as "A Singer's Romance" and "Nanette: An Aside," and do certainly seem to color the conception and conversation of the prima donna figure in *Youth and the Bright Medusa* (1920). The artistic principles tentatively urged in Willa Cather's early nonfiction, too, are echoed by remarks attributed to Fremstad and borne out by her practice. On responsibility: " 'What voice is necessary for the part I undertake, I will produce.' " On integrity: " 'My work is only for serious people.' " On interpretation: " 'It ought to mean something.' " On life: " 'We are born alone, we make our way alone, we die alone.' " The sympathies here are so fundamental that, as Willa Cather goes on to analyze Olive Fremstad's genius, the essay seems less an extension of the writer's personal standards than the unfolding of a mutual fealty to the nature and needs of art. First, Fremstad's reading is from a shaping idea, thought "so intensely experienced that it becomes emotion." The conception, however, only broadly and austerely defines the portrayal. Much of the character is kept in mental reserve. The excitement is not on stage; "the fateful drama actually went on behind her brow." Willa Cather locates the origin of Madame Fremstad's musical ideas in those "cardinal needs of humanity" that she specified in an 1899 piece on Lillian Nordica.[3] The expression Fremstad finally employs "has its roots deep in human nature, it follows the old paths of human yearning. . . ." Those old paths lead to what Bernice Slote explains as the primitive vitality behind creation, the life force of the earth.[4] Because Fremstad grew up "in a new, crude country" she had to fight "her own way toward the intellectual centers of the world." The untamed land anchors many ideas behind her impersonations. She says of her Kundry at the end of *Parsifal*: " 'There is much of my childhood in the last act. You have been to revivals? Well, so have I.' "

There is much of Willa Cather's artistic childhood in Olive Fremstad's, just as there is much of the writer's view of art in the singer's statements. The complex meshing of Willa Cather's personal experience and attitudes with the great accomplishment and career of Olive Fremstad constitutes the substance of *The Song of the Lark* (1915).[5] Other influences enter into the book, like the discovery of the Southwest, which takes on the force of a permanent preoccupation, or the attempt "to reproduce the emotional effect of the Wagner operas upon the printed page," which Cather admits to trying.[6] But *The Song of the Lark* finds its essential inspiration in the use of a singer's creative growth as an ideal analogy for the discovery and expression of all art. The portrait of an artist as diva serves too as an ingathering of Cather's association with grand opera's golden hour. In New York, as on the Nebraska frontier, she witnessed history. Edith Lewis recalls:

> We went constantly to the opera at this time. It was one of the great periods of opera in New York. Nordica and the de Reszkes, Melba and Calvé were still singing during our first years in New York. From 1905 on our old programmes continually list such names as Sembrich, Farrar, Chaliapin, Plançon, Destinn, Renaud, Mary Garden, Caruso, Amato, Homer, and Tetrazzini. Toscanini, not then half so famous, but at the height of his powers, was conducting two or three times a week at the Metropolitan. But the most thrilling, to us, of all the new stars that came up over the horizon was Olive Fremstad. We heard her nearly every time she sang.[7]

The atmosphere of music in *The Song of the Lark* is more inclusive and democratic than the posh confines of the Met, though its high pressure does gauge the other musical conditions in the novel. The Met is the summit of musical expression. Nevertheless, the origin of music is in the earth, in the sound of things and the rhythm of life. Between the physical beginning in man and the spiritual culmination are different levels of talent. There are untrained musicians who transmit the lore in their blood and many skilled lyric artists who perform the masterworks of musical heritage. The combined passion of the folk artist and the educated intelligence of the professional make up the cultural patrimony to which Thea Kronborg, the heroine, is heir. Her gradual laying claim to the double legacy is the drama of the novel. Her generous distribution of the treasure reveals to us the value of the struggle. As Thea Kronborg comes into her own as a magnificent singer, music figures the spiritual bridge between men.

II

"Friends of Childhood," the first of six sections, covers Thea's eleventh through seventeenth years, that period of her life when she was pure artist. " 'I am more or less of an artist now,' " she says to Doctor Archie when she approaches the peak of her career, " 'but then I was nothing else' " (551). She has as a girl an aesthetic freshness which allows her to experience things wholly. Her receptivity is grounded in nature. The sand hills around Moonstone, Colorado, and the Turquoise Hills ten miles off tantalize Thea with a message of freedom, courage, and aspiration. The eagle living up on a windy ridge teaches her more of the spirit and desire of man than does the most ambitious man in the town below. From people she learns a great deal, but it is small in comparison with the tidings in the naked vigor of the earth. Frequently the lesson learned from man is negative. She must preserve a certain solitude, protect her feelings from the sentimental intrusions of her sister or from the elaborate familial doings which can blot out her identity. She must hold her own against the cheap taste and rivalry of a Lily Fisher, who connives to get a show-stopper at the church Christmas concert and would sing anything which pleases the crowd. More frequently, the experience of childhood positively contributes to the development of her aesthetic sense. Among Moonstone friends Thea realizes that human relationships are matters of the heart and not applications of social or religious tenets. The final communion that Thea Kronberg creates on the Metropolitan stage at the novel's end comes back to the first trust in the social choices young Thea makes in Moonstone. A confidence shared is permanently honored. The continual and enlarging spiritual return, in fact, is one of the personal gratifications of her singing.

The accumulated wealth of childhood, apart from the unaccountable inborn power to receive the creative passion in the first place, is exemplified in four friends. Each has a different personality, but all share in a common friendliness toward one another, a love for Thea, a personal integrity; and each lives in the paradox of being a failure in the public view and a valued person to Thea. The mark of this kinship is music. Each friend is talented or appreciative of music, and in all four musical response implies the higher self which society does not discern and which the friends themselves cannot reach or release on their own.

With Spanish Johnny, the unreliable alcoholic, Thea comes nearest to the elemental impulse of the earth as it is echoed in man. The music Johnny makes on a mandolin is frenzied and exceptionally skillful, but its strength and beauty reside in the racial consciousness which is at the heart of his songs. In the second part of the novel, after Thea returns from a year of formal study in Chicago, she identifies the emotional freedom she enjoys with the Mexicans through the ethnic current in their music. Among Mexicans, and especially with Johnny, music is a felt reality and a common expression. Even their movements have "a kind of natural harmony" (289). When she sings before a "really musical people" like the Mexican neighbors, Thea receives "the response that such a people can give" (292)—pleasure and affection. Transcending social or racial fact, music unites Thea with emotional allies for whom society provides no regular means of exchange. Among the Mexicans she unearths a collective human feeling through songs of joy, love, riches, and delicate swallows: "Ultimo Amor," "Noches de Algeria," "Fluvia de Oro," "La Golandrina." The spiritual transfer with simple people is important. During her operatic career, Thea constantly draws from the deep reservoir of basic human yearning. At the close of *The Song of the Lark* the final measurement of her brilliant Sieglinde is the " 'Brava! Brava!' " of "a grey-haired little Mexican" (572) perched in the top gallery. His excitement assures us that Thea Kronborg's voice reaches the sympathetic center of those from whom she first learned music's primitive energy.

Ray Kennedy, a railroader-romancer, brings the young artist to other beginnings, those of history. From his tales of Old Mexico and the South-west Thea learns how man pulled himself up from a primitive to a civilized creature. About the Cliff-Dwellers and their cities, Ray says, "'You begin to feel what the human race has been up against from the beginning. There's something mighty elevating about those old habita-tions'" (149). Ray's own life has little of the heroism of his dreams, but he is able to communicate heroic ideals. The meaning of the human story is his gift to Thea. As a child she instinctively comprehends the time-lessness of man's fight for the civilized things which make him man, because she has within herself a yearning to create and because she re-quires direct contact with the vital source of life Ray speaks of. Later of course she does live fully by the natural pull of things in the Southwest—actually immersed in the life-water of the earth—and the conception of art which Thea achieves during this baptism is an enlargement of Ray's idealism.

Thea's closest Moonstone friend is Howard Archie, a physician, who is too timid to call a halt to an unsuccessful marriage and to leave a town he finds limiting. He cares for her from cradle to artistic coronation. The intellectual of the town, Archie is able to explain questions of religion, personal responsibility, and human destiny which puzzle Thea. He makes no concessions to her young mind; he speaks maturely. The nasty death of a tramp, who spites the town's meanness by drowning himself in the standpipe and contaminating the water supply, for example, shocks Thea; and Archie does not sentimentalize experience to lessen the shock. The indifference of everyone to the tramp's needs strikes the girl as a mockery of the Christian principles society asserts. She is also disturbed by a man's falling desperately far out of good fortune. Perplexities of these kinds will, Archie assures her, always arise, and her bookish notions of religion will not solve them. He offers in place of conventionalized restriction a doc-trine of pleasure: the important duty is "'to live . . . ; to do all we can and enjoy all we can'" (175). That she does overcome the inevitable, momentary reverses of desire and circumstance demonstrates an ability to brush ugliness and misfortune aside in favor of searching out "'the best things of this world'" (175).

A piano teacher, psychically lame like the other three Moonstone friends, has the most to do with Thea's artistic preparation. Professor Wunsch gives Thea all he can; that would be quite a bit for a normal child, but not enough for one intending to study the piano seriously. As desire outweighs discipline in his personality, so his teaching emphasizes emotion and ignores, except in a wayward fashion, the literature of the piano. Music is Wunsch's life and love; because it was not submitted to discipline of any kind, it has become an inadequate source of livelihood and an emotional frustration. The imbalance of his musicianship is not without a compensatory benefit, however. His name states what Thea receives from him—desire.

Willa Cather uses the famous lament in Gluck's *Orpheus and Euryd-ice* to represent Wunsch's tragedy. The music and myth shaping the opera reference contain as well the symbolic locus of the novel. The opera is first mentioned as one of Wunsch's favorite works of music, " 'the most beautiful opera ever made' " (89) he tells Thea, and when she shows interest, he cannot resist going over the lament. The deep feeling he brings to the melody shows the identification of his personal loss of music with the operatic hero's loss of Eurydice. As usual, Willa Cather provides a few verses of a piece to suggest background and draws upon the implied context in developing the action. The aria runs:

> I have lost my Eurydice.
> Nothing can equal my despair.
> Cruel fate, no hope is left me.
> Nothing can equal my despair.
> This is more than life can bear.
> Eurydice, Eurydice, reply!
> What torture! Answer me!
> It is thy faithful Orpheus;
> Hark to my voice that calls to thee.
> I have lost my Eurydice.
> Deathly silence,
> Hope is vain,
> What suffering,
> What torments tear my heart![8]

When Wunsch plays and Thea sings of a life without the thing one needs most, the reader is invited to participate aurally in the moment when two talents, following separate paths on the Orphic landscape, intersect. The high thoroughfare that the young girl, not fully aware of her genius, will take to success crosses the worn trail of an old man resigned to wanderings. Again, the larger service of music is to introduce the classical legend that Willa Cather is reworking in *The Song of the Lark*. Two complementary ways of deepening meaning come together. Myth holds the old human stories; music the old feelings. In this novel it is the legend behind Gluck's opera that Willa Cather uses, but her thematic sense frequently calls for a particular tonal emphasis which music supplies.

The story of Orpheus, the eponym of art, recounts the lasting drama of man's search for expression. Specifically for Willa Cather, the story glosses the relationship between art and life and the relationship between instrument and material. For Orpheus, the supreme lyric artist, the emergency of life determines the emergency of art. Only through art can he retrieve his beloved. Art can redeem life for the singer. If he can artic-ulate his grief, hell can be won over to his need. Not only must the feeling be intense, then, but the intensity must be released in communicable form and adapted to those it must sway. This Orpheus can do. But the course is parabolic. Even if art can rise to triumph over the will of hell, there remains the descent back into personal passion for which discipline of self is required. The law of hell is cunning; it makes no concession to human weakness though that weakness is the substance of the song it respects. When Orpheus must check his feelings, he fails; he looks back at Eurydice. Success in the greater task aids not at all in the lower. Art gives meaning, emotion in communicable shape, to life but does not necessarily provide a way of meeting its demands.

Willa Cather's canonical treatment of Orpheus, the artist-quester, varies. The artists in *The Troll Garden* and *Youth and the Bright Medusa* fail to enchant themselves. They duplicate the failure of the historical Orpheus. In *The Song of the Lark*, however, Willa Cather proposes a triumphant solution. It is not quite so mechanical as Gluck's union, which is arranged by Cupid, but the novel does waive the fatal clause in the pact between the singer and hell and bring together seemingly incompatible things, life and art. The marriage between life and art is brought about through the sublimation of life into art. Art for Thea Kronborg solves the crisis of life by absorbing it. When Archie expresses concern about the singer's lack of personal life, she replies: " 'My dear doctor, I don't have any. Your work becomes your personal life. You are not much good until it does. It's like being woven into a big web. You can't pull away, because all your little tendrils are woven into the picture. It takes you up, and uses you, and spins you out; and that is your life' " (546). It is toward this final integration that *The Song of the Lark* moves.

In leaving the fellowship of childhood, in embarking to seek Eurydice, Thea has only the interior "friendly spirit" (100), nourished by four soul-friendships, to guide her.

III

Thea's quest takes her to Chicago where she finds a proper discipline for her desire. Art requires hard work, she learns, especially for those few with great ability. She realizes also that she cannot be a concert pianist. The lack of early training cannot be overcome. Her true medium is the voice, the instrument through which she can unlock the strong, intimate spirit inside her. The conversion from piano to voice, like the larger artistic and intellectual ripening, is from the artificial to the natural.

Andor Harsanyi, Thea's piano teacher, accidentally discovers her real gift. Once exposed, the voice is gently encouraged to follow its natural strengths. The method Harsanyi adopts in training Thea's voice recalls Willa Cather's literary approach—as expressed in "Three American Singers"—from the controlling idea of a piece to the individual passage, from the larger feeling or intuition to interpretation, from intention to specification. The approach also corrects the aimless freedom Wunsch permitted. Thea's reading of *"Die Lorelei"* instances Harsanyi's technique. Simply singing the song does not satisfy Thea. A beautiful voice alone does not properly convey the meaning of music. The concluding bars of the song as she first sings them displease her because her conception does not mate Heine's lyric with the melody. Unless each part belongs to an inclusive conception a reading has no cogency. When she grasps the idea of a river enduring beneath the havoc above it, Thea gives the end of "*Die Lorelei*" an " 'open flowing' " (240) tone to suggest continuity. That quality pleases her and Harsanyi. Before she perceived the idea behind a melody "she wandered like a blind man surrounded by torments" (241); after the " 'revelation' " she sails with steady sureness. The beauty of the voice is always there; it is the idea which must be sought out.

Harsanyi has his own reasons for giving Thea "*Die Lorelei*"; he is suggesting a method congenial to her nature and testing the girl's ability to reach the idea behind a melody. And Willa Cather has her own novelistic reasons for giving us the song. Liszt's setting is beautiful and popular enough to evoke for the reader an atmosphere " 'reeking of a song' " (243), as Harsanyi describes the studio to his wife; but Heine's poem is Willa Cather's way of connecting an artistic discovery in a character with theme. Like the persona in the poem, Thea's mind is haunted by an indefinite "tale of past times." Though the facts of the tale are in the future, "*Die Lorelei*" foreshadows a journey beset with danger. It will be Thea's journey on the Rhine of artistic ambition, the old tale of man's need for expression. The strange splendors and exquisite allurements which in the end destroy the voyager are the countless obstacles hindering expression. "*Die Lorelei*" is the Orphic journey, the voyage perilous again.

The same intuitive grasp of a musical idea seen in Thea's singing of "*Die Lorelei*" is shown again at a symphony concert a short time later. On this occasion Thea is listening, not interpreting, and the process is reversed. By the transposition Cather suggests that instinctive sensitivity works in two directions, in appreciation as well as in execution. The exchange is doubly beneficial for the artist, as we shall come to see more clearly from Thea's appreciation of the earth's life-giving music in the Southwest. The aesthetic feeling in the concert-hall scene is more limited in effect than her response to the cañons. She is brought to a union with her aesthetic desire, but it is an impressionistic and momentary experience compared to the intellectual (as well as emotional) and permanent recognition of a creative force that comes later in Arizona. Thea has been to very few concerts and in the beginning is distracted by the novelty of her surroundings. Not until the second number is she ready to listen. Her imagination seizes on the first theme of Dvořák's Symphony in E minor, "called on the programme, 'From the New World' " (251). She visualizes her own West with wagon trails, wind, and eagles—the old sights of childhood recovered through melody. Blending into the nostalgic evocation of the past is the Walhalla motif from *Das Rheingold*, the next number the orchestra plays. Her knowledge of the opera is vague, we are informed. In Willa Cather's treatment of Thea's response, however, the Walhalla music bodes her destiny as a distinguished Wagnerian soprano. Wagner mingles with Dvořák to create Thea's New World of Music. Suggestively, Willa Cather announces a thematic image that recurs throughout her fiction in various forms and at the end of *The Song of the Lark* with complex associations: "The cold, stately measures of the Walhalla music rang out, far away; the rainbow bridge throbbed out into the air, under it the wailing of the Rhine daughters and the singing of the Rhine" (252). Thea is "sunk in twilight" now, but soon she will cross the rainbow bridge to success. In the Walhalla of her power she, as singer, will construct the rainbow bridge back to the musical spirit of her audience. The future is revealed to the reader; it is not in Thea's awareness. Her response stops at a firm decision to fight for the joy she felt in the concert hall. "As long as she lived that ecstacy was going to be hers. She would live for it, work for it, die for it; but she was going to have it, time after time, height after height" (254).

It is one thing for Thea to know that the voice and not the piano will transport her across the rainbow bridge and quite another for her to act on the knowledge. It requires a second birth, and the artistic bringing forth of the deeper self is more difficult to undergo than the first, human birth. With friends Thea's feeling and love provide the standard for singing; with the impersonal public the mind as well as soul are demanded. Approval would open the way to unusual fulfillment and self-knowledge; failure would be killing because the judgment of the voice involves a judgment of the soul. Defeat at the piano, for example, does not break her because the voice is there to absorb disappointment. Thea's fear of action is understandable from another viewpoint. Defeat is more usual than victory on the concert or operatic stage, and she has yet to meet anyone who has succeeded in the way total dedication deserves. The models have been negative. Two things do work in favor of her taking the risk, however. She cannot forget how their responsiveness to her singing gave an entrée into the "second selves" (273) of people like Ray and Spanish Johnny. And she realizes during her brief return visit to Moonstone that she cannot live in a choking moral atmosphere. The struggle would be worth while just to escape pettiness and emotional restraint. She needs glorious air to breathe. " 'I only want impossible things,' " she says brusquely to Archie. " 'The others don't interest me' " (305).

Thea's growth up to now is largely psychological. She finds out what she is not and comes generally to sense what she must be. Ironically, when she begins formal study of voice, her progress seems slow. The bitter part of every Orpheus' "bitter struggle" (221) shows itself in the acquisition of control. Discipline checks at the same time that it cleanses. Also, proximity to the profession dims the shine a tyro tends to see. The idealistic Thea encounters the hard-nosed careerist, who has finish but no fire, the coarse audience, which savors only the banality it knows, and the compromised singer, who fattens her reputation by feeding the Cerberus-audience its sop.

Encouragement of the sort she received from Archie or Harsanyi is hard to come by. The old inspiration is replaced by empty routine. Her voice master, Madison Bowers, personifies the uncongenial situation. He is good as a master but personally "cold" and "academic" (315), contemptuous of the public (and of some of his students). One might think of him as an Orpheus with the power to resist turning around to see Eurydice if only he could move hell in the first place. Thea's chief personal contact is not much brighter. Philip Frederick Ottenburg, a "florid brewery magnate," entertains her in a style to which she is unaccustomed and introduces her to the Nathanmeyers, whose knowledgeable approval of her singing and personality momentarily cheers her; but Ottenburg's interest is only ostensibly musical. The Bowers period when she tries to emerge as herself is filled with irritations intense enough to embitter Thea and to make her cynical of everyone's motives or aspirations. Everywhere about her she sees compromise, contempt, and vanity. The warmth and idealism of Moonstone and her first Chicago teacher have vanished, leaving the life of art merely another way of meeting daily hardness with comparable artistic obduracy. Icy expertise is the best attribute of this world. In Part III, "Stupid Faces," the young artist is offered two alternatives. Thea can fashion a career according to the crassitude that works so well and be assured of popular success, or she can abandon the art Bowers and his students stand for—and all art—and retain her personal integrity. A third possibility, rising above careerism, is not suggested through characterization, but it is there by inference. Again Thea moves in the dark without guidance from others. As her decision to sing was implied in music, so the future course she must take is charted in the song which she sings for Fred Ottenburg the first time they meet. Grieg's *"Tak for dit Råd"* ("Thanks for Your Advice") stands as Thea's implicit rejoinder to Bowers and all the "Stupid Faces" whose help she acknowledges and whom she will surpass. That Cather intends to emphasize this song is evident from her providing the translation of Grieg's lyric. Thea is doing the explaining:

> "Well, it goes something like this: 'Thanks for your advice! But I prefer to steer my boat into the din of roaring breakers. Even if the journey is my last, I may find what I have never found before. Onward must I go, for I yearn for the wild sea. I long to fight my way through the angry waves, and to see how far, and how long I can make them carry me.'" (338)

"Tak for dit Råd" is the singer's adieu to Chicago, and its significance derives from the perilous voyage motif of *"Die Lorelei"* and *Orpheus and Eurydice*, which it echoes. The song speaks for Thea's spiritual courage which must combat storms of hostility. With the dauntless sailor in Grieg's

air, she must carry on the struggle for guidance which comes only from the friendly spirit inside. Thea takes a high ideal to be a hard command.

IV

The fourth, fifth, and sixth parts of *The Song of the Lark* treat the liberation of Thea's "treasure of creative power" (333). Willa Cather does not delineate a rapid ascent to achievement from the desire of childhood and the direction of youth. Between consecration and action there falls a quiet pause for reflection. In Willa Cather's view of artistic growth the reposeful lull is a crucial moment. It is particularly restorative for Thea Kronborg. The pause is the retreat before the great advance, a return to the origin of all creativity—the earth. Thea's experience in the spacious, powerful cañons of the Southwest incorporates the early excitement of childhood among the open sand hills; and intellectually it goes back further, to the nature of history. Contact with the earth removes data from history to leave only the basic thing: man's continuous fight to achieve something beyond himself. That fight holds value, and it repeats itself in everyone at every stage of human development. The contest is the basis and embodiment of art. Thea achieves this understanding among rocks, air, birds, and sky, the first things which tested man's power to control and shape.

Transformation is brought about in Panther Cañon in Arizona where she lives alongside relics of the Cliff-Dweller civilization. She is able to divine the daily tone of the Cliff-Dwellers' life, and this empathy helps her to shed the Chicago bitterness and to enjoy immersion in "the earliest sources of gladness" (369). Even in extinction, ancient Indian life testifies to taste and aspiration. Its art suggests a unity between utensil and spiritual need. Especially beautiful to Thea are the jars which hold "the precious water" (377). The vessels are functional but also expressive and consecrated to the water they house. "Their pottery was their most direct appeal to water, the envelope and sheath of the precious element itself" (377). The Cliff-Dwellers transformed nature but still lived according to it. Elevation was a way of life, the vistas a way of seeing and regarding life—widely, freely. They civilized themselves. That is the ultimate heroism for Willa Cather. The severe and mighty geography dignifies, it does not falsify, the hardness of human labor.

It is while Thea is physically immersed in the "precious element" that she gains the deepest knowledge of art. Not when she practices or performs, but when she bathes in a stream comes the understanding that art is the giving of human shape to physical nature.

One morning, as she was standing upright in the pool, splashing water between her shoulder-blades with a big sponge, something flashed through her mind that made her draw herself up and stand still until the water had quite dried upon her flushed skin. The stream

and the broken pottery: what was any art but an effort to make a
sheath, a mould in which to imprison for a moment the shining, elusive
element which is life itself—life hurrying past us and running away,
too strong to stop, too sweet to lose? The Indian women had held it
in their jars. In the sculpture she had seen in the Art Institute, it had
been caught in a flash of arrested motion. In singing, one made a
vessel of one's throat and nostrils and held it on one's breath, caught
the stream in a scale of natural intervals. (378)

The experience in Panther Cañon restates one of Willa Cather's long-
standing beliefs about art. In a *Journal* piece of March 1, 1896, she wrote:
"Art is not thought or emotion, but expression, expression, always expression." The challenge is to preserve the first excitement one feels
when receiving the idea until the idea is put into words, sound, or color;
". . . that is the greatest of all the gifts of the gods. And that is the voyage
perilous. . . ."[9] In *The Song of the Lark* the voyage is from brain to voice.
The voice activates in beautiful tones the "elusive element."

That this period of Thea's life, which bears so deeply on her future
art, should be nearly without a music reference is not at all curious. The
treatment accords with Cather's idea of art and with the mythic sense in
the novel besides. For a time the singer lives on a level of pure sensation,
in a world of natural impulses where understanding "came up to her out
of the rock-shelf on which she lay" (376). She is in the source of art,
"life in the air" with its "rhythm of feeling and action" (392). The response is "not expressible in words" (376). One might call the experience
an extension of the daybreak in Panther Cañon when "the golden light"
(389) gradually soaks the gorge until everything swims "in the liquid
gold" (390). The near-absence of music implies a return to the sun.
And it is from Apollo, after all, that Orpheus receives the gift of a lyre.
With the sun one finds the inmost melody among the world's parts.

The sixth and last section of the novel brings the voyage to port.
In portraying the artist's great hour in New York Willa Cather uses two
devices to emphasize the achievement. She shifts the point of view to
Archie and defines Thea through a series of musical personages. The
limited vision of Archie preserves the "admiration and estrangement"
(500) of the non-artist before creative genius which Willa Cather re-
currently shows. Cather is fond of examining the aristocrats of experience
through democratic spokesmen. Also, up to now Thea's musical self has
been tucked in the recess of desire; the new view in a way protects the
soul's privacy. Though exposed, Thea's personality is known through
musical guises. The difference between the childhood world of aspiration
and the time of fulfillment is suggested in the title of the last part: "Kronborg." The coldness is fitting. The matter-of-fact notation of talent has
the impressiveness of a poster listing conductor and famous principal
singers without individual emphasis, thereby making genius commonplace. "Kronborg" also, appropriately enough, suggests detachment and

intimidation. Single names for Cather, after Balzac, are noble epithets, "'names that tell all and make the passer dream.' "[10]

The admiration derives from a series of Wagnerian roles which Madame Kronborg interprets. The principal ones are: Elizabeth (*Tannhäuser*), Elsa (*Lohengrin*), Venus (*Tannhäuser*), Fricka (*Das Rheingold*), and Sieglinde (*Die Walküre*). Actually there is a sixth because Willa Cather gives us two Sieglindes; the significance of duplicating the role will be taken up later. The list of appearances suggests a general movement from the more lyrical to more complex and dramatic, which hints of Madame Kronborg's style, but the important thing is that it shows the soprano's range, her rapid ascent at the Metropolitan, and her indefatigable energy.

The first important role was sung in Dresden where, thanks to the "'lucky chance' " (485) every daughter of music needs, Kronborg got to sing Elizabeth. The role and the circumstances of her debut are brought to mind during Archie's visit to the ailing Mrs. Kronborg. The doctor notices a "photograph of the young woman who must have been singing 'Dich, theure Halle, grüss' ich wieder,' her eyes looking up, her beautiful hands outspread with pleasure" (492). Willa Cather's music allusion is perfectly clear and perfectly apt. The song, which is Elizabeth's entrance and praises music itself, doubles as Madame Kronborg's artistic entrance into her personal Hall of Song. It is a joyous symbolic debut, this salutation of the hall.

> Oh, hall of song I give thee greeting!
> All hail to thee thou hallowed place!
> 'T was here that dream so sweet and fleeting,
> Upon my heart his song did trace.
> But since by him forsaken
> A desert thou dost seem—
> Thy echoes only waken
> Remembrance of a dream.
> But now the flame of hope is lighted,
> Thy vault shall ring with glorious war;
> For he whose strains my soul delighted
> No longer roams afar![11]

Elizabeth's sacred salute balances Orpheus' sad valediction. " *Dich, theure Halle, grüss' ich wieder*" heralds the triumphant induction into music for Thea Kronborg while "*Ich habe sie verloren*" signals the defeated farewell from music for Professor Wunsch.

Kronborg's move from the opera house in Dresden, which was no ordinary affiliation (first or last) at the beginning of the century, to the Met signifies her arrival at the top. But the top is where the scramble is fiercest and footing most precarious. Too many sopranos are tussling for too few roles. The surplus of talent forces major artists to take on assignments which are neither entirely suitable to their voices nor up to their expectations. Merely to survive in that era a diva needed the comprehensive repertoire of an Olive Fremstad. When Cather remarks that Kronborg sings Elsa in *Lohengrin* the first time that Dr. Archie sees her in New York, she conveys both the competitive state of affairs in opera and her heroine's capacity to cope with its demands. Kronberg's Elsa is brilliant, but, as Fred explains to Archie, " 'The fact is, *Elsa* isn't a part that's particularly suited to Thea's voice at all, as I see her voice. It's over-lyrical for her. She makes it, but there's nothing in it that fits her like a glove, except, maybe, that long duet in the third act. But wait until they give her a chance at something that lies properly in her voice . . .' " (511–512).

Her next assignment is Venus in *Tannhäuser*, but the proper role for Kronberg is Elizabeth. In Dresden it was hers; in New York she must take the lesser part. " 'Will they never let you have a chance at *Elizabeth?*' " Fred asks, and she answers philosophically, " 'Not here. There are so many singers here, and they try us out in such a stingy way' " (522).

Chance helps her out. When Madame Gloeckler breaks down after the first act of *Die Walküre* and the two likely replacements are indisposed, Kronborg is asked to finish Sieglinde, a part she has studied but never sung. Fatigued, anxious, and unable to recall a bar of the score as she rushes to get ready, once on stage Kronborg meets the challenge and turns in a magnificent performance—despite the psychological disadvantage of having to sing at a moment's notice a role she has worked on for years and hoped to do to perfection.

Always there comes the let-down. Her next role is the ungrateful one of Fricka in *Das Rheingold*, but Kronborg brings her special touch even to this secondary task. So long portrayed as a nagging, frumpy German *Hausfrau*, in Kronborg's interpretation Fricka emerges as the personification of wisdom she originally had been, glittering with a gold quality. She becomes a goddess again, her divine status restored by " 'a beautiful idea' " (539) in the singer's mind. Thea certainly is one to surprise. Even Fred, who knows Kronborg's gifts well, would not have thought Fricka her style; but after hearing the opera he realizes that she "had a distinct kind of loveliness for this part, a shining beauty like the light of sunset on distant sails" (538).

Soon she is scheduled for a Sieglinde of her own. It is a command performance. "On Friday afternoon there was an inspiring audience; not an empty chair in the house" (565). Music unifies variety. Fred Ottenburg is there, of course, along with the soprano's benefactor, Howard Archie. Andor Harsanyi, back from a successful engagement in Vienna, and his wife also are in the house. From Moonstone, from Chicago, from Europe have come Kronborg's friends; and joining them from some rare, indefinite locale is Spanish Johnny. Old friendships are present to lay spiritual claim on the voice whose growth they shared in. The older nonhuman companionships which enriched this voice are also present, for music blends the Southwest with the Metropolitan stage. " 'You're as much at home on the stage as you were down in Panther Cañon. Didn't you get some of your ideas down there?' " Madame Kronborg answers Fred: " 'Oh, yes! Out of the rocks, out of the dead people' " (554). A voice such as Kronborg's, which Wunsch recognized during its incipience as a "nature-voice" (97), is corporate, reaching down to the procreative force of the earth and up to human yearning. This is the sign and wonder of the artist's divine adoption: "Like the spring indeed, it blossomed into memories and prophecies, it recounted and it foretold . . ." (568). Of all the grace gifts the artist possesses, the most magical is the power to vault the barriers between time and place and person and construct a rainbow bridge to them all. Willa Cather does not count the curtain calls, but the fierce "clamour" (569) of the audience makes it unmistakably clear that Thea Kronborg is the kind of singer who leaves beautiful memories behind her. A soul has touched a soul.

Notes

1. "Three American Singers," *McClure's*, XLII (December, 1913), 33–48.

2. As a case in point, Farrar's reference to the " 'frozen heights,' " cited above, is strangely reminiscent of "She [Duse] is utterly alone upon the icy heights where other human beings cannot live." From *Nebraska State Journal*, November 4, 1894, p. 12; collected in *The Kingdom of Art: Willa Cather's First Principles and Critical Statements, 1893–1896*, ed. Bernice Slote (Lincoln: University of Nebraska Press, 1966), pp. 152–53.

3. "An Open Letter to Lillian Nordica," *Courier*, December 16, 1899, p. 3.

4. *The Kingdom of Art*, p. 47.

5. *The Song of the Lark* (Sentry Edition; Boston: Houghton Mifflin, 1963). All references are to the revised edition of 1937 of which the Sentry Edition is a reprint.

6. Willa Cather, Preface to Gertrude Hall's *The Wagnerian Romances* (New York: Alfred A. Knopf, 1925), p. vii.

7. *Willa Cather Living* (New York: Alfred A. Knopf, 1953), pp. 89–90.

8. *Orpheus and Eurydice*, Act III, scene i. I have taken the English translation from the *Metropolitan Opera House Libretto* (New York: n. d.), p. 9.

9. *The Kingdom of Art*, p. 417.

10. *Nebraska State Journal*, March 1, 1896, p. 9; *The Kingdom of Art*, p. 167.

11. *The Authentic Librettos of the Wagner Operas* (New York: Crown Publishers, 1938), p. 40.

My Ántonia

[Review of *My Ántonia*]   Randolph Bourne[*]

Let us turn aside [from William Allen White's *In the Heart of a Fool*]
to a novel so different that it seems impossible that it could have been
written in the same year and by an American from the same part of the
country as William Allen White. Willa Cather has already shown herself an artist in that beautiful story of Nebraska immigrant life, *O Pioneers!* Her digression into *The Song of the Lark* took her into a field
that neither her style nor her enthusiasm really fitted her for. Now in *My
Ántonia* she has returned to the Nebraska countryside with an enriched
feeling and an even more golden charm of style. Here at last is an
American novel, redolent of the Western prairie, that our most irritated
and exacting preconceptions can be content with. It is foolish to be
captious about American fiction when the same year gives us two so
utterly unlike, and yet equally artistic, novels as Mr. [H. B.] Fuller's *On
the Stairs* and Miss Cather's *My Ántonia*. She is also of the brevity school,
and beside William Allen White's swollen bulk she makes you realize
anew how much art is suggestion and not transcription. One sentence
from Miss Cather's pages is more vivid than paragraphs of Mr. White's
stale brightness of conversation. The reflections she does not make upon
her characters are more convincing than all his moralizing. Her purpose
is neither to illustrate eternal truths nor to set before us the crowded
gallery of a whole society. Yet in these simple pictures of the struggling
pioneer life, of the comfortable middle classes of the bleak little towns,
there is an understanding of what these people have to contend with
and grope for that goes to the very heart of their lives.

Miss Cather convinces because she knows her story and carries it
along with the surest touch. It has all the artistic simplicity of material
that has been patiently shaped until everything irrelevant has been
scraped away. The story has a flawless tone of candor, a naive charm,
that seems quite artless until we realize that no spontaneous narrative

*Originally published in the *Dial*, 65 (14 December 1918), 557.

could possibly have the clean pertinence and grace which this story has. It would be cluttered, as Mr. White's novel is cluttered; it would have uneven streaks of self-consciousness, as most of the younger novelists' work, done impromptu with a mistaken ideal of "saturation," is both cluttered and self-concious. But Miss Cather's even novel has that serenity of the story that is telling itself, of people who are living through their own spontaneous charm.

The story purports to be the memories of a successful man as he looks back over his boyhood on the Nebraska farm and in the little town. Of that boyhood Ántonia was the imaginative center, the little Bohemian immigrant, his playmate and wistful sweetheart. His vision is romantic, but no more romantic than anyone would be towards so free and warm and glorious a girl. He goes to the University, and it is only twenty years later that he hears the story of her pathetic love and desertion, and her marriage to a simple Bohemian farmer, strong, and good like herself.[1]

> She was a battered woman now, not a lovely girl; but she still had that something which fires the imagination, could still stop one's breath for a moment by a look or gesture that somehow revealed the meaning in common things. She had only to stand in the orchard, to put her hand on a little crab tree and look up at the apples, to make you feel the goodness of planting and tending and harvesting at last. All the strong things of her heart came out in her body, that had been so tireless in serving generous emotions. It was no wonder that her sons stood tall and straight. She was a rich mine of life, like the founders of early races.

My Ántonia has the indestructible fragrance of youth: the prairie girls and the dances; the softly alluring Lena, who so unaccountably fails to go wrong; the rich flowered prairie, with its drowsy heats and stinging colds. The book, in its different way, is as fine as the Irishman [Daniel] Corkery's *The Threshold of Quiet*, that other recent masterpiece of wistful youth. But this story lives with the hopefulness of the West. It is poignant and beautiful, but it is not sad. Miss Cather, I think, in this book has taken herself out of the rank of provincial writers and given us something we can fairly class with the modern literary art the world over that is earnestly and richly interpreting the spirit of youth. In her work the stiff moral molds are fortunately broken, and she writes what we can wholly understand.

Note

1. Editor's note: Bourne confuses Jim Burden's initial return, within a year of Ántonia's disgrace, with his subsequent return twenty years later.

The Forgotten Reaping-Hook:
Sex in *My Ántonia*   Blanche H. Gelfant[*]

Our persistent misreading of Willa Cather's *My Ántonia* rises from a belief that Jim Burden is a reliable narrator. Because we trust his unequivocal narrative manner, we see the novel as a splendid celebration of American frontier life. This is the view reiterated in a current critique of *My Ántonia*[1] and in a recent comprehensive study of Cather's work: "*My Ántonia* shows fertility of both the soil and human beings. Thus, in a profound sense *My Ántonia* is the most affirmative book Willa Cather ever wrote. Perhaps that is why it was her favorite."[2] Critics also elect it *their* favorite Cather novel: however, they regret its inconclusive structure, as did Cather when she declared it fragmented and unsatisfactory in form.[3] David Daiches's complaint of twenty years ago prevails: that the work is "flawed" by "irrelevant" episodes and material of "uncertain" meaning.[4] Both critical positions—that *My Ántonia* is a glorious celebration of American life and a defective work of art—must be reversed once we challenge Jim Burden's vision of the past. I believe we have reason to do so, particularly now, when we are making many reversals in our thinking. As soon as we question Jim's seemingly explicit statements, we see beyond them myriad confusions which can be resolved only by a totally new reading. This would impel us to reexamine Jim's testimony, to discover him a more disingenuous and self-deluded narrator than we supposed. Once we redefine his role, *My Ántonia* begins to resonate to new and rather shocking meanings which implicate us all. We may lose our chief affirmative novel, only to find one far more exciting—complex, subtle, aberrant.

Jim Burden belongs to a remarkable gallery of characters for whom Cather consistently invalidates sex. Her priests, pioneers, and artists invest all energy elsewhere. Her idealistic young men die prematurely; her bachelors, children, and old folk remain "neutral" observers. Since she wrote within a prohibitive genteel tradition, this reluctance to portray sexuality is hardly surprising. What should intrigue us is the strange involuted nature of her avoidance. She masks sexual ambivalence by certainty of manner, and displays sexual disturbance, even the macabre, with peculiar insouciance. Though the tenor of her writing is normality, normal sex stands barred from her fictional world. Her characters avoid sexual union with significant and sometimes bizarre ingenuity, or achieve it only in dreams. Alexandra Bergson, the heroine of *O Pioneers!*, finds in recurrent reveries the strong transporting arms of a lover; and Jim Burden in *My Ántonia* allows a half-nude woman to smother him with kisses

*Originally published in *American Literature*, 43 (March 1971), 60–82. Copyright ©️ 1971 by Duke University Press. Reprinted by permission of Duke University Press and the author.

only in unguarded moments of fantasy. Their dreams suggest the typical solipsism of Cather's heroes, who yield to a lover when they are most solitary, most inverted, encaptured by their own imaginations. As Alexandra dispels such reveries by a brisk cold shower, their inferential meaning becomes almost comically clear. Whenever sex enters the real world (as for Emil and Marie in *O Pioneers!*),[5] it becomes destructive, leading almost axiomatically to death. No wonder, then, that Cather's heroes have a strong intuitive aversion to sex which they reveal furtively through enigmatic gestures. In *A Lost Lady*, when young Niel Herbert, who idealizes the Forrester's sexless marriage, discovers Mrs. Forrester's love affair, he vents his infantile jealousy and rage the only way he can—symbolically. While the lovers are on the phone, he takes his "big shears" and cuts the wires, ostensibly to prevent gossip, but also to sever a relationship he cannot abide. Ingenious in rationalizing their actions, Cather's heroes do not entirely conceal an underlying fear of physical love; and the connection between love and death, long undiscerned in Cather's work, can be seen as its inextricable motif. Even in her first novel, *Alexander's Bridge*, the hero's gratuitous death—generally thought to flaw the work—fulfills the inherent thematic demand to show physical passion as disastrous. Here, as in *O Pioneers!*, a later work, illicitness is merely a distracting irrelevance which helps conceal the fear of sexuality in all relationships. *O Pioneers!* reduces the interval between love and death until they almost coincide. At three o'clock, Emil races "like an arrow shot from the bow" to Marie; for the first time they make love; by evening, they are dead, murdered by the half-demented husband.

In *My Ántonia*, Jim Burden grows up with an intuitive fear of sex, never acknowledged, and in fact, denied: yet it is a determining force in his story. By deflecting attention from himself to Ántonia, of whom he can speak with utter assurance, he manages to conceal his muddied sexual attitudes. His narrative voice, reinforced by Cather's, emerges firm and certain; and it convinces. We tend to believe with Jim that his authoritative recitation of childhood memories validates the past and gives meaning to the present even though his mature years stream before him emptied of love, intimacy, and purpose. Memory transports him to richer and happier days spent with Ántonia, the young Bohemian girl who signifies "*the country, the conditions, the whole adventure of . . . childhood.*"[6] Because a changing landscape brilliantly illumines his childhood—with copper-red prairies transformed to rich wheatfields and corn—his personal story seems to epitomize this larger historical drama. Jim uses the coincidence of his life-span with a historical era to imply that as the country changed and grew, so did he, and moreover, as his memoirs contained historical facts, so did they hold the truth about himself. Critics support Jim's bid for validity, pointing out that "*My Ántonia* exemplifies superbly [Frederick Jackson] Turner's concept of the recurring cultural evolution on the frontier."[7]

Jim's account of both history and himself seems to me disingenuous, indeed, suspect; yet it is for this very reason highly pertinent to an understanding of our own uses of the past. In the introduction, Jim presents his memoirs as a spontaneous expression—unselected, unarranged, and uncontrolled by ulterior purpose: *"From time to time I've been writing down what I remember...about Ántonia....I didn't take time to arrange it; I simply wrote down pretty much all that her name recalls to me. I suppose it hasn't any form, ...any title, either"* (p. 2). Obviously, Jim's memory cannot be as autonomous or disinterested as he implies. His plastic powers reshape his experience, selecting and omitting in response to unconscious desires and the will. Ultimately, Jim forgets as much as he remembers, as his mind sifts through the years to retrieve what he most needs—a purified past in which he can find safety from sex and disorder. Of "a romantic disposition," Jim substitutes wish for reality in celebrating the past. His flight from sexuality parallels a flight from historical truth, and in this respect, he becomes an emblematic American figure, like Jay Gatsby and Clyde Griffiths. Jim romanticizes the American past as Gatsby romanticizes love, and Clyde money. Affirming the common, the prototypical, American dream of fruition, all three, ironically, are devastated—Gatsby and Clyde die violently, while Jim succumbs to immobilizing regressive needs. Their relationship to the dream they could not survive must strike us oddly, for we have reversed their situation by surviving to see the dream shattered and the Golden Age of American history impugned. Out of the past that Jim idealized comes our present stunning disorder, though Jim would deny such continuity, as Cather did. Her much-quoted statement that the world *broke* in 1922 reveals historical blindness mistaken for acuity.[8] She denied that "the beautiful past" transmitted the crassness, disorder, and violence which "ruined" the present for her and drove her to hermitic withdrawal. She blamed villainous men, such as Ivy Peters in *A Lost Lady*, for the decline of a heroic age. Like her, Jim Burden warded off broad historical insight. His mythopoeic memory patterned the past into an affecting creation story, with Ántonia a central fertility figure, "a rich mine of life, like the founders of early races." Jim, however, stalks through his myth a wasteland figure who finds in the present nothing to compensate him for the loss of the past, and in the outer world nothing to violate the inner sanctum of memory. "Some memories are realities, are better than anything that can ever happen to one again"—Jim's nostalgic conclusion rationalizes his inanition. He remains finally fixated on the past, returning to the vast and ineffaceable image that dominates his memoirs— the Nebraska prairie yielding to railroad and plough. Since this is an impersonal image of the growth of a nation, and yet it seems so personally crucial to Jim, we must be alerted to the special significance it holds for him. At the very beginning of the novel, we are told that Jim *"loves with a personal passion the great country through which his railway runs"*

(p. 2). The symbolism of the railroad penetrating virgin fields is such an embarrassingly obvious example of emotional displacement, it seems extraordinary that it has been so long unnoted. Like Captain Forrester, the unsexed husband of *A Lost Lady*, Jim sublimates by traversing the country, laying it open by rail; and because he sees the land grow fertile and the people prosper, he believes his story to be a celebration.

But neither history's purely material achievement, nor Cather's aesthetic conquest of childhood material, can rightfully give Jim Burden personal cause to celebrate. Retrospection, a superbly creative act for Cather, becomes for Jim a negative gesture. His recapitulation of the past seems to me a final surrender to sexual fears. He was afraid of growing up, afraid of women, afraid of the nexus of love and death. He could love only that which time had made safe and irrefragable—his memories. They revolve not, as he says, about the image of Ántonia, but about himself as a child. When he finds love, it seems to him the safest kind—the narcissistic love of the man for himself as a boy. Such love is not unique to Jim Burden. It obsesses many Cather protagonists from early novels to late: from Bartley Alexander in *Alexander's Bridge* to Godfrey St. Peter in *The Professor's House*. Narcissism focuses Cather's vision of life. She valued above all the inviolability of the self. Romantically, she saw in the child the original and real self; and in her novels she created adult characters who sought a seemingly impossible reunion with this authentic being—who were willing to die if only they could reach somehow back to childhood. Regression becomes thus an equivocal moral victory in which the self defies change and establishes its immutability. But regression is also a sign of defeat. *My Ántonia*, superficially so simple and clear a novel, resonates to themes of ultimate importance—the theme of identity, of its relationship to time, and of its contest with death. All these are subsumed in the more immediate issue of physical love. Reinterpreted along these lines, *My Ántonia* emerges as a brilliantly tortuous novel, its statements working contrapuntally against its meanings, its apparently random vignettes falling together to form a pattern of sexual aversion into which each detail fits—even the reaping-hook of Jim's dream:

> One dream I dreamed a great many times, and it was always the same. I was in a harvest-field full of shocks, and I was lying against one of them. Lena Lingard came across the stubble barefoot, in a short skirt, with a curved reaping-hook in her hand, and she was flushed like the dawn, with a kind of luminous rosiness all about her. She sat down beside me, turned to me with a soft sigh and said, "Now they are all gone, and I can kiss you as much as I like." (p. 147)

In Jim's dream of Lena, desire and fear clearly contend with one another. With the dreamer's infallibility, Jim contains his ambivalence in a surreal image of Aurora and the Grim Reaper as one. This collaged figure of Lena advances against an ordinary but ominous landscape. Background and forefigure first contrast and then coalesce in meaning. Lena's voluptuous aspects—her luminous glow of sexual arousal, her flesh bared by a short skirt, her soft sighs and kisses—are displayed against shocks and stubbles, a barren field when the reaping-hook has done its work. This landscape of harvest and desolation is not unfamiliar; nor is the apparitional woman who moves across it, sighing and making soft moan; nor the supine young man whom she kisses and transports. It is the archetypal landscape of ballad, myth, and drama, setting for *la belle dame sans merci* who enchants and satisfies, but then lulls and destroys. She comes, as Lena does, when the male is alone and unguarded. "Now they are all gone," Lena whispers, meaning Ántonia, his threshold guardian. Keeping parental watch, Ántonia limits Jim's boundaries ("You know you ain't right to kiss me like that") and attempts to bar him from the dark unexplored country beyond boyhood with threats ("If I see you hanging around with Lena much, I'll go tell your grandmother"). Jim has the insight to reply, "You'll always treat me like a kid"; but his dream of past childhood games with Ántonia suggests that the prospect of perpetual play attracts him, offering release from anxiety. Already in search of safety, he looks to childhood, for adolescence confronts him with the possibility of danger in women. Characteristically, his statement that he will prove himself unafraid belies the drift of his unconscious feelings. His dream of Lena and the reaping-hook depicts his ambivalence toward the cycle of growth, maturation, and death. The wheat ripens to be cut; maturity invites death.

Though Jim has declared his dream "always the same," it changes significantly. When it recurs in Lincoln, where he goes as a university student, it has been censored and condensed, and transmuted from reverie to remembrance:

> As I sat down to my book at last, my old dream about Lena coming across the harvest-field in her short skirt seemed to me like the memory of an actual experience. It floated before me on the page like a picture, and underneath it stood the mournful line: "*Optima dies . . . prima fugit.*" (p. 175)

Now his memory can deal with fantasy as with experience: convert it to an image, frame it, and restore it to him retouched and redeemed. Revised, the dream loses its frightening details. Memory retains the harvest-field but represses the shocks and stubbles; keeps Lena in her short skirt, but replaces the sexual ambience of the vision. Originally inspired by the insinuative "hired girls," the dream recurs under the tranquilizing spell of Gaston Cleric, Jim's poetry teacher. As his name implies, Cleric's function is to guide Jim to renunciation of Lena, to offer instead the example of desire sublimated to art. Voluptuous excitement yields to pensive mood, and poetry rather than passion engages Jim:

"It came over me, as it had never done before, the relation between girls like those [Lena and "the hired girls"] and the poetry of Virgil. If there were no girls like them in the world, there would be no poetry" (p. 175). In his study, among his books, Lena's image floats before him on a page of the *Georgics*, transferred from a landscape of death to Virgil's bucolic countryside; and it arouses not sensual desire but a safer and more characteristic mood: nostalgia—"melancholy reflection" upon the past. The reaping-hook is forgotten. Lena changes from the rosy goddess of dawn to an apparition of evening, of the dimly lit study and the darkened theater, where she glows with "lamplight" rather than sexual luminosity.

This preliminary sublimation makes it possible for Jim to have an affair with Lena. It is brief and peculiar, somehow appropriating from the theaters they frequent an unreal quality, the aspect of play. In contrast to the tragic stage-lovers who feel exquisitely, intone passionately, and love enduringly, they seem mere unengaged children, thrilled by make-believe people more than each other. "It all wrung my heart"; "there wasn't a nerve left in my body that hadn't been twisted"—Jim's histrionic (and rather feminine) outbursts pertain not to Lena but to *Marguerite Gauthier* as impersonated by "an infirm old actress." Camille's "dazzling loveliness," her gaiety and glitter—though illusory—impassion him far more than the real woman's sensuality. With Lena, he creates a mock-drama, casting himself in the stock role of callow lover pitted against Lena's older suitors. In this innocuous triangle, he "drifts" and "plays"—and play, like struggle, emerges as his memoirs' motif. Far from being random, his play is directed toward the avoidance of future responsibilites. He tests the role of lover in the security of a make-believe world where his mistress is gentle and undemanding, his adversaries ineffectual, and his guardian spirit, Cleric, supportive. Cleric wants him to stop "playing with this handsome Norwegian," and so he does, leaving Lena forever and without regret. Though the separation of the stage-lovers Armand and Camille wracks them—"Lena wept unceasingly"— their own parting is vapid. Jim leaves to follow Cleric to Boston, there to study, and pursue a career. His period of enchantment has not proved one of permanent thrall and does not leave him, like Keats's knight, haggard and woebegone.

Nevertheless, the interim in Lincoln has serious consequences, for Jim's trial run into manhood remains abortive. He has not been able to bypass his circular "road of Destiny," that "predetermined" route which carries him back finally to Ántonia and childhood. With Lena, Jim seems divertible, at a crossroad. His alternatives are defined in two symbolic titles symbolically apposed: "Lena Lingard" and "Cuzak's Boys." Lena, the archetypal Woman, beckons him to full sexuality. Ántonia, the eternal Mother, lures him back through her children, Cuzak's boys, to perennial childhood.

If Jim cannot avoid his destiny, neither can he escape the "tyrannical" social code of his small town, Black Hawk, which permits its young men to play with "hired girls" but not to marry them. The pusillanimous "clerks and bookkeepers" of Black Hawk dance with the country girls, follow them forlornly, kiss them behind bushes—and run. "Respect for respectability" shunts them into loveless marriages with women of money or "refinement" who are sexless and safe. "Physically a race apart," the country girls are charged with sensuality, some of them considered "dangerous as high explosives." Through an empty conformist marriage, Jim avoids danger. He takes a woman who is independent and masculine, like Ántonia, who cannot threaten him as Lena does by her sheer femininity. Though Lena may be "the most beautiful, the most *innocently* sensuous of all women in Willa Cather's works,"⁹ Jim is locked into his fantasy of the reaping-hook.

Jim's glorification of Lena as the timeless muse of poetry and the unattainable heroine of romance requires a closer look. For while he seems to exalt her, typically, he works at cross-purposes to demean her—in his own involuted way. He sets her etherealized image afloat on pages of poetry that deal with the breeding of cattle (his memoirs quote only the last line here):

> So, while the herd rejoices in its youth
> Release the males and breed the cattle early,
> Supply one generation from another.
> For mortal kind, the best day passes first.
> (*Georgics*, Book III)

As usual, Jim remembers selectively—only the last phrase, the novel's epigraph—while he deletes what must have seemed devastating counsel: "Release the males." Moreover, the *Georgics* has only factitious relevance to Lena (though I might point out that it undoubtedly inspired Cather by suggesting the use of regional material and the seasonal patterning of Book I of *My Ántonia*). If anything, the allusion is downright inappropriate, for Virgil's poem extols pastoral life, but Lena, tired of drudgery, wants to get away from the farm. Interested in fashion and sensuous pleasure, settling finally in San Francisco, she is not really the muse for Virgil.

Jim's allusion does have a subtle strategic value: by relegating Lena to the ideal but unreachable world of art, it assures their separation. Mismatched lovers because of social class, they remain irreconcilable as dream and reality. A real person, Jim must stop drifting and study; he can leave the woman while possessing Lena the dream in remembered reverie. Though motivated by fear and expediency (as much as Sylvester Lovett, Lena's fearful suitor in Black Hawk), he romanticizes his actions, eluding the possibility of painful self-confrontation. He veils his escape by identifying secretly with the hero Armand Duval, also a mismatched lover, blameless, whose fervid affair was doomed from the first. But as a lover, Jim belongs as much to comedy as to melodrama. His affair fits perfectly within the conventions of the comedy of manners: the sitting-room, Lena's "stiff little parlour"; the serving of tea; the idle talk of clothes and fashion; the nuisance pet dog Prince; the minor crises when the fatuous elder lovers intrude—the triviality. Engaged with Lena in this playacting, Jim has much at stake—nothing less than his sexuality. Through the more serious drama of a first affair, he creates his existential self: an adult male who fears a sexual woman. Through his trivial small-town comedy of manners, he keeps from introspection. He is drifting but busy, too much preoccupied with dinner parties and theater dates to catch the meaning of his drift. His mock romance recalls the words he had used years earlier to describe a childhood "mock adventure": "the game was fixed." The odds are against his growing up, and the two mock episodes fall together as *pseudo*-initiations which fail to make him a man.

Jim's mock adventure occurs years back as he and Ántonia explore a series of interconnected burrows in prairie-dog-town. Crouched with his back to Ántonia, he hears her unintelligible screams in a foreign tongue. He whirls to discover a huge rattler coiling and erecting to spring. "Of disgusting vitality," the snake induces fear and nausea: "His abomin-able muscularity, his loathsome, fluid motion, somehow made me sick" (p. 32). Jim strikes violently and with revulsion, recognizing even then an irrational hatred stronger than the impulse for protection. The epi-sode—typically ignored or misunderstood—combines elements of myth and dream. As a dragon-slaying, it conforms to the monomyth of initiation. It has a characteristic "call to adventure" (Ántonia's impulsive sugges-tion); a magic weapon (Peter's spade); a descent into a land of unearthly creatures (prairie-dog-town); the perilous battle (killing the snake); the protective tutelary spirit (Ántonia); and the passage through the rites to manhood ("You now a big mans"). As a test of courage, Jim's ordeal seems authentic, and critical opinion declares it so: "Jim Burden dis-covers his own hidden courage and becomes a man in the snake-killing incident."[10] But even Jim realizes that his initiation, like his romance later, is specious, and his accolade unearned: "it was a mock adventure; the game . . . fixed . . . by chance, as . . . for many a dragon-slayer."

As Jim accepts Ántonia's praise, his tone becomes wry and ironic, communicating a unique awareness of the duplicity in which he is in-volved. Ántonia's effect upon Jim seems to me here invidious because her admiration of his manhood helps undermine it. Pronouncing him a man, she keeps him a boy. False to her role as tutelary spirit, she betrays him from first to last. She leads him into danger, fails to warn him properly, and finally, by validating the contest, closes off the road to authentic initiation and maturity.

Jim's exploration "below the surface" of prairie-dog-town strikes me as a significant mimetic act, a burrowing into his unconscious. Who is he "below the surface"? In which direction do his buried impulses lead? He acts out his quest for self-knowledge symbolically: if he could dig deep enough he would find a way through this labyrinth and learn the course of its hidden channels—whether "they ran straight down, or were horizontal . . . whether they had underground connections." Projecting upon the physical scene his adolescent concern with self, he speaks an analytic and rational language—but the experience turns into nightmare. Archetypal symbol of "the ancient, eldest Evil," the snake forces him to confront deeply repressed images, to acknowledge for the only time the effect of "horrible unconscious memories."

The sexual connotations of the snake incident are implicit. Later in Black Hawk they become overt through another misadventure—Wick Cutter's attempted rape of Jim, whom he mistakes for Ántonia. This time the sexual attack is literal. Wick Cutter, an old lecher, returns in the middle of the night to assault Ántonia, but meanwhile, persuaded by Ántonia's suspicions, Jim has taken her place in bed. He becomes an innocent victim of Cutter's lust and fury at deception. Threatened by unleashed male sex—the ultimate threat—he fights with primordial violence, though again sickened with disgust. Vile as the Cutter incident is—and it is also highly farcical—Jim's nausea seems an overreaction, intensified by his shrill rhetoric and unmodulated tone. Unlike the snake episode, this encounter offers no rewards. It simply reduces him to "a battered object," his body pommeled, his face swollen. His only recognition will be the laughter of the lubricious "old men at the drugstore." Again Ántonia has lured him into danger and exposed him to assault. Again he is furious: "I felt that I never wanted to see her again. I hated her almost as much as I hated Cutter. She had let me in for all this disgustingness" (p. 162). Through Wick Cutter, the sexual urge seems depraved, and more damning, ludicrous. No male in the novel rescues sex from indignity or gives it even the interest of sheer malevolence (as, for example, Ivy Peters does in *A Lost Lady*).

Also unexempt from the dangers of sex, Ántonia is seduced, exploited, and left with an illegitimate child. When finally she marries, she takes not a lover but a friend. To his relief, Jim finds husband and wife "on terms of easy friendliness, touched with humour" (p. 231). Marriage as an extension of friendship is Cather's recurrent formula, defined clearly, if idiosyncratically, by Alexandra in *O Pioneers!*: "I think when friends marry, they are safe." Turning words to action, Alexandra marries her childhood friend, as does Cecile in *Shadows on the Rock*—an older man whose passion has been expended on another woman. At best, marriage has dubious value in Cather's fiction. It succeeds when it seems least like marriage, when it remains sexless, or when sex is only instrumental to procreation. Jim accepts Ántonia's marriage for its "special mission" to bring forth children.

Why doesn't he take on this mission? He celebrates the myth of creation but fails to participate. The question has been raised bluntly by critics (though left unanswered): "Why had not Jim and Ántonia loved and married?"[11] When Ántonia, abandoned by Donovan, needs Jim most, he passionately avers, "You really are a part of me": "I'd have liked to have you for a sweetheart, or a wife, or my mother or my sister—anything that a woman can be to a man" (p. 208). Thereupon he leaves—not to return for twenty years. His failure to seize the palpable moment seems to one critic responsible for the emotional vacuum of Jim's life: "At the very center of his relation with Ántonia there is an emptiness where the strongest emotion might have been expected to gather."[12] But love for a woman is not Jim's "strongest emotion," cannot mitigate fear, nostalgia, or even simple snobbery. Nothing in Jim's past prepares him for love or marriage, and he remains in effect a pseudobachelor (just as he is a pseudolover), free to design a future with Ántonia's family that excludes his wife. In his childhood, his models for manhood are simple regressive characters, all bachelors, or patently unhappy married men struggling, like Mr. Shimerda, Chris Lingard, and Ole the Swede, for and against their families. Later in Black Hawk, the family men seem merely vapid, and prophetically suburban, pushing baby-carriages, sprinkling lawns, paying bills, and driving about on Sundays (p. 105). Mr. Harling, Ántonia's employer in Black Hawk, seems different; yet he only further confuses Jim's already confused sense of sexual roles, for he indulges his son while he treats his daughter as a man, his business partner. With Ántonia, his "hired girl," Mr. Harling is repressive, a kind of superego, objecting to her adolescent contacts with men—the dances at Vannis's tent, the evening walks, the kisses and scuffles on the back porch. "I want to have my fling, like the other girls," Ántonia argues, but Harling in- sists she quit the dances or his house. Ántonia leaves, goes to the no- torious Cutter, and then to the seductive arms of Larry Donovan—with consequences that are highly instructive to Jim, that can only reinforce his inchoate fears. Either repression of sex or disaster: Jim sees these alternatives polarized in Black Hawk, and between them he cannot re- solve his ambivalence. Though he would like Ántonia to become a woman, he wants her also to remain asexual.

By switching her sexual roles, Ántonia only adds to his confusion. As "hired girl" in Black Hawk and later as Cuzak's wife, she cooks, bakes, sews, and rears children. Intermittently, she shows off her strength and endurance in the fields, competing with men. Even her name changes gender—no adventitious matter, I believe; it has its masculine variant, Tony, as Willa Cather had hers, Willie. Cather's prototype for Ántonia, Annie Pavelka, was a simple Bohemian girl; though their experiences are similar, Ántonia Shimerda is Cather's creation—an ultimately strange bi- sexual. She shares Cather's pride in masculinity and projects both her and Jim's ambivalent sexual attitudes. Cather recalled that "much of what I knew about Annie came from the talks I had with young men.

She had a fascination for them."[13] In the novel, however, Lena fascinates men while Ántonia toils alongside them. "I can work like mans now," she announces when she is only fifteen. In the fields, says Jim, "she kept her sleeves rolled up all day, and her arms and throat were burned as brown as a sailor's. Her neck came up strongly out of her shoulders, like the bole of a tree out of the turf. One sees that draught-horse neck among the peasant women in all old countries" (p. 80). Sailor, tree, draught-horse, peasant—hardly seductive comparisons, hardly conducive to fascination. Ántonia's illegitimate pregnancy brutalizes her even more than heavy farmwork. Her punishment for sexual involvement—and for the breezy pleasures of courtship—is thoroughgoing masculinization. Wearing "a man's long overcoat and boots, and a man's felt hat," she does "the work of a man on the farm," plows, herds cattle. Years later, as Cuzak's wife, her "inner glow" must compensate for the loss of her youthful beauty, the loss, even, of her teeth. Jim describes her finally as "a stalwart, brown woman, flat-chested, her curly brown hair a little grizzled"—his every word denuding her of sensual appeal.

This is not to deny that at one time Jim found Ántonia physically desirable. He hints that in Black Hawk he had kissed her in a more than friendly way—and had been rebuffed. But he is hardly heartbroken at their impasse, for his real and enduring love for her is based not on desire but on nostalgia. Childhood memories bind him more profoundly than passion, especially memories of Mr. Shimerda. In their picnic re-union before Jim departs for Lincoln, Ántonia recounts her father's story of transgression, exile, and death. Her miniature tale devolves upon the essential theme of destructive sex. As a young man, her father succumbs to desire for the family's servant girl, makes her pregnant, marries her against his parents' wishes, and becomes thereby an outcast. His death on the distant prairie traces back to an initial sexual act which triggers inexorable consequences. It strips him of all he values: his happy irre-sponsible bachelor life with the trombone-player he "loves"; his family home in beautiful Bohemia; his vocation as violinist when he takes to homesteading in Nebraska; and his joy in life itself. For a while, a few desultory pleasures could rouse him from apathy and despair. But in the end, he finds the pattern of his adult life, as many Cather characters do, unbearable, and he longs for escape. Though Ántonia implies that her poppa's mistake was to marry, especially outside his social class (as Jim is too prudent to do), the marriage comes about through his initial sexual involvement. Once Mr. Shimerda acts upon sexual impulse, he is com-mitted to a woman who alienates him from himself; and it is loss of self, rather than the surmountable hardships of pioneer life, which induces his despair. Suicide is his final capitulation to destructive forces he could have escaped only by first abnegating sex.

Though this interpretation may sound extreme—that the real danger to man is woman, that his protection lies in avoiding or eliminating her—

it seems to me the essence of the most macabre and otherwise unaccountable episode in *My Ántonia*. I refer to that grisly acting out of male aversion, the flashback of Russian Pavel feeding the bride to the wolves. I cannot imagine a more graphic representation of underlying sentiments than we find here. Like most of the episodes in Jim's memoirs, this begins innocently, with the young bride drawing Peter, Pavel, and other guests to a nearby village for her wedding. But the happy evening culminates in horror; for the wolves are bad that year, starving, and when the guests head for home they find themselves rapidly pursued through a landscape of terror. Events take on the surreality of nightmare as black droves run like streaks of shadows after the panicking horses, as sledges overturn in the snow, and mauled and dying wedding guests shriek. Fast as Pavel drives his team, it cannot outrun the relentless "black ground-shadows," images of death. Pavel's murderous strategy to save himself and Peter is almost too inhuman to imagine: to allay the wolves and lighten his load, he wrests the bride from the struggling groom, and throws her, living bait, to the wolves. Only then does his sledge arrive in safety at his village. The tale holds the paradigm for Mr. Shimerda's fate—driven from home because of a woman, struggling for survival against a brutal winter landscape, pursued by regret and despair to death. The great narrative distance at which this episode is kept from Jim seems to me to signify its explosiveness, the need to handle with care. It is told to Jim by Ántonia, who overhears Peter telling it to Mr. Shimerda. Though the vignette emerges from this distance—and through Jim's obscuring nostalgia—its gruesome meaning focuses the apparently disjunct parts of the novel, and I find it inconceivable that critics consider it "irrelevant."[14] The art of *My Ántonia* lies in the subtle and inevitable relevance of its details, even the most trivial, like the picture Jim chooses to decorate a Christmas book for Ántonia's little sister: "I took 'Napoleon Announcing the Divorce to Josephine' for my frontispiece" (p. 55). In one way or another, the woman must *go*.

To say that Jim Burden expresses castration fears would provide a facile conclusion: and indeed his memoirs multiply images of sharp instruments and painful cutting. The curved reaping-hook in Lena Lingard's hands centralizes an overall pattern that includes Peter's clasp-knife with which he cuts all his melons; Crazy Mary's corn-knife (she "made us feel how sharp her blade was, showing us very graphically just what she meant to do to Lena"); the suicidal tramp "cut to pieces" in the threshing machine; and wicked Wick *Cutt*er's sexual assault. When Lena, the essence of sex, appears suddenly in Black Hawk, she seems to precipitate a series of violent recollections. First Jim remembers Crazy Mary's pursuit of Lena with her sharpened corn-knife. Then Ántonia recalls the story of the crazy tramp in details which seem to me unconsciously reverberating Jim's dream. Like Jim, Ántonia is relaxed and leaning against a strawstack; similarly, she sees a figure approach "across the stubble"—significantly, his first words portend death. Offering to "cut bands," within minutes he throws himself into the threshing machine and is "cut to pieces." In his pockets the threshers find only "an old penknife" and the "wish-bone of a chicken." Jim follows this anecdote with a vignette of Blind d'Arnault, a black musician who, as we shall see, represents emasculation; Jim tells how children used to tease the little blind boy and try "to get his chicken-bone away." Such details, I think, should not be considered fortuitous or irrelevant; and critics who have persisted in overlooking them should note that they are stubbornly there, and in patterned sequence.

I do not wish to make a case history of Jim Burden or a psychological document of *My Ántonia*, but to uncover an elusive underlying theme—one that informs the fragmentary parts of the novel and illuminates the obsession controlling Cather's art. For like most novelists, Cather writes out of an obsessive concern to which her art gives various and varied expression. In *My Ántonia*, her consummate work, that obsession has its most private as well as its most widely shared meanings. At the same time that the novel is highly autobiographical, it is representatively American in its material, mood, and unconscious uses of the past. In it, as in other novels, we can discover that Cather's obsession had to do with the assertion of self. This is the preoccupation of her protagonists who in their various ways seek to assert their identity, in defiance, if necessary, of others, of convention, of nature, of life itself. Biographers imply that Cather's life represented a consistent pursuit of autonomy, essential, she believed, to her survival as an artist. Undoubtedly, she was right; had she given herself to marriage and children, assuming she could, she might have sacrificed her chance to write. Clearly, she identified writing with masculinity, though which of the two constituted her fundamental drive is a matter of psychological dynamics we can never really decide. Like Ántonia, she displayed strong masculine traits, though she loved also feminine frilleries and the art of cuisine. All accounts of her refer to her "masculine personality"—her mannish dress, her deep voice, her energetic stride; and even as a child she affected boyish clothes and cropped hair. Too numerous to document, such references are a running motif throughout the accounts of Mildred Bennett, Elizabeth Sergeant, and E. K. Brown. Their significance is complex and perhaps inescapable, but whatever else they mean, they surely demonstrate Cather's self-assertion: she would create her own role in life, and if being a woman meant sacrificing her art, then she would lead a private and inviolate life in defiance of convention.

Her image of inviolability was the *child*. She sought quaintly, perhaps foolishly, to refract this image through her person when she wore a schoolgirl costume. The Steichen photograph of her in middy blouse is a familiar frontispiece to volumes of her work; and she has been described as characteristically "at the typewriter, dressed in a childlike costume, a middy blouse with navy bands and tie and a duck skirt."[15] In life, she tried to hold on to childhood through dress; in art, through a recurrent cycle of childhood, maturity, and childhood again: the return effected usually through memory. Sometimes the regressive pattern signalized a longing for death, as in *The Professor's House* and *Death Comes for the Archbishop*; always it revealed a quest for reunion with an original authentic self. In *My Ántonia*, the prologue introduces Ántonia and the motif of childhood simultaneously, for her name is linked with "*the country, the conditions, the whole adventure of . . . childhood*." The memoirs proper open with the children's journey into pristine country where men are childlike or project into life characters of the child's imagination: like Jake who "might have stepped out of the pages of 'Jesse James.'" The years of maturity comprise merely an interim period— and in fact, are hardly dealt with. For Jim, as for Cather, the real meaning of time is cyclical, its purpose to effect a return to the beginning. Once Jim finds again "the first road" he traveled as a wondering child, his story ends. Hardly discernible, this road returns him to Ántonia, and through her, to his real goal, the enduring though elusive image of his original self which Cather represents by his childhood shadow. Walking to Ántonia's house with her boys—feeling himself almost a boy again— Jim merges with his shadow, the visible elongation of self. At last, his narcissistic dream comes to fulfillment: "It seemed, after all, so natural to be walking along a barbed-wire fence beside the sunset, toward a red pond, and to see my shadow moving along at my right, over the close-cropped grass" (p. 224). Just as the magnified shadow of plow against sky—a blazing key image—projects his romantic notion of the West, so "two long shadows [that] flitted before or followed after" symbolize his ideal of perennial children running through, imaged against, and made one with the prairie grass.

Jim's return "home" has him planning a future with Cuzak's boys that will recapitulate the past: once more he will sleep in haylofts, hunt "up the Niobrara," and travel the "Bad Lands." Play reenters as his serious concern, not the sexual play of imminent manhood, but regressive child's play. In a remarkable statement, Jim says: "There were enough Cuzaks to play with for a long while yet. Even after the boys grew up, there would always be Cuzak himself!" (p. 239). A current article on *My Ántonia* misreads this conclusion: "[though] Jim feels like a boy again . . . he does not *wish* that he were a boy again. . . . He has no more need to cling to the past, for the past has been transfigured like the autumn prairie of old."[16] Such reasoning falls in naively with Jim's self-deception, that the transformation of the land to country somehow validates his personal life. Jim's need to reenter childhood never relents, becomes even more urgent as he feels adult life vacuous. The years have not enriched him, except with a wealth of memories—"images in the mind that did not fade—that grew stronger with time." Most precious in his treasury of remembered images is that of a boy of ten crossing the prairie under "the complete dome of heaven" and finding sublimity in the union of self with earth and sky. An unforgettable consummation, never matched by physical union, he seeks to recreate it through memory. Jim's ineffable desire for a child more alive to him than his immediate being vibrates to a pathetic sense of loss. I believe that we may find this irretrievable boy in a photograph of young *Willie Cather*, another child who took life from imagination and desire.[17]

In a later novel, *The Professor's House*,[18] Cather rationalizes her cathexis on childhood through the protagonist's musings, at which we might glance briefly. Toward the end of his life, Professor Godfrey St. Peter discovers he has two identities: that of his "original" self, the child; and of his "secondary" self, the man in love. To fulfill himself, "the lover" creates a meretricious "design" of marriage, children, and career, now, after thirty years, suddenly meaningless. The Professor's cyclic return to his real and original self begins with solitary retrospection. All he wants is to "be alone"—to repossess himself. For, having yielded through love to another, he has lost "the person he was in the beginning." Now before he dies, he longs for his original image as a child, an image that returns to him in moments of "vivid consciousness" or of remembrance. Looking back, the Professor sees the only escape from a false secondary life to be through premature death: death of the sexual man before he realizes his sexuality and becomes involved in the relationships it demands. This is the happy fate of his student Tom Outland, who dies young, remaining inviolate, pure, and most important, self-possessed: "He seemed to know . . . he was solitary and must always be so; he had never married, never been a father. He was earth, and would return to earth" (p. 263).

This Romantic mystique of childhood illuminates the fear of sex in Cather's world. Sex unites one with another. Its ultimate threat is loss of self. In Cather's construct, naively and of course falsely, the child is asexual, his love inverted, his identity thus intact. Only Ántonia manages to grow older and retain her original integrity. Like Tom Outland, her affinity is for the earth. She "belongs" to the farm, is one with the trees, the flowers, the rye and wheat she plants. Though she marries, Cuzak is only "the instrument of Ántonia's special mission." Through him she finds a self-fulfillment that excludes him. Through her, Jim hopes to be restored to himself.

The supreme value Jim and other Cather characters attribute to "old friendships" reflects a concern with self. Old friends know the child immanent in the man. Only they can have communion without causing self-estrangement, can marry "safely." They share "the precious, the incommunicable past"—as Jim says in his famous final words. But to keep the past so precious, they must romanticize it; and to validate childhood, they must let memory filter its experiences through the screen of nostalgia. Critics have wondered whether Jim Burden is finally the most suitable narrator for *My Ántonia*. I submit that Cather's choice is utterly strategic. For Jim, better than any other character, could control his memories, since only he knows of but does not experience the suffering and violence inherent in his story. And ultimately, he is not dealing with a story as such, but with residual "images in the mind." *My Ántonia* is a magnificent and warped testimony to the mind's image-making power, an implicit commentary on how that creative power serves the mind's need to ignore and deny whatever is reprehensible in whatever one loves. Cather's friend and biographer said of her, "There was so much she did not want to see and saw not."[19] We must say the same of Jim Burden, who held painful and violent aspects of early American life at safe distance, where finally he could not see them.

Jim's vignette of Blind d'Arnault, the black piano player who entertains at Black Hawk, is paradigmatic of his way of viewing the past. Its factual scaffolding (whether Cather's prototype was Blind Boone, Blind Tom, or a "composite of Negro musicians") seems to me less important than its tone. I find the vignette a work of unconscious irony as Jim paints d'Arnault's portrait but meanwhile delineates himself. The motif of blindness compounds the irony. D'Arnault's is physical, as though it is merely futile for him to see a world he cannot enter. Jim's is moral: an unawareness of his stereotyped, condescending, and ultimately invidious vision. Here, in his description of the black man, son of a slave, Jim's emblematic significance emerges as shamefully he speaks for himself, for Cather, and for most of us:

> [His voice] was the soft, amiable Negro voice, like those I remembered from early childhood, with the note of docile subservience in it. He had the Negro head, too; almost no head at all, nothing behind the ears but the folds of neck under close-cropped wool. He would have been repulsive if his face had not been so kindly and happy. It was the happiest face I had seen since I left Virginia. (p. 122)

Soft, amiable, docile, subservient, kindly, happy—Jim's image, as usual, projects his wish-fulfillment; his diction suggests an unconscious assuagement of anxiety, also. His phrase of astounding insult and innocence—"almost no head at all"—assures him that the black man should not frighten, being an incomplete creature, possessed, as we would like to believe, of instinct and rhythm, but deprived of intellect. Jim's final hyperbole registers his fear of this alien black face saved from repulsiveness only by a toothy servile smile (it might someday lose). To attenuate his portrait of d'Arnault, Jim introduced innuendoes of sexual incompetence. He recognizes d'Arnault's sensuality but impugns it by his image of sublimation: "all the agreeable sensations possible to creatures of flesh and blood were heaped up on those black-and-white keys, and he [was] gloating over them and trickling them through his yellow fingers"

(p. 126). Jim's genteel opening phrase connotes male sexuality, which he must sublimate, displace from the man to the music, reduce to a *trickle*. D'Arnault "looks like some glistening African god of pleasure, full of strong, savage blood"; but superimposed is our familiar Uncle Tom "all grinning," "bowing to everyone, docile and happy."

Similarly, consider Jim's entrancing image of the four Danish girls who stand all day in the laundry ironing the townspeople's clothes. How charming they are: flushed and happy; how fatherly the laundryman offering water—no swollen ankles; no boredom or rancor; no exploitation: a cameo image from "the beautiful past." Peter and Pavel, dreadful to any ordinary mind for their murderous deed, ostracized by everyone, now disease-ridden and mindless, are to Jim picturesque outcasts: Pavel spitting blood; Peter spitting seeds as he desperately eats all his melons after kissing his cow goodbye, the only creature for him to love. And Mr. Shimerda's suicide. Jim reconciles himself to the horror of the mutilated body frozen in its own blood by imagining the spirit released and homeward bound to its beloved Bohemia. Only the evocative beauty of Cather's language—and the inevitable validation as childhood memory—can romanticize this sordid death and the squalor in which it takes place. Violence is as much the essence of prairie life as the growth of the wheat and blossoming of the corn. Violence appears suddenly and inexplicably, like the suicidal tramp. But Jim gives violence a cameo quality. He has the insistent need—and the strategy—to turn away from the very material he presents. He can forget the reaping-hook and reshape his dream. And as the novel reveals him doing this, it reveals our common usage of the past as a romance and refuge from the present. *My Ántonia* engraves a view of the past which is at best partial; at worst, blind. But our present is continuous with the whole past, as it was, despite Jim Burden's attempt to deny this, and despite Cather's "sad little refrain": "Our present is ruined—but we had a beautiful past."[20] Beautiful to one who recreated it so; who desperately needed it so; who would deny the violence and the destructive attitudes toward race and sex immortalized in his very denial. We, however, have as desperate a need for clarity of vision as Jim had for nostalgia; and we must begin to look at *My Ántonia*, long considered a representatively American novel, not only for its beauty of art and for its affirmation of history, but also, and instructively, for its negations and evasions. Much as we would like to ignore them, for they bring painful confrontations, we must see what they would show us about ourselves—how we betray our past when we forget its most disquieting realities; how we begin to redeem it when we remember.

Notes

1. Terence Martin, "The Drama of Memory in *My Ántonia*," *PMLA*, LXXXIV (March, 1969), 304–11.

2. John H. Randall, III, *The Landscape and the Looking Glass: Willa Cather's Search for Value* (Boston, 1960), p. 149. See Cather's remark, "The best thing I've ever done is *My Ántonia*. I feel I've made a contribution to American letters with that book," in Mildred Bennett, *The World of Willa Cather* (1951; reprinted, Lincoln, Neb., 1961), p. 203.

3. Bennett, p. 212. Cather is quoted as saying, "If you gave me a thousand dollars for every structural fault in *My Ántonia* you'd make me very rich."

4. David Daiches, *Willa Cather: A Critical Interpretation* (Ithaca, N.Y., 1951), pp. 43–61.

5. 1913; reprinted, Boston, 1941, p. 259. When Emil finally approaches Marie to make love, she seems asleep, then whispers, "I was dreaming this . . . don't take my dream away!" The mergence of the real lover into the dream reminds me here of Keats's *The Eve of St. Agnes*—"Into her dream he melted." Here, too, the realization of love means facing the cold wintery world from which Madeline had been protected by her castle and her fantasy.

6. 1918; reprinted, Boston, 1946, p. 2. All italics in quotations from *My Ántonia* are in the original, and all subsequent references are to this text. I use this edition not only because it is readily available but also because the introduction by Walter Havighurst and the suggestions for reading and discussion by Bertha Handlan represent clearly the way the novel has been widely used as validating the American past.

7. James E. Miller, "*My Ántonia*: A Frontier Drama of Time," *American Quarterly*, X (Winter, 1958), 481.

8. See Bennett, p. 148. Cather is quoted as saying, "The world broke in two about 1920, and I belonged to the former half." The year 1922, is given in her preface (later deleted) to *Not under Forty* (renamed *Literary Encounters*, 1937).

9. E. K. Brown and Leon Edel, *Willa Cather: A Critical Biography* (New York, 1953), p. 203. Italics mine.

10. Miller, p. 482.

11. Elizabeth Shepley Sergeant, *Willa Cather: A Memoir* (1953; reprinted, Lincoln, Nebr., 1963), p. 151.

12. Brown and Edel, p. 202.

13. Bennett, p. 47.

14. Daiches says, "It is a remarkable little inset story, but its relation to the novel as a whole is somewhat uncertain" (p. 46). However, Daiches finds so many episodes and details "uncertain," "dubious," "not wholly dominated," or "not fully integrated," it might be his reading is "flawed" rather than the novel.

15. Sergeant, p. 117.

16. Martin, p. 311.

17. See the "pictures from the Wm. Cather, M.D., period of Willa's life" in Bennett, especially the photograph of Cather as a child with "her first short haircut." Note Cather's vacillating taste in clothes from the clearly masculine to feminine. It is significant that in various plays at school and at the university, Cather assumed male roles—so convincingly that spectators sometimes refused to believe the actor was not a boy. See Bennett, pp. 175–76, 179.

18. 1925; reprinted, Boston, 1938.

19. Sergeant, p. 46.

20. Ibid., p. 121.

One of Ours

[**Review of *One of Ours***]   Dorothy Canfield Fisher*

One of the most beautiful passages in Miss Cather's writing is her description (in *The Song of the Lark*) of the noble upward flight of an eagle, soaring to the sky through a flock of swallows chirping and fluttering and never rising higher than the dark walls of a canyon.

It is a passage which recurs to one's mind on reading her latest novel. We have all heard the twittering chatter which has filled the stagnant air since the end of the war. And we have all been heartsick over the pettiness and wrongheadedness of so many of the "attacks on American civilization" based as most of them seem to be on petty grounds, on uneasy self-consciousness, or wounded vanity, or a naive untraveled illusion about what life is elsewhere than in America. To read Miss Cather's novel is to see an eagle soar up through all this pettiness, on broad sure wings, carrying us in spirit with her to the heights.

Both sides of the quarrel about the war have been furiously overstating their case. And the same is true of both sides of the quarrel about the value of our American Middle-Western life. It is hard to keep a level head in the midst of all the exaggerated unfairness which has marked those discussions. Miss Cather writes as though she had never heard of their dispute, considers the case on its merits, with the calm dispassionate intelligence of an able mind and a deeply sympathetic heart. Unlike many American intellectuals, she has not lost her sense of reality in the intellectual reaction just now in fashion against the sentimental savagery of some would-be patriots or patrioteers. Unlike nearly every one else nowadays who has occasion to mention the war, she has no fear of the bitter tongues of the disillusioned, makes no attempt, as nearly all knowing writers do, to disarm them by giving occasional knowing hints that she is quite as smartly modern and skeptic as they. She does not, as a matter of fact, give them a thought, nor consider in

*Originally published in the *New York Times Book Review*, 10 September 1922, p. 14. Copyright 1922 by the New York Times Company. Reprinted by permission.

the least what they will think of her. All her thoughts, all her great brain and heart are concentrated on the meaning of the human lives she depicts, on the wonder and pathos and delicacy and power and weakness and tragedy of human beings like Claude and his mother, and the old Mahailey.

It is an amazingly rich book, rich as no other living American could write, many-peopled, complicated as life itself is complicated, but composed with a harmony and unity which only art can have. All its rich complication of varying backgrounds (presented with a wonderful ability which almost passes unnoticed in the greatness of the book as a whole), all its characters, periods, events, have one unvarying purpose, to tell the story of Claude, Claude whom we know as we know one of our very own, for whom in his baffled fineness we feel the sore, indignant, loving, helpless sympathy we would have for a dear, much-loved younger brother caught in the same *impasse*.

This is the whole purpose of the novel, to make us see and feel and understand Claude and passionately long to open the doors to his living brothers all around us, imprisoned and baffled like Claude in a bare, neutral, machine-ridden world.

The part played by the war in Claude's life has nothing to do either with the defenders or opponents of the war. For Claude, as for hundreds of thousands of other fine-natured, idealistic, inarticulate American boys, the war came as a purpose high and great enough to satisfy their high and great souls. And Miss Cather has simply told the truth about it. The war tore Claude away, as nothing else in the world could have done, away from the world where he had been born but where he did not belong, and swept him off for one glimpse of the other unknown, guessed-at world for which his lonely life had been one long nostalgia. The book is no tragedy, although it ends with Claude's death on the battlefield. He died in the world he had longed to reach, and before he had time to learn the ugliness and malice and decay which tarnishes so much of the suave ripe harmony he saw about him at last.

Miss Cather has held the scales even with an honesty of which perhaps no other American writer is capable. She shows us Claude's rare personality starving, but she shows us also the plenty amid which he starved, rich plenty for other natures, not for his. Nowhere in any of her books has Miss Cather given us a more glowing portrayal of life on the fertile Western plains, of the very throb and pulse of life lived by the seasons and not by the clock. It is enough to make some full-blooded, adventurous French boy, shut up in the gray, rigid tradition of his caste, grow heartsick with envy to read. Miss Cather's triumph is to create so masterfully this vital, exuberant, sun-flooded, gloriously living scene, and at the same time to show a young soul finding nowhere in it the absorbing aim which is all that can reconcile a seeking nature like Claude's to the act of living. It is perhaps not without intention that Claude's ancestry is all New England. Those "Summer evenings when he used to sit dumb by the windmill, wondering what to do with his life," would not have been so bitterly empty to a nature with a larger share of sensuous, easygoing capacity for compromise. It is not enough for Claude to have money, and a fine car, and a pleasant home to live in, and good health and more money to be had for the making of it. He intensely desires to "do something with his life," something shapely and harmonious. His tragedy is that in all the prosperous, full-veined, material life about him, he finds no one who can set him on his way, not even his dear, dear mother, coming down from the beautiful, serene heights on which her soul lived, to agonize with Claude, terribly to long to help him, only to add one more fetter to his chains with the narrowness of her orthodox evangelical theories and prejudices. His exquisite mother's life was passed on another plane from Claude's, and, love him more than life, as she did, grope desperately to be one with him, she could never know what it was that Claude needed, what was the lack that drained his days dry of hope. The old Mahailey, miraculous in her scriptural simplicity of heart, was oftener nearer to comforting Claude than his mother; although never in any book that I ever read is the love of a son for his mother more poignantly, more deeply imagined and portrayed.

To present this noble and tragic theme Miss Cather has so lost her personality in that of her hero that again and again the reader thinks of the phenomena known as "reincarnations." How could anything short of a reincarnation enable a mature, sophisticated, traveled cosmopolitan like Miss Cather to sink herself so wholly in this simple-hearted, great-souled, untraveled, unfulfilled American farmer? One of the beauties of the book comes from this astonishing absorption in her theme; the entire lack of any merely clever or literary writing, the entire lack of any attempt to portray mere surfaces rather than what lies under them. The massive sincerity of her style makes the work of many of her able contemporaries seem like hard, bright, detailed photographs on high-gloss paper. And yet the book is full of the most enchanting detail, of secondary characters, drawn with the utmost racy zest and color. Sometimes this color is effortlessly and insidiously sardonic, as in the matter-of-fact description of the excellent cold supper which Claude's white-faced, cold-blooded horror of a wife leaves in the icebox as an all-sufficient substitute for what a wife should be to her husband. That meal reeks with Enid's rancid self-righteousness!

Sometimes these characterizations of Miss Cather's are quietly humorous and good-natured, like the presentation of Claude's stub-fingered, perfectly-satisfied-with-life brother Ralph, who on Sunday morning "rolled out of bed and callously put on his clean underwear without taking a bath. This cost him not one regret, though he took time to polish his new-ox-blood shoes tenderly with his pocket handkerchief." That one passage tells you all you need to know about Ralph. That *is* Ralph.

The portrait of Claude's father is one of Miss Cather's best, as substantially painted as a Rembrandt. She draws to the life the vital, mocking, conscienceless, tolerant, thick-skinned, able Yankee, Ralph's father, not Claude's.

Of course, every one who reads the novel will love most of all the portrait of Claude's mother. Like everything else in this wonderful book, she is given to the reader at first hand, without the slightest formal literary description. You see her as you see a living person dear to you, by her expression, not by her physical characteristics. At the moment of Claude's death Miss Cather speaks of the disappearance of the "look that was Claude." Throughout the book she gives you "the look" that is the soul of things.

I must draw back for lack of space from any attempt at a mention of the savory gusto with which the secondary characters are drawn. Especially in the second part, Claude's great adventure in France, the canvas is filled with personages as living, with their bright liquid eyes and their frank, human look into your face, as portraits by Hals.

It is evidently Miss Cather's intention to have them all overshadowed by the figure of David, the fine, cultivated, disciplined man-of-the-world and artist, who symbolizes to Claude all that he has missed in life and might have made his own. For me, personally, the figure of David is not one of the most complete successes in the book. Compared to Claude whom by that time I deeply respect and love as one of my own, he seems rather thin, hardly worthy of all Claude's wistful, overestimating admiration. It is a little like trying to imagine Lincoln wistful and admiring before a smoothed, tea-drinking, cosmopolitan John Hay. I admit, however, that I am swept away out of this grudging feeling toward David in the beautiful and poignant passage where David plays his violin for the last time, where the music reveals to poor Claude a Promised Land of Beauty from which, quite casually, through nobody's malice, and yet irretrievably, he has been shut out. The climax of the book is there, in that cry of suffering in which hurt vanity has no part. It is an almost disinterested, impersonal anguish which Claude suffers there, such as wrings our own hearts throughout the novel, at the sight of splendid youth cheated out of its share of the glory of life, at the sight of noble human stuff wasted and warped and thrown away.

The War Lover: Claude   Stanley Cooperman*

Despite her inability to deal with army and combat realities far removed from her own experience, Willa Cather in *One of Ours* created a study of erotic war motivation unequaled until John Hersey's *The War Lover* appeared in 1959. Less clinical than Hersey, far less sophisticated in the use of military and psychological science, Miss Cather intuits what the later writer deliberately describes. Indeed, her book, beneath its sentimentality and intrusive rhetoric, can be seen as a case history of a man for whom the idea of death is the only possible aphrodisiac.

The World War I novels as a group, certainly, must be understood in terms of the nineteenth-century environment from which the Great Crusade developed. This is especially true of *One of Ours*, a novel whose protagonist goes to war as to an assignation. The definition of Claude Wheeler as a man is to be found less in his martyrdom as a soldier than in the midwestern farm life, the feminist codes, and the sterile marriage which make war a personal rather than a political necessity for him. Still searching for his own virility, Claude finds it with a phantom: the goddess who walks not in beauty alone, but in blood. She, ultimately, is the only wife he can embrace. And all the political rhetoric, the ideology of the Crusade itself, becomes a veneer applied to a deeper and far more urgent need than any external cause. "The sound of the guns had from the first been pleasant to him, had given him a feeling of confidence and safety," Claude reflects a moment before sleeping when—at last—he is in the war:

> What they said was that men could still die for an idea.... Ideals were not archaic things, beautiful and impotent; they were the real sources of power among men.... He would give his own adventure for no man's. On the edge of sleep it seemed to glimmer, like the clear column of the fountain, like the new-moon—alluring, half-averted, the bright face of danger.[1]

Here is the definition of war "lover" indeed: stimulation by violence; dutiful application of "ideals" to sanction violence; and—when the rational edifice of consciousness is most relaxed—the translation of violence into erotic fulfillment.

Just as Hersey's protagonist, however, must be admired before he is revealed, so Claude apparently lacks nothing in the way of moral and physical virtues. There is his manly good health (always a point of fascination for Miss Cather, for whom "red" and "perspiring" seem essentials of masculine beauty), his love for his mother and obedience

*From *World War I and the American Novel* by Stanley Cooperman, pp. 129–37. Copyright © 1967 by Stanley Cooperman. Reprinted with corrections by permission of Johns Hopkins University Press.

to his father, his decency, his promptness to defend helpless or insulted womanhood. Blessed with an instinctive "love of order," he regards unmastered sexual emotions as both disordered and dishonest, so that the talk of hired hands, instead of "corrupting" him, gives him a "sharp disgust for sensuality," a renewed "pride in candour." Certainly there is nothing unclean, nothing twisted about Claude. He is a good boy, a pure adolescent, an efficient farmer, a faithful husband, a generous friend, a brave soldier, an effective officer. And also like Buzz Marrow in Hersey's book, these qualities—so laudable in themselves—become for Claude an overture for death, the queen of all virtues. For if goodness surrounds Claude like a halo of midwestern sentiment, it is violence— the image of destructive power—that accompanies his every move.

Even as a boy Claude is defined by violence; the imagery of suppression, struggle, and explosion runs through Miss Cather's narrative like a trail of gunpowder on a velvet cushion. His youthful "look" is a "quick, blue flash"—a spiritual detonation that must turn inward upon itself because his environment lacks permissible targets. Ultimately he can respond fully to things or people only by means of action, thrust, imposition of will. He learns the mysteries of his own body, for example, by "imposing physical tests and penances upon himself"; he deliberately scalds himself to "conquer" fire; he walks coatless in winter to "triumph" over cold; as a young farmer he rapes rather than cultivates his property ("He . . . buried a great deal of discontent in its dark furrows. Day after day he flung himself upon the land and planted it with what was fermenting in him, glad to be so tired at night that he could not think," p. 78). A storm calls up in him a virtual epiphany:

> It was a storm that died down at last—but what a pity not to do anything with it! A waste of power—for it was a kind of power; he sprang to his feet and stood frowning against the ruddy light, so deep in his struggling thoughts. . . .
>   The stranger scrutinized Claude with interest. He saw a young man standing bareheaded . . . his fists clenched in an attitude of arrested action. (p. 119)

What the stranger sees is the basic reality of Claude himself, a frustrated violence ("storm," "power," "sprang," "frowning," "struggling," "fists," "clenched," "arrested," "action") destined to find its final release— indeed, to take its pleasure—only in the act of death.

"[T]here ought to be something . . . splendid about life, sometimes," Claude reflects in one of his frequent moments of despair, but his desire to find this something springs neither from intellectual ambition nor aesthetic sensitivity. Conditioned by an environment in which "it was beneath his dignity to explain himself," an environment where action is its own justification, Claude's attitude toward intellectuality parallels that of Hersey's Marrow, for whom men of paper (whether navigators or school teachers) are almost physically repugnant. It is less Brother Weldon's religion, for example, than his "pear-shaped head and thin, rippled hair," his "purring" voice and white necktie, that arouse Claude's disgust. Even during his brief stay at college Claude finds "no friends or instructors whom he can regard with admiration"; surrounded by a form of authority that envelopes rather than strikes, his chief reaction is one of suspicion: he suffers as one "terribly afraid of being fooled."

Triumph is the ultimate splendor for Claude, the vision of life as a target to be struck or substance to be subdued, and his personal heroes are neither talking at universities, laboring on farms, nor raising families. "There must be something more!" he says to a friend, who—in contrast to Claude—achieves a happy marriage and later goes to war reluctantly. Claude's ideal, indeed, is not flesh but bronze: the "statue of Kit Carson on horseback" in a Denver square. "[B]ut there was no West, in that sense, any more," Claude reflects. "There was still South America; perhaps he could find something below the Isthmus. Here the sky was like a lid shut down over the face of the world . . ." (p. 118). The lid, unfortunately, remains shut even after Claude falls in love. Motivated by pressures he cannot admit even to himself, he marries a woman whose facade of submission covers a will stronger than his own. One might say that in her refusal to become her husband's "South America" Enid becomes his Waterloo—until Claude's manhood is redeemed by the golden chance of war itself.

Marriage to Enid, however, is no very important matter for Claude until the loathesomely bookish Brother Weldon provides serious competition. The competition, the resistance, even more than the girl engages Claude's attention, and the courtship takes on something of the nature of a military campaign: "He hadn't seen Weldon do anything but retreat before her eager questions. He, an 'atheist,' would have given her stronger reinforcement" (p. 132). Enid herself, furthermore, unlike the vibrant and somewhat more fleshly Gladys, is ethereal, delicate, and—apparently—gentle: "The pallor of her skin, the submissive inclination of her forehead, and her dark, unchanging eyes, made one think of something 'early Christian'" (p. 123). Even her deep religious faith is, for Claude, a stimulant: "Women ought to be religious," he believes; "faith was the natural fragrance of their minds" (p. 127).

Enid's delicacy, however, proves to be unbreakable toughness, while her faith is a force of will, determination, and self; indeed, the "fragrance" of her mind rolls over the defenseless Claude like a soft and unexpected cloud of poison no less deadly for being insubstantial, and in this atmosphere Claude virtually finds himself choking. But his wound is far more serious than infected lungs. Even when the radiance of war finally clears the air of Enid and all she represents, Claude never again turns to a woman for erotic fulfillment.

Claude defines Enid—or wishes to define her—as a love *object* to be conquered, warmed by his heat rather than its own. It is essentially the same need which drives Marrow, in Hersey's book, to pursue Daphne. But Marrow becomes impotent when Daphne offers her body to him: passivity in the love-object, a basic condition for his virility, has been upset. Like Marrow, Claude is aroused only by passivity. He dreams of making love to Enid "while she was still and unconscious"; he pictures her slowly becoming "warm," feeling "what he was feeling"; she is a "statue" warmed only by his will (p. 145). After his marriage, when Enid puts him ignominiously out of their train compartment, Claude suffers "a storm of anger, disappointment, and humiliation." He feels "unmanned," and yet he does nothing because there is nothing he can do (p. 198). Unable to master Enid's will, faced with a sudden and totally unexpected realization that her being is not his own, Claude suffers an emotional and sexual shock; just as Marrow must take to his airship for the sake of his virility, so Claude dreams of "danger," follows the wonderful new war in Europe with increasing attention to atrocities and casualty reports, and looks forward to his own impending salvation through violence.

Enid herself perceives that as a result of their marriage Claude has become "a big machine with the springs broken inside"; he has been "cowed" by his delicate new wife. With his pride shattered, with gossamer threads binding him at every turn, Claude suffers and dreams—but tries "not to think . . . , and when he could he avoided thinking" (p. 208). The farm is helpful in this respect, for back-breaking labor alone permits him to sleep "like the heroes of old"; only work controls the emotional pressures building up within him. The very desperation of his labor, however, eliminates the farm as a resource, for with prosperity such narcotic action is no longer possible. The European war comes as a release—indeed, as an emotional necessity—and Claude's excitement rises with each atrocity, each report of new destructive weapons. As he reacts to rumors of the surrender of Paris, for example, Claude is strongly reminiscent of Marrow in Hersey's novel, who lovingly peruses photographs of bombing attacks. "I should think they'd burn it first, the way the Russians did Moscow," Claude says. "They can do better than that now, they can dynamite it" (pp. 168–69).

Juxtaposed with Claude's growing desperation, in other words, there are increasing references to the war—to righteous indignation, the thrill of vicarious violence. Society, of course, approves of violence only for unselfish reasons (Belgium, the *Lusitania*, Edith Cavell) and to this idealization Claude readily agrees, even sacrificing his German-American friends in the process. For his motives involve no thought of personal gain; all he desires from violence is violence itself.

Vicarious violence, however, is at best only a stopgap, especially when Enid asserts her will in pursuing missionary activities. Left to his own resources, weakened by leisure, Claude faces the precipice:

"he felt unmarried and free; free to smoke as much as he liked, and to read and dream. Some of his dreams would have frozen his young wife's blood with horror . . ." (p. 212). The very furniture of his home becomes distasteful: it is "rubbish, junk" that "exposed and condemned all the dreary, weary, ever-repeated actions by which life is continued from day to day. . . . He wondered how he was to go on through the years ahead of him unless he could get rid of this sick feeling in his soul" (p. 223). Even without Enid, Claude's freedom is limited to his dreams: the religiosity of his mother binds him just as the spirituality of his wife unmanned him.

Claude's relationship with his mother is ambiguous. "It's almost like being a bride, keeping house for just you, Claude," she remarks when his father goes away on a business trip (p. 78). Watching a snow-fall (which Claude, according to his own emotional necessities, sees as beautifully "submissive") he and his mother "clung together in the pale, clear square of the west window, as the two natures in one person sometimes meet and cling in a fated hour" (p. 87); after he enlists in the Crusade Mrs. Wheeler informs her son, "Your father talks a great deal more at home than formerly, and sometimes I think he is trying to take your place" (p. 242). And when Claude bids farewell before being shipped overseas, there is a remarkable scene indeed:

> She rose, reaching toward him as he came up to her and caught her in his arms. She was smiling her little, curious intimate smile, with half-closed eyes.
> "Well, is it goodby?" she murmured. She passed her hands over his shoulders, down his strong back and the close-fitting sides of his coat. . . . Her chin came just to his breast pocket, and she rubbed it against the heavy cloth. Claude stood looking down at her without speaking a word. Suddenly his arms tightened and he almost crushed her.
> "Mother!" he whispered as he kissed her. He ran downstairs and out of the house without looking back. (p. 263)

Small wonder that even in France Claude remembers what he never fully escapes. Admiring cathedral glass in Rouen, for example, "[h]e felt distinctly that [the light] went through him and farther still . . . as if his mother were looking over his shoulder" (p. 343).

From the moment Claude sets out on the Crusade he experiences a complete sense of well-being: the training camp is splendid, his men are fine, and he feels blessed with "purpose" and fearless in the face of danger. When his mother expresses concern about danger from submarines during his voyage, Claude brightens at the prospect: "We don't worry about that," he says. "If the Germans should sink a few troop ships it would be unfortunate, certainly—but it wouldn't cut any figure in the long run" (pp. 256–57). Claude's lack of dread will later make a sharp contrast between him and Victor, the airman. Victor's orders—service over the Verdun line—mean almost certain death, and Victor himself makes no effort to hide his bitterness and gloom at so dangerous an assignment. Claude, on the other hand, reacts like a man just given a stimulant: "the very sound of the name was grim, like the hollow roll of drums. . . . He felt more 'over' than he had done before, and a little crackle of excitement went all through him" (pp. 331–32).

On board ship, meanwhile, there are better things available than mere dreams of blood. An epidemic of influenza breaks out and Claude, working with dead or dying men, rejoices in a "sense of everwidening freedom." His enthusiasm, indeed, is finally noticed by the doctor, who comments upon so incongruous a radiance. "It was quite true," Claude admits silently; "the doctor had caught him. He was enjoying himself all the while and didn't want to be safe anywhere":

> life had never seemed so tempting as it did here and now. . . . He had them [his dying friends] on his mind and did all he could for them, but it seemed to him just now that he took a sort of satisfaction in that, too. . . . He awoke every morning with that sense of freedom and going forward, as if the world were growing bigger each day and he were growing with it. Other fellows were sick and dying, and that was terrible,—but he and the boat went on, always on.
>
> Something was released that had been struggling for a long while, he told himself. . . . But the miracle had happened . . . their golden chance. . . . The feeling of purpose, of fateful purpose, was strong in his breast (pp. 311–12).

From the time he arrives in France until the very moment of his own death Claude defends the war, quickens to violence and signs of violence, and resents any delay or interference with the purge by blood. Arguing with Gerhardt, who sees the war as a tragedy, Claude accuses his friend of being unable to understand "what hard molds and crusts the big guns had broken open" (p. 375); at the same time, however, he "grimly disapproves" of the sex adventures of the men under his command, viewing such adventures as intolerable distractions from the "legitimate business" of killing and being killed.

Before his first combat Claude's only emotion is one of delighted expectation: "They were bound for the big show, and on every hand were reassuring signs: long lines of gaunt, dead trees charred and torn; big holes gashed out of fields and hillsides. . . ." Claude marches along "wearing a stoical countenance, afraid of betraying his satisfaction in the men, the weather, the country" (p. 358). And combat itself provides no disillusion: Gerhardt may be bitter because the war has no true reason to justify such slaughter, but Claude simply admires the French landscape, joyfully convinced that "the period of happy 'youth' . . . which he had never experienced, was being made up to him now" (p. 410). Listening to French women discuss the fate of various relatives and friends ruined or dead because of the war, Claude draws the remarkable conclusion that for them "the war was life, and everything that went into it. To be alive, to be conscious and to have one's faculties, was to be in the war" (p. 416).

During a scene in a French and German graveyard, Sergeant Hicks, who had embarked on his own Crusade with high morale, suffers a vision of futility and waste. "[W]ho put 'em here, and what's the good of it?" he asks. Claude, however, is too busy admiring the noble sacrifice of the Unknown Soldier to be depressed. "Search me," he murmurs "absently," thinking that *Soldat Inconnu, Mort pour la France* was "a very good epitaph. . . . Most of the boys who fell in this war were unknown, even to themselves. They were too young. . . . The name that stood was *La France*. . . . It was a pleasant name to say over in one's mind, where one could make it as passionately nasal as one pleased and never blush" (p. 394).

After each confrontation of death, each stimulation by violence, Claude experiences a sense of peace. Following a bloody engagement in which his men are butchered, for example, he simply admires—once again—"this beautiful land, this beautiful people." His well-being is total; far from suffering under the impact of machine death, Claude enjoys an almost post-orgasmic relaxation. Certainly we feel that Claude, after he witnesses the protruding viscera and mutilated genitals of one of his own men, will remember the episode as one of those experiences he "wouldn't have missed for the world." And welcoming his own death-against-the-sunset, Claude at last achieves his own virility: "unconquerable" now is the "big machine" whose springs had been broken by Ideal Woman, by Home, by Society, and by life itself.

One of Ours is unique among the postwar novels in that technological combat reinforces rather than destroys the expectations of its protagonist. Miss Cather, of course, knew very little about the war she was describing; her picture postcard trenches, her pretty villages, her "mushroom-picking expeditions" had little to do with the impact of actual war experience. For this reason Ernest Hemingway, in "Torrents of Spring," could sneer at "this American Willa Cather who wrote a book . . . where all the last part . . . was taken from the action of *The Birth of a Nation*." Miss Cather's book, however, is valuable not so much as a treatment of war, but rather as an examination of particular psychological needs which helped fashion the bold journey into war. That technological combat shattered rather than fulfilled is something Miss Cather could not be expected to grasp in 1922, when the nature and impact of such combat was only vaguely understood by most Americans. The war lover, indeed, was unlikely to find fulfillment in the first great war of the machine, when combat threatened rather than redeemed manhood. But this is not the concern of *One of Ours*; as a study of erotic frustration and virility-through-violence, a violence made possible by a cosmetic surface of idealism and abstraction, the novel at least helps us to understand the environment from which the bold journey began. For the world of war itself, we must turn to other writers.

Note

1. Willa Cather, *One of Ours* (New York, 1922), pp. 419–20. Subsequent references to *One of Ours* are indicated parenthetically in text.

A Lost Lady

[Review of *A Lost Lady*]   Henry James Forman[*]

There is a romantic ballad somewhere in German literature about a race of giants who dwelt in Alsace. Their castle was Niedeck and their cities lay high up surrounded by a rich champaign. The refrain of the ballad is touchingly melancholic. It tells us that Castle Niedeck is now a ruin, that the cities are waste and desolate.

> Du fragest nach die Riesen,
> Due findest sie nicht mehr.
> "You ask after the giants, you find them there no more."

A dim memory this of schooldays and schoolboy German, yet it rose sharply into the reviewer's consciousness upon reading Miss Cather's brief but charming little opus. It is hardly a novel and yet it is too full and good for a short story. It is simply a little work of art.

Miss Cather is a realist. Who would dare to call her otherwise? Not this reviewer, at any rate, who has just been classifying her elsewhere as one of America's most promising realistic writers. But the memory of that German ballad emerging so insistently upon reading *A Lost Lady*, gives the show away. The truth is, Miss Cather's romanticism, long repressed, bursts forth almost in spite of her and she has painted a vivid brilliant little picture of an age that is gone not to return. One feels almost that one ought to keep Miss Cather's confidence.

"I know this is a romance," she seems to be saying, "but please don't tell a soul."

Men like Captain Forrester—a Civil War Captain this—who helped to build the Burlington, or, say, the Union Pacific, are as extinct as the Prince Alberts they used to wear. Honest, well-to-do, incorruptible, patriotic, generous to a fault—as the phrase is—old-fashioned Americans like that are not often to be found now even in the West. Modern Americans,

[*]Originally published in the *New York Times Book Review*, 30 September 1923, p. 4.

177

even with many of Captain Forrester's virtues, are too businesslike to be either so chivalrous or so generous.

And Marian Forrester—gay, handsome, very feminine, very courageous, reckless, even, somewhat weak and immoral, but as generous as her husband, the kind of woman who would be popularly described as "such a lady!"—are there any like her remaining? No. Miss Cather very fittingly describes her as a lost lady.

"You ask after the giants, you find them there no more."

> Thirty or forty years ago, in one of those gray towns along the Burlington Railroad which are so much grayer today than they were then, there was a house well known from Omaha to Denver for its hospitality and for a certain charm of atmosphere. Well known, that is to say, to the railroad aristocracy of that time. . . .
>
> When the Burlington men were traveling back and forth on business not very urgent, they found it agreeable to drop off the express and spend a night in a pleasant house where their importance was delicately recognized. . . .

Except for the American names, might not this have been the opening of a long short story by Turgenief, say, out of "The Annals of a Sportsman"?

In telling the story of Captain Daniel Forrester, and particularly of his young wife, Marian Forrester, Miss Cather keeps this note of worldly wise, yet benevolently philosophic, interest throughout. It is the note of the spacious realists, of the unhurried ones, like the Russians. It has nothing of the hot, fetid realism of some of the Frenchmen. This spaciousness and the leisured, lingering charm make the story more romantic than romance itself.

What is the story? Well, that is nothing marvelous in itself. It is the story of Captain Daniel Forrester's decline from wealth to virtual poverty because depositors in a certain bank in Denver trust in his name. He could not let them down, so he simply turned his wealth over to them.

As to Marian, whom he married under romantic circumstances, he simply worshipped her. And she was adorable—with that mysterious gift of Venus that at times makes a woman irresistible. She was as courageous in adversity as she was generous to what she regarded as her inferiors— and as frail in her morals as she was both. Even while the Captain was yet living she had a lover. After his death, well—but somehow she never lost her charm. Her vagaries in no way impaired her other qualities. To the end she was charming. Men loved her. They knew her faults as surely as Captain Forrester himself had known them, but they were fond of her. She died the wife of a rich Englishman in South America. One of the boys of her small town, subsequently a prospering engineer, saw her as an old lady in that foreign land. And still she was charming.

The Broken World:
Medievalism in *A Lost Lady*   Evelyn Thomas Helmick*

Visiting France in 1920 to complete *One of Ours*, the novel that was to win her a Pulitzer Prize, Willa Cather refused to present any of her letters of introduction, firmly declaring that she wanted to live in the Middle Ages. Her interest in that historical period was to shape two of her important novels. From her early study of the Greek poets such as Hesiod who held a theory of civilization as a process of degeneration from the age of gods, then of heroes, and from her reading of Michelet who popularized Vico's similar theory, Willa Cather had learned to view the development of the American West as a decline from a glorious past. Her novels of the matriarchal era had presented goddess-heroines as protagonists—Alexandra, Thea, Antonia; those of the heroic age present Claude Wheeler as Parsifal in *One of Ours*, Captain Forrester as a medieval king and the railroad builders as his knights in *A Lost Lady*. In this last novel, the characterization of the Captain's wife Marian as a "lost lady" becomes the chief device in one of the most successful of modern allegories by which Willa Cather marks the transition from the age of heroes to the age of lesser men in the United States and offers an analogy between that period and the comparable period—the late Middle Ages—in the evolution of the Western World.

In many ways the emerging society of the Midwest paralleled the world of Europe. As the quite feudal social structure formed, it consisted of two classes, the first composed of a few strong wealthy men, the other composed of settlers who never rose above peasant rank. Each settlement had its great house, set apart from the town, where the man of substance and authority attempted an elegant, almost courtly life with others of his station. The rigid social system was one manifestation of the struggle toward order and away from a formless, lawless past.

But the same kind of change that occurred in the late Middle Ages broke the pattern in the United States in the nineteenth century. Those changes catalogued in *A Lost Lady* begin with the investment of money by bankers and gentlemen ranchers to "develop our great West," as Cather phrases it. Some of the ambivalence she felt was expressed in an article written the same year this novel was published, admitting a certain moral victory in the attainment of prosperity under difficult conditions, at the same time condemning the materialistic attitudes soon established. The wild speculation accompanying the new commercialism led to financial catastrophe, as it does in the novel and as it had in the banking houses of Italy and Germany in the late Middle Ages. Another inevitable

*Originally published in *Renascence*, 28 (Autumn 1975), 39–46. Reprinted with corrections by permission of *Renascence* and the author.

accompaniment was the rise of a middle class unable to comprehend its place in the social structure or to appreciate the mode of the higher class. The threat of the new bourgeoisie was no less in the social and economic scheme of the West than it had been in Europe five hundred years before. Still another characteristic change can be understood here only in relation to Cather's earlier works, in which worship of the land is the chief function of the religious impulse. The desecration of Western land, not to be comprehended by Americans until generations later, is begun in *A Lost Lady* by the villain who drains a beautiful if useless marshland.

The man who can thus prevail points to a crisis of the time—the loss of heroic leaders, or at least the loss of the illusion that there were such heroes. Cather laments:

> The Old West had been settled by dreamers, great-hearted adventurers who were unpractical to the point of magnificence; a courteous brotherhood, strong in attack but weak in defence, who could conquer but could not hold. Now all the vast territory they had won was to be at the mercy of men like Ivy Peters, who had never dared anything, never risked anything. They would drink up the mirage, dispel the morning freshness, root out the great brooding spirt of freedom, the generous, easy life of the great land-holders. The space, the colour, the princely carelessness of the pioneer they would destroy and cut up into profitable bits, as the match factory splinters the primeval forest.[1]

Her strongest regret is for the demise of a class of men whose chivalric behavior had briefly provided a noble perception of the world. With the vanquishing of those men went the political, cultural, and moral ideals they represented. Even in the early novels Cather was aware that the age she was eulogizing was past—"elegiac" is the word that many critics apply to her writing. Like the historian Frederick Jackson Turner she recognized that the frontier had been a formative influence on American life, a tremendous force while it had lasted; like him she knew that it had ended before she began her study. But then she also knew, as the Old Beauty in a later Cather short story says, "Nobody ever recognizes a period until it has gone by." *A Lost Lady*, her poetic acknowledgment that the vital strength of the pioneer was no more, was begun in 1922, the year in which, as many critics have noted, she said the world broke in two. One of the consequences of her idealization of the early frontier had been to make nearly impossible for her the confrontation with the later industrial and commercial West.

Given her subject (the passing of a heroic era) and her historical sense (the awareness of the similarities between the Western United States of the nineteenth century and medieval Western Europe), it was no accident that Cather chose to structure her novel as a *roman courtois*.

Her previous "medieval" novel, *One of Ours*, is an epic or *chanson de geste* in which war is the subject; *A Lost Lady* is an Arthurian romance in which courtly love is the subject. If the first reflects the crude power of romanesque art, the second reflects the complexity and refinement of later Gothic art. The romance was an ideal, and traditional, vehicle for the expression of certain attitudes towards society. The original romance literature, Friedrich Heer says in *The Medieval World*, was nourished on the awareness of the crisis in the conscience and instincts of twelfth-century man.[2] Cather's use of the genre of courtly romance seems almost inevitable in view of her acute awareness of a moral crisis in her own time.

In addition to the theme of weakness in men and institutions, *A Lost Lady* displays all of the other prominent elements of the *roman courtois*. The plot is the classic one: a young knightly protagonist dedicates himself to the service of his lady, the wife of his king who eventually falls. Through a series of adventures, including journeys, battles (sometimes psychological), adulterous encounters (perceived rather than participated in), and many defeats, the knight undergoes his initiation into awareness of the world about him. Further, as Heer defines the *roman*, "... a woman is always at hand to transform and ennoble a man. Through his relationship with the woman the man gains access to his own soul, the deeper layers of his 'heart': his sorrowing quest for his 'queen' makes him wiser, more sensitive, more scrupulous as a person."[3] Based on this pattern, *A Lost Lady* becomes part of the tradition of such famous romances as Gottfried von Strassburg's *Tristan*, the works of Chrétien de Troyes and Malory, and Tennyson's *Morte d'Arthur*. (Cather borrows Tennyson's device of the Christmas party frame story among others.)

One of the advantages of the genre for her is that it provides opportunity for more complete manipulation of allegory. Her novels, from *O Pioneers!* on, have allegorical dimensions in their implications for historical interpretation of the West, but *A Lost Lady* is allegorical in the medieval manner, where characters are both historical and figurative, are not only themselves but representatives of something else and/or signs of their spiritual condition. Allegory and symbolism grant this story a power immediately felt if not comprehended. Yet one more attraction of the romance for Cather might have been its possibilities for experimentation in a style that was new for her. In the tradition of great writers she worked through many genres and styles in her novels (almost in the same order in which they had been established through the ages), and here she achieves an elegance and polish that had not been appropriate to her earlier novels.

From the opening page of *A Lost Lady* medieval references begin to strike the reader. Much is made of the two-fold social strata in the prairie states: there exist only the aristocratic and lower classes (homesteaders and handworkers). Adolph Blum, a young member of this latter group, understands with his "feudal mind" that a "fortunate and privileged class was an axiomatic fact in the social order" and keeps secret his knowledge of aristocratic indiscretions because he dimly perceives that these people are different. While they lead elegant lives, not much happens to the Adolph Blums of the world but weather. The two-dimensional world of the novel further divides into good and evil, as Niel Herbert and Ivy Peters recognize each other from childhood as the "natural enemies" developed by Cather in several stories. On the surface the moral dimensions are as immediately identifiable as any captured in a medieval morality play.

In its setting *A Lost Lady* seems almost a picture on a medieval tapestry, with a castle, the poplars, even a moat:

> To approach Captain Forrester's property, you had first to get over a wide, sandy creek which flowed along the eastern edge of the town. Crossing this by the footbridge or the ford, you entered the Captain's private land, bordered by Lombardy poplars, with wide meadows lying on either side. Just at the foot of the hill on which the house sat, one crossed a second creek by the stout wooden road-bridge. This stream traced artless loops and curves through the broad meadows that were half pasture land, half marsh.[4]

The plume-like shadows cast by the trees, the sharp sloping roofs of the house, the inlay on the heavy walnut furniture, the Captain's narrow iron bed, and even, his comment, "A man's home is his castle," all further establish the medieval mood.

Captain Forrester himself provides one of the strongest suggestions of medieval atmosphere by his resemblance to King Arthur. A massive man, with dun-colored mustache, a "grave courtesy," and a rigid code of behavior, he seems an anachronism even in the Western community he had helped to build. But there are many more specific references to identify him with the most famous of fisher kings. His illness, like Arthur's, begins with a fall from his horse, and his death, like Arthur's, occurs in December. The dependency of the land on the strength of its leader is a direct, almost primitive relationship: one paragraph describes the Captain's failing health; the very next paragraph describes the changing fortunes of the town of Sweet Water, including the crop failures which break the farmers' spirits. To further relate the Captain to the medieval warrior, there is a great deal of witty sword symbolism, such as his deftness with the carving knife at the table, his use of the garden shears, and later in his illness, the brandishing of two canes. But for all his posturing (the chivalric mode was indeed a series of stances), the important fact about the Captain is that he is ultimately powerless to prevent the disintegration about him—nature's decay, society's corruption, his own wife's faithlessness.

Perhaps of all the secular medieval virtues, loyalty must be deemed preeminent. The loyalties of the "lords and barons of his realm"—in this novel they metamorphose into the railroad barons—are consummately feudal; the men themselves are "great-hearted adventurers," "a courteous brotherhood" in Cather's words. As a result of her admiration for the exceptional person, she was able to see the builders of the railroads as figures of nobility at a time when it was popular to consider them "robber barons." She talks in the past tense of the "visions those men had seen in the air and followed," and yet the idea that pervades the novel accepts sadly the King's observation in *Morte d'Arthur* that "old order changeth, yielding place to new." One man who figures prominently in the story as part of the aristocratic group is Frank Ellinger, called a "prince of a fellow." This second cliché in the work of a writer notably free of clichés heightens the medieval reference. Ellinger's costume, manner, and "well-visored countenance "present him as a chivalric character. If the men are knights, the railroad is amusingly pictured as a dragon; the townspeople say that it is drawing in its horns as the Captain's town declines.

Although Marian Forrester, the long-lost lady, still retains a connection with the fertility goddesses of the earlier novels ("She was an excitement that came and went with summer"), she is chiefly an elegant, polished goddesswoman, the embodiment of the chivalric ideal. Her personality can be easily equated with the frequent descriptions of medieval society as elegant but static. She proves incapable of the kind of leadership exerted by Cather's earlier simple heroines, demonstrating the decline of usefulness of woman's intuitive powers in a male-oriented, conscious society. The story of Marian is really a series of episodes revealing, through her relationships with men of all stations, the possibilities of love. As Captain Forrester's wife, she plays the role of a beautiful queen and gracious hostess. Her husband, who understands her best even in her perfidy, can still appreciate her more than can other men. As object of the courtly worship of young Niel, she, as female principle, retains her mysterious power over him even after her charms have faded and her moral weakness is manifest. To Niel she is many things, from mother as he is injured or as he learns social graces to flirtatious woman to whom he does not respond because of innocence or righteousness. As the lover of Frank Ellinger, she is a sexual female with heightened beauty and sensibilities, but subject to the attendant jealously and vulnerability to rejection. Interestingly, she becomes real, casting off her mask and mocking manner, only at the moment her love is physically realized. As object of Ivy Peters' attentions, she loses her dignity, her authority, her reputation, and gains only material advantage from her association with him. Finally, as symbol of a privileged life, she finds admiration from the young males of the lower classes, but eventually indifference as she ages, they mature, and the class structure changes. Marian Forrester's strength in her encounters with men steadily deteriorates in the course of *A Lost Lady*. Her fall from grace, as in most myths of the Western World, is accomplished by sexual awareness and guilt, at least a guilt implied by the author, if not sensed by the characters.

Only vaguely aware of her plight, "Maidy," as her husband calls her, plays her role as lady superbly, with her long black hair to her shoulders, the velvet dress with its train, the silver-buckled slippers. Her name, of course, links her to the supreme medieval female inspiration for heroes, although ironically her power is ephemeral indeed. Her rise and fall are neatly symbolized in scenes involving the rose, that much-used sign of the Virgin. Niel first encounters her as she arranges a bunch of old-fashioned blush roses; his disillusionment begins as he carries to her an armful of wild roses, which he discards in a mud hole after a glimpse of the tawdry side of his lady. The lily, another symbol of Mary, is used ironically in connection with Marian Forrester as Niel comments that lilies that fester smell far worse than weeds. If she, in fact, allegorically represents the West in men's ideals, the tone of despair in the book becomes evident. She, however, still hopes. Exercising her aging charms, she exclaims, "I wanted to see whether I had anything worth saving. I have, I tell you! You would hardly believe it, but I still have!" Her vehemence belies her words; she, like her author, knows that her charms will never again really matter, because there are no more Captain Forresters to be attracted.

The brief hope in the era of the empire builders was soon dispelled by the men who followed, epitomized in *A Lost Lady* by Ivy Peters, whose profession—law—characterizes a conscious, masculine civilization and whose unblinking, lashless eyes identify him with evil. The scene introducing him as a youth shows him blinding a woodpecker, an act usually interpreted as mere senseless cruelty, but actually one with far greater significance in the context of the novel. The woodpecker, according to Jungian theory, is a symbol of the feminine, and much is made of the femaleness of this particular bird; thus, the cruelty foreshadows Ivy's later subjugation and ill treatment of Marian Forrester, just as Niel's inability to rescue the injured woodpecker foreshadows his later powerlessness to save his lady. This theme is carried even further as Ivy's disregard for the spiritual, the unconcious, the *anima* of man's nature culminates in his draining of the swamp on the Forrester property, in spite of the Captain's attempt to preserve that section until his death. The significance of the swamp is made clear in a passage invested with symbolic description of Niel's worship, loyalty, and submerged erotic feeling for Marian. As he is drawn to the swamp by an "impulse of affection and guardianship,"

The sky was burning with the soft pink and silver of a cloudless summer dawn. The heavy, bowed grasses splashed him to the knees. All over the marsh, snow-on-the-mountain, globed with dew, made cool sheets of silver, and the swamp milk-weed spread its flat, raspberry-coloured clusters. There was an almost religious purity about the fresh morning air, the tender sky, the grass and flowers with the sheen of early dew upon them. There was in all living things something limpid and joyous—like the wet, morning call of the birds, flying up through the unstained atmosphere. Out of the saffron east a thin, yellow, wine-like sunshine began to gild the fragrant meadows and the glistening tops of the grove. Niel wondered why he did not often come over like this, to see the day before men and their activities had spoiled it, while the morning was still unsullied, like a gift handed down from the heroic ages.

Under the bluffs that overhung the marsh he came upon thickets of wild roses, with flaming buds, just beginning to open. Where they had opened, their petals were stained with that burning rose-colour which is always gone by noon,—a dye made of sunlight and morning and moisture, so intense that it cannot possibly last . . . must fade, like ecstasy.[5]

Not understanding the worth of beauty for its own sake, Ivy drains the swamp for the profit he can make, signaling both the end of the natural beauty of the West and the end of the power of men who could appreciate it. And because the swamp stage of civilization, as Erich Neumann says, represents the early matriarchate,[6] its drying up is a symbol not only of the human dominance of nature but also of the male drive for knowledge that succeeds the female acquiesence to nature. What follows in the American context is the transformation of the West from an agricultural to a commercial and industrial society and the emergence of an urban middle class dominated by such men as Ivy and his friends, who lack all aristocratic grace.

The hope for the younger generation lies in the character of Niel, whose very name means *champion* and whose role is precisely that of the worshipping feudal attendant of royalty. His utter subjection to an unapproachable woman, his willingness to make any sacrifice to the lady he worships prove him a knight in the most romantic vein. Combining the qualities of the scholar with those of the knight, he begins his studies in law, but later decides on architecture, thus to participate in the creative life which for Cather was the only escape from an undesirable world. Even this he sacrifices for a time to care for the Captain and Marian, a chivalric decision. His feats, however, include a more dramatic rescue of his lady. It occurs when Marian Forrester, after drinking too much brandy, telephones her recently married lover. As her conversation changes to a tirade, Niel cuts the wire with his large shears, saving her in her distress from a loss of dignity.

At this point she becomes "absolutely unconscious." The lady who once had the strength of tempered steel, who was a "blade that could fence with anyone and never break," is, without the Captain, as useless as Excalibur without Arthur. Or to change the simile: "without him she was like a ship without ballast, driven hither and thither by every wind. She was flighty and perverse. She seemed to have lost her faculty of discrimination; her power of easily and graciously keeping everyone in his proper place."[7] The glory of the era she represents ends not with a bang but with Ivy Peters' grasping hand on her breast. Observing the incident, Niel thinks, "It was nothing, yet it was everything." It was the Captain, he decides, who had been the reality. Like the world view of the Middle Ages, Cather's concept of civilization held that an ideal order was the true reality. Her frontier age, like the age of chivalry, had fastened onto an ideal which could not survive the disappearance of heroes who briefly signaled the attainment of the power of consciousness. And while they prevailed they were inspired by the lady who symbolized the female principles so necessary for either a fully-developed individual or a successful society. The eventual failure of the lost lady allegorizes what Tennyson discovered as the condition of civilization in Arthur's time and his own—"sense at war with soul."

Notes

1. Willa Cather, *A Lost Lady* (New York, 1923), p. 106.

2. Friedrich Heer, *The Medieval World* (New York, 1963), p. 185.

3. *The Medieval World*, p. 181.

4. *A Lost Lady*, p. 11.

5. *A Lost Lady*, pp. 84–85.

6. Erich Neumann, *The Origins and History of Consciousness* (New York, 1954), p. 27.

7. *A Lost Lady*, pp. 152–52.

The Celibate Male in *A Lost Lady*: The Unreliable Center of Consciousness
Kathleen L. Nichols*

In Willa Cather's elegiac novel *A Lost Lady*, Niel Herbert is the youthful admirer who evokes the image of Captain Forrester's young wife, the charming Marian who brings beauty, romance, and social distinction to the prairie town of Sweet Water, Nebraska. Although Marian

*Originally published in *Regionalism and the Female Imagination*, 4, No. 1 (1978), 13–23. Reprinted by permission of the author.

Forrester is based on Cather's memory of "a woman I loved very much in my childhood,"[1] the disillusionment expressed by Niel when he discovers Marian's sexual betrayal of her aging pioneer husband has been echoed by most critics who agree that Marian is enchanting, but lost and "fallen."[2] The assumption that Niel is Cather's male "alter ego" stems, in part, from the general resemblance between this novel and Cather's earlier, more well-known *My Ántonia.*

Since both novels are stories less of the title female than of the woman's effect on the admiring male reflectors, and since both reflectors seem to resemble a common Cather type—the celibate male whose sexually-sublimated imagination redeems the past and present—, Niel is commonly viewed, as the Brown-Edel biography puts it, as "simply Jim Burden from *My Ántonia* renamed,"[3] which is to say that Cather's voice merges with Niel's as it does with Jim's. Yet one must wonder about the validity of a viewpoint, such as Niel's, which cannot comprehend why a passionate woman in the prime of her life would want to survive the demise of her pioneer husband when she could sacrifice herself on his tomb and become an untarnished memory to her young admirer. Niel's failure to understand Marian's passion for life and, even more seriously, his inability to live up to the pioneer ideals embodied in the character of her husband render suspect Niel's reliability as a center of consciousness.

As the title of this novel indicates, *A Lost Lady* is a story of *loss*, not of recovery as is *My Ántonia*, and compared to Jim Burden, Niel is much too pessimistic and ineffectual to be a celibate ideal—Cather's hope for the future, as Patricia Lee Yongue contends.[4] Most telling, however, is Cather's carefully deliberated rejection for *A Lost Lady* of the first-person narrator used so successfully in *My Ántonia*. Instead, she selected a shifting third-person perspective that separates her omniscient angle of vision from the subjectivity of Niel's limited viewpoint. The obvious reason why Cather chose to separate the viewpoints seems to have escaped most critics, but, as Dalma H. Brunauer points out, it is because "Niel Herbert is not a mouthpiece of the author . . . . Marian Forrester is a 'lost lady' in the eyes of Niel, and not of Miss Cather."[5] However, other than noting that Niel's prudery keeps him from admitting his subconscious desire for Marian Forrester, Brunauer ignores the question of *why* Niel is incapable of viewing Marian from the author's perspective.

The answer to this question is bound up in Niel's role as an autonomous character; Niel's abortive initiation experience, in fact, forms the structural basis of the novel. He is an example of what David Stouck calls the "central imaginative preoccupation" in Cather's fiction—the orphaned or motherless "child searching for the mother,"[6] a need which colors his judgment of Marian and keeps him from attaining the pioneer perspective of Captain Forrester, the idealized non-sexual father-figure. What emerges through the pattern of Niel's "celibate" responses to the past and to his lady is the story of a sexually-repressed young man's inability to accept change, growth, and adult sexuality as the waning frontier era of his childhood consciousness ushers in the "fallen" twentieth-century world of adult awareness. Through Niel's denial of sexual maturity, which bears all the symptoms of a repressed oedipal conflict, Cather explores the inherent limitations of the static childhood consciousness confronted by the modern realities of time and change.

Throughout the novel, Niel is firmly convinced that the beauty and order of his childhood were destroyed when Marian Forrester, the nonsexual lady who presided over his youthful consciousness, was transformed into a sexual woman. The omniscient narrator, however, provides background information which has been largely ignored by critics, but which suggests that Niel's view of Marian and his past is partially distorted by his unconscious need to be true to a past that predates the entry of Marian Forrester into his life. The disorder characterizing most of his childhood made its initial appearance when he lost his first lady—his mother who died when Niel was five years old. His mother, whose attitudes are reflected in her orphaned son, was a haughty southern lady who "hated" the "commonplace" West to which she had been driven only by financial necessity—the need "to turn the crown into the pound."[7] Niel is described as being "proud, like his mother," and her continual lament for her lost past—the idealized Kentucky home—establishes the basic response pattern that her son manifests when she becomes his lost world.

This pattern is revealed early in the way that Niel withdraws emotionally from his post-maternal world. In fact, he almost seems to blame his surviving family members for the sense of loss and disorder which he experiences. His father's inability to turn the crown into the pound is associated in Niel's mind with the motherless family's "air of failure and defeat" (p. 30). He thinks of his "horrid" home "where people of no consequence lived" (pp. 28–9) in terms of his mother's replacement— helpful, but disorganized Cousin Sadie, "the worst housekeeper in the world." Consequently, he "hated to have anyone come to see them" (pp. 29–30). Finally, when his bankrupt father moves to a new home in Colorado, the teenage Niel remains in Sweet Water, "clinging" to the more distinguished side of the family, as represented by his *maternal* uncle, Judge Pommeroy, a former Virginian gentleman who also was "a friend of all the great men who visited the Forresters" (p. 30). At a very young age, Niel, like his mother before him, has learned to "keep faith" with a lost past by rejecting the "fallen" world of the present.

This early loss of the mother not only influences Niel's later view of his second lady, Marian Forrester, but also keeps him from developing in his teenage years a healthy and realistic attitude toward his own emerging sexual identity and toward time and change in general. Although Marian is only an occasional, pleasant image during the six or so "unpleasant" years following his mother's death, Niel's unconscious identification of this lovely woman with his first lost lady presumably comes from his early childhood memory of Marian with her parasol, ruffles, and swirling petticoats as she descended from a carriage. Almost hypnotized by this vision of feminine loveliness from "a very different world" (p. 42), the very young child had even followed her into a church, an action which, given his tender years, suggests longing for the lost southern lady who was his mother.

Marian's hold on his consciousness begins when the twelve year old boy, who is "already old enough to see . . . that she was different from the other townswomen, and to reflect upon what it was that made her so" (p. 19), breaks his leg while playing on the Forrester property and is carried into Marian's bedroom to await the doctor. The beauty of this lady and the maternal care she renders produce several ambiguous responses in the hurt "little boy." He contentedly feels the touch of her soft administering fingers and notices "inside the lace ruffle of her dress . . . her white throat rising and falling" (p. 28). And when she kisses him lightly on the forehead, "Oh, how sweet, she smelled!" (p. 29). A child on the verge of puberty,[8] Niel is responding to Marian both as maternal presence and as sexually-attractive woman. It is the combination of these responses that contributes to the intensity of his worship of and later disillusionment with his lady.

The problem that Niel eventually will have to solve is how to retain that moment of sexual "innocence" in Marian's bed—how to keep his own sexual development from upsetting the balance between his need for the restored maternal figure and his growing attraction for the sexual woman. During his teenage years, he more or less ignores the problem and lives a double life. At nineteen, for instance, he is described as being rather cold and critical, living with "monastic cleanliness and severity, . . . and resolved to remain a bachelor, like his [maternal] uncle" (p. 33). However, the young monk's private thoughts about Marian resemble more the rhapsodies of a young lover: "[H]e had never found [a woman] so attractive and distinguished as Mrs. Forrester. Compared with her, other women were heavy and dull; even the pretty ones seemed lifeless,—they had not that something in their glance that made one's blood tingle" (p. 41). It is as though Niel can keep his relationship with Marian pure by refusing to name, and thus to recognize, the "something" that makes his blood "tingle."

But Niel's blood also tingles with something suspiciously akin to jealous possessiveness whenever Frank Ellinger, the Forrester's Denver guest notorious for his sexual escapades, is present. Niel usually delights in the admiration that Marian receives from her aging husband (who seems more like a non-sexual father than a husband-lover) and most of his men friends, but even before the young monk knows about Marian's affair with Ellinger, he is annoyed by Ellinger's "very broad, objectionably broad" shoulders, the image of which springs to his mind when Marian declares Niel's shoulders insufficiently broad for bearing her burdens (p. 78). And he feels that there is "something evil" (p. 46), although he does not know why, about the aura of male sensuality projected by this man. Niel seems instinctively to understand that the "intrusion" of Ellinger's sexuality into Marian's world could sully the "mother" and thus expose the hidden oedipal motivations behind Niel's worship of the lady. Like Hamlet (and the novel's epigraph referring to that drama invites the comparison), Niel will feel that his entire world is out-of-joint when he loses his "mother" to the sexual woman.

Although Niel is not conscious of the conflicting motivations behind his idealization of Marian, he is aware that in other respects he lives a "double life, with all its guilty enjoyments" (p. 81). Publically he may be the cold young monk chastely worshipping his lady Marian, but privately his repressed sexual interests find a vicarious release through his uncle's set of the Bohn Classics. At first glance, Cather's list of Niel's favorite books at the beginning of Chapter 7 (Book I) seems to be an irrelevant digression from the logic of the plot which has been moving swiftly toward the scene which the previously-informed reader has been anticipating for several chapters—Niel's discovery of Marian's sexuality, the revelation of which forms the turning point of the plot. And, indeed, the information on Niel's literary preferences would be excess baggage if Cather intended no more than an exposure of Marian's failure to live up to an ideal of frontier loyalty.[9] However, in terms of revealing certain contradictions in Niel's character, his literary interests are precisely to the point, for they not only show us "what he [consciously] wished his own relations with people to be" (p. 82), but also conflicting desires of which he is unaware or refuses to acknowledge. For in his reading of *Don Juan* or Ovid's erotic elegies, Niel is somewhat of a literary peeping Tom, eagerly "eavesdropping upon the past, being let into the great world that had plunged and glittered and sumptuously sinned long before little western towns were dreamed of" (pp. 81–82).

Niel's literary interests fall into two general groups that represent the two sides of his interest in Marian and thus help explain the intensity of his forthcoming reaction to the reality of Marian's sexual nature. In the first category are stories about male heroes who function, in many ways, as the literary alter egoes, safely distanced, of the sexually-repressed Niel. He becomes "beguiled" first by *Don Juan* (which his uncle said he was not yet old enough to read) and then moves on to *Tom Jones* and *Wilhelm Meister*. All three of these works concern the sexual and mental development of erring young men (all literal or emotional "foundlings"—like Niel) who leave the protective environs and illusions of their childhood, and who learn, through active involvement in the world of time, the appropriate virtues needed to insure survival or to secure a meaningful future. Since the learning experiences which make

up the "apprenticeships" of these impetuous male heroes frequently revolve around sexual initiations (often with oedipal overtones), these
stories almost seem to function as displaced sexual fantasies for the repressed side of Niel. *Don Juan*, for instance, opens with the teenage hero's
initiation into sexuality by the seductive efforts of an older woman (his
mother's friend) who (like Marian) is married to a man twenty-five years
her senior; Tom Jones is also willingly seduced by several older women,
one of whom is supposedly the foundling's rediscovered "mother." Sexual
escapades are not the focal point of Wilhelm Meister's apprenticeship,
although Wilhelm's first sexual experience is with a woman whose name
(Marianne) bears a striking resemblance to Marian's, but Goethe's insistence that Wilhelm must learn the false nature of illusions at one point
revolves around the hero's participation in a production of *Hamlet*, the
play alluded to in the epigraph of Cather's novel. Thus, indirectly, the
alert reader's attention would be brought back to the problematic relationship, with its latent oedipal overtones, between Hamlet and his mother.

Niel's private enjoyment of "sumptuous" sinners of the past is, indeed, ironic, for he will find "living creatures caught in the very behavior of living" (p. 81) less thrilling when the "sinner" is his idealized
lady. But if the literary male apprenticeship plots suggest some of the
oedipal repressions inherent in Niel's Mariolatry, the second category of
his literary interests—Ovid's erotic elegies—foreshadow what will be the
outcome of the oedipal conflict which is, unbeknownst to him, pushing
him toward the world of time and sexual maturity. Niel, we are told,
"read the *Heroides* over and over, and felt that they were the most glowing love stories ever told" and he "always went back to them after other
[literary] experiments" (p. 81). Niel's preference for the *Heroides*—even
before he discovers Marian's infidelity—is understandable, but rather
ironic, for he is essentially identifying more closely with what a (male)
author has told him is the female role and destiny rather than with the
supposedly usual male role of a Don Juan or a Tom Jones. Unlike the male
heroes, Ovid's lamenting heroines do not live and love in the present,
nor do they mature or progress towards some future goal. Instead, the
heroines, who in most cases have loved and lost, live only in the memory
of that lost love. Their grief is so overwhelming that time, as an objective
reality, no longer has meaning; in fact, the retrospective form of the
erotic elegy, plus the almost monotonous repetition of the same experience in each lamenting heroine's epistle, gives the effect of freezing time.
As one Ovidean critic suggests, these epistles of arrested female consciousness almost become "casebook studies" of the "psycho-pathology"
of love,[10] a viewpoint which sheds light on the nature of Niel's response
in Book II, for when he finds that Marian has moved beyond the static
construct which he has created to preserve her ideal form (that is, his
non-sexual childhood image), Niel himself becomes, as it were, the
Ovidean heroine refusing to betray a past ideal by entering into the

world of time, change, and maturity. Survivor's guilt will once again result in "arrested consciousness" and rejection of the post-maternal world of the present.

These progressive and conservative motivations which are simultaneously urging Niel on toward his future (and natural) maturity and irresistibly drawing him back to a static past come into open collision when Niel makes his devotional pilgrimage to (of all places!) Marian's bedroom window. Superficially, the images surrounding his journey seem to emphasize innocence and purity. He awakens early one morning "with that intense, blissful realization of summer that comes to children in their beds." However, the immediate thought of encroaching sexuality (i.e., Ellinger) drives him out into the "religious purity" of the dew-drenched dawn and fragrant meadows; he is anxious to reach Marian before explicit sexuality can awaken—"before [the sleeping] Ellinger could intrude his unwelcome presence" (p. 84). In his desire to create in Marian a "distaste for coarse worldlings like Frank Ellinger," he gathers "off the cheeks of morning" a bouquet of wild roses that will hopefully keep his lovely lady as chaste as he believes his worship is innocent (p. 85). But when he arrives at Marian's bedroom window and hears the laughing Ellinger within, he is shocked to discover that the seemingly "unstained" morning of devotion harbors active and unrepressed sexuality. Disillusioned by his failure to "save" Marian from the threat of sexuality, he utters the Shakespearian line from Sonnet 94—"lilies that fester smell far worse than weeds" (p. 87)—that critics have taken as Cather's judgment on Marian Forrester. And as he runs away from the sexual realities toward which he has been journeying, he tells himself "bitterly" that "before the dew dried ... the bloom of his existence ... was gone, like the morning freshness of the flowers" (p. 86). Innocence unfairly "betrayed" by time and sexuality is the theme of this crucial scene—from Niel's viewpoint.

Niel's Shakespearian allusion, however, suggests a broader perspective from which the theme of "devouring time" should be viewed, for this central scene is permeated with the Ovidean images and motifs of the Shakespearian sonnets. Of particular importance are the flower images apparent not only in this scene, but also in the second half of the novel. The red roses and white lilies which first appear in this central scene could, in some contexts, symbolize the Virgin Mary and thus the pure nature of the young monk's worship,[11] but the Shakespearean context of the scene suggests that the roses should be seen as symbols of passion, not innocence, and cankered roses and festered lilies as images of sexual corruption, with the latter image, in particular, implying an unnatural or distorted sexuality caused by "ingrown virginity," as one Shakespearian critic puts it.[12] Although the monkish Niel views sexuality as an external threat (namely, Ellinger), the true source of sexuality encroaching on the young celibate's devotion to his lady is suggested by his gift of "half-awake . . . flaming [rose] buds, just beginning to open" (p. 85)—that is, Niel's budding passion which sexual jealousy has nearly exposed. The image of festering sexuality is even contained within Niel's wild roses for, as any close reader of Shakespeare's sonnets is aware, the wild rose's susceptibility to corruption earned it the popular nickname of the "canker" rose.

If Niel were the hero of one of his male apprenticeship novels, this journey to his lady would mark a crucial stage in his development (a change from passive admiration to an active declaration of love) and lead to his initiation into sexuality. Niel, however, rejects the sexual revelation toward which he has been journeying, because it would lead him further away from the idealized maternal past. Instead, he tries to prolong the precariously balanced moment of early morning innocence by, as it were, nipping passion in the bud; he cuts the stems of the flowers of passion, an action suggesting symbolic castration. This denial of maturity, however, makes him even more vulnerable to the world of time and change, for the only flower more short-lived than a wild rose is a *cut* wild rose which almost immediately shows the effects of time and decay (wilts "before the dew dries"). Consequently, he himself soils his "love" by throwing the revelatory roses in a mudhole. Niel, not Marian, is the festered lily, the type which Shakespeare disapprovingly characterized as proposing "to itselfe, . . . only to live and die"—those who selfishly "husband nature's riches" onto themselves and, like the chaste Angelo in *Measure for Measure*, distort their own natures.

The Shakespearian images of transience and change which dominate this central scene continue unabated in Book II which records the death of Captain Forrester and Marian's last "betrayal" of his frontier world. If a celibate ideal exists in the novel, it is surely embodied in the Captain, but his attitudes and values differ considerably from Niel's. One of the most obvious differences between the two lies in their attiudes towards time. In Book II, roses are also associated with the Captain whose beloved rose garden surrounds his favorite object—the sun dial— on which the slowly dying man watches "time visibly devoured" (p. 111). The Captain himself is the novel's major image of passing time; each stage of his physical deterioration is likened to the slow but sure crumbling of a mountain which, despite its strength, is subject to time. Unlike Niel, however, the Captain does not reject time and change, for the dying man sees the emblem of eternity in his sundial "from the Garden of the Gods" (p. 108). Consequently, his love and loyalty for his wife are no more affected by his knowledge of time and change than they were by his knowledge of Marian's affair. As even Niel eventually surmises, the Captain "knew everything; more than anyone else; all there was to know about Marian Forrester" (p. 117), but what is most significant is that "knowing her, he,—to use one of his own expressions,—valued her" (p. 143). As Shakespeare had pointed out, it is "altered love" that makes one "time's fool," but the Captain never loses his lady because his love and loyalty are "fixed marks" which time cannot change. Consequently, those emblems of his love, the roses which he cultivates as carefully as he does his lovely wife, are not only longer lasting than Niel's cut wild roses, but are, in fact, as beautiful to him in autumn—he lovingly watches the September sunset "*glory* on his roses" (p. 114; my emphasis)—as they were in the spring of his affection. The sundial and roses, which Marian later transplants on the Captain's grave, (and the widow's annual gift of flowers for the grave) become symbols of the constant love and loyalty which he gave and received and which can survive the passage of time.

In Book II, Niel's growing appreciation of the Captain, who almost becomes a father-figure in his eyes, and the superficial resemblance between Niel's childhood aesthetic and the Captain's frontier values create the false impression that Niel's Hamlet-like attempts to set right the out-of-joint times by saving Marian from her sexual self are somehow admirable, even heroic. Yet Niel's allegiance is to an illusory stasis—an artificially recreated and preserved past—and not to the frontier virtues which, as the Captain shows, transcend, rather than deny, the world of time and change. For Niel's loyalty, unlike the Captain's, is conditional;[13] he will keep faith with Marian only if she is willing to become again the restored mother of his pre-sexually aware imagination. He sees an opportunity to expel sexuality from her world when the distraught Marian uses his telephone to call and denounce bitterly the newly-married Ellinger. In another act of symbolic castration, Niel represses her passionate outpour by cutting the telephone cord—literally, her last connection with her lover. Then, restored to her non-sexual role as Captain Forrester's wife (but too drunk and hysterical to return home), Marian can be safely undressed and put in Niel's bed while he, like a good "son," journeys to the Forrester house to care for the ailing father-figure.

The tension between this regressive movement back to a falsely idealized past and the novel's insistent drive toward a progressive future reaches its highest point when Niel gives up a year of college to help the overburdened and financially-straitened Marian care for the dying Captain. Superficially, Niel seems to be affirming the Captain's ethic— Niel had "the satisfaction of those who keep faith" (p. 142)—but in actuality what he has done is to retreat away from the future into an imaginary past. For by moving into the Forrester household where he maintains nighttime "vigils," Niel has, in essence, replaced the disordered and defeated reality of his biological family with an idealized foster home. At the Forresters, he now plays the role of dutiful son caring for his aging parents.

Niel's loyalty to Captain Forrester is motivated primarily by his need to preserve the "mother" by invoking the rights and authority of the pioneer father-figure, but when the Captain dies, Niel not only refuses to help Marian (he actively *discourages* the Captain's old friend from offering Marian financial assistance) but even rationalizes the change in his loyalties by accusing her of the unforgiveable sin of changing. "[H]is own feeling toward the lady had changed" but "it was Mrs. Forrester herself who had changed. Since her husband's death she seemed to have become another woman" (p. 152). She has indeed changed—from wife to widow—which is exactly what Niel is objecting to. To Niel, survival represents a passion for life that drives one toward the future and further away from an idealized past. From his viewpoint, Marian's survival signals her reentry into the "fallen" world of time and sexuality. For what is it that motivates his final rejection of Marian Forrester? Not her attempts to recoup her economic losses by turning to the somewhat shady lawyer, "poison" Ivy Peters (although these questionable investments do bother Niel), but his discovery that once again Marian has changed back into a sexual woman—that she is having an affair with the disgreeable Peters.[14] Niel's discovery that the Captain's widow has been released from the non-sexual restraints of the fatherly husband—that she has moved beyond the sexual inhibitions that Niel had placed on her—causes to burst forth all the hostility and anger which he had suppressed since that early morning discovery of Marian's relationship with Ellinger: "It was what he held most against Mrs. Forrester; that she was not willing to immolate herself, like the widow of all these great men, and die with the pioneer period to which she belonged; that she preferred life on any terms" (p. 169). Since that pioneer period to which he claims she belongs corresponds precisely with Niel's presexually-aware youth, what he refuses to forgive is her failure to live up to his naive and mistaken childhood image of her—the image which expressed the orphaned child's need for the lost mother.

Niel fails to become the apprenticeship hero of his own story because his desire to survive and participate in the present and future was lost with the death of his mother. After that event, he consistently reveals a resentment, in one form or another, towards all survivors—including himself—and his symbolic castrations are both an expression of allegiance to the childhood maternal ideal and an admission of guilt for having survived the lost mother. Unlike Captain Forrester, Niel is not a celibate ideal, for the life-denying basis of his non-sexual aspirations distorts his angle of vision and forces him to reject—to lose—his idealized lady until time and, eventually, her death place her beyond the world of change and adult sexuality. Only then does he recover "a bright impersonal memory" of "Daniel Forrester's wife," a memory, however, that does not redeem the present nor provide him with hope for the future. In fact, all he has at the end of the novel are unanswered questions: "Her eyes, when they laughed . . . , seemed to promise *a wild delight that he had not found in life*. . . . He would like to call up the shade of the young Mrs. Forrester . . . [and] demand the secret of that ardour; ask her whether she had really found some ever-blooming, ever-burning, every-piercing [sic?] joy, or whether it was all fine play-acting. Probably she had found no more than another . . ." (pp. 171–72; my emphasis).

Niel's final question is essentially the same one that he had asked about the secret of beautiful women when, at age nineteen, he had run away from the realities of adult sexuality and time. That her secret was to be found in her passionate will to survive and that her sexuality was one aspect of that intensity for life are answers which lie beyond the comprehension of the life-denying celibate view. But in the end, the image of the flawed sexual woman who preferred life on any terms retains in the reader's mind a brilliance and vitality more enduring than the self-justifying negations of the celibate center of consciousness who has nothing to offer but the resigned skepticism that probably no one finds joy in life. Niel's loyalty to his childhood past is a betrayal of everything the novel's celibate ideal, Captain Forrester, lived by; it causes Niel to reject his lady and to lose the promise of an ever-blooming joy possessed by Marian and by the Captain through his lovely wife.

Notes

1. Quoted by Mildred R. Bennett in *The World of Willa Cather* (Lincoln: University of Nebraska Press, 1961), p. 69.

2. This reading has been given, with little variation, in the major biographies and book-length studies of Cather. See, for instance, E. K. Brown, *Willa Cather: A Critical Biography*, completed by Leon Edel (New York: Alfred A. Knopf, 1953), pp. 228–35; John H. Randall III, *The Landscape and the Looking Glass: Willa Cather's Search for Value* (Boston: Houghton-Mifflin, 1960), pp. 174–202; James Woodress, *Willa Cather: Her Life and Art* (New York: Pegasus, 1970), pp. 199–205; and David Stouck, *Willa Cather's Imagination* (Lincoln: University of Nebraska Press, 1975), pp. 58–68. However, Ellen Moers, *Literary Women* (Garden City, New York: Doubleday and Co., 1976), p. 238, maintains that Marian is "worthy of adoration."

3. Brown-Edel, p. 229. Woodress, p. 200, uses the phrase "alter-ego," while Philip Gerber, *Willa Cather* (Boston: Twayne Publishers, 1975), p. 111, asserts that "Niel exists chiefly to represent the author and her attitude."

4. "*A Lost Lady*: End of the First Cycle," *Western American Literature*, 7 (Spring 1972), 11. However, as a narrator, Jim Burden also has limitations. For a thorough study of Jim Burden's attitudes toward sexuality and limitations as narrator, see Blanche H. Gelfant, "The Forgotten Reaping-Hook: Sex in *My Ántonia*," *American Literature*, 43 (March 1971), 60–82.

5. "The Problem of Point of View in *A Lost Lady*," *Renascence* 28 (Autumn 1974), 47. Most critics mention the problems Cather had in determining the appropriate point of view for *A Lost Lady* (see Brown-Edel, pp. 228–29), but few devote more than a paragraph to explaining the significance of her final choice. Typical is the approach of Stouck, pp. 59–66, who discusses the ironic gap in Book I between Niel's innocent view and Marian's "fallen" reality. Randall, pp. 188–90, however, does suggest some limitations in Niel's angle of vision.

6. Stouck, pp. 38; Stouck denies, however, that Niel is one of these types, but does point out, in a somewhat different context, some aspects of the erotic theme.

7. Willa Cather, *A Lost Lady* (New York: Random House, 1951), p. 30. All future references to this source will be incorporated into the text.

8. In Freudian thought, puberty is considered the period of sexual development when unresolved oedipal motivations, latent since age five (Niel's age when his mother died), would be reawakened. Since I have been unable to determine the extent to which Cather might have known or been influenced by the Freudian concepts which her era was discovering, and since the novel, in any case, moves far beyond a psycho-analytic tract, I have kept Freudian terminology to an absolute minimum. But Cather's recognition in this novel of the two most important periods of sexual development, as well as recent studies of the sexual themes in *My Ántonia*, suggest that Cather was not as oblivious to the possibility of childhood sexuality as some of her more "innocent" critics have assumed.

9. Only Randall, p. 188, tries, in a brief paragraph and with limited success, to find some significance in these references.

10. Howard Jacobson, *Ovid's Heroides* (Princeton: Princeton University Press, 1974), p. 375. Many of my generalizations about the *Heroides* are derived from this source. Jacobson also mentions that "few would now agree with [the literary judgment of] Willa Cather's Niel . . . ." (p. 3). Should Niel's belief that the *Heroides* are "glowing love stories" be read as a further irony?

11. The passing-of-the-West theme has been discussed by most of the above-mentioned critics, but, despite the novel's epigraph and Niel's allusion to the sonnets, the Shakespearian context of the time theme has been virtually ignored. Stouck, pp. 60–61, 63–64, relates, in passing, the flower images only to Marian's sexuality and "narcissism." Evelyn Thomas Helmick, "The Broken World: Medievalism in *A Lost Lady*," *Renascence* 28 (Autumn 1975), 44, sees a Virgin Mary-courtly lady reference in this flower symbolism, but her treatment of Marian as "lost" and Niel as the "hope for the future" is more complex and informative than many of the more conventional studies of the historical allegory.

12. L. C. Knights, "Shakespeare's Sonnets," *Scrutiny*, 3 (September 1934), 133–160; reprinted in *A Casebook on Shakespeare's Sonnets*, ed. Gerald Willen and Victor B. Reed (New York: Thomas Y. Crowell Co., 1964), p. 186.

13. That Niel's concept of loyalty differs from the Captain's is, to my knowledge, suggested only by two studies: very briefly in Randall, p. 190, but more helpfully in Brunauer, pp. 48.

14. Since Peters, who is not much older than Niel, has clearly functioned since Niel's childhood as Niel's foil and rival, one cannot avoid the suspicion that his peer's success has brought the sexual threat too close to Niel himself and that the motivation behind his abrupt departure from Sweet Water is (again) sexual jealousy.

The Professor's House

[Review of *The Professor's House*]   Henry Seidel Canby*

This is the age of experiment in the American novel. No sooner had the seers of the academies decided that American life was too thin and too unsophisticated for mature fiction than a flood of novels began (and this new book is one of them) in which new methods of story telling, new angles of approach, new styles were exploited in order to catch the manifold facets of an American social history that suddenly began to seem the most important, the most auspicious, and, paradoxically, the most menacing phenomenon of the century. In ten years the American novel has become, if not deep, rich. Such an outburst of technical experiment is almost irresistible to the professional reviewer. He must take the new American watch apart to see how it works, and whether its parts are certified by experience. Yet technique is not important except when it fails, and if the new technique of *The Professor's House* creaks a little, a method is only machinery after all, and we may turn to the more interesting question of what Miss Cather has got into her book.

Miss Cather, I suspect, is wearying of broad pioneer movements and sharp contrasts between flaming emotion and commonplace environment. She is going deeper, and is prepared to defend the thesis that a new country may have old souls in it. An old soul is by no means a Main Street high brow dissatisfied with crudity. He is much too civilized to be upset by a difference of opinion over the value of culture. An old soul, as the philosophers say, is driven toward recognition. Life, for him, instead of consisting of so many successes, so many quarrels, so many events that can be ticketed for a biography, is a progress in self-realization, a series of discoveries as to what experience means for *him* when stripped of illusion and in its ultimate reality. Such a soul is most likely to fall away from his closest associates; success may be a burden, an admired wife a growing problem, children who become the hard

*Originally published in the *Saturday Review of Literature*, 2 (26 September 1925), 151. Copyright 1925 by the *Saturday Review*. All rights reserved. Reprinted by permission.

worldlings that most of us are in our thirties, a depression rather than a comfort. Put such an old soul in a small western university, give him a charming wife who chooses the children's part, afflict him with two sons-in-law, one unctuous and one soured, and two daughters, one mean and one envious—and drama follows.

The Professor's House might readily have been written as a mirror of small town bickerings meticulously preserved in Miss Cather's cool, firm style. Professor St. Peter is too good for his job, and too civilized for his community; also he is a personality, with force, humor, distinction, charm. There have been two major experiences in his life, the writing of his great history of the Spanish adventurers, and his friendship with Tom Outland, the only first-rate mind that ever came into his classes. The history is written and has made him famous and financially independent. The boy is dead, killed in the war, but the patent he willed to his fiancée, the professor's daughter, has been exploited by the skilful Jew she married afterwards and has made the two of them rich and envied. Outland's fortunes, like Antony's, have corrupted better men, and brought pettiness to a family that was not necessarily committed to such a fate.

This is what happens on the smooth flowing surface of *The Professor's House*, but it is not the story; the story is beneath. The story is slow discovery by Professor St. Peter—of himself. His family have moved with prosperity to a new house, but he clings, hardly knowing why, to his attic in the old house, beside the dress forms where Augusta, the sewing woman, used to drape the young girls' dresses. Why is he happier there than in the new house? Why does his family begin to weigh upon his nerves? Why does the memory of Tom Outland grow brighter until he sits down to write his story? It is a fourth of the novel, this story, antecedent to the main action, superficially irrelevant to it—the story of an orphan adrift in the Southwest who finds with his pal a cliff dwellers' city on an unclimbed mesa, spends the best year of his life interpreting the experience of dead men, until from it he gets a perception of a life lived for ideas, a self-realization that this is how he wishes to live. Why does the professor, his work done, refuse to enjoy its fruits in travel, but rather cling to his loneliness, until, rather than face his returning family, he would, except for Augusta and the solid human nature she represents, have let the old gas stove, blown out by the wind, blow him out too?

These are the questions *The Professor's House* answers, not as a metaphysician would answer them, by analyzing the results of a self-realization which leads to new values that make the man different, but in rich and vigorous narrative. It is the difference between William James's study of religious experience and the narrative of a consignificance elsewhere always preserved. Yet I am more interested in this story than in other books of hers which are more perfectly achieved.

The soul, after all, is the greatest subject for art. We have swung in our American writing from sophisticated studies of sophisticated personalities through unsophisticated romances of simple folk to satiric narratives of commonplace people who are interesting only because they are pawns in a national society. Yet the rich, subtle natures, whose problems have no relation to success or failure as our world sees it, and who are not types of social classes or particular environments, seem always to escape the novelist, although they are probably more numerous though less self-conscious in America than in older countries where conformity is not regarded as a prime virtue. Miss Cather, one of the ablest novelists now writing in English, believes, what no Englishman or no Frenchman can be convinced of, and no native novelist since Hawthorne has practised, that there is profundity in American life. A profundity not merely instinctive such as Sherwood Anderson is revealing, but a conscious spiritual profundity which poets like Robert Frost and Edwin Arlington Robinson have long seen. This, more than *O Pioneers!*, is a pioneering book.

A Cave of One's Own   Leon Edel*

There has been for many years a vigorous resistance to literary "psychologizing" and a tendency to stop one's ears the moment a psychoanalyst arrives and starts explaining that, for example, the trouble with Robert Louis Stevenson was that he had a feeding problem when he was a baby. Having as an infant been denied his mother's milk, he sought ever after to gratify his oral needs—which was why he dreamed up his story of Dr. Jekyll and Mr. Hyde and hinged the story on the swallowing of a potion; and this was why he could hold his own at the prodigious day-long luaus in Samoa and Hawaii. This, we are further told, meant that he never really became a mature person.

It so happens that the fact is right, however much the theorizing may be specious. Mama Stevenson kept a diary when Louis was an infant, and there were some infantile feeding problems. Also Stevenson no doubt, for reasons about which we can only speculate, retained certain boyish elements in his makeup and wasn't much interested in women as characters for his fiction. But we can reply that out of his eternal boyishness grew the eternally youthful *Treasure Island*. And if there was this duality in him, how well he was equipped to trace the double sides of man's nature as he did in Jekyll and his hideous counterpart!

*From *Stuff of Sleep and Dreams: Experiments in Literary Psychology* by Leon Edel, pp. 216–40. Copyright © 1959, 1982 by Leon Edel. Reprinted by permission of Harper & Row, Publishers, Inc.

The process of applying psychiatry to literature cannot be effective if it reduces the artist to a neurosis: critics have rightly called this approach "reductive." But we are interested in how the artist triumphs over anxieties and feeding problems, all the ills of body and mind, and acquires a kind of second sight, a positive urge to create. These discussions are by no means modern: they did not originate with Freud. We have often been reminded that Charles Lamb wrote an essay "On the Sanity of True Genius" long before the advent of psychoanalysis. Men, Lamb observed, "finding in the raptures of the higher poetry a condition of exaltation, to which they have no parallel in their own experience, besides the spurious resemblance of it in dreams and fevers, impute a state of dreaminess and fever to the poet. But the true poet dreams being awake. He is not possessed by his subject but has dominion over it. . . . Where he seems most to recede from humanity, he will be found the truest to it."

Art is the result not of calm and tranquillity, however much the artist may, on occasion, experience calm in the act of writing. It springs from tension and passion, from a state of disequilibrium in the artist's being. "His art is happy, but who knows his mind?" William Butler Yeats asked in speaking of Keats. The psychologist, reading the pattern of the work, can attempt to tell us what was wrong with the artist's mental or psychic health. The biographer, reading the same pattern in the larger picture of the human condition, seeks to show how the negatives were converted into positives: how Proust translated his allergies and his withdrawal from the pain of experience into the whole world of Combray, capturing in language the very essences which seem illusory and evanescent in man's consciousness; how Virginia Woolf, on the margin of her melancholy, pinned the feeling of the moment to the printed page as the hunter of butterflies pins down the diaphanous and fluttering prize; and how James Joyce, visioning himself as Daedalus soaring over a world he had mastered, created a language for it, the word-salads of *Finnegans Wake*—but where the schizophrenic patient creates word-salads because of his madness, Joyce created them with that method in madness which Lamb was describing when he spoke of the artist's dominion over his subject. These are the victories of art over the psychic troubles which intervene at various times during our active lives.

Literature and psychology are not necessarily antagonistic, as they have been made to seem. They meet on common ground. We have for decades used psychology in criticism and in biography. When we study the motivations of Hamlet, is this not psychology? When we try to understand and speculate upon symbols in a work, are we not "psychologizing?" And in our time, when creative writers have been exposed directly to the works of Freud and Jung and use them in their writings, we must treat them for the sources that they are. How can we understand William Faulkner's *Light in August* without at least a glance at certain modern theories of conditioning and behavior? Can we deal adequately with *Finnegans Wake* without looking into Jung and his theory of the collective unconscious? What meaning can Eugene O'Neill's *Strange Interlude* and *Mourning Becomes Electra* have if they are divorced from the popular misconceptions of Freud in the 1920s? Freud himself acknowledged that Sophocles and Dostoevsky and Ibsen had the kind of glimpses into the unconscious vouchsafed him in his consulting room. The answer to the misguided use of psychoanalysis is not to close our ears but to ask ourselves: How are we to deal with this difficult material while remaining true to our own disciplines—and avoid making complete fools of ourselves?

It is fairly obvious that we can handle it only after we have studied and mastered that part of psychology useful to us, as we must master any learning. Our success will depend entirely on the extent to which we learn to use this intricate discipline. We must not run amuck; above all, we must beware of the terminology and jargon of the psychoanalysts. What we must try to do is to translate the terms in a meaningful way and into language proper to literary discipline. Critics who babble of the Oedipus complex and who plant psychoanalytical clichés higgledy-piggledy in their writings perform a disservice both to literature and to psychoanalysis. Biographers who take certain arbitrary symbols, and apply them rigidly to the wholly volatile human personality, inevitably arrive at gross and ludicrous distortions. These are matters highly complex and difficult to explain. I have accordingly sought an illustrative problem to demonstrate what I would deem to be the use—and the abuse—of psychology in the writing of biography and literary criticism.

I

My text is a novel by the American elegiac novelist Willa Cather, published in 1925 by Alfred Knopf. It fell to my lot in the early 1950s to complete a biography of Cather left unfinished by an old friend, who had died in the midst of his work. To complete the work of another is one of the most difficult tasks a writer can undertake. One has in effect to do the entire job all over again in order to seize all the invisible threads which exist in those portions already completed. My friend, Edward K. Brown, a companion of my Paris years, had written nine chapters. I found that three more were required, and in the course of my work I came on much interesting material relating to Cather's novel *The Professor's House*. This is the novel I propose to deal with. It is not a fully realized work, although it has been influential on other writers. My first and prime goal was to discover what significance the professor's house has in the story, since it is the dwelling which was given the primary place in the title.

The Professor's House is the story of a professor in a midwestern university who has achieved success but derives no particular pleasure from it. The novel is a record of his mental depression. With the money received from a prize he has won for a monumental historical work, Professor St. Peter has built a new house to please his wife and daughters. He would prefer to remain in the rented house in which he has shaped his career for thirty years. Indeed, he cannot bring himself to move out of his old study, located in the attic, where still stand the wire forms on which a dressmaker fitted the clothes for his wife and growing daughters. The attic sewing room is lit by an oil lamp. It is heated by a stove. Professor St. Peter has scorned cushion comforts. He had a "show" study downstairs and has one in the new house. But the attic room, with its silent dummies, is comfort enough for him. He clings to the old place even after the rest of the house has been emptied and the moving is over. Since the lease still has some months to run, he decides he will keep his former workroom until he has to surrender it.

His elder daughter is Rosamond, an attractive girl who has married a suave, fast-talking, pretentious, but cultivated young man named Louie Marsellus. Marsellus has, with great practicality, turned to commercial use in aviation a certain discovery made by one of the professor's former students, Tom Outland, who was Rosamond's fiancé but who was killed during the First World War. Outland bequeathed his patent to Rosamond, and since her marriage to Marsellus it has become a source of wealth. The professor loves his daughter very much, but intensely dislikes the upstart qualities of her husband, and accordingly feels a certain alienation from her. The professor's wife, however, is extremely fond of her son-in-law and his European affectations. She feels that her husband, in his withdrawal from the entire family, does not sufficiently recognize how materially its fortunes are being altered by Louie Marsellus's business acumen. There is a second daughter who is married to a newspaper columnist named McGregor. They tend to side with the father against the somewhat vulgar *nouveau riche* world of Louie and Rosamond. The latter are also building a house—in the style of a Norwegian manor, set incongruously in this midwestern community.

The first part of the book, titled "The Family," sketches for us the professor's alienation from those closest to him because of his feeling that his wife and daughters do not really understand his deeper emotional life, and his rebellion against the materialism of the college town. He has set himself apart successfully over the years. He has made for himself a French garden in this prairie setting; he has cultivated his love for French wines and delicate sauces; he has a beach house on the lake and spends long lonely hours by the water. He is a Gallic epicure isolated, like his garden, in surroundings to which he cannot ever wholly belong. He has had only one student in all the years of his teaching for whom he could feel affection: Tom Outland. He dislikes the new generation of students. He dislikes college politics. He has no real friends among his colleagues. He feels himself oppressed by the prosaic, mediocre world of the town of which his wife and daughters are so much a part. Commercial values have been exalted here over those he cherishes: the rich fabric of art related to the rich fabric of the old religion in which great cathedrals and the drama of Good and Evil exalted men to a high creativity.

The second part of the book is called "Tom Outland's Story." Here Willa Cather attempts a risky technical device, which is nevertheless time-honored in fiction. In the manner of Cervantes or Smollett she interpolates a story within a story: she gives us an autobiographical fragment written by Tom Outland and confided to Professor St. Peter. It describes a crucial episode in the young man's life. Cather explained that in writing this part of the novel she had in mind those Dutch paintings in which interiors are scrupulously rendered; in many of these there was "a square window, open, through which one saw the masts of ships, or a stretch of gray sea"; the effect is that of an inset, a picture within a picture. Having given us the interior of the professor's family life, she directs our attention to the one important window in it—the one that looks out upon Tom Outland's adventure.

The crucial episode has been his discovery of a Cliff Dwellers' village tucked into a wall of rock high in a New Mexico canyon. Here was beauty at once primitive and sophisticated. Here were houses that let in wind and sun and yet sheltered an unfathomable past. Here also was a great tower: "It was still as sculpture.... The tower was the fine thing that held all the jumble of houses together and made them mean something.... That village sat looking down into the cañon with the calmness of eternity." The Cliff Dwellers' houses are never overtly contrasted with the houses in the professor's town, but they invite contrast. In the modern town the emphasis, as my friend Edward Brown observed, is on the individual buildings. In the ancient village it is on the architectural as well as the social unity.

Tom has made his discovery with the aid of a fellow cowpuncher, Roddy. He travels to Washington in great excitement to inform the Department of the Interior, taking with him samples of the ancient pottery he found in the long-deserted houses. In the capital he is promptly wrapped up in heedless red tape; he sits in impersonal outer offices; he is met with general indifference. Civil servants seem to him strange modern cave dwellers living in rows of apartments as if in rabbit warrens; and their careerism and arrogance blot out all his hopes. He turns his back on Washington, disillusioned; he feels he has done the proper thing as a citizen, but the petty officials do not share his interest in his country's distant past. However, a still greater disappointment awaits him. Roddy, during his prolonged absence, has profited by the arrival of a German anthropologist to sell the entire contents of the cliff town. The ancient relics have been packed and shipped to Europe, and Roddy has deposited the money for Tom in a bank, thinking he has driven a good bargain. Tom, in anger at what he considers a betrayal, breaks with Roddy and then returns to the cliff town to spend a few days in magnificent solitude, hiding in the high tower his notes and records of the entire adventure. Then, descending again, he withdraws the money from the bank and uses it to go to college, there meeting the professor who becomes his guide and mentor.

The final part of the novel is a mere sketch. Titled "The Professor," it returns to the dilemma of St. Peter's isolation in his attic. Lonely and depressed, he remains there while his family is away during the summer, living a monastic dream life, with the old sewing woman turning up to act as charwoman. One day, on awakening from a nap, he discovers the room is filled with fumes from the stove, but he is incapable of making the effort to arouse himself and to throw open the window. He has lost the will to live. The fortuitous arrival of the sewing woman saves him, and there the novel ends. We can only speculate that the professor will go on living in isolation amid his family.

II

What are we to make of this novel—if we can call it a novel? It is a stitching together of two inconclusive fragments about a professor, his family, and his wish for death and the adventures of a young man alone with the past on a mesa and briefly in touch with the modern urban life of Washington. The two episodes relating to the professor hardly constitute a novel; they convey a picture of his deep depression, which nothing in the book really explains. Why does he wish for death at a time when his life has been crowned with success and when his family flourishes as never before; when indeed there is the promise of a grandchild, for Rosamond expects a baby as the book ends? The Tom Outland story fills the background of Rosamond's wealth and gives us the strange story of the intense young man who alters the whole course of the professor's life; this does not illuminate, however, the professor's final state of mind. His wish to die is at no point sufficiently motivated by the facts of the small-town life, the general hopelessness of the Philistine surroundings. To believe so intensely in art and the religion of art, and to have created so fully, and yet at the same time to be overpowered by a sense of futility and ineffectuality—these are the contradictions we discern within the professor.

Professor Brown found an inner unity which he explained in terms of the symbolism of houses within the book. It is a striking passage. There are, he points out, the two houses of the professor, and of these the old house is the significant one. The new house is wrong for him. The Marsellus-Rosamond Norwegian manor house is also wrong. It is a product of pretension and materialism, without regard for the style of the town and the essential dignity of human dwellings. The homes of the Cliff

Dwellers—for these are houses also, primitive and wind-swept on their mountainous height—possessed that dignity. In the third portion of the book, the link between these houses is established. Brown continued, speaking of this final part:

> The first and second parts of the book which have seemed so boldly unrelated are brought into a profound unity. It is in this third part of the novel that the large background of emotion, which demands rhythmic expression if we are to respond to it as it deserves, becomes predominant. In the first part it was plain that the professor did not wish to live in his new house, and did not wish to enter into the sere phase of his life correlative with it. At the beginning of the third part it becomes plain that he cannot indefinitely continue to make the old attic study the theatre of his life, that he cannot go on prolonging, or attempting to prolong his prime, the phase of his life correlative with that. The personality of his mature years—the personality that had expressed itself powerfully and in the main happily in his teaching, his scholarship, his love for his wife, his domesticity—is now quickly receding, and nothing new is flowing in. What begins to dominate St. Peter is something akin to the Cliff Dwellers, something primitive which had ruled him long ago when he was a boy on a pioneer farm in the rough Solomon valley in northwestern Kansas. To this primitive being not many things were real; . . . what counted was nature, and nature seen as a web of life, and finally of death.

The professor remembers an old poem he has read, Longfellow's translation of the Anglo-Saxon *Grave*. He doesn't recall it quite accurately (that is, Miss Cather didn't), but this is what is given in the novel:

> For thee a house was built
> Ere thou wast born;
> For thee a mould was made
> Ere thou of woman camest.

And Brown concluded:

> All that had seemed a hanging back from the future—the clinging to the old attic study, the absorption in Tom Outland and the civilization of the Cliff Dwellers, the revival of interest in the occupations of his childhood and its pleasures—was something very unlike what it had seemed. It was profound, unconscious preparation for death, for the last house of the professor.

This seems to me quite admirable literary criticism. The critic has seen the unity of the book created by the central symbol; he has penetrated to the professor's state of mind and grasped that his interest in the occupations of childhood is a stepping backward—or forward—to old age and death. But the story, as told by Cather, in reality leaves the critic helpless in one respect: There is no way to explain why the professor should at this moment of his middle years lose his will to live. We are given no clue. Cather records merely the professor's melancholy.

III

And now let us examine this ingeniously constructed novel. I have always suspected that Virginia Woolf was influenced by its structure in writing *To the Lighthouse*, a novel with a similar tripartite story, set in different moments of time, in which houses (including the lighthouse) also provide the organizing symbol. Let us look at Cather's novel, first through the understanding of symbolic statement offered us by Sigmund Freud in his book on dreams, before the development of ego psychology, and by the American psychiatrist Harry Stack Sullivan, whose theories place emphasis on personal relations.

The striking element in the story is the professor's strange attachment to his attic room, high up, old, and cramped, but safely distant from the family life in the house below. Now, people do form attachments to rooms and to houses, but the professor's attachment here verges upon the eccentric. He clearly thinks of his attic as a place of—and Cather's words express it—"insulation from the engaging drama of domestic life . . . only a vague sense, generally pleasant, of what went on below came up the narrow stairway." And later he thinks that "on that perilous journey down through the human house, he might lose his mood, his enthusiasm, even his temper."

This is much more than a professor seeking a quiet corner for his working hours. The room is "insulation." The professor withdraws from his family and at the same time makes demands on it, for care, food, attention. There is decidedly something infantile here, the security a baby feels in its possession of the mother and the breast for which it need make no return. In this attic room, tiny and snug as a womb, cradled in a warm and alive household but safe from any direct contact with the world outside, Professor St. Peter can feel taken care of and as undisturbed as an embryo.

The room, furthermore, is used by one other person—the motherly sewing woman, Augusta. Adjuncts to this mother figure are the two dressmaker's dummies. Seen as part of the sewing woman, the mother figure, these two dummies express opposite experiences of the mother: one is described as matronly, of a bulk suggesting warm flesh and re-assuring physical possession; the other is of sophisticated line, suggesting spirit and sexual awareness and interest. So the professor has in his secluded place the beloved mother, who cares for and protects him but is also of some sexual interest to him. He wants his mother to be both a mother and an erotic stimulus, and above all he wants to possess her exclusively.

Willa Cather now weaves a second story, but it is in reality a repetition of the same theme. Her hero, again a man, yearns for a high mesa, a sun-beaten plateau, and when he conquers it he finds a cave city. Caves are often feminine sexual symbols. These caves are for him inviolate and untouched, like a seemingly virginal mother preserved from others, a mother of long ago, of the infant years, who belonged only to the child greedy at her breast. There is also beautiful pottery. Pottery is again often a feminine symbol. One has only to recall some of Picasso's paintings, and how often he transforms pottery into women.

The hero cherishes these artifacts and comes to regret that he has a male companion with whom he must share them. The disinclination to share might be seen as sibling jealousy for the mother, or the kind of rivalry a boy, in his Oedipal phase, has for the father, who possesses the mother in the sexual way the boy aspires to have her. The hero is disillusioned first when his mother country, symbolized by Washington, is not interested in his discoveries and, in effect, rejects him, and then when his male friend puts the pottery to some practical use: so that we might say the boy is disillusioned when he first learns that in reality his mother is not a virgin and that his father is the cause of her having been thus despoiled. The hero angrily drives the male friend, father or sibling, away and spends a period among the caves—that is, with his mother—as blissful as a babe. He preserves a record of his narcissistic-infantile paradise, the paradise of life in the womb, of possessing the mother physically, in a notebook which he carefully secretes in the tower. Like the professor's attic room, the tower is still higher and more secluded than the dwellings, where the mother can be preserved, if not in actuality (the pottery), at least in the diary describing his intimate life with her (Outland's detailed account of the caves and their contents as he first found them). Life, its rude events and passage of time, its insistence on moving forward and routing the infant from the womb and from its mothering, also disrupts the hero's blissful eternity on his hidden mesa, in his caves, with his pottery. He has been disturbed. He seeks stubbornly at least to preserve the memory of days with his mother (the mesa, etc.), even as the professor cannot leave his cubby-hole study and would not want the dressmaker's dummies removed.

But life does move on, and in moving on it demands that we follow. The professor seeks a solution to this problem. The family which sustained him in the house below, while he took attic refuge, moves to the new house. If he follows he must accept a new room, a modern room, a room on a lower floor; he must take his place in the family on a different basis: his daughters are now married; they will have children. He must change and grow too, accept his new role as father-in-law and eventually as grandfather. He must, in other words, meet life in an adult way and recognize the demands which are being made on him to take a more active part in the lives of his grown-up children.

But the professor clings as long as he can to the old attic room, and with the life gone from the house beneath he is actually threatened with greater isolation than ever before. He has a choice: he can maintain this state of alienation from his family or he can emerge from his passive dependency and assume the active life expected of him. Appropriately enough, Willa Cather ends her story with the professor nearly suffocating in his room. To remain in the womb beyond one's time is indeed to suffocate. The tenacity of the professor's—and the writer's—determination to maintain this *status quo ante*, if only in fantasy, is illustrated in the ending of the story. It is the sewing woman— who, by the way, was sensibly eager to move to her new, bigger sewing room, to a new life, a new relationship, and cannot understand the professor's infantile attachment to the old room, the old relationship—it is the sewing woman who rescues the professor from suffocation. A mother figure has once more appeared upon the scene for the professor, who thus hangs on to his fixation even though it has brought him an immense threat. The book ends with the professor's problem unresolved, save in the sense that ultimately Mother Earth will enclose him in her womb.

IV

Psychoanalytic theory, by singling out certain primal elements in the picture, has illuminated our story and offered rather crude answers to some of our questions. The professor's death wish, undefined by the author, would appear to be due in part to lingering infantile needs, so strong that this successful adult teacher and writer, otherwise a figure of dignity and maturity, adheres to a pattern of behavior which belongs to his childhood. This he masks by rationalizations: a love for the past, a dislike of the present. But how are we to handle this material, so heavy with Freud's ideas about infantile sexuality—its insistence upon the attic as a womb symbol, its incestuous fantasies and Oedipal situation—a kind of "psychologizing" which can have meaning only to those who have worked with these concepts on a clinical level? And does this interpretation, fascinating and incredible though some of it is, tell us anything about the novel as novel? Or are we being offered a virtually meaningless diagram, highly speculative, of the unconscious fantasies of the professor, derived though it may be from the manifest material placed in the book by the author?

We all live in some form of house; and doubtless for some of us, on some unconscious level, caves and attics may be wombs and houses mothers, and the smooth curves of pottery may suggest the curves of women. But houses, and the rooms within them, are also universal facts and a universal reality. They testify to man's need for shelter and warmth. It is true that we are thrust out of the womb into the world and must inevitably acquire some shelter, by stages that start with the basket and the cradle and end in adult dwellings. And it is true that there are certain individuals who, instead of welcoming the shelters of this world, long for the unattainable state of the embryo where one was sheltered from everything. Wombs are for blissful embryos; houses for growing children and adults. We juggle, so to speak, with the obvious when we invoke such universal symbols.

And what has become of the fine social criticism in the novel? In tracing such a diagram of the professor's neurosis, it is described as a compulsive desire to cling to the past for infantile or infantile-sexual reasons. Yet the social criticism is perhaps the best part of Willa Cather's novels. They record the protest of a gifted woman against the ever increasing conformities and clichés of American life. Her voice is never more appealing than when she shows how the capital of the pioneers was converted into the small change of standardization; and that while the original settlers wrested from the land the glory of America, the sons of the settlers became real-estate agents, parceling this land out and dealing in mortgages, or front-office men—like Louie Marsellus. The anguish of Tom Outland in Washington (whatever neurotic traits he may thereby reveal) is still the genuine anguish of someone who wants government to meet its responsibilities to the past, to history.

And what of criticism of the novel itself? To label the symbols within it in terms of the clinic, or to describe the "interpersonal" relations between the professor and his family after the manner of Sullivan, gives us no help in assessing the book as work of art. We have merely used psychoanalytic ideas as instruments of quasi-clinical diagnosis. Has Cather successfully carried out her general intention? What is the explanation of the professor's happiness in the past? Why does he experience malaise in the present—a present in which, even without neurotic motivation, the malaise of aging can certainly be held to be genuine?

I have given the point of view of one critic about this novel, and a Freudian approach to the material. It is my contention that the method used in this approach leads us to a "diagnosis" which can have little meaning unless it is translated into different terms. And I hold that this translation is possible only by calling upon the resources of criticism *and* biography. Let us therefore pursue our inquiry on this third level.

Psychoanalysis is concerned with what goes on in the unconscious and how it is reflected in conscious thoughts and actions. It deals always with a given consciousness. A dream cannot be truly interpreted, as we have seen, unless it is attached to the dreamer, although it may be a pretty story and have distinct meanings for someone to whom it is narrated. These meanings, however, are not necessarily those of the dreamer, who has put into the dream personal life-symbols. The personal symbols can be understood only after a close study of their recurrent use in the weaving of that person's dream structures. As with dreams, so with the work of art. Ernest Jones has significantly said:

A work of art is too often regarded as a finished thing-in-itself, something almost independent of the creator's personality, as if little would be learned about the one or the other by connecting the two studies. Informed criticism, however, shows that a correlated study of the two sheds light in both directions, on the inner nature of the composition and on the creative impulse of its author. The two can be separated only at the expense of diminished appreciation, whereas to increase our knowledge of either automatically deepens our understanding of the other.

It is true that sometimes we have no alternative but to cling to our shreds of evidence and to speculate as best we can. But with a writer who lived earlier in our own century, we have abundant data relating to actual experience. We can attempt to determine how this experience—which she at best may have only glimpsed—was incorporated into the imaginative act.

V

Our data are derived from Brown's biography of Willa Cather and from the valuable memoir written by her friend of four decades, Edith Lewis. In these works we discover how intensely Willa Cather suffered as a little girl from an initial displacement. She was born in Virginia and lived in a large house. At ten she was taken west to the Divide, to a new house. Here she discovered also the sod houses of the early settlers, even as she was later to observe the cave houses of the Cliff Dwellers in the Southwest. We note that the professor in her novel was "dragged" to Kansas from the East when he was eight and that he "nearly died of it."

In Nebraska, Willa Cather found that nearly all the inhabitants were displaced from somewhere else, and some had been involved in a transatlantic displacement. Her later novels were to depict with deep emotion the meaning of displacement for the pioneers—from Europe and civilization to the rugged prairie. Willa Cather in her own way had shared in this experience; their anguish was hers. Then, in Red Cloud, Nebraska, where the adolescent girl began to discover the life of the frontier, there was a neighboring house in which lived a childless couple. In her own house there was the clash of temperaments and the rivalries of a large family of boys and girls; in their midst was a refined Southern-bred mother, a gentlewoman, somehow strangely aloof and exhausted by repeated pregnancies. And so this other house became a retreat; the cultivated Mrs. Wiener from France served as a kind of second mother to Willa Cather. She provided books and quiet surroundings; the future author could lie for hours on the parlor rug, reading and dreaming. A fairly circumstantial account of the two houses may be found in Cather's late story, "Old Mrs. Harris." From the small town Willa Cather went to

Lincoln, Nebraska, to attend the university, and here she discovered still another house. It was filled with robust young men, over whom there presided an Old World mother. Willa Cather had again found a home, this time as an escape from the dreariness of a furnished room. The house was that of the Westermann family, and the late William Lynn Westermann of Columbia University, a distinguished Egyptologist, testified to the accuracy of Cather's picture of life in his early home as portrayed in her novel *One of Ours*.

In 1895 Willa Cather went to Pittsburgh and worked on a newspaper. She lived in a series of depressing boardinghouses. The way in which she escaped from these into the world of the theater and music is reflected in her ever-popular short story, "Paul's Case." After five years of drab existence she met a young woman who changed the course of her life. This was Isabelle McClung, the daughter of a prominent and wealthy Pittsburgh judge, a strikingly handsome woman interested in the arts. So attached did she become to Willa Cather, the radiance of her personality, and the promise of her art, that she invited her to come and live in the McClung family mansion. The gesture might be described as protective and motherly or sisterly, and Isabelle became, indeed, during these years, a patron of Willa Cather's art. Her house was many times more elegant and spacious than the Wiener house or the house of the Westermanns. Here Cather put together her first book of verse, began to publish short stories, and finally her first volume of tales. She was given a quiet room to work in at the rear of the McClung mansion. It had been a sewing room. Still standing in it were some dressmaker's dummies.

Willa Cather remained deeply attached to this house, and to her friend. The house represented security and peace. From it she was able to face the world and build her career. Even after she had moved to New York and taken up a new abode in Greenwich Village—thus establishing her own home—and was the successful managing editor of *McClure's Magazine*, she would return to Pittsburgh for periodic visits with Isabelle McClung and uninterrupted work in her favorite room. Whether the relationship was actively or latently lesbian may not be particularly relevant here. It is clear that a deep affection and love existed between the two.

In the midst of the First World War there came a break. It followed Isabelle McClung's decision to marry a violinist she had known for some years, Jan Hambourg, who with his father and brother had a school of music in Toronto. This happened in 1917 when the writer was in her late forties. Isabelle too was no longer young. Thus a significant change was introduced into the fixed pattern of the years. And it is from this moment that the biographer can date a change in Willa Cather's works. They reflect an increasing tension and deep uneasiness. She had lost a beloved friend, an intimate companion—and who can now measure the passion and grief that came to her in middle life with this sense of loss? Her novel *One of Ours*, written in the early twenties, is an anxious book; on the surface the anxiety is related to the disillusion that followed the war and to a strong sense of betrayal by the new generation in Nebraska, which was watering down the achievements of the pioneers. For all its defects it won a Pulitzer Prize. The title of the next novel clearly conveys the state of mind of the author: it is *A Lost Lady*—and it tells of a woman who clings to a vanished past in a changing world. After this, Cather wrote *The Professor's House*.

But just before she set to work on this novel, before she had even had the idea for it, she had gone to France to visit Isabelle and Jan Hambourg. Isabelle, in her French home at Ville-D'Avray, had set aside a study for her friend. The new house would incorporate in it this essential feature of the Pittsburgh mansion. Edith Lewis testifies, "The Hambourgs had hoped that she would make Ville-D'Avray her permanent home. But although the little study was charming, and all the surroundings were attractive, and the Hambourgs themselves devoted and solicitous, she found she would never be able to work there."

Why? Miss Lewis does not tell us. But she does tell us what we have already surmised: that there are some traits of Jan Hambourg in the character of Louie Marsellus. Hambourg was a cultivated musician, widely read in French literature, and apparently as good a conversationalist as Marsellus. Willa Cather had dedicated *A Lost Lady*, one of her most popular books, to him and by this act welcomed him to the circle of her intimates. The curious thing is that she dedicated *The Professor's House* to him as well. As we compare the somewhat glib and pretentious Louie with the real-life musician, we recover similarities or exaggerations at so many points that we are prompted to conjecture whether the novelist did not find it necessary to write this flattering dedication—"For Jan, because he likes narrative"—to overcome her guilt over the unflattering portrait she had painted, or to disguise what she had done. Behind the ambiguous compliment to a man who had taken her loved one from her, we may read a considerable infusion—and confusion—of emotion: jealousy, guilt, anguish, and downright hatred. A dedication is, by its nature, so friendly an act that it is perhaps difficult to think of it as masking an animus. But two dedications plead too much: and in this instance they are not symptoms of Cather's affection for Jan. The dedications, we may guess, are really a further salute to Isabelle McClung, to whom Willa Cather had dedicated an earlier book. In later revisions, the novelist removed the Hambourg dedication from *A Lost Lady*. However much she found Jan Hambourg a civilized and cultured being, she would have preferred to have him as her friend rather than as the consort and husband of Isabelle-Rosamond.

We can now see what profound adult emotion contributed to *The Professor's House*. Willa Cather's early uprootings have only a partial meaning in explaining her attachment to a fixed abode; her mother's aloofness and her search for substitute homes readily fit into the emotional backgrounds of the novel. The Pittsburgh house with its sewing room has been transposed into the professor's frame house on the prairie. Like the professor of her fiction, Cather won a prize during her middle years; like him she achieved considerable success. The house at Ville-D'Avray becomes the new house built by the professor's family. It is no substitute for the old one, and the professor can no more share it with the newcomer to his family than Willa Cather could share the French home with both Isabelle and Jan. Isabelle was no longer a beloved figure exclusively possessed by her; she must be shared as Willa had to share her mother with her brothers, as the professor must share his daughter with Louie, and as Tom Outland shares his caves and pottery with Roddy—who betrays him.

Here we touch the heart of our psychological analysis. We can see what brought on the depression of Willa Cather's middle years in the very midst of her success, and we can understand why she wrote that "the world broke in two in 1922 or thereabouts," for we know that to her search for inner security, going back to childhood, was added the deeper sense—hardly irrational from an adult point of view—that she had been cast off, that her beloved had turned from her to another. The reality was that Isabelle had moved forward in life and had married. Willa Cather had been unable to move forward; for her there had been a "divorce," and this represented a regression. In her novel, Cather is so identified with her professor that she is unable to supply a "rejection motif" for his despair. All she could say was that the world was out of joint for him—as it was for her. This depression is described in the first part, in the account of the professor who doesn't want to keep pace with his family, although his work has been crowned with success. The professor grieves not for a lost love; he is simply alienated.

Such is the nature of our inner fantasies that they persist in seeking expression. Emotion only partly expressed continues to "want out." In the first part of the novel which emerged from these fantasies, the professor is at an impasse.

Willa Cather's fancy takes a second try—she opens a window on a further landscape, as in a Dutch painting, and here she is able to release her deepest feelings, those which tell the fuller truth. The Tom Outland story is linked to Isabelle in a curious way. It would seem that in Willa Cather's consciousness the Pittsburgh house, standing on high ground, could be identified with the mesa and the tower. For, some years earlier, when she published *The Song of the Lark*, her first novel to draw upon the Southwest, she dedicated it to Isabelle McClung with the following verses:

> On uplands,
> At morning,

> The world was young, the winds were free;
> A garden fair
> In that blue desert air,
> Its guest invited me to be.

Uplands had become Outland. The world in the "blue desert air" of the mesa is a re-creation of the feeling of freedom Willa Cather had experienced in her life with Isabelle, patron of the arts, and in the sewing-room sanctuary of the Pittsburgh mansion. But Tom Outland is betrayed twice: the maternal-paternal government rejects him; and when he returns home he finds that Roddy, his boon companion, his "loyal" buddy has denuded his cliff sanctuary of all that was precious to him. The fantasy of rejection and loss is thus incorporated into the novel.

The Tom Outland story is complete. That of the professor is not. By merging the insights gained from psychology with the biographical data that give us clues to the workings of the author's imagination, we are enabled to render a critical evaluation: we can see the crack in the façade of *The Professor's House*. The professor lives for us as a man who has given up his good fight and takes the world as preparation for the grave. Suddenly we recall his name: Professor St. Peter. He has retreated into a vale of misanthropy and despair. He has everything to live for; and for reasons unexplained and unresolved he does not want to live. The materialism of an age, the marrying off of one's children to persons we may like or dislike, the process of growing old—these are not sufficient explanation for a depression as deep and as consuming as the professor's. The world is never all that we would want it to be, and lives are lived in a constant process of change and of loves lost and won. The novel is incomplete because in the original fantasy Cather could not admit to herself that she felt deceived and cast aside; and we may conjecture that it was difficult for her to accept the triangular relationship Isabelle had in mind when she prepared a study for the writer in her French home. Moreover, Cather was in no position to state openly her feeling that Jan Hambourg was a usurper who had taken her place in the life of her dearest friend. She expressed it by creating the unpleasant Louie Marsellus and then glossed the portrait with an implicit semblance of affection in the dedications. If we wanted to pursue our psychological speculation, we might find that, to a woman as driving and masculine and as bold as Cather, the loss of Isabelle McClung brought to the surface older defeats and awakened hurts received in her younger days. The story of the professor, with which she began the novel, was too close to herself. By creating a second story she obtained the necessary distance. This does not alter the strangely childish moments in Tom Outland's behavior, suggested in the more clinical psychological interpretation. In times of trauma there are regressions. Cather had to work her way out of her broken world. Writing *The Professor's House* was one way of doing this; and the substance of the story suggests to us that the break with Isabelle had sickened her almost to death—certainly to a wish for death.

Willa Cather's later work can be read in the light of certain hesitations and misgivings within her strong stance in the world: her pride as an artist and as a "self-made" individual. Her choice of the rock as a symbol of endurance and survival in her novel *Shadows on the Rock*, her rigidity in the face of her nation's growth and change, her gradual return in her writings to childhood situations: these spring from the same overpowering isolation, the same death wish—yet struggle to live—acted out in the suffocating attic by the professor. I could find other episodes in her life to amplify what I have said. Not least is the one in which she had to uproot herself from her Bank Street apartment in Greenwich Village because a subway was being run through the area. She took refuge for a few days in a lower Fifth Avenue hotel and remained there for years. Whatever rationalizations might be offered, it was clearly difficult for her to move, and a sheltering hotel, ministering to her needs, seems to have made her reluctant to search out an apartment and re-establish a home. I am told that Cather intensely disliked being in the hotel—all the more reason, we might suppose for her to have left it sooner than she did. The world did break in two for her. One part of it moved on; she remained stranded in the other. And *The Professor's House*, in its very structure, contained this break. It is an unsymmetrical and unrealized novel because Willa Cather could not bring the two parts of her broken world together again.

And yet this novel, however much we may fault it, reveals a strong creative imagination. Its defects illustrate the imagination's gropings to fuller expression. We know that in dream we often tell ourselves a story, and as our unconscious continues to be teased by the unresolved stuff of life, we redream the dream and tell ourselves a totally different story— which, however, on examination proves to be the same story artfully disguised and metamorphosed. Tom Outland enabled the novelist to get outside herself. His sufferings could be made explicit; she was hiding from her own. And his retreat into his past, his reliving the experience high in the mountains where he had found his treasure—and a cave of his own—becomes an act of catharsis. In this way Cather's imagination, in taking the deeper plunge, carried out a self-rescue. She was able to say, through Outland, "I was robbed, robbed, robbed! My friend betrayed me! I have suffered a terrible loss. I must mourn for it and live through it and I wish I were dead." This inner statement which I extrapolate from the evidence completes the story of Tom Outland and of his creator but at the same time leaves the story of the professor incomplete.

In engaging in this kind of creative process, that of endless making and finding, the artist not only discovers intensities and relief from stress but invents new forms out of the beauties of the imaginative life. The stuff of sleep and dreams is far from inchoate and chaotic. Somewhere within we not only choose precise symbols, we find an organic structure for our parable—for ourselves.

Note

This was originally the fourth section of my book *Literary Biography* (1957), where it was entitled "Psychoanalysis." I have rewritten the chapter for the volume *Stuff of Sleep and Dreams* and was able to use material I had originally set aside out of deference to the wishes of the late Edith Lewis, Cather's executor. My principal sources among others are the Brown-Edel life of Cather, *Willa Cather: A Critical Biography* (1953); Edith Lewis's memoir, *Willa Cather Living* (1953); and E. K. Brown's *Rhythm in the Novel* (1950).

The Professor's House and Anatole France
Paul Comeau*

Critics have only recently come to regard *The Professor's House* (1925) as an integrated work of art rather than an uneven if not disjointed novel marred primarily by Willa Cather's disproportionate emphasis on Tom Outland's story. David Stouck argues convincingly that the book is unified "around the theme of power and possessions."[1] Barbara Wild suggests that another unifying element, one "which is never named but which permeates the work," is the great friendship between Tom Outland and Godfrey St. Peter.[2] And Meredith R. Machen, examining the structural and thematic resemblances between *The Professor's House* and Thomas Carlyle's *Sartor Resartus*, demonstrates that the Tom Outland section "is not an intrusion into the Professor's story."[3] Surprisingly, though, discussions of the novel's integrality completely overlook the theme of betrayal, and its corollary alienation, depicted throughout the narrative and supported strongly by the direct allusions in the first two parts to the literary and political worlds of Anatole France: St. Peter at one point likens himself to Lucien Bergeret, the protagonist of France's satire *Le Mannequin d'Osier* (1897); his son-in-law Louie Marsellus later speaks of the possibility of dining with Anatole France in Paris; and Tom Outland refers twice to the infamous Dreyfus affair in which France was involved as a writer and a French citizen. My purpose here is to analyze the significance of these four references to the kind of vision Willa Cather presents in *The Professor's House*, to show how they function in the professor's story, how they are artfully incorporated into Tom Outland's narrative, and how they finally

*This essay was written for this volume and is published by permission of the author.

serve as a psychological and emotional annotation to St. Peter's brush with death at the end of the book. For the Bergeret, France, and Dreyfus allusions not only confirm the novel's thematic coherence, they also provide a framework within which we may interpret with some confidence its otherwise puzzling ending.

To be sure, certain similarities between *Le Mannequin d'Osier* and *The Professor's House* have been noted: Lucien Bergeret and Godfrey St. Peter are both professors; both make their studies in dimly lit, ill-heated sewing rooms, which are cluttered with dressmaking forms (Bergeret's study contains one such form while St. Peter's contains two) and other sewing paraphernalia; both men have favorite pupils—M. Roux and Tom Outland respectively; and both men are ultimately betrayed by their wives.[4] But a closer reading of *The Professor's House* discloses that its relation to France's book is based on more profound correspondences than mere similarities in setting and plot. Godfrey St. Peter differs greatly from M. Bergeret in temperament and disposition, but at the time in his life when the novel opens he feels spiritually akin to his fictional counterpart, because he too must cope with betrayal and alienation in his domestic and professional lives. For Bergeret, these feelings are prompted by the discovery of his wife's infidelity and the ensuing realization that he has "no home, no home any more."[5] For St. Peter, they come to the fore when he must consider moving from "the house where he had lived ever since his marriage"[6] into a new house he has just had built to satisfy his wife Lillian. He eventually refuses to move his study to the new house or to let Augusta, the faithful sewing-woman, transfer her dressmaking forms to her new sewing room, citing M. Bergeret's case as a precedent: "If they [the mannequins] were good enough for *Monsieur Bergeret*, they are certainly good enough for me" (19). St. Peter's sudden identification with M. Bergeret and his conjunctive feeling of homelessness (a type of alienation) point up the congruity in their experiences, as their emotional and psychological disillusionments run a parallel course. In this regard, three key events in M. Bergeret's story help to illuminate the professor's present disaffection with life: Bergeret's discovery of his wife's infidelity and his subsequent alienation from her as a result of that discovery, the unexpected arrest of Senator Laprat-Teulet, and the libelous attack in a Catholic newspaper on the Jewish prefect M. Worms-Clavelin.

M. Bergeret discovers his wife's affair with M. Roux when, returning home from visiting friends one day, he finds them in the drawing room, "linked together in a violent attitude that suggested either endearment or strife, but which was, as a matter of fact, very compromising" (232). His emotions range from anger to disgust to hatred as he retreats to his study, where he confronts the wicker sewing form: "Suddenly through his tears he caught sight of the wicker-work woman. . . . This

time the headless thing appeared to be none other than Madame Bergeret herself, Madame Bergeret, the hateful, the grotesque" (99–100).
Lucien flings himself at the sewing dummy, crushes its wicker ribs, and
tosses it out the study window. This symbolic exorcism marks the end
of his friendly relationship with his wife and the beginning of a life of
pleasant solitude. But to make his seclusion complete, he must rid the
house entirely of her presence, which he accomplishes by first treating
her as "a stranger, . . . as non-existent" (132) and then firing the likeable
housekeeper Euphémie and hiring the noxious Marie to replace her.
As Lucien calculates, "the coming of Marie was like the entrance of
death into the house" (261), and the desired result is quickly achieved.
Madame Bergeret moves in with her mother, leaving her husband to
himself. The cases of M. Laprat-Teulet and M. Worms-Clavelin, though
not related directly to Bergeret's domestic and professional lives, high-
light the religious bigotry and the political abuses in his society and
generally round out the satiric design of Le Mannequin d'Osier. Laprat-
Teulet, a respected senator and a highly successful politician, is suddenly and unaccountably thrown into prison; and Worms-Clavelin, a
Jewish prefect likewise admired in his community, is embarrassed po-
litically when the public discovers that his daughter has been secretly
baptized into the Catholic Church so she can attend a convent school.
News of this deception sets off a strong display of anti-Semitism, led by
the editor of a local Catholic newspaper: "A lay, atheistic, homicidal
education is good enough for the people who maintain them! Would that
our people's eyes were opened to discern on which side are the
Tartuffes!" (212).

Separately, these events serve to animate M. Bergeret's impassive,
tedious existence, while together, they give substance and focus to the
betrayal and alienation theme in the novel. Madame Bergeret's indiscre-
tion is a betrayal of her husband's trust, just as M. Roux's actions constitute a betrayal of Lucien's confidence in and hospitality toward him.
The result is that all three parties are permanently alienated from each
other in hatred and bitterness. And, since Le Mannequin d'Osier was
written at the height of the Dreyfus controversy, the misfortunes of
M. Laprat-Teulet and M. Worms-Clavelin are particularly significant
public illustrations of the betrayal theme. Alfred Dreyfus, a captain
in the French army, was charged with espionage on 15 October 1894,
and imprisoned until his case was reviewed and he was pardoned in
1900. Because he was a Jew of German descent, his guilt was accepted
without question by many Frenchmen. Moreover, through the ineffici-
ency of the legal system, a simple military investigation into his actions
erupted into a full-blown national crisis, with Frenchmen against non-
Frenchmen, Catholics against Protestants and Jews. Anatole France
joined the Dreyfusard party in support of Dreyfus about the time
Le Mannequin d'Osier was published, so it seems likely that the cases

of Laprat-Teulet and Worms-Clavelin detail the two types of injustice and betrayal that converged in the Dreyfus affair—false arrest and anti-Semitism.

The theme of betrayal and alienation is central to *The Professor's House*, as I have indicated, but the Bergeret, France, and Dreyfus references give it emphasis and perspective. Initially, St. Peter must decide whether to move into the new house and risk betraying past memories—of his daughters, Rosamond and Kathleen, growing up, of creating his little French garden, of writing his great history of the Spanish adventurers in North America—or to live alone in the old one and risk alienating himself from his family. His dilemma centers around one memory in particular, that of his former pupil Tom Outland, who was virtually a member of the household in the early days and whose inspiration shaped the latter volumes of the history. Before being killed in the war, Tom invented the Outland engine, which Rosamond's husband, Louie Marsellus, has since marketed to great financial advantage. However, the enormous profits from the engine have sparked an excessive concern with material wealth and social status within the family, the real impetus behind Lillian's insistence on a more fashionable home. Thus, the professor instinctively views the structure as a betrayal of Tom's memory, which has already been distilled into "chemicals and dollars and cents" (132). And his tolerance of the new residence and the competition and jealousy it provokes reaches the breaking point when, ironically, Marsellus announces that the country house he and Rosamond have just built is to be called "Outland" in Tom's honor. Godfrey is outraged at the news: "This calling it after him passes my comprehension. And Rosamond's standing for it! It's brazen impudence" (47).

The betrayal of Tom's memory is unendurable to St. Peter, and Lillian's siding with Louie and Rosamond on naming the country house makes him realize how much Outland's arrival on their doorstep years ago ultimately changed the complexion of their marriage: "Lillian had been fiercely jealous of Tom Outland. As [Godfrey] left the house, he was reflecting that people who are intensely in love when they marry . . . always meet with something which suddenly or gradually makes a difference. . . . In their case it had been, curiously enough, his pupil, Tom Outland" (49). In this respect, St. Peter's story parallels M. Bergeret's, for their marriages and lives are altered greatly by the influences of their respective pupils. Where M. Roux's affair with Madame Bergeret is only a brief flirtation of little importance, though, Tom's friendship with the professor (not with Lillian) has been a lasting romance "of the mind—of the imagination" (p. 258), as Godfrey later acknowledges. Yet the implications of the Bergeret reference are more far-reaching in terms of Cather's portrayal of St. Peter's flagging relationship with his wife, for there is in the first part of *The Professor's House* a mock-discovery scene, almost a direct parody of the discovery scene in *Le Mannequin d'Osier*.

The scene involves Lillian and Marsellus, and besides substantiating the professor's belief that "Beaux-fils . . . were meant by Providence to take the husband's place when husbands had ceased to be lovers" (160), it documents the extent of Godfrey's alienation from his family. Returning home from work early one afternoon, he espies, through the drawing-room French windows (M. Bergeret also returns home early and surprises the guilty lovers in the drawing room), his wife and Marsellus in a secretive discussion of Rosamond's birthday present—an antique necklace. Louie is explaining how it will remain at the jewelers in Chicago until the birthday party: " 'That's another secret we have to keep. We have lots of them!' He bent over her hand and kissed it with warmth" (76). The professor gallantly swings himself over the balcony rail and teasingly observes that such a demonstration of affection "is always the cue for the husband to enter" (76), but concealed in his show of playfulness is the painful awareness that his once prominent place in Lillian's affections has been betrayed: "As he went upstairs he turned at the bend of the staircase and looked back at them, again bending over their little box. . . . She wouldn't have made herself look quite so well if Louie hadn't been coming, he reflected" (77).

Hence, Willa Cather works through the theme of betrayal comprehensively, relentlessly, in Book One of the novel. Kathleen, the professor's younger daughter, rallies to Augusta's aid when the trusting sewing woman loses her savings through bad investments, and sides with her father in retaining a special feeling for Tom Outland, but she is green with envy when Rosamond flaunts new furs and vents her jealousy by expressing openly her anti-Semitic feelings towards Marsellus: "Does [Rosamond] think nobody else calls him a Jew? Does she think it's a secret?" (85). Kathleen's husband, Scott McGregor, whose writing of daily prose poems for the newspaper recalls M. Roux's penchant for composing *vers libre*, dislikes both Marselluses equally and succeeds in blackballing his brother-in-law when Louie's name comes up for the Arts and Letters. And of course St. Peter sees the wrangling over Outland's patent and the money therefrom as the ultimate betrayal of Tom's memory. Through these various betrayals, the Marselluses are alienated from the McGregors, Lillian is alienated from her husband, and the professor seems unable to relate to any of them.

St. Peter's isolation from his family is actualized when, at the end of the first part, the Marselluses embark on a trip to Paris. Lillian is delighted to accompany them but nothing will persuade the professor to pass up the opportunity of living, for a few months at least, the leisurely bachelor life he enjoys so much. Like M. Bergeret, he looks forward to blessed solitude. Even Louie's argument that in Paris they might dine with such celebrities as Anatole France proves useless. "I haven't the pleasure of knowing Anatole France" (158), St. Peter explains, though one feels sure that he empathizes closely with the noted satirist of French society. This allusion to France functions in several ways. It underscores the novel's satiric intent, France himself being a satirist. It contributes to the air of contemporaneity in Book One, which contrasts so effectively with the pastoral atmosphere of Tom Outland's mesa. And finally, it recalls the earlier reference to M. Bergeret and evokes, by implication, Bergeret's exhilaration at his wife's final departure as a correlative to the professor's prospect of a quiet summer alone, editing Tom's diary.

Some years after *The Professor's House* was published, Cather wrote to a friend that she had "tried to make Professor St. Peter's house rather overcrowded and stuffy with new things; American proprieties, clothes, furs, petty ambitions, quivering jealousies—until one got rather stifled."[7] Tom Outland's story was to be a fresh contrast to the professor's both in setting and mood. This effect is achieved impressively—Tom's narrative is clearly the turquoise set in dull silver—without losing the thematic threads of the preceding section. For Tom Outland's story, like Godfrey St. Peter's, is a drama of betrayal and alienation. The alienation concept appears early when Rodney Blake, a new fireman on the railroad Tom works for as a call boy, comes sweaty and unwashed to the regular between-runs poker game. The other men object as much to his dirty appearance as to the fact that he wins the jackpot. However, despite his apparent contempt for etiquette, Rodney possesses a highly developed social conscience. An avid reader of newspapers, he "brooded on the great injustices of his time; the hanging of the Anarchists in Chicago, which he could just remember, and the Dreyfus case" (187). Blake's concern about injustice and corruption in society (his favorite book is the great social satire *Gulliver's Travels*) parallels the professor's concern and, by association, makes him philosophically akin to St. Peter, who foresees the world soon becoming "a boat on which one could travel no longer" (150). The Dreyfus reference introduces the idea of betrayal, linking it to the alienation theme while simultaneously evoking the Bergeret and Anatole France connotations from Book One.

The modern context of the Dreyfus allusion contrasts initially with the timeless pastoral setting of Tom's mesa, which is described in Edenic terms, complete with the snake that kills poor Harry the cook; and the first mummified body found is appropriately christened Mother Eve. As Tom and Rodney slowly unearth the remains of human life on the great rock, they are able to piece together, with Father Duchene's help, the history of a people's rise to civilization, a history that draws color and significance from the countless "personal" tragedies that comprise it. Mother Eve's seemingly anguished death is one such tragedy. Father

Duchene attributes it to her infidelity, to the betrayal of her husband's trust: "Perhaps when the tribe went down to the summer camp, our lady was sick and would not go. Perhaps her husband thought it worth while to return from the farms some night, and found her in improper company. The young man may have escaped. In primitive society the husband is allowed to punish an unfaithful wife with death" (223). Described here is a discovery scene not unlike those involving M. Bergeret and Professor St. Peter. Clearly, modern society has "civilized" the punishment for adultery (Bergeret inflicts on his wife a slow, psychological death), has even refined the crime itself (Marsellus merely fawns over Lillian and kisses her hand), but the husbands' feeling of jealousy and betrayal remain constant. Thus, Mother Eve's story expands the betrayal theme in Book Two and serves as a touchstone for the emotions underlying St. Peter's mock-chivalric response to Marsellus' relationship with Lillian, thereby strengthening the thematic links between Tom Outland's story and the professor's.

The betrayal and alienation theme climaxes near the end of Tom's narrative, when he travels to Washington to enlist the help of the Smithsonian Institution in excavating the Indian ruins on the mesa and when, in his absence, Blake sells the artifacts to a collector from Germany. Tom's trip to Washington resembles in sentiment, if not in detail, the professor's shopping trip to Chicago with Rosamond. St. Peter returns tired and disheartened from the "orgy of acquisition," convinced that "too much is certainly worse than too little—of anything" (154). Tom's alienating experience with the uninspired, slavish bureaucracy of the Smithsonian Institution and with the equally uninspired Bixbys, who rent him a room, gives him "a kind of low-spiritedness [he] had never known before" (233). His attachment to the mesa increases in proportion to his growing sense of alienation in Washington and this, in turn, alters his perception of the plateau and its treasures. Almost instinctively he begins to view it as "a world above the world" (240) and the artifacts as the inheritance of his ancestors, which now belong "to this country, to the state, and to all the people" (244). As a result, he is bitterly angry at Blake for betraying their ancestors' "trust" (244) by selling the treasures: "You've gone and sold your country's secrets, like Dreyfus" (243), he rages. Blake counters by affirming Dreyfus' innocence, "a point he would never pass up" (243).

This second allusion to the Dreyfus affair, a symbolic as opposed to the hitherto domestic rendering of the betrayal and alienation theme, functions on direct, indirect, and ironic levels of meaning. On the direct level, it evokes Dreyfus' alleged betrayal of his country as an analogue to Blake's selling the artifacts. On the indirect level, it calls up the idea of social injustice, characterized by false accusation and anti-Semitism inherent in the Dreyfus controversy, again strengthening the thematic links between the first two parts of the narrative; for although anti-Semitism is not an issue in Tom Outland's story, it is an underlying theme in the professor's, and comes to the fore when Kathleen perversely attacks Marsellus for being Jewish. And on the ironic level, the reference undercuts the disdainful tone of Outland's accusations against Blake, since Tom's anger leads to a more profound betrayal than Dreyfus', the betrayal of Rodney's friendship. This represents Cather's last overt mention of the literary and political worlds of Anatole France, but the four allusions she makes to these worlds have been so carefully and insistently woven into the dramatic, thematic, and emotional fabrics of the first two parts of *The Professor's House* that they carry over into the third by the power of suggestion alone. Indeed, this is precisely Willa Cather's style of writing, to strike one note and then to let the reverberations carry over and blend naturally into the next note. Accordingly, the evocations of the Bergeret reference are echoed in the France reference, are present though somewhat muted in the Dreyfus references, and rebound with new strength of implication in the concluding section entitled "The Professor."

After witnessing his wife's infidelity and after learning of M. Laprat-Teulet's imprisonment, M. Bergeret pessimistically concludes that life is "a constant catastrophe, . . . a never ceasing ruin, . . . and endless prospect of misery," and that "to live is to destroy" (196). With respect to the characteristically dramatic flair with which he declaims life and self, M. Bergeret is not at all like Professor St. Peter, but the fundamental problems each grapples with—the meaning of life and of his own place in the overall scheme of things—are essentially the same. And their solutions to these problems, though intensely personal, corroborate the importance of life and action. For M. Bergeret, life is affirmed when he drives his wife from the house, since "to live is to destroy" and he successfully demeans his wife. For St. Peter, the process of affirmation is more complex and dangerous, because his perceptions of life and self are intimately tied up with his memories of Tom Outland. To go on living, he must somehow relinquish these paralyzing alienating memories of the past without betraying them and thereby betraying the most intellectually creative period of his life.

The act of relinquishing is an inevitable, even a necessary one, as Willa Cather intimates in an early *McClure's* article on the creative richness of youth: "The individual possesses this power for only a little while. He is sent into the world charged with it, but he can't keep it a day beyond his allotted time. He has his hour when he can do, live, become. If he devoted these years to caring for an aged parent—God may reward him but Nature will not forgive him."[8] Tom Outland's summer alone on the mesa is his "hour," his "high tide" (253), during which time he perceives the true meaning of filial piety. He intuits that to analyze the past, to reread his diary, to go back and "unravel things step by step," is to risk losing "the whole in the parts" (252). And although he is frightened by his own "heartlessness" in forgetting about Blake, he senses the necessity of it, for Nature would not forgive him if he misused his hour.

The essence of "happiness unalloyed" (251), however, is that one "can't keep it a day beyond his allotted time," and the penalty is that what follows must then somehow be endured. Hence, Tom's summer on the mesa ended and "troubles enough came afterward" (253). This, we imagine, has been the professor's experience as well. St. Peter's hour to "do, live, become" arrived when Outland appeared on his doorstep. Inspired by Tom, he was able "to see old perspectives transformed by new effects of light" (258), in the same way that Tom's vision of the mesa changed when he could finally see it "as a whole" (250). In one sense, the price of fulfilling his hour has been as great for the professor as it was for Tom, because he has lost Lillian just as Tom forfeited Blake's friendship. Both misfortunes are unavoidable in Cather's scheme, for in the pursuit of their high tides exceptional people like Tom and Godfrey must be freed, "by a sort of right to personal solitude, . . . [from] the usual human sense of responsibility to lifetime relationships."[9] In a more profound sense, though, St. Peter's loss has proved greater than Tom's, since the resiliency of youth allowed Tom to rebound quickly, whereas the relative inflexibility of age has made the very idea of change unbearable to the professor. Godfrey therefore tries to prolong his hour by clinging to the place (his old study) and the companion (Tom Outland) of his past triumphs. But editing Tom's diary is as dangerous as the young man sensed rereading it would be, for it encourages St. Peter to go back and "unravel things step by step."

Book Three of the novel begins with just such a process of unraveling, from which the professor concludes that his life, specifically his education in France, his marriage, and his friendship with Tom Outland, has been a series of fortunate accidents. Unlike M. Bergeret's life of "never ceasing ruin," St. Peter's has been so successful that he would not choose to live it over for fear of worse luck. Consequently, as he continues to analyze the events of his past, his reaction to the present is not Bergeret's regret and hostility but rather indifference; and where hostility is an animating force, indifference is a disabling one. Even the idea of death is not unattractive to him: "But now he thought of eternal solitude with gratefulness; as a release from every obligation, from every form of effort" (272). His subsequent debate with himself over whether he is morally obliged to escape from the gas-filled study, when by accident the wind extinguishes the old stove and slams the window shut, indicates how close he comes to losing the whole (his life) in the parts (his recollections), as one critic has rightly observed.[10]

When St. Peter regains consciousness after his near asphyxiation and ponders Augusta's fortunate arrival at the old house, he admits that "if he had thought of Augusta sooner, he would have got up from the couch sooner. Her image would have suggested the proper action" (279–80). He had tried to act at the moment of agonized strangulation, but to no avail; it was Augusta who pulled him from the room. The symbolism of Augusta's action exceeds the limits of M. Bergeret's affirmation of life in *Le Mannequin d'Osier*, because it implies community instead of solitude. This idea of community, however, is very different from that of close family ties to which St. Peter has been accustomed, for it is predicated on the adoption of Augusta's philosophy of self-denial, as Godfrey realizes: "He had never learned to live without delight. And he would have to learn to . . ." (286). But in fact his acceptance of Augusta's stoical approach to life as an alternative to constant grieving, to death itself ("eternal solitude"), represents a kind of resolution to the betrayal and alienation theme not offered by France in his book. M. Bergeret sits alone at the end of his story and justifies his own alienation and the betrayal of his family by arguing that life is essentially destructive. St. Peter, on the other hand, affirms life and action more positively by deciding to remain a member of his natural family, and of the larger family of mankind, though it means living "without joy, without passionate griefs" (282). Among other things, his decision precludes the kind of intense emotional relationships he once shared with Lillian and Tom Outland, but where there is no such intense commitment there can be no real betrayal or alienation. The professor can therefore "face with fortitude the *Berengaria* and the future" (283).

Clearly, then, the value to Willa Cather of *Le Mannequin d'Osier* lay in the emotional, dramatic, and thematic support it supplied for St. Peter's story. Certainly, her artistic purpose was different from France's, as revealed by her inclusion of a second dressmaking form in the professor's study. Whatever else these two forms may represent, together they symbolize Godfrey's final need of Augusta's "remedial influence" (280) to point him in the right direction. In a similar fashion, I believe that *Le Mannequin d'Osier*, as the major literary source for *The Professor's House*, provided Willa Cather with the same sense of imaginative direction, the same emotional and psychological sureness of purpose, that Augusta provides for Professor St. Peter.

Notes

1. *Willa Cather's Imagination* (Lincoln: Univ. of Nebraska Press, 1975), p. 99.

2. " 'The Thing Not Named' in *The Professor's House*," *Western American Literature*, 12 (February 1978), 264.

3. "Carlyle's Presence in *The Professor's House*," *Western American Literature*, 14 (Winter 1980), 276.

4. These comparisons are outlined by Wolfgang Fleischmann in "Willa Cather's *The Professor's House* and Anatole France's *Le Mannequin d'Osier*," *Romance Notes*,

1 (Spring 1960), 92–93, and by John Hinz in "A Lost Lady and *The Professor's House*," *The Virginia Quarterly Review*, (Winter, 1953), 78.

5. Anatole France, *The Wicker-Work Woman*, trans. M. P. Willcocks, in *The Works of Anatole France*, Autograph Edition (New York: Gabriel Wills, 1924), VIII, 110; hereafter cited in the text.

6. Willa Cather, *The Professor's House* (Toronto: Macmillan Co., 1925), p. 11; hereafter cited in the text.

7. *Willa Cather on Writing* (1949; rpt. New York: Alfred A. Knopf, 1962), p. 31.

8. Quoted by Elizabeth Shepley Sergeant in *Willa Cather: A Memoir* (1953; rpt. Lincoln: Univ. of Nebraska Press, 1967), p. 204.

9. Ibid., p. 220.

10. David Stineback, "Willa Cather's Ironic Masterpiece," *Arizona Quarterly*, 29 (Winter 1973), 329.

My Mortal Enemy

[Review of *My Mortal Enemy*]   Louis Kronenberger*

For several reasons, some of them not altogether significant, Miss Cather's latest story will doubtless be compared with *A Lost Lady*. Both books are short. Both have something of the same framework, the same approach. Both carry us out of one age into another. And both have to do, though only one of them makes the fact explicit, with a lost lady. Again Miss Cather has taken a woman of charm, of rich personality, of sensitive intelligence, and shown how the attrition of circumstances and of temperament wears her down, brings her to an unfitting end. But this time, unfortunately, though it is only fair to suppose that her exact aims are different, Miss Cather has fallen short, rather far short, of her earlier level. Her lost lady is not so real, not so moving, not so delightful. Her background, if less ambitiously attempted, is much less significantly achieved. Her approach, through the eyes of a second person, is by no means as sensitive and significant as Niel's to Mrs. Forrester in *A Lost Lady*. And *My Mortal Enemy* is dangerously, destructively briefer.

Nellie Birdseye, who tells the story of Myra Henshawe, stands outside its limits. Miss Cather's method of giving us one character through the eyes of another is not, of course, new, but the interpreters of *My Ántonia* and *A Lost Lady* had a real relationship to them, dwelt inside their plots. They gave them more verisimilitude than Nellie gives this. They gave them a viewpoint and an interpretation which Nellie does not give to this. She simply tells us about Myra Henshawe at two periods of her life when she knew her. As a young girl she spent a week in New York with Myra when she and Henshawe had been married some twenty years. Originally, deep in love, they had eloped and Myra, by that act, had given up a fortune. When Nellie first knew them their happiness was beginning to grow clouded. They lacked money. Myra needed wealth to live, to expand, to be happy, to be fine. She had pride

*Originally published in the *New York Times Book Review*, 24 October 1926, p. 2. Copyright 1926 by the New York Times Company. Reprinted by permission.

and a generous but violent nature. There were quarrels, scenes, necessary adjustments.

Ten years later Nellie met the Henshawes again, in very reduced circumstances out West, with Myra an invalid. Her whole life spoiled by poverty and its annoyances, a beautiful love ended, a nature roused to bitterness and violence by self-denials and failures, she is but the wreck of her old self. She is slowly dying—face to face with her own dual nature, her "mortal enemy"; alone with the husband she has ceased to love and with herself. She makes, just before the end, a deathbed revolt to freedom and peace by running away.

Miss Cather's methods are always as engrossing as her material, and a good bit of the effectiveness of her earlier novels lies in the individuality of their form. Most obvious are her use of a secondary character to interpret the chief character, which colors and enriches *My Ántonia* and *A Lost Lady*, and her use of incident in place of situation or analysis for purposes of revelation. Both these characteristics are conspicuous in *My Mortal Enemy* and both, for almost the first time, largely unsuccessful. Nellie is a colorless, artistically meaningless character, and her impressions are correspondingly without color or meaning. The book is a succession of incidents, and they do not reveal enough. One seriously doubts whether, in its effect as well as in its form, it can be called a novel; it has no real continuity, forms no organic whole. We are given a woman's character and the end of a great love largely through incident and exposition, and we only get characteristics, contours. We do not really know the woman. We do not really know her life. The book implies much, but connotes little. That is its weakness, and it is a serious one.

One is forcibly struck by the increasing tendency toward brevity which Miss Cather's novels reveal—*The Song of the Lark*, *My Ántonia*, *A Lost Lady*, *My Mortal Enemy*—each a study of a woman, and each shorter than the last. Compression and selection grow naturally stronger in most good writers as they master their medium. But in *My Mortal Enemy* they have been carried too far. All bones and no flesh is never a wise method. In this instance Miss Cather has done even worse—though she has used very little, she has not always used the bones. Significant things are left out, and the reader is left not only unsatisfied, but also puzzled.

Though in actual merit *My Mortal Enemy* is perhaps Miss Cather's least important book, it does have a certain value as regards Miss Cather's development. Immeasurably inferior to *A Lost Lady* that it is, according to every concrete standard by which it can be judged—style, form, tone, lifelikeness, plot—it does impress one, somehow, as a "later" book. It belongs in the same period as *The Professor's House*. For with *The Professor's House* Miss Cather began delving into the innermost, fundamental nature of a character, into his mind and soul. One gets the feeling that she was trying to delve so here, and that in part at least, the groping and confusion of her character are responsible for the groping, the confusion, the incompleteness of her method. She seems to be finding life more complex, more elusive, more irreducible than she once did. The simplicity, the openness, the warmth of an Ántonia no longer deeply interest her. She is absorbed by a sophisticated, troubled, neurotic woman here, a woman lost far less circumstantially than Marian Forrester was; and she is lost also. Marian Forrester lives, Myra Henshawe does not even begin to live; but Myra Henshawe is, without question, a "harder" character to realize. But if this book is greatly inferior to *A Lost Lady* for one reason, it is greatly inferior to *The Professor's House* for another. That book eluded her exact grasp also, but it had rich connotations, moments of depth, which *My Mortal Enemy* has not. This book fails in all ways to be prehensile. It does not coalesce. The whole is not as great as the sum of its parts, and it should be greater.

A Falling Out With Love:
My Mortal Enemy
Harry B. Eichorn*

Does love conquer all? In the mid-twenties Miss Cather seemed to think that much of the conventional wisdom about love was wishful thinking. She was more aware of the limitations of love than of its power. In *The Professor's House* she brought her protagonist to the conclusion that falling out of love is the saddest experience in life, and in *My Mortal Enemy*, her grimmest novel, she re-examined this idea. There are obvious similarities between *The Professor's House* and the story of Myra Driscoll Henshawe, the heiress who rejects her fortune and her religion to marry for love, only to end her life by rejecting her husband and returning to the faith of her childhood. Both Godfrey St. Peter and Myra turn against their marriage partners and sacrifice human ties in their attempts to recapture the past. In both stories money plays a significant role in precipitating the characters' problems. Both characters turn, in their discovery of human limitations, to thoughts of death and thoughts of religion. These similarities, however, only emphasize the more significant differences. The two characters are hardly alike in their temperaments. Godfrey is generous, fastidious, and restrained, while Myra is selfish, flamboyant, and violent. If sudden wealth brings on many of Godfrey's problems, Myra blames her unhappiness on poverty. Finally, the religion which enables Myra to resolve her problems is not available to Godfrey.

*Originally published in *Colby Library Quarterly*, 10 (September 1973), 121–38. Reprinted by permission of *Colby Library Quarterly* and the author.

Neither is it available to Nellie Birdseye, the narrator of *My Mortal Enemy*. Nellie, a teacher who, like Myra, grew up in the town of Parthia in southern Illinois, reveals nothing about herself except the part that Myra has played in her life, but the impact of Myra on Nellie has been devastating. From her earliest years, Nellie had idealized the story of Myra's elopement as a romantic legend of love on the grand scale, but her first meeting with the real Myra started a process of disenchantment that deepened with further acquaintance. Seeing Myra finally reject her husband as her mortal enemy, Nellie has come to distrust human love itself. At the same time, Myra's religious conversion has an inhuman ferocity that makes it unappealing to Nellie. The novel is thus the account of a double disillusionment, in which the story of Myra Henshawe leaves Nellie Birdseye with an emotional poverty as severe as Myra's financial poverty. Nellie's experience suggests that, after all, there may be something sadder than falling out of love—falling out *with* love before one has ever fallen in.

Nellie's distrust of romance colors her manner of narrating the story. Looking back at the events many years after they have occurred, she seems to take a wry pleasure in recalling her youthful illusions, and she records only the details that have impressed her by their glamor or their drabness. Her consistency in doing this invests many of the early descriptive passages with an ironic tone that seems to have escaped the notice of many readers. It also makes Nellie a perfect vehicle for Miss Cather's theory of the "unfurnished" novel, according to which an artist is to present scenes by suggesting details rather than by enumerating them. Nellie does not describe her home town at all, except for the Driscoll estate. She dismisses the rest of the town as a place where nothing interesting ever happened. Her attitude toward her home town suggests, in an indirect and unemphatic way, that a sensitive young person from the country is especially susceptible to the glittering appeal of a big city and to violent disillusionment.

Nellie's reactions to people and events are not the only ones that the novel conveys (her Aunt Lydia is often a foil, as extreme in the caustic tone of her matter-of-fact comments on Myra as the young Nellie is in her enthusiasm), but her consciousness is the source of all the information the reader receives. Miss Cather has so arranged the story that Nellie can plausibly be present at all the scenes which reveal the personality of Myra Henshawe.

The first of these scenes is Myra's visit to Aunt Lydia around the turn of the century, some twenty-five years after her wedding. Nellie recalls Myra's disappointing plumpness and her own feeling of awkwardness at this first meeting. Myra puzzles Nellie by her emotional warmth in greeting her husband and by her high-handedness in telling him that she has given his six new shirts to the son of their janitor in New York. Oswald Henshawe, in fact, is more attractive to the fifteen-year-old Nellie; he is close to her conception of a romantic hero, with his "military air," his eyes, "dark and soft, curious in shape—exactly like half-moons," and his apparent nobility of character: "There was something about him that suggested personal bravery, magnanimity, and a fine, generous way of doing things."[1]

The appearance of Myra twenty-five years after "that winter night when Love went out of the gates and gave the dare to Fate" (25) is a disappointment to the young Nellie Birdseye. Contrasting the diminished scale of Myra's life with the "pomp and dramatic splendour" of her great-uncle's funeral, Nellie feels, after that first meeting, that "John Driscoll and his niece had suddenly changed places in my mind, and he had got, after all, the more romantic part" (27). Myra's grand gesture seemed to deserve more than a commonplace life, but she and Oswald have been only "as happy as most people," according to Aunt Lydia, while for Nellie "the very point of their story was that they should be much happier than other people" (25).

Myra feels this disappointment, too, as Nellie learns when she and Aunt Lydia visit the Henshawes in New York during the Christmas holidays. The qualities that Nellie has already seen in Myra become sharper, and more bewildering. The Henshawes' apartment on Madison Square is the last word in luxury and taste to Nellie, and she cannot understand Myra's craving for more wealth and prestige. At the same time, Myra's generosity to her friends makes Nellie feel that "her chief extravagance was in caring for so many people, and in caring for them so much" (54). She promotes her young friends' love affairs with enthusiasm but also with guilt, because as she says, "love itself draws on a woman nearly all the bad luck in the world" (38). In this bitterness and self-pity Myra can turn not only against love but also against her husband, in a violent quarrel which leaves Nellie feeling "a conviction that I should never like Mrs. Myra so well again" (66).

Nellie's liking for Myra revives, though, at their next meeting ten years later on the west coast. Nellie is now a college teacher; the Henshawes have fallen into poverty, partly because of Myra's ambitions for Oswald, and Myra herself is mortally ill. Illness, rather than taking away the forcefulness of her personality, has only increased it: "She looked strong and broken, generous and tyrannical, a witty and rather wicked old woman, who hated life for its defeats, and loved it for its absurdities" (80).

In her illness and poverty Myra becomes more conscious than ever of the fortune she threw away to marry Oswald. Her illness makes her "acutely sensitive to sound and light" (86), and the most painful circumstance of her life in a run-down hotel is the noise of her neighbors overhead. She tells Nellie, "Oh, that's the cruelty of being poor; it leaves you at the mercy of such pigs! Money is a protection, a cloak; it can buy one quiet, and some sort of dignity" (83). Many years before, when her uncle was threatening to disinherit her, he warned her of the importance of money: "It's better to be a stray dog in this world than a man without money. I've tried both ways, and I know. A poor man stinks, and God hates him" (22). Now Myra feels that old John Driscoll was right. She complains that her marriage has brought her only unhappiness. When Oswald tries to remind her that they were happy at least in their younger years, she denies even this: "We were never really happy. I am a greedy, selfish, worldly woman; I wanted success and a place in the world" (91).

Since her marriage took away her chance of wealth, Myra blames Oswald for her unhappiness. She reproaches him for not getting her away from their noisy neighbors. She locks him out of her room. The more demands she makes on him in her illness, the more resentful of him she becomes. She tries to explain her increasing hostility toward Oswald in a conversation with Nellie. "People," she says, "can be lovers and enemies at the same time, you know. . . . A man and woman draw apart from that long embrace, and see what they have done to each other. Perhaps I can't forgive him for the harm I did him. Perhaps that's it. When there are children, that feeling goes through natural changes. But when it remains so personal . . . something gives way in one. In age we lose everything; even the power to love" (105).

With no love for the present, Myra turns away from human relations and finds comfort in thoughts of death, the past, and religion. Her favorite retreat from the noisy apartment is a lonely cliff overlooking the Pacific, where she can lean against a cedar tree and look off to sea. For her the cliff is "like the cliff in *Lear*, Gloucester's cliff" (87), and she tells Nellie she would like to see it at dawn, because "that is always such a forgiving time" (89). In her aversion to her husband, she begins remembering her uncle. She speaks admiringly of his "violent prejudices" (97) and of his ability to get what he wanted, whether in helping his friends or in crushing his enemies. When her illness worsens and the thoughts of her dead friends crowd in upon her, she returns to the Catholicism of her childhood. In her last recorded words she talks about religion, and asks, "Why must I die like this, alone with my mortal enemy?" (113). She receives the Sacrament and makes a final escape to her cliff, where, as Nellie says, "there was every reason to believe she had lived to see the dawn" (118).

Perhaps the first question that a brief sketch of Myra Henshawe raises is: How could Nellie's liking of her survive their very first meeting? Myra's unpleasant qualities—her vanity, avarice, self-pity, and willfulness—are so obvious that it seems beside the point to emphasize them as if Miss Cather were not aware of them. Miss Cather seems to have realized that a woman like Myra could still have a personal magnetism about her. She has shown Myra's shortcomings with rigorous objectivity and yet made them parts of a complex and consistent personality, almost incredibly complex for such a brief story. And she has made Myra, both in her own career and in her effect on Nellie, suggest things larger and deeper than herself.

In nearly every episode of Myra's life there are conditions which, if emphasized, might have made her more likable. Conversely, in her more likable moments there are personal flaws that reduce her appeal. For instance, the account of the elopement hints strongly that religious bigotry is the only basis of John Driscoll's opposition to the marriage, but there is no attempt to draw sympathy toward Myra by suggesting that her marriage was a triumph of principles over prejudice. The emphasis, instead, is on Myra's headstrong recklessness. On the other hand, Myra's unmistakable avarice appears to be not a purely selfish craving for money but the wish to be a Lady Bountiful to her friends. If there is vanity in her dispensing of gifts and hospitality, there is also a genuine warmth in her solicitude for her friends' needs, and she can be as intense in her friendships as she is in her hates. Furthermore, the account of Myra's jealous suspicions about her husband is not without the suggestion that Oswald may have given her cause by duplicity and perhaps by infidelity, though the story does not reveal more than Nellie could have known about the topaz sleeve-buttons given to Oswald by a girl "from a breezy Western city, where a rich girl can give a present whenever she wants to and nobody questions it" (43). Oswald is still wearing the sleeve-buttons ten years after the quarrel with Myra, and it is significant that Nellie notices them in a scene describing Oswald's friendship with a girl who works on a newspaper, a scene immediately following Myra's locking of her bedroom door. Finally, Myra's return to her religion is such a mixture of heroism and self-indulgence, of repentance and vanity, that it makes the end of her life at once admirable and repellent. The effect of all of these shadings of motivation and responsibility is to make Myra a vividly realized character whose actions are always consistent but whose essence eludes easy formulation.

Myra is a vain woman. She needs at all times to think well of herself. One expression of her vanity is her self-dramatization. Nellie's Aunt Lydia speaks once, not completely invidiously, of "Myra's dramatics" (68). It is through "Myra's dramatics" that Miss Cather has attempted to explain her significance by suggesting similarities and differences between Myra and other characters in literature, specifically and appropriately the literature of the theatre. Her method is light-touched and elusive; the suggestions come from brief references to characters and from echoes of phrases in plays. It is a method more suitable for poetry than for prose fiction, perhaps, but Miss Cather thought of it as the mark of excellence in any art. A brief investigation of some of the more readily identifiable allusions will serve to illustrate one of Miss Cather's ways of giving an overtone and an emotional aura to the story of Myra Henshawe.

Myra has what Marcus Klein, in his introduction to the Vintage Edition of *My Mortal Enemy*, has called a taste for greatness. She describes her head as one that "would have graced one of the wickedest of the Roman emperors" (77). One of her friends is Helena Modjeska, whom Nellie remembers for her portrayal of tragic queens. It is altogether appropriate, then, that the story of Myra should contain some specific allusions to several plays of Shakespeare, each of which deals with royalty.

The first of these allusions, already noted, is to *King Lear*.[2] There are several correspondences between incidents in *My Mortal Enemy* and such details of the play as Lear's unreasonable disinheriting of Cordelia, Gloucester's hasty rejection of Edgar, and the wholesale violations of natural human relationships that occur throughout *King Lear*. Miss Cather's specific reference, however, is to "Gloucester's cliff." In the play, as in the novel, the cliff has an association with death. At the beginning of Act IV, Gloucester has just had his eyes plucked out by Cornwall, and he realizes that he has been blind all along to the real attitudes of his two sons. Now in despair, he asks Edgar, who is disguised as a mad beggar, to lead him to one of the cliffs at Dover, where he intends to kill himself:

> There is a cliff, whose high and bending head
> Looks fearfully in the confined deep:
> Bring me but to the very brim of it,
> And I'll repair the misery thou dost bear
> With something rich about me: from that place
> I shall no leading need. (IV, i. 76–81)

Edgar, of course, does not carry out this request but deceives his father in order to save him. When Gloucester thinks that he is at the edge of the cliff, he gives Edgar a purse containing a jewel. Then, bidding Edgar leave him, he jumps. Edgar convinces the old man that a miracle has saved his life, whereupon Gloucester recovers from his despair and resolves to suffer with patience.

There is certainly an echo of *King Lear* in the description of Myra's death. She hires a Negro cabman to drive her to the cliff, gives him a ten-dollar gold piece, and tells him to leave her there. There are also differences, which show that Miss Cather has not merely tried to give stature to Myra by linking her with Gloucester. On the contrary, she has emphasized the contrast between the two characters more than the parallel. Myra, for instance, cares about no one's misery but her own, and there is "something rich" about her in her manner of dying even more than in her gold piece. She could easily paraphrase Gloucester's words to describe her own death: "And I'll repair the misery *I must bear* with something rich about me." Unlike Gloucester, Myra actually does choose her way of dying, and though she has suicidal thoughts like him, she does not try to kill herself. The time she spends on the cliff arouses thoughts of reconciliation and relief, and she dies peacefully on the cliff, clutching a crucifix.

Perhaps the key to Miss Cather's alteration of Shakespeare lies in her emphasis on the details of the cliff itself. Shakespeare, interested primarily in the human drama, stresses only the fearful height which makes the cliff serve Gloucester's thoughts of self-destruction. Miss Cather has emphasized the panoramic view of the sea, the color of the sunlight at different times of the day, the bareness of the land, and above all, the lone tree growing out of the rocky ground. Unlike Shakespeare, she has the romantic's sense of the cliff as landscape.

In the chapter following Myra's discovery of Gloucester's cliff, there is a brief reference to two other plays of Shakespeare in Nellie's description of Myra's reading habits: "Myra's eyes tired quickly, and she used to shut a new book and lie back and repeat the old ones she knew by heart, the long declamations from *Richard II* or *King John.* As I passed her door I would hear her murmuring at the very bottom of her rich Irish voice: *Old John of Gaunt, time-honoured Lan-cas-ter*" (99).

The significance of Myra's quotation of the opening line of *Richard II* depends on the context of the passage in the novel. Myra has just been talking about her uncle. John of Gaunt, of course, is King Richard's uncle, and Miss Cather seems to be suggesting an ironic contrast between Myra and King Richard in their relations with their uncles. John of Gaunt dies telling Richard that his irresponsible rule will bring trouble to England. Richard immediately seizes all of his dead uncle's property in order to finance his Irish wars, but by this action he brings his own downfall by giving Bolingbroke a pretext for leading his successful rebellion. Myra Henshawe comes to blame her misfortunes on her rejection of John Driscoll's advice, but, unlike King Richard, she is not able to get possession of her uncle's property.

Myra is also like King Richard in many ways—in her vanity, in her prodigality, and especially in her eloquent expression of self-pity after she has fallen into poverty. The second half of *My Mortal Enemy* contains many passages that seem to echo lines in *Richard II.* When Myra is recalling her youth, she says: "Ah, *we* wouldn't be hiding in the shadow, if we were five-and-twenty! We were throwing off sparks like a pair of shooting stars, weren't we, Oswald?" (79). In *Richard II* the Earl of Salisbury says, in contemplation of King Richard's defeat:

> Ah, Richard, with the eyes of heavy mind
> I see thy glory like a shooting star
> Fall to the base earth from the firmament. (II, iv, 18–20)

In the final days of Myra's illness, when she begins to attribute the noise of her neighbors to Oswald, she says, rather strangely: "He'll wear me down in the end. Oh, let me be buried in the king's highway!"

(109–110). Her words seem to recall the words of King Richard when Bolingbroke's forces are in front of Flint Castle:

> Or I'll be buried in the king's highway,
> Some way of common trade, where subjects' feet
> May hourly trample on their sovereign's head;
> For on my heart they tread now whilst I live;
> And buried once, why not upon my head? (III, iii, 155–59)

Myra's final desperate act of self-assertion in choosing the place of her death may well reflect the words that Shakespeare has given King Richard:

> Our lands, our lives and all are Bolingbroke's,
> And nothing can we call our own but death. (III, ii, 151–52)

If Myra identifies herself with King Richard, she probably identifies John Driscoll with the hero of *King John*, the other play she likes. King John is the uncle of *three* characters in the play, and his various dealings with them lead to consequences which provide a humorous contrast to the fate of John Driscoll. King John has a niece, Blanch of Spain. Whereas John Driscoll phrases his opposition to Myra's marriage as "a cold, business proposition" (22), King John tries to promote a marriage, for purely political reasons, between Blanch and Lewis, the Dauphin. Nothing could be more unlike the romantic adventure of Myra's elopement than the cool compliance of Blanch in her words to Lewis:

> My uncle's will in this respect is mine:
> If he sees aught in you that makes him like,
> That any thing he sees, which moves his liking,
> I can with ease translate it to my will;
> Or if you will, to speak more properly,
> I will enforce it easily to my love.
> Further I will not flatter you, my lord,
> Than this: that nothing do I see in you,
> Though churlish thoughts themselves should be your judge,
> That I can find should merit any hate. (II, i, 510–20)

More like Myra is the Bastard Faulconbridge, son of Richard Coeur-de-Lion and thus nephew of King John. The Bastard comes before King John to dispute his dispossession by Sir Robert Faulconbridge, and when the king decides in favor of the Bastard, young Robert Faulconbridge protests. King John then satisfies both of them by giving Robert the disputed land and knighting the Bastard, who henceforth becomes the king's most loyal defender. The Bastard pleases King John by his earthy wit and his good looks. John Driscoll likes Myra for the same reasons: "Myra's good looks and high spirits gratified the old man's pride. Her wit was of the kind that he could understand, native and racy, and none too squeamish" (19–20). King John's other nephew,

Arthur, is the claimant to his throne. The king's resistance to Arthur's claim leads to war and eventually to the deaths of both of them. In his conduct of the war, King John arouses the wrath of the Church by plundering monasteries. His action is in contrast to that of John Driscoll, who enriches the Church with his own money.

It is not by accident, then, that Myra spends her days repeating speeches from *King John*, for she can find in the play a reminder of her own youthful years with John Driscoll. Myra is like Blanch in that her uncle tries to influence her marriage, like the Bastard in that she pleases her uncle by her humor and good looks, and like Arthur in that she unsuccessfully challenges her uncle's authority; but she is unlike Blanch in that she defies her uncle's wishes even though he tries to prevent her marriage rather than to promote it, unlike the Bastard in that her disinheritance marks the end of her friendship with her uncle rather than its beginning, and unlike Arthur in that her uncle's method of resisting her challenge improves rather than impairs his relations with the Church.

Though the allusions to *King John* and *Richard II* are less emphatic than the allusions to *King Lear*, Miss Cather has used all three plays for the same purpose: to let the reader know more about Myra than Nellie can tell him. The most intelligent observer in the world cannot be a mind reader, and Miss Cather has carefully permitted Nellie to reveal only what she can see and hear. When Myra is silent, Nellie can only wonder about her thoughts, as she herself remarks at one point: "During those nights and days when she talked so little, one felt that Myra's mind was busy all the while—that it was even abnormally active, and occasionally one got a clue to what occupied it" (111). Miss Cather has given the reader more of these clues to Myra's thoughts during the months of her illness. Just as the story of Gloucester's attempted suicide shows Myra's thoughts about her death, the echoes of *Richard II* in her speech show her thoughts about her decline, and the relationships in *King John* show her thoughts about her youth. After all, a woman capable of using the words of King Richard II to complain about her noisy neighbors is entirely capable of fancying herself the niece of King John.

The unobtrusiveness of the allusions does not make Myra's awareness of their relevance to herself implausible. It suggests, rather, that this relevance is not apparent to Nellie. If, as Nellie says, Myra knows long declamations from these plays by heart, her relating of them to herself is altogether consistent with her personality as revealed throughout the novel. Her awareness of the parallels is within the range of her vanity, and her awareness of the contrasts is fuel for her self-pity.

By her use of Shakespeare, Miss Cather has, without violating the consistency of her narrative method, given the reader an opportunity to bypass Nellie and to see into the mind of Myra Henshawe herself. If

Nellie is not aware of Myra's Shakespearian vision of herself, it is because she thinks of Myra in different terms. For Nellie, Myra suggests not the characters from Shakespeare's plays but the tragic heroine of an Italian opera. Just as Miss Cather has used Shakespeare to define her heroine's character, she has suggested the significance of Myra's story by her use of Bellini's *Norma*.

The allusion to *Norma*, unlike those to Shakespeare, is anything but brief and inconspicuous. It covers nearly two full pages and forms the climax of one of the most memorable scenes in the novel. At the end of Myra's New Year's Eve party, Helena Modjeska turns from looking at Madison Square in the moonlight and asks her friend Emilia to sing something from *Norma*. Oswald turns off the lights, and Madame Modjeska sits by the window in the moonlight as Emilia sings the "Casta Diva" aria. "It was," Nellie recalls, "the first air on our old music-box at home, but I had never heard it sung—and I have never heard it sung so beautifully since" (60). Then Nellie describes her thoughts about the scene: "For many years I associated Mrs. Henshawe with that music, thought of that aria as being mysteriously related to something in her nature that one rarely saw, but nearly always felt; a compelling, passionate, overmastering something for which I had no name, but which was audible, visible in the air that night, as she sat crouching in the shadow. When I wanted to recall powerfully that hidden richness in her, I had only to close my eyes and sing to myself: *Casta diva, casta diva!*" (60–61).

Though this passage is emphatic and prominent, its implications are not transparent. As one might guess from Miss Cather's handling of Shakespeare, the relevance of the "Casta Diva" aria to the story of Myra Henshawe includes more than the author has explicitly told the reader. It depends on the context of the aria in the opera and on the context of Nellie's words in the novel.

The aria itself is a lyrical prayer for peace. The heroine, standing in the sacred grove of the Druids with moonlight shining upon her face, asks the moon goddess to calm the savage hearts of her countrymen, to temper their bold zeal, and to spread upon the earth the peace that reigns in heaven. Though this prayer is, to be precise, only the first part of the aria, it is probably all that Nellie hears on this occasion. Indeed, Emilia could not sing the rest of the aria without the aid of a mixed chorus. It is this prayer for peace that Nellie says she associated with Myra for many years.

Nellie admires primarily the beauty of the music, but Miss Cather has so described the whole scene as to associate the aria with Nellie's early romanticized conception of Myra. The emphasis on moonlight throughout the passage connects the aria to the New Year's Eve party, at which Myra reaches the peak of her glamor. In the early pages of the story Miss Cather has consistently used the imagery of moonlight to suggest Nellie's illusions: in her fascination with Oswald's "half-moon eyes" (47); in her first misty-eyed glimpse of New York, where "the dull gold dome of the *World* building emerged like a ruddy autumn moon at twilight" (32); and in her fascination with Saint Gaudens' Diana in Madison Square during the reverie which leads Myra to call her "moon-struck" (35). This linking of the aria with Nellie's illusions suggests further that Nellie, at the party, does not realize how deceptive is the aria itself. A person who knows the music as merely "the first air on our music-box at home" and has never heard it sung before is not likely to recognize how incongruous this prayer for peace is with Norma's position as high priestess of the god of war. Nor is she likely to know that the real reason for Norma's sudden pacifism is her love for the enemy leader, whom she has secretly married in violation of her vows as a priestess.

Nellie presumably knows more about *Norma* by the time she is telling the story, since she compares Emilia's rendition favorably with others that she has heard. The "many years" during which she associates Myra with the aria continue until the scene in which Myra calls Oswald her mortal enemy. The descriptive details of this scene connect it with the "Casta Diva" scene. It occurs in Myra's room, and the time is again the early hours after midnight. The room is darkened again, and Nellie notes the stillness of the city just as Madame Modjeska does in the earlier scene. One detail is different, and it changes the atmosphere completely: there is no moonlight. In this room Myra's candles are the only source of light. The scene is the climax of Nellie's loss of her illusions about Myra. Her discoveries show—though Nellie does not point it out—that just as there is a relationship between the aria and her first impressions of Myra, there is also a resemblance between the real Myra and Norma herself.

The resemblance is in the conflict of loyalties that both women find between religion and romantic love. It is only a partial resemblance, with differences in the personalities of their lovers, but the most important difference is in the final resolution of the conflict in the two stories.

Norma's love for Pollione raises the issue more intensely at the outset than Myra's love for Oswald. Pollione, as the Roman proconsul, is the commander of the forces that hold the Gauls in subjection. Besides, he openly despises the Druidic religion, in which Norma's father, Oroveso, is Arch-Druid. John Driscoll's hatred of Oswald seems, on the contrary, to be a one-way affair. Norma is aware that her love for Pollione has brought her into conflict with both her religion and her country. She says at one point that Pollione's heart would be, for her, a substitute for life, fatherland, and heaven.

Though Norma is very much in love herself, she is beginning to have doubts about Pollione's constancy. She has good reason, because Pollione has grown tired of her and has fallen in love with a young virgin of the war god's temple. Norma soon discovers his infidelity, and her immediate reaction is furious jealousy. She turns on him with insults and threatens vengeance if he leaves her. When she sees that she cannot move him by love, by insults, or by threats, her fury gives way to despair. She feels that she has lost the man for whom she broke her vows. Her feeling of loss intensifies her guilt, and she decides to end her life. But as long as there is any hope of recovering Pollione, she is willing to have him back at any cost. She submits even to letting her rival try to send him back to her. In spite of her threats of vengeance, when Pollione finally defies her by invading the priestesses' quarters in the temple, she finds herself unable to strike him. Instead, she makes a last appeal by threatening to kill her children and her rival. In this way, she says, she could make Pollione as unhappy as herself. She finds, however, that she is unable to carry out this threat, and she denounces herself to the Druid assembly as a perjured priestess who must now become a human sacrifice to the war god. By this act she regains Pollione's love and admiration. He asks her to pardon his infidelity. She does so and in turn wins forgiveness from her father. She and Pollione go willingly to the flames with the hope that their sacrificial death will purge their guilt and seal their love forever.

In sacrificing her life, Norma is able to resolve the conflict between religion and human love, but Bellini permits her only a tragic resolution of the problem. She cannot keep her lover and her life, and she must first lose her lover and despair of recovering him before she comes to the point of acknowledging her love publicly. Her very acknowledgment is a desperate show of force rather than a manifestation of love. The cause of her desperation is jealousy, and her self-denunciation removes the cause of jealousy by bringing her lover to a new admiration for her.

If jealousy is the driving force in Bellini's heroine, it is a quality that Myra shares with her. Just as Pollione fears Norma's jealous wrath, Oswald tries to prevent the outbreaks of Myra's jealousy, and after her death, he remembers her jealousy as the cause of all her bitterness toward him. He tells Nellie: "Of course, she was absolutely unreasonable when she was jealous. Her suspicions were sometimes—almost fantastic" (121).

Myra has the same jealousy as Norma, but she is in a less flattering situation. The intensity of Norma's passion makes her an undoubtedly impressive heroine, and her personality retains its stature in spite of Bellini's insistence on her superiority to everyone around her. Miss Cather has given Myra the same personality as Norma but has looked at her more objectively. Myra's emotions are just as violent as Norma's but her experiences are not so spectacular and her conflicts are not so one-sided. She does not have to face such drastic punishment for her marriage; she does not have a husband who is so overtly dishonorable or a rival who is so guileless and accommodating. Her personality involves her in the same problems, but because of her situation the problems are more complex, and the resolution of them is more severe.

Myra is not a priestess married to a proconsul but merely an heiress married to a clerk. Her marriage had been a bold gesture of defiance, but the conflict between religion and human love in her life is of her own making: she need not have broken with the Church to marry Oswald, but this break was merely part of her break with everything else. To her, the most important consequence of her marriage is her disinheritance. Like Norma, after several years of marriage she feels dissatisfaction, but she is not able to find so obvious a cause of that dissatisfaction as her husband's desertion. Oswald is quite content with the arrangement of his life, whatever that might be. If Myra does not have the righteous position of a deserted wife, neither does she have the anomalous task of trying to reclaim the love of a man she scorns. Her jealousy can feed only upon suspicions. Unable to find a simple reason for her dissatisfaction, Myra connects her unhappiness to human love itself, and she tries to find happiness by turning against her husband.

Myra shares Norma's need to dominate her husband and her surroundings. The thwarting of this need by any feeling of helplessness drives her to more and more desperate acts of self-assertion. Her lack of wealth makes her haughty toward the rich. When she is unable to learn Oswald's secrets, she leaves him. When her illness makes her dependent on Oswald, she resents his nursing and tries to withdraw from him in any way she can. The most dramatic way is by returning to her religion. Just as Norma begins to feel remorse for the violation of her vows only when she has lost her power over Pollione, Myra's preoccupation with thoughts of death, guilt, and religion begins on the same day that she declares that love has destroyed her.

In her return to her religion, Myra retains her jealousy in her hoarding of money "for unearthly purposes" (102) and in her choice of the place of her death. Her death has nothing in it of Norma's voluntary sacrifice of her life. Myra can only "meet the inevitable in the way she chose" (117). She sacrifices not her life but her husband. For Norma, on the contrary, there is no question of sacrificing Pollione: he has already rejected her. Myra's reconciliation with her religion does not reconcile her with her husband. For her, there is no resolution of the conflict between religion and human love except in having one at the expense of the other. If Norma cannot have both her lover and her life, Myra's return to her religion leaves her with neither.

The end of Myra's story shows how completely the "Casta Diva" aria is "mysteriously related to something in her nature that one rarely saw" (60). It is Nellie who thinks of Myra in terms of the aria, and the variations between the outcomes of Myra's romance and Norma's are the measure of Nellie's disillusionment. Just as Miss Cather had used Shakespeare to suggest the life that Myra wishes she could have lived, she has used Bellini to suggest the life that Nellie would have preferred for her. By the device of these allusions, she has filled the story with characters whose hovering presence in the background serves to define the personality and the fate of Myra Henshawe. If this is a technique usually associated with poetry, Miss Cather may have been providing a clue to it by making Nellie an admirer of the modern poets.

While Miss Cather has resolved the conflict between religion and human love more severely for Myra than Bellini has for Norma, she has brought Nellie Birdseye's experiences to an even more severe conclusion. Myra's return to her religion gives her something that enables her to face death confidently, but Nellie has lost the ability to face life confidently. She ends her story by saying that the memory of Myra's last words has made her doubt that any love story can end happily. Her observation of Myra has destroyed her faith in human love, but she cannot adopt Myra's religious faith. She finds such a faith not only inaccessible but repulsive. Nellie does not explicitly describe her reactions to Myra's conversion, but since she is a teacher of literature, her values are presumably humanistic. Though she is willing to believe that Myra finds peace and satisfaction, she is clearly appalled by a religious enthusiasm that carries otherworldliness to the point of rejecting human relationships and human responsibilities altogether. "Religion," Myra says near the end of her life, "is different from everything else" (111). It is so different, in fact, that it is irrelevant for Nellie, whose disillusionment leaves her hopeless.

Is Nellie's hopeless conclusion also Miss Cather's? The novel offers no grounds for thinking otherwise. The compactness and starkness of *My Mortal Enemy* suggest that Miss Cather had full confidence in the accuracy of this conclusion and in her talents as a writer. Some may find it ironic that the book in which she gained the surest control of her art expresses her most despairing vision of life, but is it really? She was soon to make a journey to New Mexico and to discoveries that would brighten her spirits and give a new serenity to her later novels. Is it not, rather, entirely consistent with her devotion to her art that, when life seemed to fail her, her art saved her?

Notes

1. Willa Cather, *My Mortal Enemy* (New York, 1926), 15. Subsequent page references to this book appear in the text.

2. All quotations from Shakespeare are taken from *The Works of William Shakespeare* (Globe Edition: London, 1907).

Death Comes for the Archbishop

[Review of *Death Comes for the Archbishop*]

Henry Longan Stuart*

In *Death Comes for the Archbishop* Miss Willa Cather has given us an account of the episcopate of one of those devoted servants of the Catholic Church who carried its doctrines to the New World.

The Congregation De Propaganda Fide has had to face many knotty problems during the four centuries of its existence, but probably no single one where so many possibilities for mistake and disaster existed as that which confronted it after the taking possession of New Mexico for the United States by General Kearny in the summer of 1846. The religious destiny of a new district "larger than Central and Western Europe, barring Russia" suddenly became a matter of urgent concern. And everything about the new territory was cryptic and unprecedented. Missionaries and enthusiasts such as accompanied the Spanish conquistadores wrote some of the most splendid chapters in the history of the Catholic Church. But to administrators of a later and more sober day they bequeathed some terrible dilemmas. Everywhere abandoned missions and ruined churches bore witness to Indian warfare as terrible in its character as the desert raids which wiped out the African Church in the fifth and sixth centuries. Even the character of the neophytes who had withstood the storm and the pastors around whom they rallied was a debatable question. There was too much reason to fear that for the former religion had become a matter of a few pious practices grafted upon a paganism never really abandoned in the heart and that, for the latter, the corruption almost inevitable when isolation overtakes an infant church was calling for stern disciplinary measures if the seed sown in the blood of so many martyrs was not to be choked in thorns and brambles.

These are the times and conjunctures that seldom fail to produce extraordinary men, or, rather, that call forth from men who in normal

*Originally published in the *New York Times Book Review*, 4 September 1927, p. 2. Copyright 1927 by the New York Times Company. Reprinted by permission.

times might have spent their lives blamelessly and anonymously, unsuspected resources of heroism and initiative. Such a one was Jean Marie Latour, successively Vicar Apostolic Bishop and Archbishop of Santa Fe for thirty-eight years.

At the very beginning of any consideration of such a book, a question of literary conscience poses itself. The newly aroused interest in American history as dramatic material of the first order is having many results, some good, some less so. But it is quite plain that it is producing and will produce in the future a type of book which falls under no category hitherto familiar. This new type may be roughly defined, not so much as an historical novel, as a superimposition of the novel upon history. And it is not taking its place among forms hitherto recognized without a certain accompanying mysterification. No one who has followed current literature within the last few years will have any difficulty in recalling instances in which such outstanding landmarks in our history as the gold rush of 1848 on the Pacific slope, or the acquisition of Alaska have been dealt with in very lighthearted fashion. For the smaller fry whose mission is merely to entertain the question how far established fact is adhered to is hardly worth putting. But for a writer of Miss Cather's calibre, it is in its place. The facts of the Santa Fe episcopate are accessible in any standard book of reference. We know that its first Bishop was John Baptist Lamy, that his life followed, chronologically at least, the limits given it by Miss Cather. We may suspect that in the new setting she has given it an enormous amount of tradition collected upon the spot is enshrined. Nevertheless, the mere transposition of Latour for Lamy, for a man not forty years dead, is a little disquieting. Does it bespeak a resolution to have done with the tyranny of fact, an enfranchisement from the limitations hitherto accepted, more or less loyally, by those who make the historical novel their concern? And may not the new fashion quite possibly be laying down snares for the feet of generations to come, little versed in documentation and quite ready to take the word of so fascinating a writer in matters of fact as well as of fancy?

This reservation made, it is sheer critical duty to go and admit that Miss Cather has succeeded in producing a truly remarkable book. To begin with, it is soaked through and through with atmosphere, not of the facile sort acquired by the mere descriptiveness, but by the relation of every scent and sound to the senses and nerves of one who sees the barren upheaved land and breathes the intoxication of its barrenness for the first time.

Moreover, by an artistry that is as beautiful as it is rare, every perception of this fantastic diocese and of the violent and generous children who are his charge is allowed to reach us through the perceptions of a thoroughly civilized man, of gentle birth, but from the province where feudalism lingered intact, and the stubbornness of whose sons is a French proverb, cultured, a little aloof and filled with pity for something vaguely fine and doomed to perish that he sees around him. Bishop Latour, though he accepts all hardships with equanimity and good grace, has no discoverable austerities. He likes good cheer, good wine and architecture, shudders retrospectively, like Mrs. Trollope, at the memory of frontier Cincinnati, and to the day of his death never loses a certain feeling of satisfaction as he washes his hands in the big silver bowl that was the gift to him of a lordly Spanish parishioner. His Indian guides love him for his good manners, for his unostentatious courage and for the respect with which he listens to their tales of the old religion, satisfying himself with an "Our Father," recited together before pastor and neophyte roll themselves in their blankets. His hand is forbearing and patient, even when armed with the thunder of Rome, and ready to fall upon recalcitrant Padre Martinez, the bullnecked tyrant of Taos, who leads the life of a patriarch of the Old Testament amid his herds and women. His belief in God and his faith is crossed, as it is crossed among so many scholarly Christians, by a scepticism as to the power of average human nature to correspond with the message offered.

When officiating on the enchanted mesa of Acoma,

> he had never found it so hard to go through the ceremony of the mass. Before him, on the gray floor, in the gray light, a group of bright shawls and blankets, some fifty or sixty silent faces; above and behind them the gray walls. He felt as if he were celebrating mass at the bottom of the sea for antediluvian creatures, for types of life so old, so hardened, so shut within their shells, that the sacrifice on Calvary could hardly reach back so far. Those shell-like backs behind him might be saved by baptism and divine grace, as undeveloped infants are, but hardly through any experience of their own, he thought. When he blessed them and sent them away it was with a sense of inadequacy and spiritual defeat.

Many figures, some familiar, come into the story Miss Cather has to tell us. There is our childhood friend Kit Carson with his dignified Mexican wife. "There is something curiously conscious about his mouth, reflective, a little melancholy—and something that suggested a capacity for tenderness. The Bishop felt a quick glow of pleasure in looking at the man." There is Father Vaillant, blundering, warm-hearted and enthusiastic type of the older missionary school of Jogues and Lallemant, who leaves his rich Denver parishioners ("men who owned mines and sawmills and flourishing businesses; but they needed all their money to push these enterprises") and goes back to beg among his poverty-stricken Mexicans, who gave "if they had anything at all." There is the guide Jacinto, who takes his Bishop during a blizzard into an ancient haunt of fear and superstition, after first swearing him to secrecy, and lets him listen to the roar of a subterranean torrent moving in utter blackness under ribs of antediluvian rock. There are legends, beautiful and terrible, of Fray Baltazar, who made his rock bloom like the rose and paid for gluttony with his life, of Fray Junipero, who met the Holy Family at the foot of three cotton trees in the desert. From the riches of her imagination and sympathy Miss Cather has distilled a very rare piece of literature. It stands out, from the very resistance it opposes to classification, in the authentic line, and at no great distance either, of such masterpieces of our literature as *Eothen* and *Arabia Deserta*.

Summary of *Death Comes for the Archbishop*: The Cathedral and the Stagecoach
John H. Randall III*

I have remarked earlier that in her novels Willa Cather often employs a double protagonist, one of whom symbolizes the heart, the other the head, and that the two stand for different aspects of Willa Cather herself, and represent the sophisticate and the provincial dwelling side by side in her own breast. In Father Vaillant and Archbishop Latour she has presented the two different ways of life which interested her, the one in her youth, the other in her age. The two can be symbolized in the images of the cathedral and the stagecoach: the great stone pile by means of which the Bishop hopes to perpetuate his personality, and the rough jolting vehicle inside of which Father Joseph would lean forward to greet an incoming guest. The cathedral is beautiful but it is a little cold, a little remote from human needs (at least in the sense in which the Bishop envisions it); above all it is stationary and unchanging. The stagecoach is much humbler, rather ugly, but is designed for human needs and is warm with human life within; and most important of all, it is dynamic, constantly moving on to seek new places. These two images could serve as tropes not only for Willa Cather's two clergymen, but also for her conception of art and life themselves. Throughout most of her career Willa Cather had tried to combine the two and achieve some sort of balance. Here again she tries to combine them by having Father Vaillant and the Bishop set up a household together almost as if they were a married couple. Once Father Vaillant leaves for Colorado, however, the balance is upset, and the Bishop is exposed again to the pangs of loneliness. But Willa Cather quickly intervenes, insisting that the Bishop isn't really lonely at all. It is easy to see the

*From *The Landscape and the Looking Glass: Willa Cather's Search for Value*, by John H. Randall III, pp. 306–10. Copyright © 1960 by John H. Randall. Reprinted by permission of Houghton Mifflin Company and the author.

Bishop in his solitude as a type of the author herself who has given up everything for art, and wondering whether after all the choice really was worth while. But the later Willa Cather is not so clear-headed as the younger one had been; she refuses to admit that any conflict between art and life exists; so she tells us that the Bishop's solitude is not solitude after all.

In her *Commonweal* letter Willa Cather writes of *Death Comes for the Archbishop*: "As a writer I had the satisfaction of working in a special genre which I had long wished to try."[1] This statement is highly revealing. For the genre she is writing in is that of local color; *Death Comes for the Archbishop* fits all the specifications for a local-color story which I have previously set up.[2] Its characters are mostly stereotypes or, if not this, are (with a few notable exceptions) sentimentally rendered; even its two heroes are not related to their environment in any clear way, and, although Father Vaillant comes to life from time to time, the Bishop remains rather vague. The setting of the book is probably its best feature. Willa Cather gives a good realistic description of the Spanish Southwest, but uses it romantically; that is, she uses the landscape and the Catholic Church together as an exotic and exciting backdrop for what little action the book contains; she uses it the way local-color writers make use of their backgrounds. The book is permeated with a strong feeling of nostalgia for an earlier and, it is implied, a better time in which the problems of a commercial and industrial civilization simply had not arisen. The idea of recovery of the past can be found in Willa Cather's writing as far back as *My Ántonia*; one need only recall the note of Populist nostalgia on which that novel ended. But now it has become so important to Miss Cather that it forms the major theme of the entire book.

Now local-color fiction, charming as it may be, is a minor genre because it takes a limited view of things and one implying an escape from life. Thomas Love Peacock could have used it to justify his "mental rattle" theory of poetry. Since it is more concerned with the presentation of picturesque surroundings than of human problems, it very often neglects to describe struggle and conflict. This is just what Willa Cather tells us she wanted to do when she writes: "I had all my life wanted to do something in the style of legend, which is absolutely the reverse of dramatic treatment."[3] It is true that omitting conflict from a book is the reverse of dramatic treatment, but such a literary method loses more than it gains. Conflict is the essence of life, and it is the essence of nearly all novels. The reason that we can accept a work of literature as an interpretation of human experience is that the conflicts it portrays are in some sense an extension of our own. The absence of struggle, far from being a virtue, is a handicap in this narrative. It is precisely because of the lack of struggle that *Death Comes for the Archbishop* is less memorable than the prairie novels or *A Lost Lady*.

But leaving aside for the moment the value of what she is attempting, does Willa Cather accomplish in the book what she says she does? Does she consistently omit conflict and deal with the lives of the two fathers in the style of legend? The answer is no. Willa Cather doesn't treat *Death Comes for the Archbishop* like a fresco by Puvis de Chavannes; she doesn't give great and little happenings equal importance. On the whole she gives much more importance to little things: to chance sense impressions, the gold-ocher color of a hill, the delicate taste of a soup. This is neither medieval nor saintly. And in spite of what she says in the *Commonweal* letter we find her reverting to the novelistic technique she had practiced before. Her dialogue is like that in a realistic novel; even she realized that it resembled "the old trite phraseology of the frontier."[4] The aura of realism which surrounds the book contradicts her avowed intention of imitating legend. Moreover, although she says she wished to omit conflict entirely, she occasionally fails to do so; one can say of the book that when it's good, it's dramatic. A few parts of it are very dramatic indeed: for example, the legend of Fray Baltazar and the scene between Bishop Latour and Padre Martinez. But, except in the case of Fray Baltazar, she never shows the conflict resolved. Miss Cather's comments on her aims and ideas are frequently illuminating, but they do not always have much bearing on the work referred to. Her capacity for self-criticism was small.

Because of her tendency to eliminate conflict from the novel, one feels that the order which Willa Cather stresses so much is a spurious order; that human problems have been ignored rather than transcended. The realities of the situation she deals with are put on a Procrustean bed, and if any should fail to fit in with her ideas, so much the worse for them. It is this distortion of what life is like in favor of her preconceived view of what it should be like that makes her later fiction so much less interesting to read than her earlier work. She was very much interested in presenting an image of life without conflict, without tension between opposing claims, and this apparently is more than life has to offer. Evidence of this can be found even in her presentation of the things which now interest her, especially in her treatment of landscape. In her pioneer novels enjoyment of nature had been a reward for struggling with nature. Now nature is enjoyed tourist-fashion for its own sake. Her evasion of the serious problems she had treated in previous novels becomes most marked when she is dealing with ritual. Instead of the mysteries of life and death, Willa Cather invites us to consider the mysteries of the gourmet's dinner table. Instead of sowing and harvesting and the cycle of the seasons we find cooking and eating and the preparation of three meals a day. Religious ritual has given way to domestic ritual.

Thus the order which in earlier books had grown out of the material itself and had been based on a fairly frank confrontation of human conflict is here forcefully imposed by the author with no regard for the material because Willa Cather felt an extreme reluctance even to suggest the idea of conflict. In *Death Comes for the Archbishop* she gives a convincing picture of neither the inner discipline which constituted the strength of the pioneers nor the external discipline responsible for the functioning of the Catholic Church. This lack of any real order in her vision is emphasized by the loose episodic construction of the novel. The fact that Willa Cather wrote a poorly organized book extolling the virtues of order does not argue well for her insight. There is something inherently ludicrous in a disorderly praise of order. Discipline, one would think, should begin at home.

Of all the books Willa Cather ever wrote, *Death Comes for the Archbishop* is by far the most popular. It ran through eleven editions, was translated into eight languages, and is known to people who have never read anything else of Willa Cather's. Many consider it to be the crowning glory of her achievement. In spite of this, it is not a good book. The reason is that her anxiety for order stultified her creative urge and crippled her vision of life. *Death Comes for the Archbishop* falsifies the facts as she herself had previously seen them; for she asks us to admire the Bishop as both a pioneer and a deeply religious man, whereas in the book he is neither. Pioneers have to struggle, but the Bishop lets Father Vaillant do his struggling for him. Religious men have to face the problem of evil and suffering, but this too is carefully avoided. In *My Ántonia* she had used the vegetation myth as a means of confronting and transcending the great problem presented by the fact of death. Now the only allusion to the fertility myth occurs in connection with Indian snake worship, and there it is found disgusting.

A great deal of Willa Cather's trouble with *Death Comes for the Archbishop* seems to stem from her confusion of art with life. She does not realize that things which are ugly in the living, such as intense conflict, suffering, and pain, can be rendered beautiful by the ordering process which constitutes the essence of art. Instead, she forms her own special variant of the genteel tradition by trying to avoid all mention of ugly things. The result is a vision of life which is pitifully maimed and inadequate; at times it seems superficial and unconvincing, at times downright dishonest in its ignoring of the issues raised. What remains? Some beautiful description of landscape and a well-conceived minor character or two. At the end of her most famous essay Willa Cather remarks: "The elder Dumas enunciated a great principle when he said that to make a drama, one needed one passion and four walls."[5] She followed this principle in her prairie novels, but in *Death Comes for the Archbishop* she has given us four walls and left the passion out.

Notes

1. "On *Death Comes for the Archbishop*," in *Willa Cather on Writing* (New York: Alfred A. Knopf, 1949), pp. 11–12.

2. Randall had previously defined local color as "a relatively minor literary genre which can be described as having three characteristics: romanticized or sentimentalized characters, a realistic setting (which is, however, used romantically and exploited for its exotic qualities), and a generally escapist tone" (editor's note).

3. "On *Death Comes for the Archbishop*," p. 9.

4. Ibid., p. 10.

5. "The Novel Démeublé," in *Willa Cather on Writing*, p. 43.

Narrative Without Accent: Willa Cather and Puvis de Chavannes
Clinton Keeler*

In a letter to the editor of *Commonweal* Willa Cather describes the genesis of *Death Comes for the Archbishop*. She had seen Puvis de Chavannes' frescoes of the life of Ste Geneviève and had determined to do something similiar in prose. "Something without accent" were her words, "something in the style of legend, which is absolutely the reverse of dramatic treatment."[1] Although several critics have mentioned the similarities between the narrative and the painting, none has examined these similarities in any detail. A comparison of the painting and the novel not only sheds light on the novel but also provides an alternative to the cul de sac which criticism seems to have reached. Some critics, analyzing her work on the basis of biographical influences, feel that Miss Cather's writing too often culminates in withdrawal and escape from reality. The *Archbishop* is a failure, according to John Randall, because it avoids conflict, ugliness and pain, and omits deep emotion.[2] More recent critics make the opposite judgment. The novel is superb; further, although there are only two notable departures from the essential historical facts behind the story, the author's main concern is not with the historical matrix itself, but with a profounder meaning behind the facts.[3] In this view there is a deeper engagement with reality—not an escape.

The familiar arguments about what constitutes a true engagement with reality can be extended indefinitely with little profit. But where these discussions end in point-blank contradictions, a study of the painting that started the writing provides insight into the contradictions themselves. Is the *Archbishop* commendable because it demonstrates the

*Originally published in *American Quarterly*, 17 (Spring 1965), 119–26. Copyright 1965 by the Trustees of the University of Pennsylvania. Reprinted by permission of *American Quarterly* and Lorene Keeler.

"solid virtues of an inspiriting past" in contrast to the "mercurial shifts of practical reality"?[4] Or is it deplorable as a "vision of life which is pitifully maimed and inadequate . . . at times superficial . . . at times downright dishonest"?[5] Underlying this dispute is the question of Cather's basic attitude toward the historical materials. An examination of the painting of Puvis de Chavannes clarifies this attitude.

First a few details from the memorialization of Geneviève are relevant. As the leader of her people against the Huns in 451, she was made the patroness of Paris. Also, she is said to have established the church of St. Denis; in the latter part of the eighteenth century the Panthéon was built on the site of her tomb. In the 1870s Puvis de Chavannes was commissioned to paint a memorial on the walls of the Panthéon.

At a time when art was being given new directions by Renoir, Monet, Gauguin and others, Puvis de Chavannes was an enigma. He avoided the new optical analysis of the impressionists and returned to the monumental painting of the Renaissance. Comments about his work sound rather like those about Cather's novel. To André Michel, reviewing Chavannes' exhibit of 1888 in the *Gazette des Beaux-Arts*, Puvis was "disdainful of actuality," and yet curiously, one day, "in the great confusion of philosophers and doctrinaire realists, he might be not simply the most noble but one of the most suggestive and the most *documentary* painters of our times."[6]

Ste Geneviève, like Latour in Cather's novel, had built a church; and like the novel, the mural completed by Puvis represented a monument combining religious and patriotic themes. Commenting on this quality in the frescoes, the biographer Vachon said that they suggest immediately the great painters of the Florentine Renaissance.[7] The mural "L'Enfance de Sainte Geneviève" is divided into four panels with a frieze. In a central panel the child Geneviève is shown in the countryside of Nanterre, where she is recognized by Saint Germain. The women are kneeling before the bishops; the countrymen regard the scene with respectful curiosity. The accompanying panels portray scenes of arrested life: the sick are brought to be healed, a woodsman or shepherd and his family watch Geneviève at prayer, and scattered throughout are details of daily life—peasants, sheep, fowls and cattle.

There is little reason to describe the minutiae of the painting, because the main interest in comparison with the *Archbishop* lies in the style. Yet it can be pointed out that as Geneviève's mission is foretold by the bishops, so Latour is commissioned by the Cardinal in the Prologue. Like Geneviève, Latour prays before a rustic or natural cross: Latour and Geneviève minister to the country people; they build a church; they are, in short, legendary figures in the early history of their country. To compare, say, the historical reality of the woodsman in the painting with that of a figure like Kit Carson in the narrative would be absurd. Yet this point should be made: it is no more ridiculous, considering the aim of the painter, to criticize the image of the woodsman as not being his-torically accurate for the fifth century, than it is to criticize the fictional Carson for being unlike the actual trapper. The painting and the narra-tive are highly stylized.

Movement in the *Archbishop* is like that of a viewer moving from picture to picture, panel to panel. It is a commonplace in criticism to note the effect of tableaux in the *Archbishop* from Latour's youth to his death. Whatever is claimed for the work, it is not dramatic action. A scene in Rome opens the story; a scene in New Mexico, with parallels from earlier passages, closes it. One writer suggests that the book is like a triple triptych. In this view, the very divisions of the narrative are comparable to the sound of the Angelus which rouses the Bishop from sleep in the clear air of the new land.[8] *Triptych* connotes the pictorial quality of the narrative. But whatever the term of comparison, the appear-ance of immobility, definitive in Puvis' painting, is clearly present in the novel.

Concerning the more important matters of style, it has been said that the frescoes of Ste Geneviève are marked by the characteristics of the monumental style. First, static figures are arranged in groups without the suggestion of motion. Progression is given by the movement of the viewer from panel to panel. Puvis himself implies such by referring to the first panel as a prologue. Moreover, there is little distinction between fore-ground and background, a quality that echoes medieval painting. The word *immobility* may be used appropriately for both the static quality and the flatness of the painting, since the figures do not suggest move-ment, nor is the eye of the viewer made to travel long lines of perspec-tive. Whatever unity the work has cannot be said to derive from merging lines or converging action.

Secondly, Chavannes' paintings are marked by the use of light and color. There are flat tones, few contrasts and no vivid colors. The total effect of color in the painting is that of monotones overlaid with a kind of pale light, which, metaphorically, seems to put a distance in time or space between the viewer and the objects viewed. The translucent quality suggests a patina in which all lines are softened; or the light seems a medium in which all objects and figures are suspended outside of time.

The immobility, flat tones and pale light, and the detachment or dis-tance, then, give the paintings the effect of a stylized monument, rather than the vigorous color and contrast, say, of a Renoir or a Gauguin. Similarly, there is a flatness, a lack of emphasis in the *Archbishop*. The opening scenes at Rome are a combination of landscape and still life: "It was early when the Spanish Cardinal and his guests sat down to dinner. The sun was still good for an hour of supreme splendour, and across the shining folds of country the low profile of the city barely fretted the sky-line—indistinct except for the dome of St. Peter's bluish grey like the flattened top of a great balloon, just a flash of copper light on its soft metallic surface."⁹ Yet this panoramic scene is not treated in any more or less detail than the dinner table or the "long gravelled terrace and its balustrade—blue as a lake in the dusky air" in the foreground. The Spanish Cardinal is hardly stressed more than the allusion in the conversation to the dancing girl who had become *croyante* and who was singing in the new opera by Verdi. Perhaps significantly, the last anecdote of the prologue deals with an El Greco painting of St. Francis. The painting alluded to is, of course, filled with contrast in light and dark, with the tortuous El Greco lines—but the scene in which the portrait is discussed is as calm as the soft summer air surrounding the Sabine hills. The suggestion of intense feeling is framed by stillness, and this precisely describes Willa Cather's attitude toward her materials. The emotions of her characters are framed by a kind of detached calm. More relevant to the main theme of the story is the character of Vaillant as opposed to that of Latour. One critic complains that whereas the energy of Joseph is always threatening to break through the plan of the novel, to humanize the narrative with his "hopeful rashness," the author always subdues this impulse and preserves the thoughtful, but artificial order represented in Latour. Vaillant, says this critic, represents life; Latour represents art. Cather has confused art and life, and her so-called order is specious, lacking in conflict and therefore in humanity. It would be better, from this point of view, to have *one* main character who suffered within himself conflicts between beauty and morality.¹⁰

In other words, the author has avoided an internal conflict, and has put the opposing qualities in different characters, as in a morality play, or a legend. This assuredly results in some flatness in characterization. Yet if the theme has to do with the interrelation of moral and aesthetic order and primitive energy, it must be appropriate to have the quality of the main character—a love of order—dominate the book. The Cardinal says of the new candidate in the prologue: "He must be a man to whom order is necessary, as dear as life."¹¹ The dominance is expressed in small quiet details—the Bishop's taste in art, in food, as well as in, say, his treatment of the mutinous Father Martinez. The events that reveal character have a likeness—an equality of stress—that suggests a medieval tapestry.

Puvis wrote that he wanted the central figure of Geneviève in his painting to provide the tone for the whole scene; and Cather, similarly, makes Latour's character suffuse the whole narrative. This is done, however, not by making the action involve the Bishop at every point, but by presenting the scenes in a style which presupposes the value of order and restraint—a value that distinguishes the Bishop. The effect then is that of the clarity, order and light which pervade the frescoes.

Indeed, the effect of light, literally represented in the narrative, is so marked that Randall objects to it as a substitute for action: "The effect is a good deal more passive and static than the previous effects obtained in earlier novels. She now uses tonal climaxes with light instead of emotional climaxes of action."[12] In the prologue which sets the mode of light and color for the whole book, the author writes, "The vehemence of the sun suggested motion. The light was full of action and had a peculiar quality of climax—of splendid finish. It was both intense and soft...." Since she has so clearly stated her goal, to write something "which is absolutely the reverse of dramatic treatment," and has so clearly begun in this graphic mode, it seems irrelevant to criticize the lack of conflict. Puvis spoke of the light in his painting: "The general aspect was tender and soft, like the soul of that child which must...bathe the whole composition."[13] This kind of light, relating the events to the theme, pervades the novel. The light on the "carnelian colored" hills outside Santa Fe, the great plain near Acoma "glittering with rain sheets but the distant mountains bright with sunlight," the mesa itself, where "the bare stone floor of the town and its deep worn paths were washed white and clear," the Indians kneeling in the grey light like antedeluvian creatures, and the Archbishop's new cathedral, "yellow, a strong golden ochre, very much like the gold of the sunlight that was now beating upon it."[14]

The westward movement of the light *is* the action, and the color of the sun is fittingly assigned to the Bishop's monument, the cathedral of native stone. The symbolic overtones of the scene are typical: Latour is aging; it is late afternoon. Once again the Bishop and Vaillant have ridden *west*. They look up at "the rugged wall, gleaming gold above them. 'That hill, *Blanchet*, is my cathedral.'" The use of light after the manner of Puvis de Chavannes has enabled Willa Cather to deal with two commonplace and difficult subjects, the westward movement and religion, in a delicately stylized manner that almost always preserves the novel from hackneyed plot and the merely picturesque scene. Such are the uses of immobility, flatness and light that Willa Cather brings from painting to fiction. The last quality, *distance* or detachment, is perhaps the most significant, and yet the most difficult to analyze.

In his essay on "Point of View in the Arts" Ortega y Gassett distinguishes in painting "proximate vision" from "distant vision."[15] In his words "the *proximate vision* and the *distant vision* of which physiology speaks are not notions that depend chiefly on measurable factors, but are rather two distinct ways of seeing." So, for example, if we picture an earthen jar in a foreground and landscape in the background, our eyes are focused on the jar and we sense its very surface, even the tactile quality. The objects in the background are blurred, hardly identifiable. There is a central object, a "luminous hero" as Ortega says, "a protagonist standing out against a mass, a visual plebs." This earthen jar represents proximate vision. But when the eye reaches the distant horizon, the optical hierarchy disappears. The field is homogeneous; everything is equal in a kind of optical democracy. All tactile or textural quality has, of course, disappeared. This is distant vision, in which there is little focus.

One further characteristic of distant vision is the hollow space between us and the object. Proximate vision, then, analyzes, treats each object with respect for its volume, roundness, solidity. Every external object is as real as every other. Distant vision overlays the object with the medium contiguous to both object and eye—namely, space. One can almost say that space *unifies* the field.

In a most convincing manner Ortega demonstrates his thesis that the history of the arts in Europe has been a record of the painter's point of view changing from proximate to distant vision [from preoccupation with "bulk" to preoccupation with "hollow space"—editor's clarification]. Quatrocento artists seem to paint each object separately. Later Velasquez paints objects veiled by space. A single point of view dominates. Here space is a governing idea. Then the impressionists retreat further toward the eye itself, and the process of *seeing*, the breaking up of the light, receives the attention. Finally in cubism, painting has gone into the consciousness itself and from the external realities of the quatrocento, painting has receded into the mind: from *things*, through *sensations* to *ideas*; or from external reality, to the subjective reality, and finally the intrasubjective. To summarize Ortega's somewhat complex idea: the evolution of Western painting consists in "a retraction from the object toward the subject, the painter himself."

It is significant that when impressionists were directing the point of view of art further inward, Puvis de Chavannes went back to an earlier period. His monumental style seems created by a desire for a "calm poetry inspired by the history and legends of civilization."[16] He goes back toward the Renaissance for the clarity of his individual figures, and their flatness and their lack of accent suggest the distant vision as defined by Ortega. His works, like earlier art, may be wanting in cohesion, but the idea of distance, and especially the overlaid light, imply a special [detached] attitude toward the events of history.

That is to say, the idea of distance or space develops into a style in which historical events are monuments. These monuments are illumined by the painter, but they are neither copies of the "actual" nor projections of arbitrary forms in his mind. It is surely this quality that Michel had in mind when he said that Puvis de Chavannes might sometime be regarded as the most documentary of painters.

What has been said of the painter applies precisely to Willa Cather. Writing at a time when the innovations of Joyce and others had led fiction *within* the mind, within the process of consciousness, Cather turned to an earlier period. The distance, the detachment, with which she treats her historical subjects has the effect of the monumental style. Historical events are contained in that style not as "actuality," or as anarchic forms within the mind, but as events ordered by a tradition. In this tradition, as in a legend, light is a correlative of belief, and space is a correlative of freedom. Thus the style and the subject are closely related.

The sunlight and distance of the Southwestern landscape are important subjects of the narrative. The manner in which the light and the space are used, the manner of stasis instead of accent, of distant vision instead of perspective, of suffusion of light instead of dramatic action, is parallel to what is "monumental" in Puvis' frescoes.

For Willa Cather's characters, belief illuminated and ordered history. For the novelist herself, space in the land implied the freedom in which belief erected monuments. The Archbishop built his church of native golden stone where there was "[s]omething . . . wild and free, something that . . . lightened the heart, softly, softly picked the lock, slid the bolts, and released the prisoned spirit of man into the wind. . . ."[17]

Notes

1. *Willa Cather on Writing* (New York, 1949), p. 9.

2. John Randall, *The Landscape and the Looking Glass* (Boston, 1960), p. 310.

3. Edward & Lillian Bloom, *Willa Cather's Gift of Sympathy* (Carbondale, 1962), p. 236.

4. Bloom, p. 236.

5. Randall, p. 310.

6. André Michel, "Exposition de M. Puvis de Chavannes," *Gazette des Beaux-Arts*, 2ᵉ pér., t. XXXVII (1888), p. 44.

7. Marius Vachon, *Puvis de Chavannes* (Paris, 1895), p. 108. Good reproductions of the mural are in this volume or in Arsene Alexandre, *Chavannes* (London, n.d.).

8. Robert Gale, *Explicator*, XXXI (May 1963), item 75.

9. *Death Comes for the Archbishop* (New York, 1951), p. 4.

10. Randall, p. 276.

11. *Archbishop*, p. 8.

12. Randall, p. 291.

13. J. Buisson, "Pierre Puvis de Chavannes, Souvenirs Intimes," *Gazette des Beaux-Arts*, 3ᵉ pér., t. XXII (1899), p. 19.

14. *Archbishop*, p. 241.

15. José Ortega y Gassett, "On Point of View in the Arts," *Partisan Review*, XVI (August 1949), pp. 822–24.

16. *Dictionary of Modern Painting*, eds. Carlton Lake and Robert Maillard (New York, n.d.) p. 239.

17. *Archbishop*, p. 276.

Willa Cather's Archbishop:
A Western and Classical
Perspective   John J. Murphy*

The hero rather than setting or situation is the main thing in *Death Comes for the Archbishop*. Willa Cather admitted that for a long time she had no intention of writing the novel: "the story of the Church and the Spanish missionaries was always what most interested me; but I hadn't the most remote idea of trying to write about it."[1] What changed her mind were stories she had heard about Archbishop Lamy of Santa Fe and her discovery of Howlett's biography of Bishop Machebeuf. She was intrigued by the reaction of the French priests to the people and country of New Mexico, the Western experience as filtered through the hero she would fabricate from these and other sources, a hero at once "fearless and fine and very, very well-bred. . . . What I felt curious about was the daily life of such a man in a crude frontier society." In this way she revealed her interest in creating a Western hero, one sharing the experiences of Leatherstocking, the Virginian, and even Huckleberry Finn, yet responding to these experiences with a more cultivated sensibility. Beyond this local or national type are similarities to the heroes of classical literature, particularly Aeneas, whose destiny was to shape a new culture in Italy by transplanting the home gods of Troy. Thus Archbishop Latour reflects Cather's cyclical view of history, in which the American experience repeats the European, and our West the larger West.

I

Jean Marie Latour is introduced wearing buckskin like Natty Bumppo, although the far western setting of the novel demands an equestrian hero like the Virginian. Cather opens with "a solitary horseman, followed by a pack-mule, . . . pushing through an arid stretch of country somewhere in central New Mexico."[2] This horseman is atypical, however: "Under his buckskin riding coat he wore a black vest and the cravat and collar of a churchman" (p. 19). Even aside from his calling, he is unusual: "His bowed head was not that of an ordinary man,—it was built for the seat of a fine intelligence. . . . There was a singular elegance about the hands below the fringed cuffs of the buckskin jacket. Everything showed him to be a man of gentle birth—brave, sensitive, courteous. His manners . . . were distinguished." Cather presents us with the cultivated counterpart of the naturally attractive hero described by Wister's narrator at the beginning of *The Virginian*: "in his eye, in his face, in the whole man, there dominated a something potent to be felt . . .

*Originally published in *Western American Literature*, 13 (Summer 1978), 141–50. Reprinted by permission of *Western American Literature*.

by man or woman:"[3] Wister's tall stranger and Cather's young priest
are knights-errant in the wilderness, rescuing those in need, righting
wrongs, bringing law to lawless regions.

The Virginian's exploits range from pranks to gun duels, but there
is always decency about them. The rescue of Molly Wood from the river,
while a humorous situation, is of a maiden in distress, the kind of affair
Natty Bumppo specialized in in the New York forests. The Virginian's
role in lynching the cattle thieves is of more serious dimension, a haunt-
ing episode leading to tears for his old friend Steve. This and the famous
gun duel with Trampas jeopardize his relationship with Molly, but he is
forced into them by the corrupt condition of Wyoming law. In trying
to justify the hero's actions, Judge Henry explains to Molly, "We are in
a very bad way, and we are trying to make that way a little better until
civilization can reach us" (p. 314). Even the Wyoming bishop cannot
really condemn the Virginian's action under the circumstances.

New Mexico too is in a bad way, and Latuor has to contend with
similar lawlessness. "The Lonely Road to Mora" episode combines the
hero's rescue of the female in distress and a situation of self-defense.
After the terrified Magdalena warns the priests about the murderous
Buck Scales, Latour draws his pistol on the outlaw. When Magdalena
escapes, Latour watches over her until the buckskin-clad, conventional
Western hero, Kit Carson, takes her home to his wife. In a more
amusing vein, and more befitting a courtly type, is Latour's administering to Isabella Olivares during the difficulty she has admitting her age.
Latour's confrontations with the wayward native clergy make him a kind
of frontier lawman forced to compromise in imperfect situations until
the appropriate time for action. Rather than "lose the parish of Taos
in order to punish its priest" (p. 157), he allows the excesses of Father
Martinez to continue until he can get a strong replacement. Martinez,
Gallegos and Lucero, a trio of clergymen as lawless as any company of
cattle rustlers, challenge the new bishop's authority by practices as varied
as political intrigue, gambling, hoarding money and siring children.
Patiently but firmly, Latour replaces them, although Lucero and Martinez
organize a rival church of their own.

Cather's hero shares with Natty Bumppo concern over the exploitation and destruction of the land by new settlers. Natty complains that
white men's explorations "always foretell waste and destruction"[4] and
demonstrates less wasteful Indian methods of hunting and fishing.
Latour is sensitive to the Indian respect for nature: "it was the Indian's
way to pass through a country without disturbing anything. . . . It was
the Indian manner to vanish into the landscape, not to stand out against
it. . . . They seemed to have none of the European's desire to 'master'
nature, to arrange and re-create. They spent their ingenuity in the other
direction; in accommodating themselves to the scene in which they found
themselves" (pp. 233–34). Just as Natty laments the sacrificing of

New York forests for the ugly, jerry-built structures of Templeton, Latour is disturbed by the proliferation in Santa Fe of "flimsy wooden buildings with double porches, scrollwork and jack-straw posts and bannisters painted white" (p. 271), which destroy the setting of his golden Romanesque cathedral. He is forced to contend with the confusions of life brought about by the discovery of gold in Colorado, where wandering prospectors and their followers crowd into the mountains, pollute the water and succumb to fever. Latour assigns these Colorado problems as the special task of Father Vaillant, who eventually becomes the bishop of Denver.

Also, Latour's Indian companionships associate him with Cooper's hero. Natty's lifelong friendship with Chingachgook and his relationship with Uncas and Hist have their parallels in Latour's dealings with Jacinto and especially the Navajo leader Eusabio. Like Natty, Latour is able to communicate with Indians. At Laguna, he talks with Jacinto about Indian names and legends. The Navajo Eusabio becomes Latour's friend for life, and his desert home the place Latour visits during a period of spiritual aridity. The two men share Christianity, concern for the welfare of the Navajos, and a respect for each other reminiscent of Natty and Chingachgook. The nobility of both relationships and the silent inter-course characterizing them are suggested in a meeting between Eusabio and Latour after the death of Eusabio's son: "At first he did not open his lips, merely stood holding Father Latour's very fine white hand in his very fine dark one, and looked into his face with a message of sorrow and resignation in his deep-set, eagle eyes" (p. 221). The scene recalls Natty's attempt to comfort Chingachgook at the grave of Uncas, when he declares, "Sagamore, you are not alone," and Chingachgook grasps his hand with warmth of feeling.[5]

Celibacy and perpetual boyhood also characterize the Western hero. Natty Bumppo's refusal to involve himself with Judith Hutter and his foolishness in the unequal affair with Mabel Dunham illustrate the bachelor aspect Wister ridicules in the story of the rooster fleeing Judge Henry's ranch because of a fear of petticoats. The Virginian himself decides to move on when the community begins to fill with young mar-rieds and a school is contemplated:

> ". . . Well if this hyeh Territory is goin' to get full o' fam'ly men and empty o'game, I believe I'll—"
> "Get married yourself," suggested Mr. Taylor.
> "Me! I ain't near reached the marriageable age. No, seh!" [P. 42]

This reminds us of Huck Finn's constant efforts to avoid the complexities of society by moving on, by lighting out for new territory to escape that "cramped up and smothery" feeling in conflict with the easy freedom of the raft, where one floated "wherever the current wanted," where one could throw off the restraints of civilization and go naked, "day and night."[6] The threat marriage and domestic life represent to the perpetually boyish Western hero is most clearly dramatized in Crane's "The Bride Comes to Yellow Sky," when gun-happy Scratchy Wilson desists from his constant pistol dueling with Sheriff Jack Potter when confronted with the news of Potter's recent marriage. Wilson calls off the feud, muttering, "Married!" Wilson "was not a student of chivalry; it was merely that in the presence of this foreign condition he was a simple child of the earlier plains."[7]

Wilson seems an extreme case beside Latour, whose celibacy is a condition of his religious vocation; nevertheless, the churchman leads a bachelor life like typical Western heroes and most Cather heroes. Near the end of the novel, when the elderly Latour grows homesick for New Mexico while visiting Clermont, we are made aware of this boyhood existence, now a kind of reward for a life of service: "In New Mexico he always awoke a young man; not until he rose and began to shave did he realize that he was growing older. His first consciousness was a sense of the light dry wind blowing in through the windows, with the fragrance of hot sun and sage-brush and sweet clover; a wind that made one's body feel light and one's heart cry 'To-day, to-day,' like a child's" (p. 275). The Old World could not bestow this youth, but the wind of the "light-hearted mornings of the desert, . . . that wind . . . made one a boy again. He had noticed that this peculiar quality in the air of new countries vanished after they were tamed by men and made to bear harvests." This resembles the Virginian's hankering after an undomesticated territory without schools. The atmosphere of freedom becomes necessary for Latour: "he had come back to die in exile for the sake of it. Something soft and wild and free, something that whispered to the ear on the pillow, lightened the heart, softly, softly picked the lock, slid the bolts, and released the prisoned spirit of man into the wind, into the blue and gold, into the morning, into the morning!" (pp. 275–76).

II

Latour is a variation of the typical Western hero, and his life spans the epoch of far-western expansion: "he had come with the buffalo, and he had lived to see railway trains running into Santa Fe" (p. 273). Yet, Cather takes us beyond the world of Leatherstocking and the American West. *Death Comes for the Archbishop* opens in the gardens of a villa in the Sabine hills, beneath which Rome spreads before a setting sun, the dome of St. Peter's the distinctive feature on the horizon. The discussion concerns bringing the order of the Roman Church to the vast New Mexican territory. Besides two references to the romances of Fenimore Cooper, one of the discussants, a New World missionary, is referred to as "an Odysseus of the Church," and he compares the job to be done in New Mexico to cleaning out an Augean stable. The American West is thus given classical perspective and Cather's priests the status of classical heroes. As a missionary of Roman law and order, Latour suggests Aeneas. There are surprising resemblances between them. Although Cather might have been aware of the Virgilian aspect of Latour's ship-wreck in Galveston harbor, the fated dimension of his tasks and his communication with the world beyond are unmistakable similarities.

Aeneas' destiny is to bring about the Roman peace, when, as Jupiter foretells, "the age of violence [shall] be mellowing into peace."[8] Unlike the typical American Western hero, Aeneas is not confused about being on the side of civilization. Hector charges him in a dream to save the holy things and gods of Troy and plant them in an Italian home (II, 291–97). Despite the jealousy of Juno and the stumbling blocks she sends his way, Aeneas manages to fulfill Jupiter's prophecy. His mother Venus is always there to help him, of course, to maneuver a friendly reception in Carthage, to direct him to the golden bough, to cure his wounds before the final contest with Turnus. As discussed over dinner by a few ecclesiastics, Latour's destiny seems hardly so awesome: "He will have to deal with savagery and ignorance, with dissolute priests and political intrigue. He must be a man to whom order is necessary— as dear as life" (p. 8). However, a mysterious world operates here too. In "The Lonely Road to Mora" incident, for example, the warning given the priests by Magdalena "seemed evidence that some protecting power was mindful of them" (p. 70). Cather's inclusion of the stories of miracles like Guadalupe, where the Virgin appeared to Brother Juan, requested a church to be built and imprinted her portrait on his coarse garment, suggests manipulation by the other world. Latour's experience with the peasant Sada before the Mary altar in "December Night," when "The beautiful concept of Mary pierced the priest's heart like a sword," is essentially a visitation from above: "He received the miracle in [Sada's] heart into his own, saw through her eyes . . ." (p. 218). A few chapters later he takes Vaillant to the golden hillside from which his Romanesque cathedral will be built and explains how he discovered this singular hill by chance, when he had to divert his route due to a washout. "Oh, such things are never accidents, Jean," responds Vaillant (p. 242). The rescue of Latour in the red-hilled desert through the discovery of the pastoral oasis of Agua Secreta is given supernatural dimension by Cather's balancing this episode with the one in which Junipero Serra is entertained by the Holy Family in the desert.

Confrontation with the other world is not always beneficent, how- ever. Aeneas is frequently tortured by Juno and her lackeys, especially during the war with the Rutulians, about which Venus complains to Jupiter:

Now Juno is dredging up the Underworld—a province
Hitherto unexplored—and has suddenly loosed Allecto
On the earth, to spread delirium through the Italian towns. [X, 39–41]

Also, Aeneas himself suffers chilling experiences in the underworld during
his search for his father Anchises. After entering a dark cave, he witnesses
the shapes of Death, Agony, and War, and unfortunate souls occupying
places of mourning and punishment, those experiences Dante would
employ in his own great poem, which D. H. Stewart has applied to
Cather's novel.[9] The self indulgence of Gallegos, sensuality of Trinidad,
avarice of Lucero, and lusts and seductions of Martinez, accompanied
by the heresy and discord sown by the latter two, provide Latour with
underworld experiences and enough opposition to require heroic effort.
The diabolical dimension of this crew is suggested in the death scene
of Lucero, when, surrounded by candlelight, he perceives Martinez
in torment and utters his last words, "Eat your tail, Martinez, eat
your tail!" (p. 171). Even the vanity of Doña Isabella has other-
worldly ramifications, since it jeopardizes the building of the cathedral,
symbol of the success of Latour's mission. However, Latour feels most
at a loss when confronted with the superstitions of the Indians. "Snake
Root" includes material on the ceremonial fire and snake worship,
practices confirmed by Jeb Orchard and by Latour himself when, in
the foul-smelling cave, he witnesses Jacinto flattened against the rock
and listening at the oval hole in the rear wall. "The Mass at Acoma"
contains both aspects of Latour's difficulties. While the Indians cluster
about him in their shawls and blankets, he feels threatened and
ineffectual: "He felt as if he were celebrating Mass at the bottom of
the sea, for antediluvian creatures; for types of life so old, so hardened,
so shut within their shells, that the sacrifice of Calvary could hardly
reach back so far" (p. 100). He begins to long for the comfort of his
own tradition: "He was on a naked rock in the desert, in the stone age,
a prey to homesickness for his own kind, his own epoch, for European
man and his glorious history of desire and dreams" (p. 103). The
Acoma legend of Fray Baltazar, the final part of this book, is a com-
pendium of most of the excesses of the native clergy.

   In addition to the missionary dimension and the influence of
other-worldly supportive and opposing forces, there are specific qualities of character shared by Aeneas and Latour. Wendell Clausen has
pointed out the piety of Virgil's hero, his awareness and acceptance
of fate, even when the cost is loss of almost every human attachment.[10]
When compared to Odysseus or Achilles "Aeneas is almost devoid of
passion or personality," "seems curiously inert," and "more burdened
by memory than any other ancient hero." His "actions may be described
as valiant, patriotic, devoted; but more and more he becomes the hero
who acts in some other and higher interest, like a priest." All these
qualities describe Latour, who, firmly, but knowing pain and terror, had

decided to leave his native France for missionary work in the New World. Perhaps a greater sacrifice for Latour occurs when, beyond mid-life, he relinquishes Father Vaillant for the Colorado missions. He had recalled Vaillant from Tucson because he wanted his companionship, yet he suggests to his vicar the need for a priest at Camp Denver. Latour is disappointed at Vaillant's enthusiastic willingness to leave Santa Fe: "he was a little hurt that his old comrade should leave him without one regret. He seemed to know, as if it had been revealed to him, that this was a final break; that their lives would part here, and that they would never work together again" (p. 252). At this point he confesses his motives for recalling Vaillant: "I sent for you because I felt the need of your companionship. I used my authority as a Bishop to gratify my personal wish. That was selfish, if you will, but surely natural enough. We are countrymen, and are bound by early memories" (p. 253). These words suggest both the burden of memory and the sadness of what duty demands, and, as he returns home from his leave-taking from Vaillant, Latour reflects on these demands: "He was forty-seven years old, and he had been a missionary in the New World for twenty years—ten of them in New Mexico. If he were a parish priest at home, there would be nephews coming to him for help in their Latin or a bit of pocket-money; nieces to run into his garden and bring their sewing and keep an eye on his housekeeping" (p. 255). However, back in his study he successfully transforms his loneliness into something positive: "It was just this solitariness of love in which a priest's life could be like his Master's. It was not solitude of atrophy, of negation, but of perpetual flowering" (p. 256).

Latour's lack of passion, bordering on coldness for some readers, and the difficulty he has making friends are more than compensated for by the presence of supporting characters. In effect, Cather's method is to embody in others the qualities in which her hero seems deficient. Martinez rather than Latour is her passionate character; however Martinez was "like something picturesque and impressive, but really impotent, left over from the past" (p. 141). Next to Latour, the buckskin-clad Kit Carson is the typical adventurer, the more legendary hero of the frontier, but Carson proves brutal in his treatment of the Navajos and is dismissed as "misguided" (p. 293). Vaillant is warmer, more popular and more active than Latour, who in his humility feels inferior to his vicar. This is obvious when he requests Vaillant's blessing before one of their separations: "Blanchet, . . . you are a better man than I. You have been a great harvester of souls without pride and without shame—and I am always a little cold—un pédant, as you used to say. If hereafter we have stars in our crowns, yours will be a constellation. Give me your blessing" (pp. 261–62). Latour feels that his somewhat quieter work in Santa Fe pales beside the more aggressive and celebrated mission in Colorado. However, Vaillant's work depends upon Latour, for he was responsible for Vaillant coming to the New World, had "to forge a new will in that devout and exhausted priest" (p. 299), and directed his missionary work, including Colorado.

Clausen concludes his consideration of Aeneas by noting Virgil's "perception of Roman history as a long Pyrrhic victory of the human spirit" and his suggestion of a less than optimistic view of Rome's future by having Aeneas depart from the underworld through the gate of ivory, the gate of false dreams. Cather's comments about the failure of the twentieth-century priests of New Mexico to respect the old mission churches and their decorations, and her generally pessimistic view of the outcome of Western pioneer endeavor cast Latour's accomplishments in similar light. Maybe this is why her novel is, from beginning to end, riddled with the light of the setting sun. Yet, there is something everlasting in those "fearless and fine and very, very well-bred" qualities of her hero. Her combining of the Western tradition and the classical tradition and the perspective of death from which the novel is written suggest Latour's timelessness. Facing death, when life reveals itself as "an experience of the Ego, in no sense the Ego itself," he acquires an insight outside of "calendared time": "He sat in the middle of his own consciousness; none of his former states of mind were lost or outgrown. They were all within reach of his hand, and all comprehensible" (p. 290).

Notes

1. *Willa Cather on Writing* (New York: Alfred A. Knopf, 1962), pp. 6–7.

2. *Death Comes for the Archbishop* (New York: Random House Vintage Books, 1971), p. 17. Subsequent references are to this edition.

3. Owen Wister, *The Virginian, A Horseman of the Plains* (New York: Pocket Books, 1956), p. 6. Subsequent references are to this edition.

4. James Fenimore Cooper, *The Deerslayer; or, The First War-Path, A Tale* (New York: D. Appleton and Company, 1892), p. 44.

5. *The Last of the Mohicans, A Narrative of 1757* (New York: D. Appleton and Company, 1892), p. 442.

6. Samuel Langhorne Clemens, *Adventures of Huckleberry Finn*, ed. Scully Bradley, Richard C. Beatty, and E. Hudson Long (New York: Norton Critical Editions, 1962), pp. 96–97.

7. *Stephen Crane: Stories and Tales*, ed. Robert W. Stallman (New York: Random House Vintage Books, 1955), p. 285.

8. *The Aeneid of Virgil*, trans. C. Day Lewis (Garden City, New York: Doubleday Anchor Books, 1952), p. 21 (I, 291). Subsequent references are to books and lines of this edition.

9. "Cather's Mortal Comedy," *Queen's Quarterly*, 73 (1966), 244–59.

10. "An Interpretation of the *Aeneid*," *The Aeneid/Virgil*, trans. John Conington, ed. Wendell Clausen (New York: Pocket Books, 1965), pp. vii–xv.

Shadows on the Rock

[Review of *Shadows on the Rock*]　　　　　Wilbur Cross[*]

Sometimes a novelist's art may be summarized in a happy title. Twice Edith Wharton thus betrayed her art. *The House of Mirth* was in the end everything but a house of mirth. *The Age of Innocence* was anything but an age of innocence. As in these novels, Mrs. Wharton's attitude towards persons and things has been consistently ironical. Likewise, Sinclair Lewis's *Main Street* and *Babbitt* by their very titles forecast the drab life of Middle Western towns, with satirical intent.

Willa Cather's art has passed through several phases. In *O Pioneers!* and *My Ántonia*, her subject was mainly the early settlers on Nebraska plains among Yankee, Bohemian, French, German, Scandinavian, and Russian immigrants. There they are as she saw them in the flesh in her childhood and youth. Subsequently, she moved her scene south to Colorado and eventually to New Mexico also, where she sojourned later. But of gross observation there is little or none. Everywhere she selects significant incidents, rarely working them too hard, for bringing out the characteristics of the men and women whom she depicts. When as in *The Song of the Lark* she becomes more liberal with incident, she succeeds less well. The novel which she can best manage is comparatively short, like *A Lost Lady*, which in the opinion of many, still remains her masterpiece.

Outwardly, Miss Cather has moved far in her method. At first she adopted the traditional form of the novel, rather loose in construction. Then, as in *The Professor's House*, she began to experiment with the biographical manner, which she has come to like best of all. *A Lost Lady* is her study of a situation such as we almost always have in the novels of Edith Wharton. But throughout all of Miss Cather's work there is a lyrical quality which at times rises to genuine poetry. You see it in her earliest work. No one, for example, can ever forget the way she brings

[*]Originally published in the *Saturday Review of Literature*, 8 (22 August 1931), 67–68. Copyright 1931 by the *Saturday Review*. All rights reserved. Reprinted by permission.

into *My Ántonia* the plough magnified to a great black image against a glorious sunset as a symbol of the life on the Nebraska prairies. The lyrical mood, which climbs to its height in *Death Comes for the Archbishop,* is the prime characteristic which separates Miss Cather from her two outstanding contemporary novelists.

Her title, *Shadows on the Rock,* the happiest one yet, seems to have behind it a philosophy of life and of art too. Are we but shadows projected upon a scene, whether the scene be on the plains or on the slope of a fortress? Or are the men and women, whom we observe and watch everyday or whom we read about in old books, but shadows to us after all? Can we penetrate the inner consciousness and tell the world what is going on in the mind, as Virginia Woolf and others profess to do? Well, Miss Cather will do the best she can and leave it to her readers to determine whether she ever gets behind the shadows. She does not fall into the old fallacy of thinking that she sees things as they are. Nobody knows what they really are. She renders them as they appear to her, well knowing that they may appear to others differently. Nothing quite exists outside the mind that perceives, infers, reasons. Miss Cather's mind has a romantic glow.

In the time of which she writes in her latest novel, Quebec was not much more than a village of two thousand inhabitants living on the slope of the fortress and down by the river. For its economic existence, it relied upon trading with the Indians; too often, furs for brandy. It was, too, the outpost for missionary work with them, along the St. Lawrence and far back in the woods. Vast domains were explored and claimed for France. It was a New France north of a New England. Miss Cather's purpose is to tell about the life of the people on the rock, far from home. Most of all she dwells upon the mentality of the immigrants who brought into the wilderness with them the ideas of a well-ordered universe which had become fixed in their minds by the teachings of the Catholic Church when they were children in France. God and the angels were always near them in the beauty of the landscape, in the sun and the moon and the stars, and in the many miracles God wrought for their happiness. So there was little or no sickness for the home they had left beyond the sea. What was tragic in their lives is kept well in the background. Everywhere the colony is invested with a poetic glamour by beautiful descriptions of the rock through the changing seasons of the year.

> It was the first day of June. Before dawn a wild calling and twittering of birds in the bushes on the cliff-side above the apothecary's back door announced clear weather. When the sun came up over the Ile d'Orleans, the rock of Kebec stood gleaming above the river like an altar with many candles, or like a holy city in an old legend, shriven, sinless, washed in gold.

There is no study of character in detail. There is nothing comparable to the great missionary priests in *Death Comes for the Archbishop*. The tone is subdued to a poetic atmosphere which must be maintained. Purposely the sketches are slight and delicate like the pastels of Latour or Watteau. Action is reduced to a minimum. Of political history just enough is given to fix the time and the scene; no more. Characters come and go in glimpses. Here and there is comment or an anecdote or a short strip of biography. Quarrels are indicated rather than described. The clash between Bishop Laval and his successor, Saint-Vallier, is but a clash of temperaments. The hardships of Pierre Charron, the fur trader, who subsisted in the woods with the Indians on dried eels and dog meat boiled with blueberries, are toned down by a half-humorous narrative. So throughout. So far as the story is held together, it is by Auclair, the apothecary and medical advisor to the Count de Frontenac, and by Auclair's charming daughter, Cécile, about whom we learn most as we see them in their daily routine or on an evening reading aloud Plutarch or La Fontaine. Indeed, the apothecary's shop, where men and women of all classes go for herbs to cure their ills, is the center towards which the tale drifts, until we come to the lyrical afterglow in the death of Frontenac, who as he lies dying waves a feeble gesture with his left hand as a silent command that the priests and nuns kneeling by the bedside rise and draw back. The last battle must be fought alone. The great shadow passes on and leaves the rock in full splendor. A new age is at hand.

A novelist who tries an unaccustomed form must expect that many readers will be disappointed. It is always a risk. Why not another *Lost Lady* or another *Death Comes for the Archbishop*? Miss Cather willed otherwise. *Shadows on the Rock* is quite of another kind. In some respects it resembles Sterne's *Sentimental Journey* where scenes and characters separate and coalesce at the command of the author, and at last fall into an exquisite harmony of tone and atmosphere. The characterization, because it is brief, must be deft. Necessarily, much is left to the imagination. Miss Cather loves particularly the eyes. Of Saint-Vallier, Auclair remarks to his daughter: "What restless eyes he has, Cécile; they run all over everything, like quicksilver when I spill it." And Cécile's eyes, when her heart was touched, grew dark "like the blue of Canadian blueberries." In other instances, it is a hand or a gesture or a movement of the face that subtly reveals character. It is all a delicate art, more difficult than the art of the traditional novel. Few have ever measurably succeeded. Miss Cather is among these few.

The French-Canadian Connection:
Willa Cather as a Canadian Writer   Benjamin George*

Willa Cather's vivid and poetic rendering of the landscape of the Great Plains of the United States and her sympathetic treatment of the struggle of sturdy immigrant girls towards the promises of the American Dream would seem to mark her as a distinctively American writer. Yet she came to hold a close affinity with Canadian ideals and attitudes, pointedly different from those of her own national ethos. While the development of those ideals and attitudes may be traced throughout her work, they come into clearer focus in her work after World War I and reach their culmination in her Canadian-set novel, *Shadows on the Rock* (1931).

Set in the New France of the seventeenth century, *Shadows on the Rock* demonstrates Cather's belief in the value of maintaining the continuity of the traditions of European civilization in the New World as opposed to the delight and pride which her compatriots have traditionally taken in their attempts to create a new and better society in the New World. In a related choice of values, Cather makes quite clear in *Shadows on the Rock* that in the great conflict between civilization and nature which dominates so much of the literature of the New World, she sides, as does the Canadian tradition, with civilization. Appropriately then, Cather depicts nature, not in the light of the tradition dominant in American literature, as the source of that which is good, innocent and ennobling, offering regeneration for society freed from European conventions, but rather as a threat to civilization, as a force ready and waiting to snuff out the accomplishments of puny man in its formidable midst.

The development and intensification of these views on Cather's part to the point of her formulation and expression of them in *Shadows on the Rock* mark her realization and her concern that the genteel way of life which she valued had disappeared from the new post–World War I American scene. Viewing with disdain and contempt the elements of modernism and materialism which overtook American society in that era, Cather could find the genteel values which she so admired only in the past or in more traditional societies, particularly in France. France was to Cather, quite simply, the very source of civilized life. Even as early as 1895, seven years prior to her first visit to France, she wrote that, "most things come from France, chefs and salads, gowns and bonnets, dolls and music boxes, plays and players, scientists, and inventors, sculptors and painters, novelists and poets. . . . If it were to take a landslide into the channel some day there would not be much creative power of

*Originally published in *Western American Literature*, 11 (Fall 1976), 249–61. Reprinted by permission of *Western American Literature* and the author.

any sort left in the world."[1] Her admiration was successively reaffirmed by the seven visits she made to France over the course of her life.

By a happy accident of literary history, Cather discovered France in the New World. Worn by her father's death and her own attack of the virus in the spring of 1928, Cather and her friend and companion, Edith Lewis, decided against their usual route through Maine to Grand Manan Island, off the coast of New Brunswick, where Cather had summered since 1922, and chose a new route through Quebec. There on the rock of Quebec, Cather found a city which, with its preservation of its physical and social past, had not only maintained French culture in the New World, but had also managed to resist the trends of modernism and materialism which were sweeping the United States.

Lewis's account of the author's reaction to Quebec vividly and succinctly conveys the special appeal of that city to Cather:

> . . . from the first moment that she looked down from the windows of the Frontenac on the pointed roofs and Norman outlines of the town of Quebec, Willa Cather was not merely stirred and charmed—she was overwhelmed by the flood of memory, recognition, surmise it called up; by the sense of its extraordinarily French character, isolated and kept intact through hundreds of years as if by a miracle, on this great un-French continent.[2]

Cather spent ten days exploring the city and, according to Lewis, was so utterly charmed by her discovery that she set immediately to reading Canadian history and interviewing local historians. She returned to Quebec several times after that first visit, including once in mid-winter when the city was deep in snow.

Quebec was a great discovery for Cather, for she found there respect for the maintenance of the traditions of the past and European culture, making for a refuge of all she valued in the midst of a world which she found distasteful. Quebec's particular physical setting accentuated these qualities, for situated as it is on a rock, it met the physical demands of the setting which she had used for the location of ideal worlds in her fiction since her youth, that of an enchanted bluff or great rock. In his article, "Willa Cather and The Big Red Rock," Philip L. Gerber has carefully traced the development of the symbolic qualities of that setting in Cather's work from her introduction of it in an early short story "The Enchanted Bluff" (1909).[3] Gerber summarizes much of the development of that setting with the explanation that the rock as symbol climaxes for Cather, "her rejection of twentieth century life, which she saw as an agony of blatant commercialism. . . ." Gerber best describes what the rock did, in fact, mean to Cather in his conclusion to his article, "From her wasteland there rises always the rock, strong, defiant, reaching for the clouds to postulate all the affirmative values of character, fidelity, idealism, civilization, culture, religion, ethics and order. . . ." Cather's best known use of the rock is as the setting for *The Professor's House* but the rock as symbol reaches its final culmination in the Quebec-set novel where it is a part of the title itself.

Clearly then Cather found in French Canada something other than French culture, which had disappeared in the United States. That she did not see the same respect for maintaining the continuity of the traditions of European culture in English Canada, though she had visited Toronto and other areas often before her visit to Quebec, demonstrates both the difference in degree in living up to a set of common ideals between English and French Canada and English Canada's greater similarity to the United States. In her novel *Shadows on the Rock*, Cather does, nevertheless, express her admiration of and sympathy for ideals and attitudes which are characteristic of both English and French Canada.

Shadows on the Rock is composed of a series of vignettes which follow a complete cycle of seasons through the course of the year October, 1697, to November, 1698. The novel is concluded by a brief epilogue set in 1713. Cather's use of the historic past as setting is important for it is in that colonial period that Cather can treat the confrontation between the settlers from the Old World and the environment of the New, and can thereby depict the ideas and attitudes which governed that confrontation and which led to the preservation of European civilization in the Quebec of her own day.

While the lives of historic personages, local legends, political events and tales of adventure are all treated in the vignettes, they are all incidental to the daily lives of the central character, Euclid Auclair, a widowed apothecary, and his twelve-year-old daughter, Cécile. While Auclair misses his beloved France, he is well aware of the problems of that country and is thereby able to contrast the Old and the New France. Cather is American author enough to seize this opportunity to present the injustices and iniquities of the Old World. In taking the reader back to Auclair's Parisian days, Cather explains the basis of his decision to leave France for the New World:

> Gradually there grew up in Auclair's mind the picture of a country vast and free. He fell into a habit of looking to Canada as a possible refuge, an escape from the evils one suffered at home, and of wishing he could go there. . . . He could not shut his eyes to the wrongs that went on about him, or keep from brooding upon them. In his own time he had seen taxes grow more ruinous, poverty and hunger always increasing. People died of starvation in the streets of Paris, in his own parish of Saint-Paul, where there was so much wealth. All the while the fantastic extravagances of the Court grew more outrageous. The wealth of the nation, of the grain lands and vineyards and forests of France, was sunk in creating the pleasure palace of Versailles. The richest peers of the realm were ruining them-

selves on magnificent Court dresses and jewels. And, with so many new abuses, the old ones never grew less; torture and cruel punishments increased as the people became poorer and more desperate. The horrible mill at the Châtelet ground on day after day. Auclair lived too near the prisons of Paris to be able to forget them.[4]

Cather develops this motif throughout the novel by her consideration of the King's ingratitude to Frontenac, the political maneuvers of the Church, and the reactions of other settlers to the world of Versailles.

Cather's demonstration of the iniquity of the Old World is, however, strongly tempered, if not set aside in Shadows on the Rock, by her major theme, the value of preserving the civilization of Europe in the New World. She makes no suggestion whatsoever that the iniquities of the Old World constitute a justification for disregarding it or for breaking the ties that bind the colony to the parent country. Cather adheres then to a Canadian rather than to an American attitude. While recognizing the evils of the Old World and seeing the New World as a refuge from them, she through Auclair and the other settlers of Quebec, expresses her belief that the evils of the Old World can be corrected in the New without surrendering the advantages of a civilization developed over the centuries or the stability and order which that civilization can provide.

Although aware of the injustice of the Old World, Auclair, himself, is a devotee of France and her traditions. He remains a loyal servant to his lord Frontenac and maintains the culture of France in his home. Both he and his deceased wife have impressed upon their daughter the value of maintaining French civilization in the New World for and of itself and because it is the bulwark by which they prevent themselves from sliding into what they see as the abyss of barbarism awaiting them on all sides.

Cather's chief means of expressing her belief in the value of preserving European culture is her treatment of domestic manners which for Cather are the very basis of civilized life, and the principles which she establishes through her valuation of their continuity must apply, in her scheme of things, to the larger institutions of society. Cather depicts the transference of French civilization in the form of domestic activity by having Madame Auclair, a model French housewife, pass on to Cécile, daughter of New France, her high standard of domesticity with the warning that only the preservation of such matters can, in fact, protect them all from the influence of the New World.

Madame Auclair, we are told, "had brought her household goods without which she could not imagine life at all" (26), and succeeded with them in transforming their Quebec home into a replica of their French one. As long as Madame Auclair lived, Cather assures us, "she tried to make the new life as much as possible like the old" (27).

Recognizing the fact of her fatal illness, Madame Auclair devotes her last days to passing on her manners to her daughter so that, Cather writes, Cécile "would be able to carry on this life and *this order* (italics mine)" (27), after Madame Auclair's death. Cather effectively makes her point in one of Madame Auclair's set speeches to Cécile in which the mother seems to advocate the maintenance of European civilization not to Cécile alone but to the New World at large.

> After a while, when I am too ill to help you, you will perhaps find it fatiguing to do all these things alone, over and over. But in time you will come to love your duties, as I do. You will see that your father's whole happiness depends on order and regularity, and you will come to feel a pride in it. Without order our lives would be disgusting, like those of the poor savages. At home, in France, we have learned to do all these things in the best way, and we are conscientious, and that is why we are called the most civilized people in Europe and other nations envy us. (28)

Cather emphasizes the point in her summation of the process of the transference of cultural values:

> Then she [Madame Auclair] would think fearfully of how much she was entrusting to that little shingled head; something so precious, so intangible; a feeling about life that had come down to her through so many centuries and that she had brought with her across the wastes of obliterating, brutal ocean. The sense of "our way,"—that was what she longed to leave with her daughter. She wanted to believe that when she herself was lying in this rude Canadian earth, life would go on almost unchanged in this room with its dear (and, to her, beautiful) objects; that the proprieties would be observed, all the little shades of feeling which make the common fine. The individuality, the character, of M. Auclair's house, though it appeared to be made up of wood and cloth and glass and a little silver, was really made of very fine moral qualities in two women: the mother's unswerving fidelity to certain traditions, and the daughter's loyalty to her mother's wish. (29)

To underscore the appreciation of the preservation of European civilization by the community at large, Cather has the apothecary's shop and home a source of delight to all levels of society in Quebec, with the townspeople seizing upon any opportunity to stop there.

Cather conveys her theme on the public as well as on the private level. She depicts as the great day in the life of the colony the spring arrival of the ships from France, and presents it in vivid detail as a veritable feast day which celebrates the renewal of European ties. Conversely, the saddest day is the day of the autumn departure of the ships. Moreover, the attention which Cather gives to both state and church as additional links to Europe throughout the novel consistently reinforces the image of a colony tightly bound to the Old World in both the temporal and spiritual realms. Through her concentration on the domestic aspects of daily life, the relations of Count Frontenac with the king, and the personalities, ritual and legends of the Church, Cather ties the colony on the rock of Quebec closely to the parent civilization of France and assures the reader thereby of the preservation of gentility, spiritual values, respect for tradition, stability, order and permanence.

Clearly then Cather is not presenting a colony determined to create a new society in the New World which in turn would lead the way for the Old World, as was the aim of the Puritans of New England—best expressed by John Winthrop's "For wee must consider that wee shall be as a city upon a Hill, the eies of all people are upon us." Rather, in contrast to that American notion of the City upon a Hill, Cather creates an image for the Canadian ideal in her conception of a City upon a Rock. Whereas the settlers of the City upon a Hill saw themselves as being in the forefront of movements in Europe and aimed at creating a new society which would show the way to Europe, only eventually to forego the tie and pursue an independent destiny, the settlers of the City on a Rock see themselves as the faraway extension of Europe and exert their efforts towards preserving and protecting their cultural inheritance and maintaining the ties which will enable them to do so.

That which their civilization has to be protected against is, initially, the overwhelming, hostile and forbidding wilderness which surrounds it, threatening always to snuff it out. Cather has then recognized the Canadian settlement as garrison and the wilderness as threat to the garrison as the opening scene of her novel well illustrates.[5] Set on Cap Diamont, highest point on the Rock of Quebec, the opening scene depicts Auclair watching the autumn departure of the ships from France and surveying below him, the city of Quebec and the surrounding area. With the departure of the ships, Auclair is led to muse upon the isolation of the colony in the New World. The notion of isolation which Auclair introduces is intensified by his reference to the city below him as a "French strong-hold" and his recognition that the threat to the stronghold and the civilization it embodies is the wilderness which surrounds it. Cather's depiction of the wilderness as a threat stands as one of the finest treatments of that particular theme found in literature by or about Canadians and Canada:

> On the opposite shore of the river, just across from the proud
> rock of Quebec, the black pine forest came down to the water's edge;
> and on the west, behind the town, the forest stretched no living man
> knew how far. That was the dead, sealed world of the vegetable king-
> dom, an uncharted continent choked with interlocking trees, living,
> dead, half-dead, their roots in bogs and swamps, strangling each other
> in a slow agony that had lasted for centuries. The forest was suffoca-
> tion, annihilation; there European man was quickly swallowed up in
> silence, distance, mould, black mud, and the stinging swarms of insect

life that bred in it. The only avenue of escape was along the river. The river was the one thing that lived, moved, glittered, changed,—a highway along which men could travel, taste the sun and open air, feel freedom, join their fellows, reach the open sea. . . . reach the world, even! (7)

In this scene, reminiscent of the opening of Richardson's *Wacousta* with the same emhasis on the waterway as the avenue of escape through the threatening wilderness, Cather well depicts the garrison mentality, the view of nature, which many critics have seen as the dominant one in Canadian literature, and the theme of survival itself which both literary critics and historians have pointed out as a most distinctively Canadian motif.

Cather demonstrates the effects which the wilderness combined with the loss of European standards could have on civilization in the New World through the Harnois incident. During this incident, in which Cécile leaves the Rock for the first and only time during the novel, she visits the Harnois family on the Ile d'Orléans, in the middle of the Saint Lawrence. Cécile is repulsed by the crude, dirty and unkempt life led there, as Cather well illustrates in the following description of Cécile's reaction to the children of the Harnois family:

> The little girls wore moccasins, but no stockings, and their brown legs were badly marked by brier scratches and mosquito bites. When they showed her the pigs and geese and tame rabbits, they kept telling her about peculiarities of animal behaviour which she thought it better taste to ignore. Cécile was not at all sure that she liked these children with pale eyes and hay-coloured hair and furtive ways. (221)

The life of the Harnois family has drifted away from European standards and Cécile learns only too well the difference it has made. Cather connects the setting of the island with the forbidding wilderness with which she opens the novel through her attention to the mosquitoes, as though they were manifestations of the evil forces of nature itself. The contrast between the effects of the mosquitoes in the wilderness and in Auclair's home, where they are dispelled by a European import, supports Cather's argument. She writes that ". . . the kitchen where they ate was very hot and close for Madame Harnois shut all the doors and windows to keep out the mosquitoes. There were mosquitoes at home, . . . too, but her father drove them away by making a smudge of eucalyptus balls, which were sent to him from France every year" (222).

At bedtime, Cécile balks at having to share a dirty bed with four unwashed girls covered with mud and the blood of mosquito bites. Rather than sleep in such squalor, Cécile sits up all night. The misery of her situation leads her thoughts to her mother, and her strict maintenance of French standards of civilized life, and Cather here presses her point, for Cécile remembers, "how her mother had always made everything at home pleasant, just as here everything about cooking, eating, sleeping, living, seemed repulsive" (224).

The scenes of life at the Harnois' stand in utter contrast to those at her father's home. There on the Île d'Orléans, while not in the forest, itself, but then not on the rock either, the Harnois have lost the traditions of European civilization on the domestic level, and have allowed the natural world to affect them, reducing them to barbarians. Cather has Cécile learn the lesson well. Safely back in her own kitchen, the girl delights in her domestic implements and realizes an important point by which Cather is able to expand her own concern with daily domesticity to civilized life itself:

> These coppers, big and little, these brooms and clouts and brushes, were tools; and with them one made, not shoes or cabinet-work, but life itself. One made a climate within a climate; one made the days,—the complexion, the special flavour, the special happiness of each day as it passed; one made life. (230)

Granted that frontier life is not highly complimented by many American writers either, the values of nature in American literature being saved for the true wilderness, it is important to note that Cather does extend her negative views of the wilderness beyond the immediate area of Quebec, in terms of reports of European men losing their way and freezing, starving, or suffering from Indian depravity. Safety—and survival—is with civilization, and civilization is on the Rock, above but surrounded by the forest.

Cather's presentation of Pierre Charron, a heroic voyageur and a friend of the Auclairs, further demonstrates her sympathy with the Canadian rather than the American attitude towards the world of Nature. Depicted as a Canadianized version of Natty Bumppo, Charron is described as one "who shot up and down the swift rivers of Canada in his canoe; who was now at Niagara, now at the head of Lake Ontario, now at Sault St. Marie on his way to the fathomless forbidding waters of Lake Superior" (199). Indeed to both the elder Auclairs, he more than anyone else, "realized the romantic picture of the free Frenchman of the great forests which they had formed at home on the bank of the Seine" (200). To further intensify this image of Charron as the natural man, Cather has Charron speak out harshly against those connected with Versailles and the inequities of the Old World. Born in Canada, he regards himself as a Canadian rather than a Frenchman. He is clearly then Cather's New World man, and in keeping with her American tradition, he is associated with both the world of nature and with high moral principles.

Cather does, however, distinguish him from Natty Bumppo and his literary descendants in a very telling way. Rather than spending a lifetime in the wilderness according to the tenets of Cooper for Natty

Bumppo, Charron is very much a part of his society. Even as a voyageur, he returns periodically to Quebec and in a symbolic transference of power, demonstrative of the growth in the colony, Cather has Charron take over as Auclair's protector after Count Frontenac dies and attributes to both Frontenac and Charron many of the same sound qualities of leadership. In the epilogue, we learn that he has married Cécile, that he has built a spacious and comfortable home in the upper town, and that the couple is "well established in the world" and is "raising four Canadians of the future" (323), all male. The world of the wilderness may then serve as a source of dangerous excitement, but neither it nor the romanticized freedom it may provide are meaningful ends in themselves, not even for a man such as Charron. No American New World Adam is he, free and celibate in the forests, for he finds values in life in civilization complete with Eve, domesticity, and family ties.

Cather closes her novel with a conclusion of the initial period of settlement in the colony and a preview of the new nation to come. Power has been symbolically transferred from the French to the Canadians, and Charron and Cécile stand as the founders of a new people. Cather's marriage of the two and her presentation of them as the Adam and Eve of the Canadians well illustrates her depiction of the Canadian version of the New World Dream. Through Charron, Cather presents the natural man of the New World who stands firmly against the degeneration of European society but not against society in general. Through Cécile, who, though French born, thinks of herself as Canadian, Cather presents the notion of a New World identity which is inclusive rather than exclusive of a sense of identity with the Old World. Combined, these features—the natural man with ties to society, the disapproval of the immorality of the Old World, along with the maintenance of its civilization—make for Cather a Canadian identity.

In Quebec, then, Cather found a society built upon a rock which came as close as any she ever found to meeting her fictive notions of the City built upon a Rock, for there she found a world which cherished the past, which maintained its traditions, which represented the preservation of European civilization in the New World, and whose roots were those of her most admired country, France. She responded to the situation with a series of vignettes around a central core of characters in that society's past and in doing so conveyed her understanding and appreciation of the historic processes which led to the development of that society.

In doing so, Cather revealed her sympathy with Canadian ideals and attitudes as opposed to the American counterparts. While a number of her compatriots also expressed one or another of these views in their response to the twenties or more particularly to the Depression, it is Cather's treatment of a constellation of views, similar to a constellation of those characteristic of Canadian literature, which is so striking. In a letter which she sent to an appreciative reviewer of *Shadows on the*

Rock, Cather explains her understanding of the Canadian situation and makes quite clear her recognition of its difference from that of the United States:

> To me the rock of Quebec is not only a stronghold on which many strange figures have for a little time cast a shadow in the sun; it is the curious endurance of a kind of culture, narrow but definite. There another age persists. There, among the country people and the nuns, I caught something new to me; a kind of feeling about life and human fate that I could not accept, wholly, but which I could not but admire. . . . Those people [the early settlers of Quebec] brought a kind of French culture there and somehow kept it alive on that rock, sheltered it and tended it and on occasion died for it, as if it really were a sacred fire—and all this temperately and shrewdly, with custom always tempered by good sense.
>
> It's very hard for an American to catch that rhythm—it's so unlike us. But I made a honest try. . . .[6]

If we accept E. K. Brown, eminent critic of both Canadian literature and Willa Cather, as the judge of the success of Cather's honest try, then the attempt was very successful indeed for he has written that,

> It is far too little to say of 'Shadows on the Rock' that it is the best novel drawn from the rich material of Canadian history. Beside it William Kirby's 'Golden Day' is clumsy and external, Charles G. D. Roberts' 'Forge in the Forest' conventional, and Gilbert Parker's 'Seats of the Mighty' merely facile. Nor would any historical novels written by French Canadians sustain a comparison with Miss Cather's craftsmanship and vision.[7]

In *Shadows on the Rock*, however, Cather has done more than write a fine Canadian historic novel or give expression to her views about the past and civilization; she has in fact articulated a Canadian ideal.

Notes

1. James Woodress, *Willa Cather, Her Life and Art* (New York: Western Publishing Company, 1970), p. 233.

2. Edith Lewis, *Willa Cather Living* (New York: Alfred A. Knopf, 1953), pp. 153–4.

3. *College English*, 19 (January, 1958), 152–7.

4. Willa Cather, *Shadows on the Rock* (Boston: Houghton Mifflin Company, 1938), pp. 36–7. All further quotations from the novel are taken from this edition.

5. In his "Conclusion" to *The Bush Garden: Essays on the Canadian Imagination* (Toronto: Anansi, 1971), pp. 213–51, Northrop Frye has explained the concept of the "garrison mentality" in Canadian literature.

> Small and isolated communities surrounded by a physical or psychological 'frontier,' separated from one another and from their American and British cultural sources: communities that provide all that their members have in the way of distinctively human values, and that are compelled to feel a

great respect for the law and order that holds them together, yet confronted with a huge, unthinking, menacing, and formidable physical setting—such communities are bound to develop what we may provisionally call a garrison mentality. (225)

6. *Willa Cather on Writing: Critical Studies on Writing as an Art*, with a forward by Stephan Tennant (New York: Alfred A. Knopf, 1949), pp. 15–17.

7. "Homage to Willa Cather," *Yale Review*, 36 (September, 1946), 89.

The Last Four Books

[Review of *Obscure Destinies*]   Henry Seidel Canby*

These "three new stories of the West" make the reviewer pause. Here
is no bold experiment in a new type of fiction such as has characterized
Miss Cather's novels, nor any new terrain studied closely for a texture of
life refreshingly different from our own. This is the West of Miss Cather's
early novels, a country where roads are ankle deep in summer dust, incredibly beautiful by moonlight, a country where the corn will burn up
in a single torrid day, or it is the high sage brush plains of Colorado,
familiar to us before. It is a country where many people are mean and
commonplace, where there is little generosity of living; and into it her
imagination plunges deep for recollections of great souls that make a
contrast and a salvation.

"Great souls" sounds like a rhetorical description of Miss Cather's
unfaltering realism, but this, nevertheless, is what distinguishes these
stories. They contain all the elements of that country of disillusion which
the sociological novelists have made wearisomely familiar. In "Neighbour
Rosicky," the work is hard, the family does not get on, the American town
girl who marries the Bohunk's daughter longs for cheap amusements. In
"Old Mrs. Harris" the little Colorado town has every horror of prying
neighbors and cheap convention. The family's pride is to keep up appearances, and the husband's easy shiftlessness, and the spoiled wife's selfish
egotism, are only euphemisms for the exploitation of a poor old grandmother who believes that after forty the old should go to the kitchen
and youth have its way. In "Two Friends" a dose of political claptrap
breaks down a life-long friendship which was a symbol of the possible
excellence of human values in a town where everything else was commonplace.

Yet, while it would be most misleading to say that Miss Cather views
these dreary possibilities as an optimist might, a difference, but no such

*Originally published in the *Saturday Review of Literature*, 9 (6 August 1932), 29.
Copyright 1932 by the *Saturday Review*. All rights reserved. Reprinted by permission.

280

crude difference, distinguishes her work from the passionate drabness of the school which sees America only as a lost opportunity. She looks with keen eyes and unafraid, a little deeper. In "Neighbour Rosicky" she has drawn a full-length portrait of a good man, good in the sense which takes little account of principles but much of character and personality. It is so much harder to write of such a character, to make him live, to make you love him, without one concession to tricks of sentiment or appeal to conventional reactions. Rosicky, the ex-tailor's boy, happily at home at last on the land, would be to you just a Bohunk with a pleasant face. He is never anything else through the story, and yet a great soul is manifest. Grandma Harris is a pure essence of that stiff conventionality which holds itself fast in the respectable just above the level of the poor white. Beside the warm flexibility of temperament of her neighbor, the Jewish Mrs. Rosen, she is crystallized prejudice. The grandchildren that love her, and for whom she drudges without understanding the meaning of sacrifice, will be ruined, one feels, by just such ideas as she lives by, when their hearts, like the oldest's, grow harder. A bare difference of a degree of angle, a shift in the lens, and she would be a ridiculous old woman, killing herself to keep the house respectable, a stupid martyr to selfishness. The lens is not shifted. She remains a stupid old woman, a victim of selfish and futile respectability, but she is a great soul. Mrs. Rosen sees that.

And in the last story, "Two Friends," something still more difficult is attempted. Mr. Dillon and Mr. Trueman—the Irishman and the old American—are themselves characters of depth and color. Dillon with his imperious head on a small, wiry body, his musical, vibrating voice, and his air of superiority amounting to arrogance; Trueman who made you feel solidity, "an entire absence of anything mean or small, easy care-lessness, courage, a high sense of honor"—these two men represented success and power in the community. But it was not their souls that were great, it was their friendship. As they sat in their chairs at night on the brick sidewalk it was a "strong, rich, outflowering silence between two friends, that was as full and satisfying as the moonlight. I was never to know its like again." And it was precisely that friendship which gave solidity and meaning to the little town which would have seemed so commonplace to others, which *was* commonplace, except for this node of influence.

It is remarkable how easily and surely, like all the really competent novelists, Miss Cather builds up these stories, without one trick, without one undue emphasis, with every significant detail, not sparing the human weaknesses, never flattering, never ignorant of cruelty, ugliness, disappointment, never afraid of humor, as of Trueman's rear that "looked a little like the walking elephant labelled 'G.O.P.' in *Puck*," nor of beauty, as of "the soft, dry summer roads in a farming country, roads where the white dust falls back from the slow wagon-wheel." And this is perhaps why, in an unsentimental period, she can make great souls where others deal in stereotype, caricature, or studio photograph. The West is a little more human, and our imagination a little richer, for Grandma Harris and Neighbour Rosicky.

[Review of *Lucy Gayheart*]   Dorothea Brande*

Sometimes it seems that Willa Cather is an artist doomed not to be understood by her own times. Those who were young when the stories were written which later appeared in *Youth and the Bright Medusa* can never read her without a reminiscent recapturing of the excitement and joy to which they were once stirred, nor, sadly, without an unjust feeling that some tacit agreement between themselves and the author of these stories has not been fully met. Even less can the younger reviewers, handicapped by having been taught by the new psychology to criticize fiction by standards more suitable to the psychiatrist's laboratory than the artist's workroom, understand an author who uses only the materials which seem to her pertinent to her subject, refusing staunchly to handle those which her newest critics invariably try to thrust upon her. It is probably fortunate for all of us that Miss Cather goes quietly along her own way, offering book after book which we cannot fail to recognize and receive as the work of a true artist, although—some for one reason, some for another—seldom quite so generously as we should like.

That is what makes reviewing such a book as Miss Cather's *Lucy Gayheart* a thankless task. More than probably she fulfilled her own intention, and we have had evidence before this that her intention was often better than any we could have dictated to her. In addition, Miss Cather is unsurpassed in craftsmanship. Few novelists can do what she does so unerringly: she brings her *story* unobtrusively to a full circle; her characters then go on, truly created, alive independently even for us, who so often and so inconsistently complain that they were never fully living. Surely no author ever had a better right than Miss Cather to paraphrase Sargent's bitter epigram: "A portrait is a picture that has something wrong with the mouth." Miss Cather in her solitude must feel that our definition of a novel should be "A book which has something wrong with the end . . . or some character, or a motive."

At least she must have the satisfaction, for what it is worth, of knowing that her books are a vital element in the lives of her readers. While *Lucy Gayheart* was still running serially it already had the importance that gives rise to living gossip: "She killed off her hero at the end of the

*Originally published in the *American Review*, 5 (October 1935), 625–29.

first part, and her heroine at the end of the second," we said; "what's left for the end?" No insignificant book raises such a question as that.

Well, what was left for the end is justification enough for a dozen novels, and yet I too want to join in the chorus of scolding and complaint, and say in my turn that if the book had been much shorter, if, indeed, it had been kept to the dimensions of a long short story, not even the most obtuse reader could have failed to see the pertinence of every element in it to that ending. Of course she did not "kill off" the hero or the heroine of her book at all, although the character who gives her name to the novel does drown at the end of the second section. For the hero—or heroine, as you choose—is none of the characters of the story, but the sense of life; and Miss Cather says so as openly as she can without bustling into the middle of her own scene. But since she did spend so much time in drawing Lucy, and in drawing the singer, Sebastian, they come to have at once too much and too little presence: too much if they are to be seen as vehicles of life, too little if we are intended to feel them as individuals.

Since the story of the book is well enough known by now, I shall only summarize it briefly. Lucy Gayheart, after a childhood in a small Western town, goes to Chicago in pursuit of music. Always vividly although undiscriminatingly in love with life, she learns through a relationship with Sebastian, whose practice-accompanist she becomes, the justification for her intense joy in living. The relationship is not quite love, is more intense than friendship, and after entering it she is unable to marry the cautious, prosperous suitor at home, in whose heart and memory she is destined to live on at the end of the book. Before she has learned to disentangle the gift of appreciation from the man who gave it to her, Sebastian is drowned. Crushed by his death, she returns to her home. Slowly, through long months, she tries to regather her life, for the blow has almost destroyed her sense of her own identity. Then just as she begins to understand—"What if Life itself . . . were like a lover waiting for her in distant cities?"—she also is drowned.

With an unfailing touch, Miss Cather saves this from being gratuitous tragedy. If Lucy had drowned before her moment of illumination, the book would have fallen to ashes; Lucy would have died without transfiguration. As it is, she lives on; and surely few novelists would have saved the treasure of Lucy's three childish footprints across the old cement walk to spend as Miss Cather does. The pattern of the book is at once subtle and clear: only Tolstoi's use of the railroad station in *Anna Karenina* returns to me at the moment as so surely handled as Miss Cather's scenes on the icy river. Every element of the opening pages is used again at the scene of Lucy's death, and yet there is not an obvious item among them. And then, with the generosity of the artist there comes that added gift of the footprints, withheld until it can bring its own relief and comfort: "Was there really some baffling suggestion of quick motion in those impressions,

Gordon often wondered, or was it merely because he had seen them made, that to him they always had a look of swiftness, mischief and lightness? As if the feet had tiny wings on them, like the herald Mercury." And, when the book closes: "As he was leaving the Gayhearts', he paused mechanically on the sidewalk, as he had done so many thousand times, to look at the three light footprints, running away."

Since the book has its successful pattern, since the closing section is no anticlimax, but embodies the very feeling of continuing life that its author intended, what possible complaint can there be against *Lucy Gayheart*? Yet the chorus of wistful complaint arises, however much it has been set off with appreciation and praise. Because Miss Cather knew so much about her Lucy, took us so close that we heard her breathe and knew her thoughts, she seems arbitrarily to have denied us some deeper knowledge that we needed, and which Miss Cather herself must have had. The relation between Lucy and Sebastian is ambiguous, not merely subtle; Lucy's sense of life—that central focus of the book—is never convincingly vivid for all the author's reiteration of it. Lucy's father and sister are stock figures, and Lucy herself too oblivious to them to lend them any part of her own rather fitful reality.

That is the type of complaint her readers must make against Miss Cather—surely the most satisfactory captiousness a writer can be asked to bear: that she does so well, we want her to do better, to give us what she herself has taught us to expect. And that is something as near perfection in art as the novel has been able to come.

[Review of *Sapphira and the Slave Girl*]

Dorothy Canfield Fisher*

The people of our times are turned towards embittered skepticism by calamity almost beyond human imagining. Helpless spectators of the horrifying spread of human slavery, readers of 1940 are forced into a suspicion that a happy ending to any story can be no more than a cheap and sleazy veil thrown over but not hiding the ugly figure of truth. To such saddened readers, aching with shame for humanity, Willa Cather presents a lovely story of escape from human slavery, which is not only literally and factually true, but deeply and symbolically the truth.

The book is very quiet in tone, slight and short—about half the length of the usual novel, with a good deal of space given to minute, affectionate and enchantingly detailed descriptions of the background of life in a rural

*Originally published in *Book-of-the-Month Club News*, December 1940, pp. 2–3. Copyright Book-of-the-Month Club News. Reprinted by permission.

district of Virginia, near Winchester, in 1856. Hardly a page in it is without a thumbnail vignette, clearly drawn, of the exact aspect of place or person, as they were on the date of the story:—"A short, stalwart woman in a sunbonnet, wearing a heavy shawl over her freshly ironed calico dress"—there is a plain, pre–Civil War country woman, every item chosen to make her different from a modern country woman visually vivid.

The home of the miller, where the action takes place, is like an old, finely-executed, pen-and-ink drawing with every tree, every walk, every plant set precisely in its place. Nor are all these details visual ones. The story of how the miller's wife happened to own the land in Back Creek is told from 1747 to 1759, long before the birth of any of the characters of the book. The annual mowing of the meadows by eight scythe-swinging Negro field-hands is as brilliant with carefully selected detail as the best Breughel painting of peasant life. The talk of the Negro slaves is almost startlingly real, every shading preserved, the difference carefully marked between the language used by house servants when speaking to their white masters and when talking together in their own cabins.

But, although all this is utterly charming, Miss Cather's book is no period piece. Vivid as it is, the background is, outdoors and indoors, in its proper place back of the characters, back of the action. It is not in the book for its own sake, in spite of the loving care lavished on it. The reader's attention is wholly fixed on the story, one of the many variations on one of the oldest of human themes, a prison, a human being in it, the effort to escape, the uncertainty as to whether escape is possible. The use of the wonderfully described background is the sound legitimate use of setting a real world around real human beings.

And yet, although the story is on the always exciting theme of attempted escape from prison, although the men and women, black and white, are profoundly human and living, one feels a relaxed, mellow lack of intensity which, although it is agreeable in the extreme, seems at first rather odd in a story made up of the crudest and most violent elements. The tale is of the cruelly ruthless attempt made by a jealous elderly wife to use the unrighteous power over other human beings given slave owners, to wreck and blight a blooming, dewily innocent, and virtuous young girl, hardly more than a child.

Mrs. Colbert, the wife of the miller, complacent with the stupid self-esteem of the provincial over-valuation of material possessions, cold, calculating, relentless, is an appalling old woman of exuberant Elizabethan wickedness. Portrayed by Faulkner, in livid purples and bloody reds, she would have had the reader, his hair standing on end, shouting for help. But in Miss Cather's book we accept her as those around her accepted her, without heroics.

The same sort of almost dreamy quality is found in the portrayal of Nancy's tragic situation. Her danger, her trapped struggles to escape from the doorless, windowless prison in which slavery kept her, make an exciting story. But we are not excited by it. We believe fully in the stealthy, threatening footsteps which so terribly frighten Nancy: but Miss Cather does not try, as Hemingway does, to make us, too, hear them with a physical shudder. We follow the plot with the closest, most sympathetic attention, but—we realize at the end of the book—almost as though we knew all along, that Nancy was sure to be saved from the villainous plot to destroy her, that the nobility, integrity, sense of the sacredness of human dignity, felt by the miller and his magnificent daughter, cannot but conquer the forces of evil, as right cannot but in the end be stronger than wrong.

As soon as we begin the exquisitely written Epilogue, we see why the book has, for all its savage story, a lovely mellow bloom, why, as we read, we half know that it is all going to come out all right. We see that it is not just a story, it is poetry, poetry in the sense of emotion remembered in tranquility. We see that it is, and has been all along, a tale told to a little girl, held in her memory for a lifetime, recurring to her mature mind with the special moonlit, seen-in-a-mirror quality of stories remembered from childhood. And as we realize this, we see how it frees us from the turbid, immediate, imitation-emotion of literally realistic stories, and permits us calmly to see in perspective the golden human values of the tale.

Those values are infinitely consoling and comforting to us, shocked as we are by the recurring, ever-nearer dangers to our own freedom. The book bids us have faith.

[Review of *The Old Beauty and Others*]   Charles Poore*

Willa Cather was born a Virginian and died a New Yorker and wrote most memorably about Nebraska and the West. The three stories in this, her last book, suggest those places in point of view or mood or setting. One is a wreath for an international enchantress of the Nineties. One is a tale of youth and the prairie years. One is the soliloquy of a Western rich man facing his mortal enemy at last. In the pleasure they give and the mastery they show they belong with her finest and most characteristic work, with *My Ántonia*, and *A Lost Lady*, and *Death Comes for the Archbishop*. Yet nothing in them, true fragments though they are, tells us so much, perhaps, about Willa Cather as a choice she made not long before her death a year ago last April.

That was when she unexpectedly answered a question. The question—put by an industrious anthologist—was: What, among the works

*Originally published in the *New York Times Book Review*, 12 September 1948, p. 3. Copyright 1948 by the New York Times Company. Reprinted by permission.

of others, do you wish you had written? It went to a lavish variety of literary celebrities. Upton Sinclair chose a bit from Isaiah; Henry Canby chose a bit from his bible, *Walden*; Irwin Edman went straight to George Santayana. Miss Cather said she wished she had written the ballad of "The Mary Gloster," by Rudyard Kipling.

Why, of all things, did she choose that? Why didn't she choose something from Turgenev or Henry James or the Sarah Orne Jewett who had counseled her: "One must know the world so well before one can know the parish," or the Walt Whitman who had given her the title for *O Pioneers!*? Miss Cather used explanations as sparingly as she used words in writing *Shadows on the Rock* or *My Mortal Enemy* or *Sapphira and the Slave Girl*, or *Lucy Gayheart*—or the stories in *The Old Beauty and Others*.

And, on the rare occasions when she did explain, she did so with a glowing asperity that sometimes burned middle-class critics hell-bent on being as proletarian as all getout.

"Literalness," she said in an essay called "The Novel Démeublé," "when applied to the presenting of mental reactions and of physical sensations seems to be no more effective than when it is applied to material things. A novel crowded with physical sensations is no less a catalogue than one crowded with furniture."

Also these words, which might well be above every writer's desk and in every school that tries to teach writing:

"Whatever is felt upon the page without being specifically named there—that, it seems to me, is created. It is the inexplicable presence of the thing not named, of the overtone divined by the ear but not heard by it, the verbal mood, the emotional aura of the fact or the thing or the deed, that gives high quality to the novel or the drama, as well as to poetry itself."

All her later books are true to that principle. In some of the earlier ones, such as *The Song of the Lark*, there is too much archaeological furniture. Perhaps in *The Professor's House* and *One of Ours*, too. It was, then, the conciseness of Kipling's "Mary Gloster," as well as the fortitude in the deathbed portrait of a tough and picturesque old titan—like the titans of her West—who got things done, who scorned the soft and the cheap, the rust that tarnished the scabbarded blade, that appealed to her:

> *Never seen death yet, Dickie?*
> *Well, now is your time to*
> *learn,*
> *And you'll wish you held my*
> *record before it comes to*
> *your turn.*
> *I've made myself and a million;*
> *but I'm damned if I made*
> *you.*

It has what Unamuno called "the tragic sense of life" that you will find in all Miss Cather's books. It shows "the inevitable hardness of human life," which, Thea Kronborg said toward the end of *The Song of the Lark*, all real artists must learn. It is not out of key with the spirit of the Marian Forrester of *A Lost Lady*, who "mocked outrageously at the proprieties she observed, and inherited the magic of contradictions." And it would not be despised by Father Latour, in *Death Comes for the Archbishop*, who went over the splendor of his memories tranquilly, and who said with a smile: "I shall not die of a cold, my son. I shall die of having lived."

All of a piece throughout, then, Miss Cather's stories return again and again to her themes: youth lost and fortitude maintained, daring and art and valor. The old values, she frequently likes to suggest, are better than the new. The giants lived yesterday; pygmies rule today.

Now that is a bracing stand to take. The trouble with it is that it really won't stand an awful lot of discussion. For what is a fine old value to me, may have been a pretty shocking and revolutionary notion to my crusty great-grandfather. As Anon has said, there must once have been people who thought that romance went kiting out of the sea when those new-fangled things called sails took the place of the good old paddles and the dugout canoes of the good old days.

Yet you know very well what Miss Cather means when Gabrielle Longstreet, the heroine of "The Old Beauty," living out her last days at Aix-les-Bains, in 1922, a significant place and date to Miss Cather, says: "I think one should go out with one's time."

And, like Yeats' dying lady, "with the old kindness, the old distinguished grace," mourning what Ezra Pound called "the old men with beautiful manners," who will come no more, Gabrielle, once the toast of two continents, is soon on her way to her final resting place. Where? Why, at Père-Lachaise cemetery in Paris, of course. Hadn't it also been fashionably chosen by "Adelina Patti, Sarah Bernhardt and other ladies who had once held a place in the world"?

There is a faint ghost of absurdity to trouble us here. But please don't think Miss Cather wasn't aware of it. Her use of the word fashionable indicates that, without specifically naming it. What she was doing here was what she once said in a letter to *The Commonweal* a novelist should do—presenting "the experiences and emotions of a group of people by the light of his own. . . . whether his method is 'objective' or 'subjective.'"

Incidentally, that mention of Patti and Bernhardt is itself a quintessence of Catherism, a touch of the Willa Cather whose stories frequently show how much she admired great old-time singers and actresses as well as the ruins of the Southwest.

In the second story in *The Old Beauty and Others*, called "The Best

Years," there is a wonderful picture of the Nebraska country at the turn of the century, when Miss Evangeline Knightly, the young school superintendent, was on her way to see a promising youngster who died young before finding the bright Medusa. Years later Miss Knightly, who had long since married and gone away, as Miss Cather's characters so often do, comes back for a postscript visit, in homage to nostalgia and the tidy ending (as Miss Cather's characters so often did).

A pert young modern, "a wide-awake, breezy girl with blond hair and crimson lips," is now the district superintendent. We are told that the former Miss Knightly "liked young people who were not in the least afraid of luck or responsibility," though the liking does not seem to be overwhelming. Anyway, when she explains that she would prefer a horse and buggy rather than an automobile to visit the schools again, the red-lipped blonde brightly says:

"I get you. You want to put on an old-home act. You might phone around to any farmers you used to know. Some of them still keep horses for haying."

To which Miss Cather's heroine answers nothing—nothing whatever—though you can feel the air quiver with what must have been her reaction to that bit of jazz-age sauciness. And again something is felt on a page without being specifically named there.

The story's explicit moral is that "our best years are when we're working hardest and going right ahead when we can hardly see our way out." But there is no comment on that, either. The commentary, if any, comes in the last story, "Before Breakfast," when the self-made Henry Grenfell, in his island retreat designed for peace of mind, goes back over the years and finds their climax singularly disturbing.

In a preface to a new edition of *The Song of the Lark*, written at New Brunswick, Canada, in 1932, not far from the scene of "Before Breakfast," Miss Cather had said: "Success is never so interesting as struggle—not even to the successful, not even to the most mercenary forms of ambition."

After revising *The Song of the Lark*, she was still critical:

"The interesting and important fact that, in an artist of the type I chose, personal life becomes paler as the imaginative life becomes richer, does not, however, excuse my story for becoming paler. The story set out to tell of an artist's awakening and struggle; her floundering escape from a smug, domestic, self-satisfied provincial world of utter ignorance. It should have been content to do that. I should have disregarded the conventional design and stopped where my first conception stopped, telling the latter part of the story by suggestion merely. What I cared about, and still care about, was the girl's escape; the play of blind chance, the way in which commonplace occurrences fell together to liberate her from commonness. She seemed wholly at the mercy of accident; but to a person of her vitality and honesty, fortunate accidents always happen."

Finally, in "Before Breakfast," we have a perfect Cather touch when Grenfell recalls saying to his wife and son, who have grown away from him, that while they are at the symphony, he is going to hear John McCormack sing "Kathleen Mavourneen." And his wife in her "innocent, well-bred way," says:

"Dear me! I haven't heard McCormack sing since he first came out in Italy years and years ago. His success was sensational. He was singing Mozart then."

There are few shouts in Miss Cather's writing. But the murmurs are incomparably clear.

Willa Cather's Last Four Books   David Stouck*

I

In her major novels Willa Cather explored the archetypal dimensions of the human imagination: *O Pioneers!*, with its vision of the new land and its heroic settlers, is written in the epic mode; *My Ántonia*, with its quest into the author's personal memories, is a pastoral; *The Professor's House*, which chronicles an ugly tale of human greed, is largely satiric, and *Death Comes for the Archbishop*, with its saintly missionary priests, portrays the disciplined, timeless world of the paradisal imagination. But what of those books written after *Death Comes for the Archbishop*, particularly those last four volumes (*Obscure Destinies, Lucy Gayheart, Sapphira and the Slave Girl, The Old Beauty and Others*) which critics agree mark the decline of Miss Cather's art? Can these books, from a writer of such depth, be as undistinguished and insignificant as has been suggested?[1] The answer is at once affirmative and negative. With the exception of the long story, "Old Mrs. Harris," the later writing lacks the imaginative energy which found consummate expression in the earlier novels. But the vision which underlies these books is precisely one which discounts the urge to expression through art; for it was the author's conviction in later years that not art but only life truly matters in the end. Consequently Willa Cather's last fictions occupy that paradoxical, but not uncommon, position of works of art pointing to their own devaluation.

As a romantic Willa Cather believed in the absoluteness of the artist's vocation.[2] Her major novels were all written as egotistic expressions of an individual consciousness seeking to know and understand itself. Even as apparently selfless and disinterested a book as *Death Comes for the Archbishop* reflects a way of life achieved by the author after she

*Originally published in *Novel: A Forum on Fiction*, 7 (Fall 1973), 41–53. Reprinted by permission of *Novel* and the author.

had gone through a nadir of despair over her failure in human relationships. But the last novels and stories posit quite a different relationship between art and human consciousness. No longer driven by the Faustian urge to power through her writing, Miss Cather came to view her lifetime dedication to art as placing selfish and consequently tragic limitations on the demands of life itself. Again Miss Cather was following a path well-worn, to use one of her favorite images, by the "pilgrims" of the imagination. The futility of life's sacrifice to art had been dramatized more emphatically by artists who arrested their work in early or mid-career: by Rimbaud, for example, who went to Abyssinia to make his fortune in the slave trade; by Hardy, who ceased writing fiction after publishing his most powerful novel, *Jude the Obscure*; or by Hart Crane who, in his quest for the ideal, despaired of the mediacy of poetry and committed suicide. For Willa Cather the implications of her vision were never as wholly irrevocable or tragic, yet instinctively she moved toward that same juncture where art terminates in the mute acceptance (or, in Crane's case, hopeful transcendence) of life.

The change is first evident with the publication of *Obscure Destinies* in 1932. Willa Cather's achievement of self-mastery with its fictional flowering in *Death Comes for the Archbishop* (1927), her supreme work of art, was irremediably shaken in the following years which brought the disruption of her apartment life in New York and the death of her father in Nebraska. The fictional consequence of this reversal was *Shadows on the Rock* (1931), a book set in seventeenth-century Quebec, but pervaded throughout by a very personal feeling of homesickness and the desire to retreat into a world that never changes. However, it was the illness and death in 1931 of the author's mother which determined the direction of her writing for the remaining years. For her father Miss Cather had felt nothing but affection, but her relationship with her mother had always been difficult; indeed, much of her youthful behavior was in deliberate contravention of her mother's wishes.[3] However, with the passing of time and the prospect of her mother's approaching death, Miss Cather's attitude softened considerably. Edith Lewis's account is valuable here not only for suggesting the author's change of heart, but for giving an incisive portrait of the woman (Miss Cather's mother) who was to play such an important role in the last fiction: "The long illness of Mrs. Cather . . . had a profound effect on Willa Cather, and I think on her work as well. She had come to understand her mother better through the years—her strong-willed, imperious nature, full of quick, eager impulses—quick to resent, quick to sympathize, headstrong, passionate, and yet capable of great kindness and understanding. She realized with complete imagination what is meant for a proud woman like her mother to lie month after month quite helpless. . . ."[4] With her mother's death a source of conflict integral to Miss Cather's imaginative life was gone, leaving her with only a deep sense of her own thoughtlessness and perversity. Where the novels of her middle years had found characters and settings in the world at large, the later fiction returns the author to her personal past once again in Nebraska and Virginia. But what is most significant is that these books are shaped throughout by a desire to see that world, at last, equally and with compassion. The imaginative tension for great art is largely gone, but in its place we have the artist's wisdom, her resolve—her testament to life which is poignantly simple and reassuring.

II

Miss Cather's last writings are informed throughout by a profound regret that youth in its self-absorption is so often cruel and indifferent, that greatness in any endeavor is achieved at the cost of human sympathy. The most moving expression of this final vision in her art is "Old Mrs. Harris," the second story of *Obscure Destinies*. Here Willa Cather no longer attempts to prove herself in recreating the characters and incidents from her past, nor does she seek in them some way of resolving the tensions in her own private life; rather her attitude is one of remorse and humility, as though writing were a form of penance and its only objective were to win forgiveness from those remembered persons by means of their sympathetic embodiment in a work of art. In "Old Mrs. Harris" Willa Cather recreates the characters and a period in her life (specifically her mother and grandmother as she remembered them from adolescence) which previously she had viewed with little affection. In this story, remembering the past is not an escapist pleasure, but a confrontation with guilty memories evaded for much of a lifetime.

The art and the reprise of "Old Mrs. Harris" lie in the subtlety with which point of view is managed. Although the controlling perspective is ultimately the author's—the grown Vickie remembering a sequence from her childhood—the story is narrated so that the three women in the family, while not understanding each other, emerge nonetheless as sympathetic individuals. Miss Cather in effect describes the tragic undertow of this story herself in her essay on Katherine Mansfield when she singles out that author's ability to reveal the many kinds of relations which exist in a happy family: ". . . every individual in that household (even the children) is clinging passionately to his individual soul, is in terror of losing it in the general family flavour. As in most families, the mere struggle to have anything of one's own, to be one's self at all, creates an element of strain which keeps everybody almost at the breaking point."[5] In "Old Mrs. Harris" sympathy at first appears to be reserved for the grandmother alone: the story begins with Mrs. Rosen's visit to Grandma Harris, and from the neighbor's vantage point the old woman appears to be the drudge in her daughter's household and the victim of her son-in-law's ineffectuality in business. But as we are taken inside Mrs. Harris's thoughts we find that as a Southerner she accepts her role in her daughter's kitchen and is grateful to be able to follow her daughter's fortunes in this customary way. Also the picture of her daughter from the neighbor's eyes as haughty and selfish, jealous of any attention paid to her mother, begins to soften as the old woman reflects that while her daughter is indeed proud, she at the same time has a "good heart." The old woman, moreover, admits to herself that, because Victoria had been the prettiest of her children, she had spoiled her. Mrs. Harris could have been wholly idealized if the author had retained only a granddaughter's perspective, but the tension in the family is felt from the daughter Victoria's point of view as well. At the Methodist social we are given a glimpse into her motives and feelings. We see her giving money spontaneously to the children of the poor laundress and know that the gesture is not intended to be patronising; we also feel with her the intended reproach when one of the meddlesome townswomen implies that Victoria exploits her mother in the kitchen. Victoria could have been a wholly negative character, but sympathy is elicited for her in thus exposing her vulnerability.

The portrait of Vickie, however, is the most complex for hers is the "guilty" perspective; because she is a projection of the author's younger self she is viewed at once most critically and most sympathetically. Vickie's desire to go to college, to escape the cramped existence of an overcrowded family in a small midwestern town, blinds her to the feelings and needs of those around her. The measure of regret the author feels years later is suggested in the homely incident when the family cat dies. Vickie is so absorbed in her studies that she pays little attention to the death of the cat and her grandmother explains to the other children: "Vickie's got her head full of things lately; that makes people kind of heartless."[6] It is a seemingly trivial incident, but it is steeped in the self-recrimination which underlies the story. When Vickie learns that in spite of the scholarship she has won there will not be enough money for her to go to college, she sees everyone as her enemy; she even refuses her grandmother's comfort.

The failure of sympathy and understanding in the family reaches a dramatic crescendo at the end of the story where the members of the family become so engrossed in their personal problems they do not realize the grandmother is dying. Here each of the women gives bitter expression to her frustration and despair as the grandmother looks helplessly on. Victoria asks her mother in an accusing tone if she is sick and says: "You ought to be more careful what you eat, Ma. If you're going to have another bilious spell, when everything is so upset anyhow, I don't know what I'll do" (p. 175). When Vickie hears that her grandmother is ill and her mother lying down in her room she thinks "wasn't it just like them all to go and get sick, when she had now only two weeks to get ready for school, and no trunk, and no clothes or anything?" (p.

185). But our sympathies are never one-sided: Vickie's selfish indifference is tempered by our knowledge that she is apprehensive and full of
self-doubt about going away to school; and we learn that the attractive
Victoria is to bring yet another child into the crowded house. The interweaving of multiple viewpoints renders movingly the imaginative tension
at the heart of the story: while the memories of hidden longings and
isolation are vividly recreated through Vickie's viewpoint, the narrative
overview at the same time creates the mother and grandmother with
sympathy and compassion. But it is a tragic ambience which surrounds
the tale, for the understanding and forgiveness have come too late. The
prototypes from life (and it is to life that we are directed in Miss Cather's
last writings) are now gone, and compassion can only be expressed in
art. The most moving image in the story is that of the poor servant
woman, Mandy, washing old Mrs. Harris's feet. The power of this image
derives from the Keatsian paradox that the servant's gesture of compassion is momentary but complete, while its artistic recreation must always
be compensatory. The homely details of childhood are nowhere in Miss
Cather's writing so lovingly described; but that affection is a quietly
tragic emotion for art, though timeless, can never replenish life.

In the same collection and written in the same mode, "Two Friends"
is a brief but moving recollection of a misunderstanding between two
businessmen in a small pioneer town. Their friendship has a rare and
imaginative intimacy, and to the narrator as a child it betokens an
exciting sense of life's potential. But the two men quarrel over politics
and never speak to each other again. Both men die a few years afterwards
and this vignette from childhood closes on a quiet note of regret for
"something broken that could so easily have been mended; something
delightful that was senselessly wasted. . ." (p. 230).

The spirit of self-exorcism in which "Old Mrs. Harris" was written
is pursued even more relentlessly in *Lucy Gayheart* (1935). Of all Willa
Cather's novels *Lucy Gayheart* has probably received the greatest amount
of negative criticism; the charge is usually that of contrivance and sentimentality. But if one perceives its design, *Lucy Gayheart* appears less
contrived. The novel is built around three tales of love, three tales of
remorse and reprise. In a letter to a friend Miss Cather suggested that
the novel doesn't pull together until one reads the last part.[7] It is in the
final section, or Book 3, that we look at the novel through the eyes of a
character who is filled with guilt and remorse over his actions in the past.
Although Book 3, like the rest of the novel, is written in the third person,
it is narrated from the viewpoint of Harry Gordon living on in the small
Nebraska town of Haverford, twenty-five years after the heroine's death.
Gordon had loved Lucy Gayheart, but he had not understood her. She
had gone to Chicago to study piano and there had fallen in love with a
singer, Clement Sebastian. Smitten in his pride, Gordon only thought of
revenging himself on Lucy, of making her suffer. When Lucy came back

to Haverford after Sebastian's death, he refused, in spite of her plea, to help or comfort her, withdrawing into the exclusive confines of his unhappy new marriage and the family bank. On the last day of her life, he had refused to give Lucy a ride in his cutter out of the cold wind. Book 3 takes place following old Mr. Gayheart's death; his winter funeral had made the townspeople feel "almost as if Lucy's grave had been opened." Harry Gordon, now fifty-five, reflects on the years that have elapsed since Lucy's death and admits to himself that he had gone to great lengths in order to make her suffer. The day on which she drowned "he refused Lucy Gayheart a courtesy he wouldn't have refused to the most worthless old loafer in town" (p. 220).[8] Subsequently his sense of guilt over her death has been the preoccupation of his life. He thinks of it (and his marriage) as a "life sentence" and his friendship with Lucy's father as an "act of retribution." He will never leave Haverford, for his home town is the place of his sorrow and his penance. The last section of the novel is a brief but sharply etched account of twenty-five years of remorse; but its mood creates a frame around the whole of *Lucy Gayheart*, for the book opens several years after Lucy's death, recalling the girl's vital presence in the town and mourning her loss. One of the song-cycles that Clement Sebastian performs is Schubert's *Die Winterreise*, the songs of a rejected lover who is psychically resurrected in the dead of winter to experience again and express the anguish of his loss.[9] Although Gordon is not a singer the musical metaphor applies to him most aptly for his winter memory becomes the controlling perspective in the novel—an extension of the author's lamentation in her remorseful old age.

In "The Old Beauty," written the year after *Lucy Gayheart* was published, Willa Cather touches once again on the major preoccupation of her last writings—her theme of regret and of confronting one's past honestly. Gabrielle Longstreet, the old beauty of the title, was once the rarest flower in London's brilliant society of the nineties. Recalling his acquaintance with her in those years is a very agreeable nostalgic experience for Seabury, the central consciousness, for those "deep, claret-coloured closing years of Victoria's reign" appear to him from the 1920's as a more noble and more gracious period in human history. But on renewing his friendship with Gabrielle Longstreet, who is living anonymously as Madame de Couçy in France, he finds that her recollections of those years are steeped in regrets. In her youth she had been surrounded by countless unsolicited admirers; they were men of achievement, but she had simply taken them for granted. Now in her old age she has come to recognize their greatness and is filled with remorse that she once held them so lightly. She says to Seabury: "You may remember that I was a rather ungrateful young woman. I took what came. A great man's time, his consideration, his affection, were mine in the natural course of things, I supposed. But it's not so now. I bow down to them in admiration . . .

gratitude. They are dearer to me than when they were my living friends, —because I understand them better" (p. 33).[10] Her chief pleasure now is to read what those men wrote and what has been written about them. In spite of his nostalgia the past has its disagreeable aspect for Seabury as well. Gabrielle recalls to him that the last time they met he had found her in the embraces of a vulgar American businessman. Seabury had gone to China after the incident and had not seen her since. This preoccupation with confronting the past brings the story to its abrupt denouement. The automobile in which Seabury and Gabrielle are riding narrowly misses colliding with a small car driven by two vulgar young American women. Gabrielle dies shortly after this incident and our sympathy for the old beauty is complete. However, that sympathy does not derive, as critics have repeatedly suggested, from a simple juxta-position of the old order against the new; rather it is extended to a heroine who, in the two American women, has caught a glimpse of herself in her youth. Outward appearances and life styles change but Gabrielle nonetheless marks in them her own thoughtless nature and perhaps her vulgarity too. It is a brutal confrontation, but in this moment of truth the old beauty is pardoned and redeemed.

III

The quest for some mode of redemption or release runs as a com-plementary theme throughout the last fiction to the statement of remorse. Earlier, in *The Professor's House*, Willa Cather found that the misery of failure in human relationships could only be transcended by relinquish-ing the desire for power and possessions in both human and material terms.[11] In the last books the exorcism of man's lust for power still re-mains the antidote to the futility of ambitions and desires which leave only sorrow and regret in their wake.

In *Lucy Gayheart* Clement Sebastian's love for the heroine is pre-sented as the most positive relationship in the novel. Unlike Harry Gordon, Sebastian loves Lucy in a detached, selfless way—as an embodi-ment of life's vital essence and not as a beautiful creature he must possess in order to enhance his own life. Each of the characters in the novel must learn that only the selfless, impersonal love of Christian teach-ing can survive the vicissitudes of human emotion. Love that is posses-sive will always be destructive. This is the nature of Mockford the pianist's attachment to Sebastian and both men drown, Mockford drag-ging Sebastian into the water. In contrast Sebastian had loved Lucy genuinely because her feeling for him "seemed complete in itself, not putting out tentacles all the while. . . . In her companionship there was never the shadow of a claim" (pp. 80–81). Lucy is forced, after Sebas-tian's death, to redirect her love from an individual to "Life"; she learns this from Mrs. Ramsay, her aged confidante. Harry Gordon, whose possessive love is virtually the cause of Lucy's death, learns the same from Lucy's father, a man who lived life without any claims and died without regrets. That Sebastian had earlier gone through the same experience is suggested when Lucy remembers the words from Mendelssohn's *Elijah* that he had sung for her in the beginning: *"If with all your heart you truly seek Him, you shall ever surely find Him"* (p. 185).

Willa Cather's preoccupation with power and possessiveness is nowhere as strikingly in the foreground as in her last novel, *Sapphira and the Slave Girl*, with its focus on the question of slavery. Dramatic conflict in this novel of pre–Civil War Virginia stems from the fact that Sapphira Colbert is a slave owner while her husband and daughter are in essence abolitionists. To Sapphira, an aristocrat, slavery is a natural part of the order to which she was raised, but for her husband and daughter the ownership of a human being is morally wrong. The attitudes to slavery are an essential expression of character in this novel; it is Sapphira, the slave owner, who experiences jealousy (the passion of possession) in relation to her husband whom she suspects of an amorous attachment to the slave girl, Nancy Till. The miller and his daughter, on the other hand, are indulgent and compassionate towards others: Henry Colbert is a gentle, understanding master and Rachel Blake is a Sister of Mercy at the bedsides of the sick.

For the author herself, however, the question of power devolved upon the nature of art. All her life her writing had been her means of conquest, and during the crisis of her middle years it had been her way of transcending failure in personal relationships as well. But in the last phase she came to suspect even the circumstances and motives of her craft. A commitment to art is first seen as having potentially tragic consequences in "Old Mrs. Harris." Throughout the summer of the story Vickie, the artist's embodiment of herself as a child, turns away from her family to the Rosens, the cultured neighbors, who encourage her to be a scholar. We naturally feel sympathy for her desire to escape the overcrowded house and the drabness of a small, midwestern town in the romantic world of the arts. But there is a dark dimension to this youthful self-absorption imaged in the slight but telling details of Vickie's reading. In the Rosen's library she pauses in an illuminated edition of *Faust* over a picture of Gretchen entering the church and Faustus gazing from behind a rose tree with Mephisto at his shoulder. Allegorically the scene suggests the fundamental opposition between experience and abstract knowledge (life and art) in the legend. Unaware of its implications Vickie expresses an urgent desire to be able to read the German in which the text is printed, thus making a Faustian wish. Between the first and second parts of the book she finds the *Dies Irae* hymn, and while for Vickie it only represents a test of her Latin, for the author it betokens a perspective from the other end of life—the day of judgment. It is from this perspective that Vickie's choice has tragic implications. Her youthful absorption in art blinds her to the plight of her mother and grandmother. She sees them instead as enemies and her response to their suffering is selfish indifference. The final feeling in the story is tragic because art can never redeem the losses it once incurred.

In *Lucy Gayheart* the truth the heroine must discover is that art and an artist's career will always be second in importance to living itself. In the first section of the novel we are essentially looking at the world through Sebastian's eyes and it is he who gives expression to those feelings which underlie all of Willa Cather's last writings. After the death of a close friend this disillusioned artist reflects grimly: "Life had so turned out that now, when he was nearing fifty, he was without a country, without a home, without a family, and very nearly without friends. Surely a man couldn't congratulate himself upon a career which had led to such results. He had missed the deepest of all companionships, a relation with the earth itself, with a countryside and people" (p. 78). This repudiation of art as a vocation inimical to the gratifications of life emerges as the central concern in the second section of the novel which more properly gives us Lucy's point of view. Sebastian has drowned and Lucy, whose passion is eternally frustrated, must find some way of continuing to live. The answer is first spoken by Professor Auerbach, her music teacher in Chicago, who says to her prophetically "You will learn that to live is the first thing" (p. 134). In her home town it is Mrs. Ramsay, the elderly widow of one of the town's first citizens, who gives Lucy the same advice somewhat augmented: "Life is short; gather roses while you may. . . . Nothing really matters but living. Get all you can out of it" (p. 165). The importance of Mrs. Ramsay's words to Lucy is anticipated earlier when Mrs. Ramsay's daughter reflects on the change that has come to her mother with the years. Once the older woman's sympathy for Lucy would have been passionate and very personal; now it was "more ethereal. More like the Divine compassion" (p. 147). Mrs. Ramsay also suggests to Lucy that in the end one's career comes second in importance to living, that accomplishments are only the ornaments of life. Consequently it is surprising at first that a concert at the Opera House should renew Lucy's desire to live. But Miss Cather has chosen this symbolic turning point very carefully; for what is important to note is that it is not the work of art itself—the often sung opera *The Bohemian Girl*—which inspires Lucy, but rather its rendition with such freshness and compassion by the aging soprano. "Her voice was worn, to be sure, like her face, and there was not much physical sweetness left in it. But there was another kind of sweetness; a sympathy, a tolerant understanding. She gave the old songs, even the most hackneyed, their full value" (p. 181). It is the human element which transforms the tired songs into a moving, living experience. In feeling the urge to live once again Lucy has followed Mrs.

Ramsay and recognizes that it is not an individual she loves, but "Life itself" (p. 184).

IV

The priority of life over art and achievement is implicit throughout Willa Cather's last four books and gives them their special direction both in theme and form. The most joyful assertion of life's triumph is "Neighbour Rosicky" from *Obscure Destinies*. In this story the focus is again on death, but unlike the other stories in this collection death is seen as the natural fulfillment of life. The Rosickys have not been infected by the American urge to "get ahead"; they refuse, for example, to sell the cream off their milk in spite of the profit it would bring. Mary Rosicky says: "I'd rather put some colour into my children's faces than put money into the bank" (p. 25). In the description of the Bohemian kitchen with the geraniums blooming on the window ledge, the plentiful food and strong coffee on the table, there is a rich sense conveyed of life being lived fully in the present. We feel after he has died that neighbour Rosicky's grave must be snug and homelike, for his death does not leave regrets, a sense of a life wasted; rather it affirms the privilege of existence. In relation to Willa Cather's writing as a whole "Neighbour Rosicky" is a kind of pendant or coda to *My Ántonia*; it gives us a later picture of that same Bohemian family that served as prototypes for the characters of the famous novel. But there is a significant formal difference between the novel and the story: the highly self-conscious narrator Jim Burden, whose education and experience in the world are undermined by a sense of failure, has been eliminated from the story so that our focus rests squarely on the Bohemians themselves. There remains a vestige of Burden in the doctor, but his appreciative presence never distracts us from the subjects; rather it gives accent to the richness and fullness of their lives.

In the last books Willa Cather virtually abandons the descriptive-reflective style of her major novels and adopts more dramatic modes of narration. For the primary objective of her writing is no longer self-expression but the desire to see human relationships from as many vantage points as possible—drama being the stylistic corollary of her shift from "romantic" artist to apologist for life. We have already seen how in "Old Mrs. Harris" the author subtly manipulated the narration so that we view all three women sympathetically. In *Lucy Gayheart* and *Sapphira and the Slave Girl* dramatic scenes replace the earlier narrative method of remembered or reported action, and through multiple viewpoints we are urged to recognize in these scenes the complexity of motive behind every human act.

Much of *Sapphira and the Slave Girl*, with its evocation of a landscape and people, is still told in the loose anecdotal style, but smoldering beneath the descriptions of Virginia and the pre–Civil War way of life is a mordant drama of jealousy and revenge, the action of which is carried forward in fully dramatic scenes. The novel opens at "The Breakfast Table" when Sapphira announces to Henry her intention of sending Nancy to Winchester, and closes with Sapphira's moving repentance and her decision to invite her daughter to come and stay at her house. Such scenes in between as Martin Colbert's sexual pursuit of Nancy and Nancy's flight to Canada, which Miss Cather would formerly have avoided, are dramatized in considerable detail. As a result we see the characters as complex individuals, neither wholly good nor wholly bad, but engagingly and sympathetically human. Sapphira at first appears a malignant force; she is proud and coldly vengeful and sets out to ruin Nancy in order to punish her husband. But we are also made aware that her illness is a heavy burden and that her suspicions of her husband are not without foundation. In contrast we see the miller poring over his Bible down in the mill, striving to be a righteous man. But if Sapphira is too domineering, then her husband is too weak. He is fond of Nancy, as a father of a daughter, but does nothing to protect her from his nephew's advances; his role in helping her escape is a clandestine, non-committal gesture of leaving some money unguarded in his coat pocket. We see these two characters most equably through the eyes of Rachel Blake. She realizes that by nature she is not equipped to understand her mother, for Sapphira is indeed harsh, often cruel, with her servants and patronizing towards her husband. But she sees her mother's kindness— her indulgence with Tansy Dave and her affection for Old Jezebel—and realizes that Sapphira genuinely likes to see her servants happy. On the other hand, while Rachel shares her father's quiet sympathetic nature, she sees clearly his moral cowardice. The full humanity of Sapphira and the miller is disclosed in their last scene together where they recognize their mutual failings and strengths. The miller tells his wife that she is a good woman because she has relented and offered Rachel their home for the winter, but Sapphira says "Not so good as Rachel, with her basket!"[12] The miller returns that there are different ways of being good to people, and sometimes keeping them in their place is also being kind. The full measure of sympathy the author feels for her characters is evident in Sapphira's penitential recognition of her shortcomings; she says contritely to the miller: "We would all do better if we had our lives to live over again" (p. 269).

Willa Cather's affirmation of life through sympathy and understanding is further reinforced by the implications of the epilogue to *Sapphira and the Slave Girl*. The narrator here is the author as a child, "something over five years old," and the scene of Nancy's return has that vivid but incomplete quality of childish recall. The temporal remove of this scene from the authorial present of 1940 renders the story of Sapphira and the miller even more remote in time; we view them now from the sober perspective of human mortality. But although Sapphira and the miller are dead, there is a strong suggestion of their survival in the characterization of the child-narrator's mother and father. The mother is energetic and impatient and dominates the room, while the father, like the miller, is removed from the scene, probably in his room in the basement making shoes for the paws of his shepherd dog. In "Old Mrs. Harris" Willa Cather did a portrait of her parents in the Templetons. The essential nature of that couple reappears in Sapphira and the miller, though here Miss Cather was purportedly portraying her great-grandparents. But Rachel Blake's assessment of her mother could substitute for the description of Victoria Templeton without any disruption to that character: "Mrs. Colbert, though often generous, was entirely self-centered and thought of other people only in their relation to herself. She was born that way, and had been brought up that way" (p. 220). And like the evasive and ineffectual Mr. Templeton the miller concedes all authority to Sapphira: "You're the master here, and I'm the miller. And that's how I like it to be!" (p. 50). In going back to her earliest memories for her final novel Willa Cather was probably rehearsing for the last time the essential drama of her imaginative life—the child indulged by a gentle father and disciplined (perhaps in her own eyes rejected) by a strong-willed and unsympathetic mother. The pattern is constant and coherent throughout Willa Cather's fiction. Nancy's dilemma with Sapphira prefigured in the countless rejected or orphaned protagonists who mourn their "lost lady." If this hypothesis is correct then *Sapphira and the Slave Girl*, despite the control and detachment of its execution, is a genuine work of compassion and understanding—a subtle novel of human relationships and intimations of mortality.

In the other two stories of the posthumous collection, *The Old Beauty and Others* (1948), the final theme is worked out more explicitly. "Before Breakfast," a story of regret, does not conclude with death, like "The Old Beauty," but with an affirmation of youth and life. The protagonist of this brief tale is Henry Grenfell, a self-made man who has worked his way up from a messenger boy with Western Union to a senior partner of a powerful corporation. As an old man, however, he looks back on a remarkably successful life not with satisfaction but with grave misgivings. What was it all for, he asks himself. His three sons have turned out well, two of them brilliantly, but he admits to himself despairingly that they are "as cold as ice." In the past Grenfell has always found solace on his island retreat in the North Atlantic, but this year a geology professor (two of Grenfell's sons are also professors) has spoiled the island by coming to study its formation and thereby including it in the dynamic world of information and progress from which Grenfell seeks to escape. It is the geologist's presence which forces the crisis in Grenfell's soul; however, he does not rest the blame for his sense of failure and despair on forces external to himself: "The bitter truth was that his worst enemy was closer even than the wife of his bosom—was his bosom itself!" (p. 156). In contrast to Gabrielle Longstreet self-confrontation is for Grenfell a salutary and necessary prelude to his reawakening to life. It is the sight of the geologist's daughter out swimming in the Atlantic which capitulates his reaffirmation of living. Her pink-skinned fragility in the cold water, coupled at once with her vitality, proclaims to him that life will continue to renew itself and that humanity will endure in spite of its destructive urge to power. The degree of his understanding and acceptance is measured by his final reflection which good-humoredly incorporates the images of progress over which he has despaired: "Anyhow, when that first amphibious frog-toad found his water-hole dried up behind him, and jumped out to hop along till he could find another—well, he started on a long hop" (p. 166).

In the last story she was to write Miss Cather followed through her affirmation of life to the point of totally dissolving the dramatic conflict upon which her art was based. According to her biographers, "The Best Years," written in 1945, was inspired by a last visit with her brother Roscoe and her purpose in writing the story was to recapture something of the pleasure and intimacy of their childhood together. It is easy to see this as the author's last nostalgic glimpse of her past, but in view of the direction in which her imagination was instinctively moving its implications are more profound, more far-reaching. For in this story of a young school teacher whose weekend visit at home is to be one of her last before an early death, the picture of the author's family has radically altered. The mother, Mrs. Ferguesson, is still a definite, energetic person, but the selfishness of Victoria Templeton and the cold authority of Sapphira have disappeared. There is no conflict here between mother and daughter; on the contrary the mother's authority and organization are so totally benevolent that, for Lesley Ferguesson, being at home was a soothing feeling that went through her "like getting into a warm bath when one is tired" (p. 96). The father is still recognizable as a failure in practical terms, but there is no sense of his dreamy nature being a source of real conflict. Here "Wide Awake Farm" where Mr. Ferguesson takes his regular afternoon siesta is a purely comic rendering of Mr. Templeton's evasiveness and the miller's cowardice. In the last sequence of the story Lesley's school superintendent, Evangeline Knightly, returns fifteen years after Lesley's death for a visit with Mrs. Ferguesson. The feeling of love and accord imaginatively achieved between 'mother' and 'daughter' is here consummated. Instead of writing a daughter's eulogy for her dead mother, Miss Cather reverses the situation and lets the mother speak words of love for her lost daughter. Imaginatively this scene could have had the childish petulance of 'You'll be sorry when I'm gone,' but instead it bespeaks a recognition that perhaps in her own way her mother did truly love her.

V

When Willa Cather died in 1947 she left an unfinished story which in accordance with her wishes was subsequently destroyed. Its title was to have been "Hard Punishments," and its setting the Avignon of the medieval popes. Miss Cather had been working spasmodically on this long story after she finished *Sapphira and the Slave Girl*; however, after the death of her brother Roscoe in 1945 she never went back to it or any other writing. Critics have discussed the possible directions Miss Cather's imagination would have taken in her new work, which in both time and place represented a significant departure from all her other writing.[13] But in a letter to a friend Miss Cather clearly defines, I believe, that direction herself when she says that she has no more interest in writing since her brother's death, for she realizes nothing in life really matters but the people one loves.[14] At this point there is a very personal relevance to the author's reflection on the world's great artists and their last works.

Art is too terribly human to be very "great," perhaps. Some very great artists have outgrown art, the men were bigger than the game. Tolstoi did, and Leonardo did. When I hear the last opuses, I think Beethoven did. Shakespeare died at fifty-three, but there is an awful veiled threat in The Tempest *that he too felt he had outgrown his toys, was about to put them away and free that spirit of Comedy and Lyrical Poetry and all the rest he held captive—quit play-making and verse-making for ever and turn his attention—to what, he did not hint, but it was probably merely to enjoy with all his senses that Warwickshire country which he loved to weakness—with a warm physical appetite.[15]*

An artist's abandonment or renunciation of his craft, however, does not invalidate his life's work. On the contrary it places it in the more meaningful context of experience achieved, for the artist's path is a circuitous one which returns its pilgrim to life. That Willa Cather, unlike many of her American contemporaries, travelled the full road is not always recognized. But the words of Wallace Stevens are a worthy reminder: ". . . we have nothing better than she is. She takes so much pains to conceal her sophistication that it is easy to miss her quality."[16]

Notes

1. The popular critical consensus of Willa Cather's later fiction is reflected in James Woodress's recent biography, *Willa Cather: Her Life and Art* (New York: Pegasus, 1970). While Professor Woodress sees *Obscure Destinies* as still in Miss Cather's best vein of writing, he finds *Lucy Gayheart* sentimental and not up to standard. He considers *Sapphira and the Slave Girl* the work of a disciplined intelligence, but lacking the passion of the author's best work. He views the three stories published posthumously (*The Old Beauty and Others*) as interesting but distinctly minor pieces.

2. For a comprehensive discussion of Willa Cather's commitment to art see the second of two essays by Bernice Slote in *The Kingdom of Art: Willa Cather's First Principles and Critical Statements, 1893–1896* (Lincoln: University of Nebraska Press, 1966), pp. 31–112. See also the chapter entitled "The Artistic 'Chain of Human Endeavor' " in Edward A. and Lillian D. Bloom's *Willa Cather's Gift of Sympathy* (Carbondale: Southern Illinois University Press, 1964), pp. 116–152.

3. See Mildred Bennett, *The World of Willa Cather* (Lincoln: University of Nebraska Press, 1961), pp. 26–31.

4. Edith Lewis, *Willa Cather Living* (New York: Alfred A. Knopf, 1953), pp. 156–157.

5. Willa Cather, *Not Under Forty* (New York: Alfred A. Knopf, 1936), pp. 135–136.

6. Willa Cather, *Obscure Destinies* (New York: Alfred A. Knopf, 1932), p. 142. All further references are from this text.

7. Unpublished letter to Carrie Miner Sherwood (Willa Cather Pioneer Memorial, Red Cloud, Nebraska), July 1934.

8. Willa Cather, *Lucy Gayheart* (New York: Alfred A. Knopf, 1935), p. 220. All further references are from this text.

9. For a fuller treatment of the musical motif here and elsewhere in Willa Cather's fiction see Richard Giannone, *Music in Willa Cather's Fiction* (Lincoln: University of Nebraska Press, 1968). The discussion of *Die Winterreise* is on pp. 213–231.

10. Willa Cather, *The Old Beauty and Others* (New York: Alfred A. Knopf, 1948), p. 33. All further references are from this text.

11. For a fuller discussion see my article entitled "Willa Cather and *The Professor's House*: 'Letting Go With the Heart,' " *Western American Literature*, VII (Spring 1972), 13–24.

12. Willa Cather, *Sapphira and the Slave Girl* (New York: Alfred A. Knopf, 1940), p. 268. All further references are from this text.

13. See George N. Kates, ed. "Willa Cather's Unfinished Avignon Story," in Willa Cather, *Five Stories* (New York: Vintage, 1956).

14. Unpublished letter to Irene Miner Weisz (Newberry Library, Chicago), October 22, 1945.

15. From an undated fragment of criticism entitled "Light on Adobe Walls" in *Willa Cather on Writing: Critical Studies on Writing as an Art* (New York: Alfred A. Knopf, 1962), pp. 125–126. Foreword by Stephen Tennant.

16. *Letters of Wallace Stevens*, selected and edited by Holly Stevens (New York: Alfred A. Knopf, 1966), p. 381.

INDEX

Note: *Titles of works other than Cather's do not appear in this index. Check pages listed under particular authors for discussions of their works.*